CULTURE TROUBLES

For Emile

PATRICK CHABAL
JEAN-PASCAL DALOZ

Culture Troubles

*Politics and the Interpretation
of Meaning*

The University of Chicago Press

The University of Chicago Press, Chicago 60637
C. Hurst & Co. (Publishers) Ltd, London WC1B 3PL
© Patrick Chabal and Jean-Pascal Daloz, 2006
All rights reserved. Published 2006
Printed in India.

15 14 13 12 11 10 09 08 07 06   1 2 3 4 5

ISBN: 0-226-10040-5 (cloth)
ISBN: 0-226-10041-3 (paper)

Cataloging-in-Publication data have been requested
from the Library of Congress.

CONTENTS

PREFACE

There is clearly today renewed interest in cultural issues. From the notion that we all live in multicultural and hybrid societies to the fear of the so-called 'clash of civilisations', concerns about culture are now ubiquitous. Yet there is little consensus either on what it actually is or about what its influence on our lives might be. It seems that culture matters, but how it matters is not clear. The question of the relationship between culture and politics is even more opaque. Politicians pay homage to the cultural heritage of their constituents while attempting to manipulate cultural symbols for partisan purposes. Political scientists for their part range widely in their approach: from those who reject the very notion of culture to those who view it merely as instrument or ideology.

Both of us have worked in comparative politics for several decades and we have felt increasingly frustrated by the inability of our discipline to offer clearer insights into the relevance of culture for comparative analysis. Our previous book *Africa Works* was an attempt to use a cultural methodology that would make possible the task of accounting convincingly for the evolution of postcolonial African politics. Although the book was well received and has now become a standard reference on the subject, some reviewers suggested to us that our approach raised theoretical questions, which deserved fuller examination.

One critical line implied that to talk about the effects of culture on politics was culturalist because it implied a determinist explanation of behaviour—"culture drives politics"—and presumed a 'hierarchy' of cultures—"West is best". Another suggested that an explanation of politics that incorporates culture is an implicit argument in favour of 'identity politics'—that is again a determinist view in which agency derives from putative notions of self. These were valid points for debate and we concluded that there was now a need for systematic discussion of theory and methodology.

Culture Troubles is thus an attempt systematically to re-examine the relationship between culture and politics. Although we are both political scientists, we claim neither specialist knowledge in epistemology nor an equally precise knowledge of all polities across the globe. We have taken as our starting-point those social scientists (including a large number of anthropologists) who have special knowledge of that question, from either a theoretical or an empirical standpoint. Our interests and expertise have combined well. Between the two of us we have worked on a wide range of countries, from Africa to East Asia by way of North America, Scandinavia and South Asia. Patrick Chabal, who has special interest in questions of method, identity and belief systems, had overall responsibility for the Introduction, Parts II and III. Jean-Pascal Daloz, who is a specialist on élites and symbolic representations, took the lead in Parts I and IV as well as the Conclusion.

This book has been many years in the making and would not have been possible without the support, help and encouragement of a large number of colleagues and friends. Of these we mention only a few: Peter Burke and Yann Fauchois, who took an interest in the project from its inception; Michael Dwyer, who saw the potential of the book right away, and Farzana Shaikh, who provided detailed comments on several drafts. Patrick Chabal acknowledges the support of his colleagues at King's College London and the opportunities offered by his institution for sabbatical leave, including one at the University of Basel where he advanced writing of this book. He also offers collective thanks to the members of the Africa-Europe Group for Interdisciplinary Studies (AEGIS), who have made it possible for him to keep up lively intellectual contacts across Europe over the past decade. Jean-Pascal Daloz is grateful to his home institution, the CERVL (Institut d'Etudes Politiques de Bordeaux), and to the Universities of Uppsala and Oslo for facilitating his research. Both authors express their gratitude to Emil Udhammar for organising in Uppsala the first public presentation of the book.

P. C.
J.-P. D.

INTRODUCTION
THE POLITICS OF CULTURE

'To see ourselves as others see us can be eye-opening. To see others as sharing a nature with ourselves is the merest decency. But it is from the far more difficult achievement of seeing ourselves amongst others, as a local example of the forms human life has locally taken, a case among cases, a world among worlds, that the largeness of mind, without which objectivity is self-congratulation and tolerance a sham, comes.'[1]

Understanding politics in settings other than our own has always been a perilous exercise. Comparing the politically significant actions of men and women across the globe is even more fraught. Only the naïf, the zealot or the foolhardy engages in such an enterprise without sustained forethought. There is so much that can be misunderstood; so much that is habitually misunderstood—as appears obvious from the most cursory reading of what the foreign press has to say about us. What our own people write of others seems, somehow, to be less distorted, less wrong. There may well be merit in comparing the quality of journalism in varying countries of the world, probably to comfort ourselves further in the belief that 'we' are rather more unbiased than 'they'. However, the question continues to nag: how can we be sure? By what reference point do we compare?

Of course scholars profess devotion to more stringent canons of objectivity and write, accordingly—at least one hopes so. Political analysts employ methods that minimise the risk of shallow comparison. They make plain their assumptions. They justify the use of the concepts they deploy. They explain why they use particular theoretical frameworks. They give good reasons for the comparisons they undertake. They are open about the limitations of their investi-

---

[1] C. Geertz, 1983, 'Introduction' in C. Geertz, *Local Knowledge: further essays in interpretive anthropology*, p. 16.

1

gations. Yet for all that the attempts to explain the politics of 'others', and even more to compare them to 'ours' remain, more often than not, unconvincing. Frequently such accounts amount to superficial, or even facile, statements, when not tautologies. If 'others' do what they do because they are not 'us', then there is little gained by the explanation. Stated in this stark form, the charge may appear inaccurate, or perhaps unfair. But is it?

To take, first, a simple and relatively frivolous example, it is not clear at all that political scientists have provided convincing explanations as to why in Europe sexual indiscretions have such divergent consequences for elected politicians. The cliché is that the Protestant North is more repressed and will tolerate no foible while the Catholic South is more lax and will easily excuse roguish behaviour.[2] That is common sense; but how reliable is common sense for political comparison? Is there not more to it than seems on the surface to be the case, such as important distinctions between a more rigid Calvinism and a more tolerant Lutheranism? Perhaps the more relevant explanation of the differences lies in local perceptions of elected officials, or of politicians *tout court*, rather than of sexual behaviour *per se*. What if that which may appear to be a similar peccadillo is actually seen to carry vastly dissimilar political connotations: a flaw in one country, an asset in another? It would follow that a superficial emphasis on the difference between two cases in this respect only obscures the more significant conclusion that politicians everywhere seek to display the qualities that may strengthen their position.

However, let us look at a more difficult instance: the use of extreme violence in politics. A Sri Lankan woman suicide bomber kills Rajiv Gandhi. Palestinian youth blow themselves up deliberately to take the lives of Israeli civilians. A Saudi engineer working in Germany chooses to fly a passenger plane into the World Trade Center. Is there a good explanation for deeds that to us in the West appear so particularly 'evil'? Can one meaningfully compare such disparate acts of carnage with other forms of political protest? Are we witnessing a 'clash of civilisations'[3] between people who willingly use their own

---

[2] The cliché as presented here applies to males. It might be argued that the reverse is true for women: the North is more liberated and free; the South more conventional and constraining.

[3] The reference here is, of course, to S. Huntington, 1996, *The Clash of Civilizations and the Remaking of World Order*. We shall return to this author, not just because his

body as a weapon to kill others and those who do not? Or, if the situation is a trifle more complicated than common sense intimates, how do we devise a means of comparing such 'political' action with others, less violent, more familiar and (perhaps) more palatable to us? Are we to say that Muslims, or perhaps Third World people, are more 'fanatical' than Westerners; and if so why?[4] Or are we to argue that desperation is the key to such behaviour; but then how do we measure desperation? What, in any event, is the more 'immoral' violence: suicide bombing or the 'collateral' damage caused by carpet-bombing?

Finally, moving away from the titillating or the shocking, let us enquire into a more mundane political question: what is political accountability? In the West today what it is, is inescapably conflated with how it is exercised—in this instance through the holding of periodic multiparty elections. Politicians compete on the basis of party 'programmes' and, once elected, govern by means of parliamentary systems. Accountability is imposed *a posteriori*, as it were, through the next series of polls.[5] Nevertheless, we know that such a procedural definition does not exhaust the meaning of political accountability. How then do we assess such a process in settings where either there are no such electoral contests or where these are very fundamentally flawed, at least in 'respect' of the Western norm? Is there a non-ethnocentric notion of accountability? And if there is, can we make sense of it? How do we know, really, whether rulers are accountable to the ruled in countries where the practice of politics does not conform to what the standard textbooks on political theory postulate, or rather assert?

What, if anything, do these examples suggest in respect of political science? At the very least analysis must be contextual if it is to enlighten. In order to explain, and even more to compare, we need to

---

writings have become so influential but mainly because they provide the most consummate demonstration of the dangers of equating culture with values. Therefore, our critique of Huntington's views are not primarily concerned with the ways in which he divides the world into 'cultural zones', but turn on his conceptual approach to the question of assessing the relevance of culture in comparative politics. See Part I, Chapter 3.

[4] For an interesting discussion of the Third World and Development, see A. Escobar, 1995, *Encountering Development*.

[5] A. Przeworski, S. Stokes, and B. Manin (eds), 1999, *Democracy, Accountability and Representation*.

know why such occurred in a particular case and not in another. We should understand the specific circumstances of the event, or the process. But that is not enough. We may be able to account for the facts of the case without perceiving their rationale. François Mitterrand had a daughter born out of wedlock, a fact known to many in France for years, and yet this state of affairs had no bearing on his political career. When Wafa Idris, an apparently 'secular' young nurse, became the first female Palestinian suicide bomber in Israel, her action brought shame rather than pride to her family. In Pakistan the country's more Westernised and affluent socio-economic élite applauded the overthrow of a democratically elected government by a military officer on the grounds that the greed of politicians makes them 'illegitimate'. In all three instances the difficult question is why. In all three instances the beginning of a plausible answer may appear when we realise we ought to seek to explain these events from a *local* perspective: that is, how do the people concerned *make sense* of what has happened.

Unravelling what makes sense to the actors and their contextually relevant 'spectators' is to enter the realm of the interpretation of meaning: that is, to make the effort to decode the significance of such events from the other's viewpoint. To do that is inescapably to address the issue of culture. Mitterrand's tenure of power was not invalidated, probably because in France there is a tacit consensus that a politician's secret love life is not a liability and can, in some circumstances, also be a political asset. Perhaps Wafa Idris blew herself up because her vision of martyrdom was coloured by a very 'secular' notion of the sacrifice required for national liberation in hopeless Palestine. The Pakistani élite probably care little about democratic accountability because they operate in a political environment that gauges government purely from a practical viewpoint: which ruler allows them greater leeway for the accumulation of wealth? Of course it would be possible to suggest, in all these cases, as in others, that it is merely well considered 'self-interest' that is the most likely common thread. Possible, but hardly convincing. More probably, what links these (rather random) examples is the obvious realisation that the cultural aspects of politics have everything to do with explaining them. Indeed, plausibility suggests an interpretation of cultural factors.

Yet comparative politics aspires to achieve more than the mere explanation of discrete events and processes. It aims at uncovering similarities in the behaviour of political actors. It is thus not sufficient to account for Mitterrand's durability, Wafa Idris' violent sacrifice, or the disabused beliefs of the Pakistani élite. The ambition is to contrast the lineaments of Mitterrand's tenure to that of politicians elsewhere in the West, to assess Wafa Idris' death in the context of other forms of political terrorism, to compare the Pakistani élite to that of, say, India or other South Asian societies. Comparative politics seeks to advance such evaluation by means of a 'scientific' approach: using a theoretical framework that proposes the examination of a number of 'variables', assumed to be valid in the various settings under examination. In other words, it posits the conceptual approach by means of which the comparison is to be undertaken. However, such a method is not well suited to the comparison of the more cultural features of politics or, as we see it, to the interpretation of meaning that ultimately lies at the heart of the discipline.

WHY COMPARATIVE POLITICS CANNOT HANDLE CULTURE

The grounds on which present day political science fails to account satisfactorily for cultural factors are self-evidently complex and it is not our intention here either to simplify the discussion of the scholarly foundations of our discipline or to engage in superficial polemic. All social sciences aim to generate insights that are more revealing than mere common sense and all are inherently constrained by the theories they employ. Theoretical disputation, therefore, is not directly our concern. Instead we want to tackle the use of culture in political science from a more practical standpoint. To this end we need in the first instance to understand why it is that comparative politics as it is currently practised, at least in the West, is singularly ill-equipped to integrate cultural 'variables'.[6] Why, in other words, are political scientists so reluctant to exploit the insights made available to them by other social sciences, like anthropology, which attempt to provide an 'interpretation' of cultures?[7]

[6] For a recent synthetic presentation of the current debates within the discipline of comparative politics, see M. Lichbach and A. Zuckerman (eds), 1997, *Comparative Politics*.

[7] C. Geertz, 1973, *The Interpretation of Cultures*.

An answer to that question demands that we address at least three problems. The first is the question of theory in political science. The second concerns the instruments used within the discipline, that is concepts and measurements. The third has to do with the pitfalls of evidence: how to do (good) research in the field and how to collect (valuable) data.

The question of theory in political science

As a modern discipline, political science has deep roots in three other human or social sciences—history, sociology and economics—although it has also been influenced by other disciplines such as anthropology or psychology. Its modern incarnation is a product of a very specific context: the Second World War and the ideological struggle between East and West or capitalism and socialism. Indeed, the field of politics was born in the United States during the 1940s out of a theoretical debate between American and exiled European social scientists, who sought to forge a new 'scientific' discipline able to help them explain the various forms of political governance—democratic and totalitarian—which seemed to define the middle part of the twentieth century. A decade later they also attempted to erect a conceptual framework that would encompass the political future of the newly independent countries of Asia and Africa. A further decade onwards they aimed to integrate into comparative analysis the turbulent evolution of Central and South America.

In broader terms the genesis of politics as a social science owes much to work done previously—the Scottish pioneers of political economy; English political theorists including Locke, Burke and Mill; Marx and the Marxist approach to development; Weber's historical, socio-economic and political work; and, to some extent, the French sociological school going back to Comte and Durkheim. In the Anglo-Saxon world it sought to differentiate itself sharply from the contemporary historiography of modern politics, of which perhaps the two more important strands were the British empirical tradition and the *Annales* School in France.[8] In France, on the other hand, political science marked itself out from the institutional weight

---

[8] For one comprehensive review of the relationship between history and social theory, see P. Burke, 1992, *History and Social Theory*.

of the study of constitutional law and evolved in much closer affinity with historians, particularly of the Annales School. The founders of the modern discipline of political science in the United States, who were deeply influenced by the work of Talcott Parsons and Edward Shils,[9] had lofty scientific ambitions and believed that it was possible to construct 'a' theory of politics, 'a' conceptual apparatus, which would enable scholars systematically to study this one crucial societal activity. In this they were the proud descendants of their nineteenth-century predecessors, Darwin and Marx (though, of course, they were ideologically anti-Marxist), who both undertook to make explicit the 'laws' of development in their respective fields, and of Max Weber who toiled hard to establish the parameters of comparative socio-political analysis.

The historical context within which political science grew—the consolidation of Bolshevik rule in Russia and the rise of Fascism in Western Europe—could not but influence deeply those who wished to contribute to an understanding of the processes by which democracy was eschewed in favour of (left or right) despotism. The bulwark provided by the United States against totalitarianism quite naturally induced political scientists to address the issue of the rise, consolidation and preservation of liberal democracy in the context of a very unstable world, which was soon engulfed in the Cold War. In this respect, then, the first two generations of American political scientists were also soldiers in the struggle to promote the spread of democratic regimes throughout the world. This may explain why scientific certainty and ideological conviction presided over the birth of the sub-field of political science with which we are concerned: comparative politics. There is no space here to assess the work of the pioneers in political science, but a short appreciation of the founders of comparative politics may be useful.

Although the field of comparative politics can perhaps be said to have originated in the work of Montesquieu, we are here interested

[9] Parsons was a sociologist but with an ambition to conceptualise the whole of the social sciences. See Talcott Parsons' classic texts: T. Parsons, 1937, *The Structure of Social Action*; 1951, *The Social System*—; and T. Parsons and E. Shils (eds), 1951, *Towards a General Theory of Action*. See here also R. Merton, 1968 [1949], *Social Theory and Social Structure*. For a critical survey see B. Wearne, 1989, *The Theory and Scholarship of Talcott Parsons to 1951*.

in its modern post–War incarnation, which was from the outset concerned with political development.[10] From the 1950s onwards, therefore, comparativists wanted not just to contrast institutions, actors and processes across the Western (European and North American) world but also to weigh them against what was happening politically elsewhere on the globe. Partly because of the assumptions made by social scientists such as Parsons[11] and Deutsch[12], and partly because of the ideological context of the time, theorists of comparative politics assumed a linear form of political development leading in due course to the consolidation of liberal democracy as practised in the United States and most European countries. Hence they posited the ultimate Westernisation of politics across the planet. Here they echoed the work of developmental economists who, spurred by Walt Rostow's classic work, adumbrated the same linear evolution through the several stages of growth that were in the end to result in the blossoming of capitalism throughout the world.[13]

Therefore, comparative politics was not content to contrast polities across the globe. It also aimed to combine the insights derived from examining differing political settings with a general notion of political development. Unsurprisingly it was a child of its time in that it dealt in grand theory, capable both of accounting for the unfolding of myriad political events in the most diverse areas of the world and of providing the type of policy advice that was supposed to hasten the advent of democracy where it did not yet exist. The key issue here is not so much the ideological assumptions underlying such an approach as the conviction that there was 'a' general theory of political development, upon which comparative politics could be erected. In this respect it truly was an attempt to provide an anti-Marxist model

[10] As perhaps best illustrated in the work of Gabriel Almond: G. Almond and G. B. Powell, 1966, *Comparative Politics*; G. Almond and S. Verba, 1963, *The Civic Culture*.

[11] For a critique of Parsons' approach to culture, see M. Schmid, 1992, 'The Concept of Culture and its Place within a Theory of Social Action: a critique of Talcott Parsons' theory of culture' in R. Munch and N. Smelser (eds), *Theory of Culture*.

[12] Karl Deutsch, who had left Germany because of the Nazis' rise to power, developed a functionalist theory of politics. See K. Deutsch, 1963, *The Nerves of Government*.

[13] W. Rostow, 1958, *The Stages of Economic Growth*.

of politics, demonstrating the historical superiority of Western democracy. In this respect too it was as teleological as Marxism.

The consequence of such an intellectual genesis is that the field of comparative politics has always been prone to grand theories.[14] We return to this critical issue in Chapter 1. Suffice it here to highlight some of the effects of this tendency. First, there has been a clear ethnocentric bias since, implicitly or explicitly, analysis is grounded in developmental assumptions that posit a linear, when not a singular, form of modernisation resulting in Westernisation. An advanced industrial society is *ipso facto* taken to move in the direction of liberal electoral democracy.[15] Second, the choice of the concepts used to study polities comparatively has been driven by the need to assess the extent to which 'similarly developed' political systems exhibit similar characteristics. Here we might point to the large body of work devoted to the discussion of party politics in Western societies, all based on an agreed notion of the ways in which such political organisations 'represent' their constituencies. Third, the hypotheses comparative politics proposes to test are very largely based on the assumption that they will confirm that where there is political 'development' the same (socio-economic) conditions bring about the same outcomes. So, for instance, it is widely held that economic growth results in a higher level of education and that education brings about greater civic participation. Finally, the discipline is predicated on notions of causality that are believed to obtain in modern, Westernised, societies. Modernity, for example, has long been assumed to cause the increasing secularisation of society.

The bias towards grand theory, however disguised in textbooks of comparative politics, has, for reasons that are easy to understand, had a fateful effect on the discussion of culture within the field. The scientific pretensions of our discipline have made it difficult to devise ways in which cultural factors can be sufficiently well defined to afford proper conceptualisation and effective hypothesis testing. By its very nature culture is a 'soft' concept, both subjective and contextually bound, prone to the kind of elusiveness that makes it resistant

---

[14] See here, *inter alia*, A. Kohli *et al.*, 1995, 'The Role of Theory in Comparative Politics', *World Politics*, 48.

[15] For an intriguing discussion of the necessity to rethink liberal democracy, see S. Chan, 2002, *Liberalism, Democracy and Development*.

to a simple definition. What is culture? What are its boundaries? How does it impinge on politics? How can we compare cultures, even within the supposedly similar societies that make up the modern, industrialised, Western world? Furthermore the notion of culture, whatever it is taken precisely to mean, is often seen in the field as being much too closely related to that of individual habits, tastes, preferences, ways of life, personal beliefs and the like. As such it is believed by most political scientists to belong more readily to psychology, or cultural studies and the arts.[16]

Such a reluctance to take into account the relevance of cultural factors to politics has, in our minds, resulted in the existence of a very large black hole at the core of comparative theory.[17] Broadly, our discipline has used one of two strategies to 'deal' with culture. On the one hand it has sought to conceptualise 'political culture', a concept that suggests a double agenda: identifying those cultural factors, or political 'values', that most directly influence political behaviour and development *and* studying the processes of socialisation that result in certain forms of political dynamics.[18] The pioneering work on 'civic culture', undertaken from the early 1960s by American political scientists, illustrates the attempts made to understand why some countries were more 'deficient' in their democratic practices than the standard bearers of modern politics.[19] The conclusion that some societies are more 'civic' minded than others may strike us today as a trifle quaint, but there is plenty of current research following the same methodological path.[20] Equally there has always been a trend in comparative politics towards the discussion of those 'values' that are more, or less, conducive, for instance, to democratic politics.[21]

On the other hand, our discipline has considered culture as a residual category. The reasoning here is that because culture cannot

---

[16] For one possible approach (which we do not share) to some of these factors, see R. Le Vine, 1973, *Culture, Behavior and Personality.*

[17] Comparative politics as a discipline seemed strangely reluctant to avail itself of the insights of political anthropology.

[18] See here, for a relatively insightful early example, L. Pye, 1962, *Politics, Personality and Nation Building.*

[19] See here for instance, G. Almond and S. Verba, 1963, *The Civic Culture.*

[20] Contrast here two books on Italian 'political culture': the more anthropological approach of E. Banfield, 1958, *The Moral Basis of a Backward Society,* with the more quantitative one in R. Putnam, 1993, *Making Democracy Work.*

[21] A full discussion of these issues occurs in Chapter 3.

be properly operationalised, it cannot be meaningfully compared.[22] However, it is recognised that political action is influenced by what are often defined as 'subjective' factors—many derived from customs, habits, creeds and values—which must, therefore, be taken into account. The argument is not that those elements are unimportant but simply that they merely 'colour' the political process and as such are not a primary, or causal, factor of the changes that take place. They may explain the complexion of certain events but they do not determine the processes at work. Since comparative politics is a social 'science' it must aim to assess and contrast those attributes of the political system that its own theory posits to be the most relevant to its development. Thus culture merely helps to fine tune or refine an interpretation of politics in specific settings, but it does not contribute to an explanation of the fundamental changes under examination.

Hence it can be seen that the notion of theory in comparative politics as it has evolved over time is inimical to a cultural approach. For reasons connected with the very genesis and identity of the discipline, there is no satisfactory manner in which the analysis of politics can integrate in a meaningfully comparative way either the study of culture itself or the role of culture in politics. There is even less chance that the field will find means of conceptualising culture so that it can advance our comparative analysis of societies across the world. And there is virtually no possibility that the discipline as it currently stands can manage to provide an account of the dynamics, over time, of dissimilar political systems in markedly distinct environments. We develop this argument in more specific detail in the next two sections.

The demands of comparative analysis: concepts and measurements

Comparative politics seeks to generate insights by means of recognisably operational concepts and measurements, both quantitative and qualitative, which can be applied to the most diverse case studies. The impetus here is not so much the acquisition of further knowledge about the exercise of power in its relevant context but the eval-

---

[22] This critique raises the thorny problem of incommensurability in the social sciences: in this instance, how *can* we compare vastly different cultures?

uation of ostensibly similar institutions, actors, events or processes in
different settings. However, the difficulty of evolving comparative concepts lies in the quest for universal relevance. The theoretical ambitions of the discipline demand that the conceptual framework and its
attendant methodology be clearly in place before any research is
undertaken. Thus right from the beginning there is a tension between the wide ranging nature of comparative analysis—both in
terms of geographical diversity and as regards the vast range of possible questions to investigate—and the requirements that 'scientific'
standards be met.

The notion of science that informs this quest is exacting since it
derives, implicitly or explicitly, from that commonly accepted in the
'hard' sciences as applied to the social sciences (outlined perhaps most
cogently by Karl Popper): the validity of scientific enquiry lies in the
testing of hypotheses.[23] In practice this implies that the concepts used
must meet two tough criteria. First, they need to be relevant to the
study of the politics of modern Western industrialised societies: that

is, to have been successfully tested empirically in our own settings.
Second, they must relate causally to the overall grand theory
deployed, which in most cases requires that they be significant to the
understanding of Western political development. Needless to say,
such an approach inevitably tends to privilege ethnocentric conceptual frameworks over those that may be argued to be more appropriate for non-Western, or non-industrial, societies.

To return to a previous example, the comparative examination of
political parties proceeds on the assumption that parties, *qua* political
organisations, perform similar 'functions' in the different societies
under study, whether in Norway, Canada or Nigeria. Hence their
study ought to make possible an understanding of similar processes in
different countries. The task of the comparative analyst is not, therefore, to assess the extent to which parties in Nigeria are indeed as significant vehicles for the representation of public opinion as they are
in Norway or Canada, but merely to 'test' how differently they allow
political actors to compete in elections. The concept of 'political
party' thus derives from that which has been formed in the context of
those Western industrialised societies where they first emerged and is
applied, virtually wholesale, to other countries with a vastly different

[23] K. Popper, 1965, *Conjectures and Refutations.*

historical experience and cultural complexion. Equally, the empirically confirmed hypothesis that multiparty competition, as it has evolved in the West, is causally consequential for the creation and sustenance of democracy is applied *tel quel* to settings, such as post-colonial Africa, where the evidence tends to suggest otherwise.[24]

Thus the very universal claim of the concepts used in comparative politics, although derived from the historically and culturally specific context of the advanced West, imposes on the discipline a methodology that may not promote the understanding of the deeper political processes at work in many non-Western societies. Indeed it can be argued, as is clear from the evidence presented in our previous book,[25] that a study of the contrasts between parties in Canada, Norway and Nigeria would obscure rather than illuminate the appreciation of why it is that in the West African country the key to making sense of party politics lies in an analysis of the cultural context within which clientelistic power is exercised. In this specific instance, then, whatever the 'scientific' aim of a book devoted to the comparative analysis of political parties, the inclusion of a chapter on Nigeria would, because of the nature of the concept deployed and of the assumptions underlying the hypothesis about the causal relationship between multiparty competition and democracy, go against the aim of explaining why in that country Western-style democracy has failed to flower.[26]

We show throughout the book how the theoretical imperatives of the current comparative mainstream 'over-determines', as it were, the choice of concepts and why this undermines the discipline's very *raison d'être*, We want at this stage primarily to highlight why this conceptual issue and the related one of measurement are intimately connected to the question of culture. In the concrete example discussed above, it is apparent that the use of the concept of political party and the testing of hypotheses linked to the role of parties in democratic systems, are predicated on three key assumptions. The first is that Western politics is most fully embodied in a system where political

---

[24] See P. Chabal, 1998, 'A Few Reflections on Democracy in Africa', *International Affairs*, 74 (2).

[25] P. Chabal and J.-P. Daloz, 1999, *Africa Works*.

[26] The argument that there is today a functioning democracy in Nigeria immediately raises the question of whether there are different 'cultural' notions of what 'functioning' means.

representation is best conveyed through political parties, and that the legitimacy of such parties is refreshed in the course of electoral political competition. The second is that the cultural differences that may exist between Western democratic countries are not such as to invalidate either the representative nature of political parties or their legitimacy as the proper conduit for the expression of political opinion. The third is that multiparty electoral competition is considered beneficial to the health of democracy, regardless of the cultural variations that may be found between Western polities.

When it comes to measurement, similar problems arise. Our discipline's instruments of choice are based on questionnaires, surveys and statistics—seen as the most convincing and most comparable 'hard' data. We shall see below how critical the question of evidence is, but it is useful at this juncture to re-assess the cultural implications of the notion of measurement in comparative politics. Whilst there is no denying the usefulness of this type of quantitative information, we must question its universal validity. Above and beyond the fact that most countries in the world have very poor, and highly unreliable, statistics, there is every reason to doubt that the gathering and interpretation of such data is equally significant in every case. Again it is assumed that Western democracies share relatively similar standards of objectivity and professionalism but, even if that is true (which is debatable), such cannot be taken for granted elsewhere. Comparisons of income inequality, for instance, are only as good as the figures on which they are based and the gathering of information on wealth, income and revenue is by no means a straightforward matter, even in Western societies—for reasons, incidentally, which have a great deal to do with culture. It is quite simply fanciful to assume that it is possible to obtain meaningful cross-country data on the link between, say, affluence and political participation.

The unreliability of statistical evidence, however, is as nothing compared to the untrustworthiness of questionnaires, opinion polls and surveys—so often the lynchpin of the discipline. Students of comparative politics have systematically tested their hypotheses about political dynamics and changes by means of cross-national surveys—from the early 1960s study of 'civic culture' to the current evaluation of democratic norms in Black Africa. Then, as now, it has been accepted practice to send into the field armies of researchers, equipped with questionnaires essentially drawn from those in use in the Western countries, where the surveys originate. Although it is frequently claimed that the questions asked are adapted to local circumstances, what is never put in doubt is the validity of the methodology. And yet there are strong grounds for thinking that such polls are dangerously unreliable when used beyond the fairly narrow confines of the societies in which they are common currency and, crucially, where there are no additional means by which to cross check their soundness.

The aim here is not systematically to review the shortcomings of such surveys, but it may be useful to indicate why eschewing cultural factors matters. In the first instance a number of fairly obvious points need reiterating. The political questions asked are only meaningful if they are drawn from a previous knowledge of the historical and socio-cultural context concerned. In addition, the presentation of the questions, as well as the manner in which they are asked, both of which are undoubtedly linked to the cultural context in which they were framed, do influence results. Furthermore, the extent to which such polls are taken seriously, or even understood, hinges on the perception of the relevance of surveys generally (are people used to this form of research?) and on the opinion they have of the rationale of the particular survey being undertaken (what does it mean to me that I should be asked these questions?) Finally, the interpretation of the raw data must be made within culturally significant parameters. This in itself means that such surveys can be seriously exploited as only one piece of a large jigsaw, the other elements of which are equally important, if often left implicit. In all this, culture is paramount.

For instance, the reading of a questionnaire about public trust in politicians hinges largely on the analyst's knowledge of those general contemporary factors that condition the wider view taken by the electorate of the most recent causes for trusting/distrusting politicians. Such opinions generally have deep cultural roots, which an outside observer may fail to know or appreciate, as the case of Mitterrand highlights. We would all be sceptical, if not downright suspicious, of a poll conducted by a foreigner with scant knowledge of our own society, especially if the results were manifestly to run counter to our 'self-image'. Yet there is scarcely a moment's hesitation in undertaking surveys in (most frequently 'exotic') societies that differ

Both the ways [survey] one finds *have* *no good + cir [?] how* *doesn't work anyway*

radically from our own and of which we have only superficial experience. Employing 'local' researchers is merely a palliative, as becomes
obvious if we think of the difficulties that would arise were a foreign
researcher to ask us to conduct a predetermined survey based on
questions that appeared to us trivial, irrelevant or grounded in unwarranted assumptions.

Our intention here is not simply to make plain the fact that comparative political scientists are all too often insufficiently critical of
the concepts and measurements they deploy. It is rather to stress that
such a predicament makes it difficult, if not impossible, to integrate
any cultural perspective into comparative analysis. This is so not just
because there is very little explicit acknowledgement of the cultural
context or content of the main concepts used, but also because the
methods of measurement employed are so steeped in the tacit acceptance of Western cultural norms that they risk having very little relevance to the understanding of the other settings to which they are
applied. Conversely, because cultural factors do not easily lend themselves to the methodology and assessment framework most commonly adopted in comparative analysis they tend to be ignored,
devalued, or cast off into a very large residual category of so-called
'subjective' elements.

The pitfalls of evidence: field research and the collection of 'facts'

The situation discussed above is made intractable by the practicalities
of field research and the realities of the quest for 'facts'. Unlike economists who draw evidence primarily from statistical data or anthropologists who commit long periods in the field so as to immerse
themselves within the one community they aim to study, the comparativists' search for evidence is more ambiguous and, certainly,
more schizophrenic. Their method pulls them into two incompatible
directions. On the one hand, they must attempt to extend the comparative range of their enquiries, that is to access as large as possible a
sample of case studies.[27] The consensus here is that the greater the
number of cases the sounder the conclusions are likely to be. On the
other hand, they must seek to maximise the use of hard, or primary,

---

[27] We are leaving aside here those who engage in two-country or 'dyadic' comparisons, which in the nature of things are easier to operationalise.

evidence, the collection of which presupposes original research at the local level. The assumption in this instance is that the validity of the data is commensurate with the proximity of the source to the actors concerned.

As a consequence, comparative politics has proceeded in two quite distinct directions. The first has brought about the production of wide ranging studies about specific questions in the field, most commonly related to the types and workings of political, often democratic, systems. Here the aim has been either to produce typologies, then examine in detail how differences within sub-types matter, or to seek the patterns of political processes and change that help better to characterise the polities in question. The former has generated, among others, a large body of work on the constituent parts of multiparty systems: parliaments, parties, bureaucracies, civic associations and the like.[28] The latter has resulted in interesting studies on, for example, secularisation in the West, the trend away from ideology in advanced industrial societies, the causes of military rule or the dynamics of democratisation within authoritarian societies.[29]

Research in these areas is conducted primarily by means of a series of parallel surveys within the different countries concerned. Frequently, large numbers of students are mobilised to carry out polls in a number of areas at the same time, or at least within a limited time-frame, since in this instance contemporaneity matters. Methodology and research tools are standardised. The key to success is a tight conceptual agenda, clearly defined hypotheses, closely supervised surveys, and well-managed interpretation of the data by a single scholar or a group of closely collaborating colleagues. The danger lies in the fog engendered by too much data from so many different contexts. The temptation is to look for the smallest common denominator or to simplify results excessively.

This type of research is singularly ill-suited, for both conceptual and practical reasons, to the incorporation of cultural factors into political analysis. Comparative work of this kind makes use of

[28] On political parties, for instance, see the evolution in approach between two comparative volumes: J. La Palombara and M. Wiener (eds). 1966. *Political Parties and Political Development* and C. Boix, 1998, *Political Parties, Growth and Equality.*

[29] For one example, see R. Luckham and G. White, 1996. *Democratisation in the South: the jagged wave.*

concepts that are deemed to be relevant to a large number of different countries and seeks to test general hypotheses. Such an approach cannot easily accommodate an interest in the (necessarily) diverse cultures to be found in these numerous cases. Furthermore, its conclusions depend on the examination of a huge bank of data, most of it of a quantitative, or quantifiable, nature. Interpretation habitually hinges on some form of regression analysis. So that, for instance, the testing of the hypothesis that industrial societies become increasingly secular cannot be based on a case by case study of the nature of 'religiosity' in the different countries but must rely instead on a statistical computation of generally agreed indices of secularisation. Equally, the hypothesis that political parties in the West are becoming decreasingly 'ideological' and increasingly issue-oriented, can only be tested by means of a systematic examination of their manifestos and policy statements rather than by an in-depth study of, say, separate working-class cultures in industrialised countries.

The second area in which comparative analysts have been active is the in-depth study of particular polities, more akin to the country monograph. The ambition in this case is quite different and, in turn, can go in two directions. First, it can be a matter of wanting to answer a very specific question, which is important to comparative politics. Are there good political reasons why Singapore achieved such high rates of economic growth? Why did Muslim Turkey establish a secular state?[30] Or, second, it can be an attempt to study in detail specific aspects of a particular country so to advance the comparative knowledge of certain types of political systems. How relevant was socialist ideology to the postcolonial evolution of Guinea? What is the role of the military in Chile?

Research here follows more traditional patterns. It is usually the work of a single scholar who resides in the country under study for some considerable time and seeks to combine the search for documentary evidence with interviews or other direct contacts with the political actors concerned. Here success depends on a clear conceptual framework, a tight methodology, a solid background preparation, good contacts in the field, initiative, willingness to adapt and, of course, luck. The danger in this instance is of being diverted, either

[30] The recent surge of Islamic parties raises the question of whether secularism goes against the country's deep Muslim culture.

because of the lack of fit between the prepared research project and the situation on the ground or because of the pressures of immersion within a single society. The temptation is to over-generalise from the one case study.[31]

In this instance there is naturally a much greater chance that research is concerned with matters of culture. By its very nature an in-depth political study of a particular country, region or community requires a minimal understanding of the appropriate historical, socio-economic and cultural context. The very best such studies have been the result of the acquisition of the type of local knowledge and of the interaction with the local population more usually achieved by anthropologists than political scientists. Indeed, the early years of comparative politics produced a number of first-rate monographs on (mostly newly-independent) Third World countries that have stood the test of time.[32] In our perspective it is no coincidence that these books incorporate culture into political analysis, for scholars conducting research in areas new to the field had perforce to make the effort of understanding the socio-cultural world within which they were working. Nevertheless, even when such monographs displayed considerable local knowledge, they did not lead to a more cultural approach to the study of politics—as is demonstrated, for example, by David Apter's more theoretical publications from the same period[33]—and this for very significant reasons, which need briefly to be explored.

These scholars paid attention to culture not because they invested the field with an approach that placed such consideration at the heart of their enquiry, but simply because they realised they could not address the questions they had set out to explore without first acquiring sufficient understanding of the local context. Since there was in most cases no body of political work to which they could refer, and since most of the literature on the country was either of an historical or anthropological nature, clearly the background information that framed their work was heavily influenced by their knowledge of such contextual data. Both of these factors meant that their conclusions

---

[31] An issue discussed in detail in the Conclusion.

[32] For Africa, see J. Coleman, 1963, *Nigeria: background to nationalism*; D. Apter, 1955, *The Gold Coast in Transition* and 1961, *The Political Kingdom in Uganda*.

[33] D. Apter, 1965, *The Politics of Modernization*.

were much more sensitive to cultural factors than has since been the case in the discipline. Nevertheless, such early comparative scholars were keenly aware of the need for their work to help develop their newly established field. For this reason they made every effort to produce 'scientific' studies, based on a rigorous conceptual structure, which had little time for the 'softer' issues of culture. Furthermore, they worked within the decidedly teleological framework of political development theory, which meant they partook of the view that cultural factors would become increasingly less relevant as these newly independent countries 'matured' politically—that is, Western-ised. Understanding culture was useful but it was not what the discipline was about.

Our conclusion that comparative politics cannot 'handle' culture should not be misconstrued. It is neither an attempt to discredit the field as a whole nor a claim that political science is a spent force. The way social sciences evolve is rarely the result of the Kuhnian shift of paradigm that is so frequently cited, though more rarely understood, by scholars not working in the 'hard' sciences.[34] The clash of par-adigms cannot be resolved, once and for all, scientifically. Competing approaches offer alternative ways of explaining the world that are not necessarily reconcilable, as shall be explained in the Conclusion. Ana-lytical trends, however, change incrementally, often imperceptibly, and never straightforwardly, both in their theoretical focus and in their methodology.

However, within such a context it is our contention that the present insistence on the part of a growing number of political sci-entists upon the need for the discipline to become more 'scientif-ically rigorous' is misplaced. Indeed, the seemingly irresistible rise of rational choice theory is in danger of taking comparative politics down a theoretical blind alley in which the mirage of quantitative precision will ultimately dissolve in a grotesque distortion of the political realities which ordinary men and women confront in their everyday existence. Having shown how the field of comparative poli-tics is largely unable to integrate the cultural factors that give mean-ing to our lives, we now turn to a discussion of culture, thus laying down the foundations of our approach.

[34] T. Kuhn, 1962, *Structure of Scientific Revolution*.

WHAT IS CULTURE AND HOW DOES IT MATTER?

It would be tempting, but ultimately futile, for students of comparative politics to attempt to conceptualise culture by searching for a comprehensive definition, identifying in the process all its politically significant constituent parts. The very method that consists in seeking to list the attributes of human life that could be classified as cultural is itself the outcome of the vain quest to endow political science with the quality of 'hard' sciences. It is indeed precisely because such a quest has more often than not been unsuccessful that political scientists have been induced to look upon culture as a residual category, fit only to reclaim those areas of politics for which there was no good conceptual home. It is also for this reason that a good number of cultural analyses have appeared to be constructed on weak theoretical grounds, placing them immediately on the defensive within a discipline with aspirations to the highest scientific ideals.

Our approach starts from the opposite premise. Culture is not to be defined exhaustively, by reference to all the possible elements that might come to represent what it is at a particular (and inevitably frozen) point in time. Culture is best understood as an environment, a constantly evolving setting, within which human behaviour follows a number of particular courses—many of which are contradictory.[35] We discuss below how best to employ such an 'unorthodox' manner of characterising the concept, but we want first to make clear how we think culture matters for comparative political analysis. Our view is that culture is not merely an additional dimension of politics that requires attention. It is quite simply one of the key fundaments of social life, the matrix within which that which we understand as political action takes place. In other words, the field of politics itself has to be examined within its appropriate cultural milieu, as it were. Far from being a residual category, culture is in some sense that which constitutes the coordinates, the mapping, or the very blueprint of politics.[36]

---

[35] Some of the earliest, and most fruitful, reflections on the notion of culture in society go back to the British philosopher David Hume. See here particularly D. Hume, 1976, *A Treatise of Human Nature*, Book III.

[36] As Clifford Geertz writes: "As interworked systems of construable signs (what, ignoring provincial usages, I would call symbols), culture is not a power, something to which social events, behaviors, institutions or processes can be causally attributed; it is a context, something within which they can be intelligibly—that

The key here is an analysis of culture as a *system of meanings* and not primarily as *values*.[37] To look at culture in terms of values is to approach the question from a normative and, not infrequently, ethnocentric perspective—making it difficult, for instance, to explain 'cultural' differences within a single society. To look at it in terms of meanings, on the other hand, is to attempt to reveal the language in which people, who may disagree about values, or political ends, can do so within a shared perspective. An explanation of the cultural context no longer requires an explicit definition of culture in terms of norms, beliefs and values—or even an analysis of how these differ from our own. Our work, therefore, offers a study of politics that is different from the standard (political science) approach in terms of 'political culture', as has hitherto been developed in comparative politics. It also provides an analytical framework that is at variance from that adopted in a volume like *Culture Matters* where, again, culture is largely equated with values.[38]

Therefore, our enterprise is not only an effort to explain how culture is germane to comparative analysis. It is an attempt to show how the very business of political science needs theoretically to be grounded in a proper cultural perspective. This does not mean that culture necessarily 'explains', even less 'determines', the outcome of political action. Rather, it implies that the elucidation of such action calls for proper recourse to theories that allow relevant consideration of the appropriate cultural environment(s). It is in this sense that what we propose in this book is congenial to what Marc Ross writes of cultural analysis in a recent, and quite comprehensive, panorama of comparative politics:

[I] argue that two distinct, but not unrelated, features of culture are relevant to comparative politics. First, culture is a system of meaning that people use to manage their daily worlds, large and small; second, culture is the basis of the social and political identity that affects how people line up and how they act on a wide range of matters.[39]

---

is, thickly—described." C. Geertz, 1973, 'Thick Description: toward an interpretive theory of culture' in *The Interpretation of Cultures*, p. 14.

[37] We discuss this in detail in Chapter 3.

[38] L. Harrison and S. Huntington (eds), 2000, *Culture Matters: how values shape human progress.*

[39] M. H. Ross, 1997, 'Culture and Identity in Comparative Political Analysis' in Lichbach and Zuckerman (eds.), 1997, *Comparative Politics*, p. 42.

Culture is not simply 'relevant' to comparative politics. Much more fundamental, comparative politics can only be meaningful insofar as it succeeds in making sense of the cultural environment that provides the very framework within which local politics take place. But let us now explain more specifically how we approach the concept of culture.

Definition(s): universal questions; local knowledge

As should be clear by now, we do not think it useful to endeavour to present a single and comprehensive definition of the notion of culture, even less one that would be geared to politics as such. Like many others, we are stimulated by the work of Clifford Geertz, itself a reflection on comparative analysis deeply informed by the historical legacy of a number of social scientists. Partly because Geertz is one of those rare scholars to write with style and partly because his formulations are conceptually compelling, it is easiest to develop our views from three of his best-known statements.

[T]he culture concept to which I adhere has neither multiple referents nor, so far as I can see, any unusual ambiguity: it denotes an historically transmitted pattern of meanings embodied in symbols, a system of inherited conceptions expressed in symbolic forms by means of which men communicate, perpetuate, and develop their knowledge about and attitudes towards life.[40]

Let us unpack what this characterisation implies for political analysis. The key notion here is that culture is a 'system of inherited conceptions expressed in symbolic forms'. This makes it plain, first, that what may appear merely as a conglomeration of discrete 'values' is in fact an inter-related and structured whole. Second, it highlights the historical dimension of culture, which is to be understood not as being simply the current 'language' of norms and habits (synchronically) but as the living environment, evolved in the *longue durée* (diachronically). Finally, the emphasis is clearly placed on the fact that culture is expressed in symbolic form, and not, as is sometimes believed, only in factual statements. Comparative analysis, therefore, must concern itself with all three aspects of culture, and not just with

---

[40] C. Geertz, 1973, 'Religion as a Cultural System' in C. Geertz, 1973, *The Interpretation of Cultures*, p. 89.

those that may appear to be more directly applicable to the business of politics. A cultural analysis of politics is one that builds into its theoretical approach a discussion of culture rooted in the three dimensions outlined above.

Further, Geertz writes:

> The concept of culture I espouse... is essentially a semiotic one. Believing, with Max Weber, that man is an animal suspended in webs of significance he himself has spun, I take culture to be those webs, and the analysis of it to be therefore not an experimental science in search of law but an interpretive one in search of meaning. It is explication I am after, construing social expressions on their surface enigmatical.[41]

The second key element of Geertz's proposition is thus that the concept of culture is first and foremost semiotic, in the sense in which it is defined above.[42] This is critical and needs re-asserting forcefully not only because it is an aspect of the question that is habitually eluded in political science but also because it is one of the central tenets of our method, as is explained in Chapter 8. The reason this notion of culture is unpalatable to political scientists is because it touches on what appear to be 'subjective' characteristics of human action—the words and symbols by which people recognise and express themselves. An acceptance of such a conception of culture would imply a research agenda with which most political analysts are uncomfortable, since it puts a premium on the assessment of meanings as they matter to the individuals who make up each distinct society. This is a demanding requirement, but we believe it is imperative to place it at the heart of comparative analysis, if we are to advance the heuristic value of our discipline.

Indeed Geertz's reminder of Weber's understanding of culture should be a timely prompt to comparative analysts for, whatever our view of the German social scientist, it cannot be disputed that he was

---

[41] C. Geertz, 1973, 'Thick Description: toward an interpretive theory of culture' in *ibid*, p. 5.

[42] Whether Geertz would today be unhappy with the use of the concept of 'semiotic', which he would see as being aligned with the structural approaches he dislikes, is an open question. We, for our part, are in agreement with his original formulation and do not follow the structuralists on this point. We are concerned with meanings and not merely 'signs'. For a more general discussion of the author, see K. Rice, 1980, *Geertz and Culture* and, more particularly, S. Ortner, 1997, *The Fate of Culture*.

the pioneer of comparative historical sociology and that there is much to be gained by re-examining his methods. One of the limitations of current political theory is its short-term memory, ignoring as it does the fact that the residual notion of culture so frequently employed has only a very recent pedigree. As explained above, it was only born within the ambit of the post–Parsonian approach. Until then European social science took the notion of culture (or in the case of France, 'civilisation'[43]) very seriously. In any event, the central consequence of such an approach to culture is, as Geertz points out, that the task of the analyst is the search for meaning, and that the instrument to be employed is, as is discussed below, the 'art' of interpretation.

Finally, addressing specifically the issue of culture and politics, Geertz comments:

Culture, here, is not cults and customs, but the structures of meaning through which men give shape to their experience; and politics is not coups and constitutions, but one of the principal arenas in which such structures publicly unfold.[44]

This statement is useful in that it focuses attention both on the object of political analysis and on the method most relevantly used to study politics. By suggesting that politics is an 'arena', rather than a 'black box'[45], Geertz goes right to the heart of the question. From this point of view, what is consequential is not so much the study of functional equivalents within the body politic but the translation of the meanings, the symbols, of what is 'political' in a particular society into a language that lends itself to comparative analysis.[46]

It may be thought at this stage that our discussion of the concept of culture is all too Geertz-centred, or at the very least excessively dependent on an anthropological notion. Are none of the definitions used in political science of any use?[47] The question is not purely rhe-

---

[43] For a synthetic treatment of that question, see D. Cuche, 1998, *La notion de culture dans les sciences sociales.*

[44] C. Geertz, 1973, 'The Politics of Meaning' in C. Geertz, 1973, *The Interpretation of Cultures*, p. 312.

[45] As it is in much American classical political science since the days of Karl Deutsch. See K. Deutsch, 1963, *The Nerves of Government.*

[46] On the question of political symbolism and politics as theatre, see Chapter 10 and Conclusion, where these are discussed explicitly.

[47] There is, of course, a body of work that defines culture in terms of the symbolic and, along with this, approaches to politics that take symbolism seriously. See

torical because the answer is important to our approach. For reasons expounded at length above, we hold that political theory as it is commonly understood today propounds a concept of culture that is inimical to the type of analysis we propose.[48] Not only does it seek to narrow down the scope of culture to variously operational common denominators, often dubbed variables, but it fails to take seriously the question of the 'webs of significance', which Weber quite rightly considered critical for comparative analysis. And the German scholar himself demonstrated how a well-considered effort to interpret meanings in this way could be accomplished through a systematic study of historical sources, which could result in the production of an insightful comparative analysis. The current resurgence of interest in Weber's work is proof, if proof be needed, that his method is once again of interest to social scientists dissatisfied with the state of their disciplines.[49]

We make no apology for taking as our starting point a conceptual perspective best expounded by an anthropologist. Nor do we feel it incumbent upon us to defend Geertz's position on the subject, even if we recognise that it has also been contested by his professional colleagues.[50] Ours is not a quest for a 'definitive' characterisation of culture but for an approach that manages to respond to the dilemmas faced by practitioners of comparative politics as they grapple with the contextual and historical complexities of their very diverse case studies. In our previous work on Africa we found it immensely rewarding to integrate some of the most illuminating insights derived from anthropology. Indeed, there scarcely seems to be any disagreement today among Africanists that such combined approaches are ulti-

---

here, for instance M. Edelman, 1971, *Politics as Symbolic Action*. For us, however, this author takes an excessively instrumental view of culture. Other more recent approaches worthy of note are to be found in A. Dörner and L. Vogts (eds), 2002, *Wahl-Kämpfe*.

[48] For instance, E. Ringmar, 1996, *Identity Interest and Action* offers a less than wholly convincing cultural explanation of Swedish intervention in the Thirty Years War as an alternative to rational choice theory in *Identity Interest and Action*.

[49] Of course, Weber was influenced by nineteenth-century evolutionary theories and believed, for instance, in the gradual 'rationalisation' of politics over time. However, one can find rich conceptual insights without subscribing to such teleology.

[50] For a recent discussion of Geertz's work in context, see F. Inglis, 2000, *Clifford Geertz*.

mately fruitful. Furthermore, and more generally, we believe firmly
that the most convincing comparative accounts of political processes
are those that have combined solid historical research with the use of
concepts from appropriate relevant other social sciences.[51]

Relevance: explaining the complexities of actual politics

Our advocacy of a cultural approach to the comparative study of
politics does not simply derive from an *a priori* bias. It issues from the
conviction that our discipline as it now stands is in danger of reducing
the scope of its activities to a primarily quantifiable, focus. It is, in
other words, liable to forget that the only justification for what we do,
other than to construct models in the air, is to further the understanding of political processes across the world. Comparison is warranted if it provides a more plausible account of what is happening,
either in a single or in a series of settings. The 'science' of politics can
only aim at explaining political events and processes more credibly
than mere 'common sense' when its theoretical framework enables a
new, and more meaningful, elucidation of the facts.[52] Otherwise it is
otiose, purely self-serving.

Of course, theory in the social sciences provides a simplified model
of how human beings behave and form social relations over time, but
the litmus test of theory, here as in the natural sciences, is how it facilitates the explanation of observable events. Or, to put it differently,
how it allows us meaningfully to unpack the complexities of real life.
Comparative analysts should explain, not simply paraphrase, actual
politics. And they can scarcely hope to do that unless they begin to
develop methods that allow them to integrate a cultural approach—
that is, not just pay lip service to a few self-evidently important cultural factors, like ethnicity or language, but to disentangle the relevant
webs of significance that impinge on political action. Why is this? Let

---

[51] For an example of such a scholar who, however, did *not* use the cultural approach
we advocate, see B. Moore, 1966, *Social Origins of Dictatorship and Democracy.*

[52] On common sense Geertz again provides us with a pithy comment: '[C]ommon
sense [is] a cultural system; a loosely connected body of belief and judgement,
rather than just what anybody properly put together cannot help but think…
Common sense is not a fortunate faculty, like perfect pitch; it is a special frame of
mind, like piety or legalism. And like piety or legalism (or ethics or cosmology) it
both differs from one place to the next and takes, nevertheless, a characteristic
form.' C. Geertz, 1983, 'Introduction' in C. Geertz, *Local Knowledge*, pp. 10–11.

us explain by reference to Africa, that much-maligned continent that we know well.

It is generally argued by comparative analysts in the field that there is in sub-Saharan Africa, as elsewhere in the world, a trend towards democracy. On the face of it the evidence is strong, since in the last decade most countries have held (single or repeated) multiparty elections.[53] Furthermore, recent comparative research appears to confirm, by means of large-scale surveys, that there is increasing support among the population at large for democratic systems.[54] Based on such work, then, it would seem legitimate to conclude that Africa is indeed moving in the same direction as other regions of the globe. This would not be an inaccurate inference, given the limited procedural definition that is usually given of 'democracy' (meaning simply the holding of regular, relatively free and fair, elections), but it would be a highly misleading one, for several important reasons.

First, it would convey the impression that the direction in which politics is evolving in Africa is, in some meaningful way, taking the continent towards a model akin to that found in the West.[55] In fact, the opposite is the case, since whatever the effects of multiparty elections, they have emphatically not led to political behaviour that resembles substantively those to be found in Europe, North America, or even Southeast Asia. Second, it would imply that the characterisation of present day African polities as 'democracies' is an insightful manner of conceptualising the exercise of power in those countries. Again, not only is the reality totally at variance with this conclusion but the emphasis on the 'democratic' nature of current African governments tends to obscure the actual complexities of the present situation. What we find south of the Sahara are, with few exceptions, (functioning or collapsed) clientelistic regimes that have, more or less reluctantly, adopted the procedures of multiparty elections. By stressing how 'democratic' these procedures may be we divert attention from

---

[53] A comprehensive analysis of democratisation is to be found in M. Bratton and N. van de Walle, 1997, *Democratic Experiments in Africa*.

[54] See the ongoing University of Michigan Afrobarometer project conducting surveys on key political issues, many of which are related to 'democratisation', in a number of African countries.

[55] The following argument is drawn from P. Chabal and J.-P. Daloz, 1999, *Africa Works*, and P. Chabal, 2002, 'The Quest for Good Government and Development in Africa: is NEPAD the answer?', *International Affairs*, 78 (3).

the significance for analysis of the actual exercise of power in these countries.

This example is not intended simply to demonstrate the limits of the current comparative work on Africa, although it is of course impossible to ignore them, but to illustrate the reasons why the failure to integrate a cultural approach into a study of the continent has vitiated our understanding of its present predicament. This is not to imply that a stress on contemporary political transitions is irrelevant. Multiparty elections in Africa have brought about important changes, such as much greater freedom of expression, which bear examination. It is, rather, that the incorporation of African politics within the broader field of comparative democratic studies has led to the adoption of what we would call an 'a-cultural' (and, incidentally, a-historical) theoretical framework, generating a highly misleading account of politics on the continent. Therefore, such a model does not in our eyes meet the basic 'scientific' criterion of plausibility.[56]

Our work on Africa has shown how a cultural approach makes it possible to understand the extent to which the exercise of power, south of the Sahara, is predicated on a personalised concept of politics. This explains, first, why relations of legitimacy, representation and accountability are primarily vertical, between patrons and clients. Second, it provides clear reasons why, on the continent, there has been so little political institutionalisation—in the sense in which Max Weber defined it—and that whatever institutionalisation had taken place by independence was undermined by the logic of informal political relations that prevailed afterwards. It makes plain why such a pattern induces political élite to seek to accumulate wealth—both to display their political 'substance' and to have the means to redistribute to those on whose support they depend. Finally, it reveals why present transitions are unable to change the nature of politics in Africa. The holding of regular multiparty elections, which is usually equated with 'democratisation', has come about largely because of outside pressure, but the realities on the ground are that, more often than not, it is democracy that has been adapted to the logic and rigours of clientelism and not, as so often proclaimed, the reverse.

What lessons can we draw from this African example? Three remarks are relevant to the claim that a cultural approach helps to explain

[56] Our notion of 'scientific' is made clear in Chapters 7 and 8.

the complexities of real politics. The first is that it is clearly necessary to build into any account of sub-Saharan politics a method for conveying what the notion of power means for the local actors, from the top to the bottom of society. This entails an ability to explain what 'makes sense' to them and, in the context of Africa, it implies research into areas of social, cultural and religious life—such as, for instance, the occult—that may be less relevant to other regions of the world. Second, it means that we must go beyond the surface of political processes—such as here multiparty elections—to probe deeper into the significance of political change. Most people in Africa conceive of 'democracy' in terms of personalised politics and not in terms of institutionalisation. Finally, it shows that the best way to compare African political systems with those found elsewhere is not to focus primarily on their procedural complexion but to attempt to contrast how political forms of 'exchange' like legitimacy, accountability or representation actually take place.

Application: the 'art' of interpretation

Making progress in the use of culture in comparative analysis entails developing the means to understand such webs of significance as are relevant to the questions we ask. This, as is suggested above, rests on the issue of translation, or as we would put it, the 'art' of interpretation. For an elegant elaboration of what is meant by translation in this context, we turn, yet again, to Clifford Geertz:

'Translation'… is not a simple recasting of others' ways of putting things in terms of our own ways of putting them (that is the kind in which things get lost), but displaying the logic of their ways of putting them in the locutions of ours; a conception which again brings it rather closer to what a critic does to illumine a poem than what an astronomer does to account for a star.[57]

Such a 'poetic' view of translation is evidently not a mode of interpretation to which social scientists would readily adhere, and it is certainly one from which rational choice theorists would recoil. Can one base analysis on such a very personal vision of what webs of significance might mean in different settings? Is this not a far too 'ethnological' approach, useful for in-depth case studies but unsuited to the broad comparative canvas? These objections are well taken and

[57] C. Geertz, 1983, 'Introduction' in C. Geertz, *Local Knowledge*, p. 10.

go straight to the tension that lies at the heart of our discipline: how to reconcile specific local knowledge with the general sweep of trends and processes? There is no easy answer to that question, but there is a price to pay for ignoring it.

Geertz's contrast between the calling of the astronomer and that of the critic points to the key issue at stake. The choice between the one and the other is not arbitrary, whimsical, but derives from the nature of the 'problem' to be solved. There is room for both; it is simply that each does a different job. Of course, a poet could account for a star (many have) and an astronomer could explain a poem (rather fewer have), but what they would be doing would be distinct. Stars, after all, are poetic; and poems are metric. There is merit in recounting the particular sentiment a star may unleash in one single soul. Equally, the algebraic patterns of rhymes can be scientifically elegant. But this is not the issue. The point of a poem is how it says what it says, not whether a computer can identify its architecture. The interest of a star usually resides in the data it provides about the motion of celestial bodies or the creation of the universe. More generally, therefore, our argument is that the method employed derives from the problem at hand, not from *a priori* theoretical or ideological choice.

Therefore, the claim that analysis rests on the 'art' of interpretation issues from the recognition of the fact that comparisons demand the ability of 'displaying the logic of 'their' ways of putting things in the locutions of 'ours'. This can only be done if we take seriously the job of trying to reveal what that logic might be—that is, to make sense of the behaviour of political actors in their own, specific and local, settings. Interpretation, therefore, is far from arbitrary. It is, we would argue, scientific, in that it requires a systematic approach: the disciplined use of theories and concepts as instruments for the 'translation' of the material to hand. Hence the 'art' of interpretation is for us based on clearly identifiable methods, which can be explained and, more importantly, replicated. The way(s) in which those methods are applied, on the other hand, ought to be determined by the contextual factors most relevant to the case studies under examination.

Let us take as one example the comparative study of what is all too blandly called corruption—as though it were a straightforward issue.[58]

---

[58] See here how corruption is understood by the influential NGO, Transparency International, which publishes a yearly *Global Corruption Report*.

The standard comparative approach consists in providing a definition of the phenomenon, commonly based on juridical terms; putting forward a number of hypotheses about what factors may most usefully correlate with corruption; and setting out to gather the data to test such suppositions. Our approach would differ in every respect. We would not attempt to offer a tight, or closed, definition of corruption other than to say that the phenomenon touches on the tension, in each society, between what is deemed to be desirable and what is seen locally to be permissible. We would then develop concepts about the best way to approach that question and emphasise that what is at stake is essentially the way in which different societies consider and sanction illicit transactions. We would then explain why there may well be significant differences in the meanings of 'licit' and 'legal', why in any event such notions might differ significantly from those current in the West. We would finally study the 'moral and political economy of corruption' in various countries with a view to disclosing the nature of that tension within each society. Only then would we hazard a comparison between the instances under examination.

Therefore, our concern would not be to compare corruption *per se*, but to contrast the varying logic of illicit acts in the different case studies. We will develop this example at greater length later on, but here we would like to explain how it impinges on our understanding of interpretation. Comparing corruption in different societies consists in being able to explain to ourselves, and to those who read our books, why avoiding tax in Italy, making corporate donations to political parties in South Korea, pilfering funds from the state in Nigeria, pocketing a commission on a commercial transaction in Kuwait, or giving a job to a poorly qualified acquaintance who went to the same public school in Britain are all illegal but widely perceived as 'culturally legitimate' acts within each one of those countries.[59] The point here is not to establish a hierarchy of illicit acts and cast a comparative moral judgement so as to identify which is worse, nor even to see which form of corruption is more detrimental to, say,

---

[59] We do not mean to imply here either that all members of a particular society behave in the same ways or that there are not significant differences between groups within a given society. Nor, as we will show later, are we suggesting that there are 'national' tendencies in this respect. We are here simply concerned to show how our approach differs from that currently in vogue—whether in comparative politics or in other forums where comparisons are made.

economic growth—about which much of interest can be said. It is, rather, to understand how in every society individuals and groups exploit the tensions between the desirable and the permissible, seeking at every opportunity to make use of the loopholes, or interstices, through which such corruption can be achieved.

However, the 'art' of interpretation is not just about 'a' scientific method. It is also about the narrative of comparative analysis, that which Geertz calls the work of the critic. Explaining what makes sense to others, the logic of what they do, depends on our ability to find the right 'locutions' in our own analytical language. Here too present trends in political science are adverse, for they tend to narrow down comparative discourse to jargon-like utterances that merely attend to the lowest common denominator. In the case of corruption what is comparatively least interesting is a statement such as, for instance, 'There is more corruption in societies where economic growth is low'. The banality of the conclusion, true as it may well be, is made worse by the fact that the formulation lacks any real critical insight. What is interesting about corruption is not so much why it exists, but how it affects politics. To give texture to that question is to try to articulate the complexities of what corruption actually 'means' in these different settings. How do the Italians, South Koreans, Nigerians, Kuwaitis or British express their form of corruption, how do they use language both to justify and condemn such activities?

For this reason we are mindful of the need to write about the phenomena we attempt to compare by means of a language that is attuned to the terrain in which we are working. We cannot, of course, merely translate the words that are used by the actors themselves, but we can find more original ways of reflecting what those words mean by allowing ourselves to stray far beyond the constraints of social science terminology. There is, clearly, a thin line between language that sheds light on what is happening in any given society and facile metaphors with implicit meanings that may distort what is being discussed. It is, for example, debatable whether the expression 'the politics of the belly', as employed by a French political scientist to conjure the complex links between political and economic power in Africa, evokes in the Western reader the image that is most illuminating.[60] This is because, in this case, 'the politics of the belly' immediately points to

---

[60] J.-F. Bayart, 1989. *L'Etat en Afrique: la politique du ventre.*

corruption whereas what is interesting in the book in question is the extent to which modern political practices are anchored in the cultural and historical roots of African politics.

The point here is less to focus attention on the (admittedly) intricate question of corruption than to illustrate the extent to which both interpretation and enunciation can be made meaningfully 'scientific'. What is at stake is not just the 'right' language but the critical method best suited to comparative politics. Although there are no obvious standard means of understanding and accounting for different political 'arenas', there are approaches that are more attuned to the job of listening, interpreting and rendering in the appropriate language the realities we study—as the book will show in some detail.

The cultural methodology advocated here is not one beholden to any particular theory, either in political science or anthropology. We seek to use a notion of culture that is enabling, and not restrictive; open ended, and not constraining; enlightening, and not obscuring. This is the measure of our undertaking. The validity of the analysis we claim does not lie in the accuracy, or pedigree, of our definition of the notion of culture, but only in the extent to which it helps explain political acts, events and processes within a comparative perspective. We have found Geertz's approach helpful both in the manner in which it conceptualises culture and in the framework it proposes for looking at politics as an 'arena'. However, ours is not a Geertzian 'model'—insofar as that exists—but, as we shall show at the end of the book, a call for an eclectic methodology.

Culture Troubles is an attempt to develop a cultural approach to the comparative study of politics. The goal is to provide a conceptual framework and a method suited to the demands of a discipline aiming to study a large number of different polities across the globe. The structure of the book is designed to show how our work builds upon, but also differs significantly from, the mainstream of political science. The three main tasks we set ourselves are simple to outline. We want, first to define the parameters of enquiry—that is, make clear what it means to compare. Second, we seek to look into the question of how to compare, or stated more simply, how to ask the appropriate comparative questions. Finally, we aim to show how it is possible to enunciate comparative insights going beyond the common bounds of ideology and causality that have so constrained our discipline.

The book is in six distinct parts. The five sections that follow this Introduction endeavour, respectively, to discuss the current approaches to the question of culture in contemporary political science, to delineate our understanding of the notion and role of culture in politics, to develop our method and to show how it can be applied to distinct settings. We conclude with a call for theoretical eclecticism.

Part I concentrates on the framework within which political theory has tackled the question of culture. We provide a critique of the main approaches extant and refute the most common objections to cultural analysis. We then discuss the demands made on theory as it seeks to assess diversity while avoiding reductionism. Finally, we lay out the analytical foundations of our methodology.

Part II focuses more specifically on the ways in which it is possible to integrate culture into political analysis. It addresses some of the thornier issues in our field and attempts to show how the approach we favour makes it possible to come to some plausible comparative conclusions on the matter. Here we discuss the relationship between culture and identity, the implications of a cultural analysis for the understanding of power in society and, lastly, what is the relevance of culture for political change.

Part III explains our method, or, in other words, reveals the sinews of our approach. Consistent with the notion of culture outlined above, we advocate a methodology that rests on two central pillars: the need to think *inductively* and *semiotically*. What does this mean in practice? The first, induction, is an argument in favour of a strong link between the understanding of the terrain and the type of methodological instruments deployed to explain its politics. A semiotic reasoning consists in an analysis firmly grounded in the study of meanings and the translation of what makes sense to the actors concerned.

Part IV shows how our method offers new insights into comparative analysis. Here we examine two key issues: the question of the State and the meanings of representation. Following a discussion of how the State came to be constituted we explain how a cultural approach is indispensable to an appreciation of the State that illuminates its (formal and informal) workings in three different settings: Nigeria, France and Sweden. We then analyse the diverse and complex connotations of the notion of political representation in these same three areas.

The Conclusion brings together the strands of our argument and validates our advocacy of what we call an eclectic approach. It shows why present day paradigms are largely mutually exclusive and why, therefore, our eclectic method is conceptually and theoretically more open. We end the volume with an illustration of how our approach offers a methodology with which it is possible to develop a dynamic comparative analysis of political leadership.

Part I. FRAMEWORK

One of the main outcomes of research in the social sciences, particularly ethnology and anthropology, is to have shown that the cultural
environment within which we live influences our perception, understanding and organisation of the world that surrounds us. Once
human groupings had evolved from a purely instinctive relationship
with the world, they began to elaborate a variety of complex sets of
codes, or rituals, that were often incompatible with those of other
bands. Culture, which is meant to distinguish us from animals, is thus
infinitely multiple.

Clearly these cultural systems have had a *deep influence* on how we
live. The ways in which we create order out of our surroundings,
make sense of the myriad interactions we experience, and give meaning to our lives, are all ultimately dependent on the cultural legacy we
have inherited. Whether we cultivate or reject such bequest, this very
process of socialisation leaves indelible traces.[1] Thus it is not possible
to conceive of a life devoid of culture. Indeed, it is hard to conceive of
meaningful behaviour other than within a cultural context.

Linguists and anthropologists have shown how our perception of
the world was mediated by language. Are we not in effect imprisoned
by its grammar, vocabulary and even syntax?[2] An individual brought
up in an idiom in which time is a fluid concept finds it difficult to
come to terms with one in which past, present and future are clearly
delineated linguistically. Is it significant, for instance, that some West
African languages do not have words to express colour?

---

[1] It has been shown that different peoples have differently developed senses (vision,
hearing, smelling etc.). Therefore, it is probable that we do not even inhabit the
same sensorial world. Culture thus affects even the most basic of our attributes as
human beings.

[2] One might refer here to the work of B. Whorf (a disciple of E. Sapir) who, on the
basis of empirical research among the Hopi Indians, argued that the language
spoken by an individual determines his/her conception and perception of the
world. This is an issue that linguists have been debating for over a hundred years.

Equally, there are huge gaps between the non-verbal aspects of different cultures. Peoples living in the extreme north, in a world with no apparent reference points, where the horizon disappears in a blur of glaring white, manage to find their bearings by means of a complex set of calculations involving the direction and smell of the wind as well as the texture of snow. Space is always understood, or conceptualised, by reference to cultural attributes. In some parts space is conceived in terms of artificial lines and conventional measures (the Greenwich meridian or the mile). Yet in other settings, reference is made to surfaces and intersections.[3] The same goes for notions of time. If in Northern Europe and North America punctuality is highly prized, to arrive on time in Sub-Saharan Africa is to display inferiority. The mighty always appear late: the mightier, the later. On another register, concepts of what is legitimate and illegitimate are eminently variable. Finally, aesthetic taste belongs to the realm of extreme relativism.

As a result, there is no end to the possibility for misunderstanding or incomprehension in cross-cultural relations. To look someone in the eye, a virtue in some societies, is construed as insolence in others. Conversely, to avert one's eye may be perceived as a sign of respect or of deviousness. Interrupting someone could be an indication of forthrightness and involvement or, alternatively, of effrontery. Ensuring that one's breath does not reach the other person can be seen as highly hygienic in one place but as an unacceptable display of detachment in another. The same goes for maintaining a suitable distance with one's interlocutor. Studies have shown that North Americans instinctively step back when addressed by South Americans, whereas the latter continue to seek closer proximity: each one interpreting social distance in the opposite fashion.[4] Similarly, the culture we have received might privilege frankness or tact, the exhibition or concealment of emotion, the cult of efficiency or of the slow meandering in which the exhibition of activity is more important than the end-result. There are countless other examples of what makes, or does not make, sense to the other.

Comparativists who favour a cultural approach—that is, the setting of distinct representations of the world, dissimilar social attitudes

---

[3] It is worth remembering here that in Japan it is neighbourhoods, or intersections, that are named and not the streets.

[4] See here Edward Hall's work, in particular, 1966, *The Hidden Dimension*.

or different political discourses within their appropriate context—are often met with resistance because they appear to cast doubts on some of the most cherished beliefs held within their own society. Equally, they are wont to show that our own models, even if they appear all conquering, are not universal. This frequently leads to a hostile reaction or to the naïve plea that such considerations are in any event superficial, or irrelevant.

A long intellectual tradition in Western thought rests on a voluntarist notion of the *politic*. For Aristotle it was the embodiment of the nature of man, its realisation; for Hobbes it was the instrument that enabled man to transcend the 'state of nature'. Politically committed analysts take as their point of origin the painful gap between the principles they advocate and the socio-cultural realities extant. If their overt aim is to reveal to their fellow man the mechanisms that shackle society, their ultimate ambition is clearly to convince them of the righteousness of their own conception of the desirable political and sociological organisation.

Such an approach is not merely the preserve of the ideologues. Confusion between scientific ambition and intellectualist posturing is widespread among social scientists. For this reason, we wish at this early stage of our discussion to note that one of the main reasons why a cultural approach is unpalatable to so many (analysts or intellectuals) is because it is by definition non-dogmatic and non-teleological. As will be shown in Chapter 1, this is because it eschews the universalist pretensions of grand systemic explanation—whether in the guise of human values or explanatory schemes for human development. The cultural comparativist starts from the premise that the realm of politics cannot be taken for granted but needs to be studied within the plurality of systems of meanings whence it arises. The very definition of the *politic* and the way it is articulated with other spheres of social activity are far from simple or resolved issues.

It is often argued that a cultural approach rests on conveniently shaky definitional foundations. For this reason it is important to chart carefully the specificities of rival concepts, to explain the debates that surround their use, and to assess the position of the competing interpretations. This will make possible an appreciation of their heuristic value and a sharpening of our own perspective on the question. To this end Chapter 2 discusses the key question of how independent the cultural variable may be and will assess the import of a number of reductionist approaches.

Another charge is that a method focusing on differences is likely to evolve into a form of hyper-culturalism that would make comparison difficult, if not impossible. We take the opposite view—namely that a scientific approach requires a systematic and rigorous study of what is dissimilar. Instead of seeking to identify vague, or contrived, convergences, comparative analysis should seek to take seriously the differences to be found between distinct worlds of meaning. This is only possible if we move away from a normative reading of cultures—either in terms of values or in terms of those 'political cultures' that appear more 'civic'. Our approach is also clearly distinct from the post-modernist, the chief aim of which seems to promote the recognition of 'dominated' identities and to encourage resistance to the hegemonic tendencies of dominant cultures.

A scientifically grounded cultural approach does not *exalt* differences; it seeks to take their meanings *seriously*.

1

CRITIQUE OF GRAND THEORY

An approach such as the one presented in this book stems from scepticism in respect of universalising conceptual frameworks. There is a deep and irreconcilable distinction between the work of the intellectual,[1] in search of *the* key that will unlock social processes and that of the interpretativist scholar, who is driven by the ambition to understand what makes sense within a given context. By its very nature a cultural methodology is prone to question established theories in the social sciences and point to the limits of existing and sometimes well-established models.

However, the interpretativist methodology is frequently criticised for a number of reasons, which ultimately amount to the charge that it does not meet the criteria of a social 'science'. We will return to this question throughout this volume, but we want in this chapter to address two sets of interrelated issues. The first is essentially a critique of the influence of grand theory on the study of comparative politics. The second is an in-depth discussion of some of the most frequent charges levelled at a cultural approach.

THE UNIVERSALIST FALLACY

Although we would argue against all universalist theories in the social sciences, it seems to us that there are three strands in the literature that have had strong resonance in the field of comparative politics: politically driven approaches, the use of historical parallels and the de-

---

[1] 'Intellectual' here is used as in the French tradition, referring to someone with some degree of education who, because of his/her supposed competence and conviction, is ready to intervene in public debate and sometimes to participate in political campaigns. More broadly, it refers to those scholars or academics who also pursue a political agenda.

ployment of teleological systems. It is undoubtedly the case that a large number of political scientists are motivated in their work by a commitment to a particular political cause or ideology. Equally, as concerns the evolution of the non-Western world, most students of comparative politics seek to assess the extent to which these societies are likely to Westernise politically and economically. The first part of this chapter discusses the analytical implications of such tendencies.

The hazards of dogmatism

From the work of Aristotle to present day comparative politics our discipline has always been framed by normative concerns. Classical political thought pursued a philosophical approach aimed at uncovering the nature of 'good' government. Typologies invariably proposed ideologically conceived and ethnocentric hierarchies between more and less desirable systems of governance.[2]

It is tempting but ultimately misleading to think that modern attempts to make political analysis more 'scientific' have resulted in heuristic neutrality. On the one hand, numerous analysts simply equate the realm of politics with that of social conflict and seek to develop an argument that supports their quest for the ideal polis. This is as true of those who defend a particular model (for example, American-style polyarchy) as it is of those (like Marxists) who are critical of existing societies. On the other hand, and this is more pernicious, a number of political scientists who claim to be devoted to comparative analysis, and not to the quest for the 'public good', continue to use normative approaches. The problem arises from the determination to apply the same hypotheses to all and every political setting.[3] This results in unwarranted simplifications and, more generally, to the fitting of what is dissimilar into analytical schemas drawn from the experience of the analysts' own society. It is this (implicit or explicit) dogmatism that is detrimental to comparative insight and which a cultural approach avoids by means of rigorous scientific neutrality.

[2] The main exception is Montesquieu, who (within the limits of his period and environment) began to think about the political implications of the fact that customs and habits were relative.

[3] For a discussion of some of these pitfalls, see here B. Badie and G. Hermet, 1990, *Politique comparée*.

Those who, like intellectuals or policy-oriented researchers, have a clear political agenda (such as Marxism or development theory) do not see politics as the product of specific societal and cultural sedimentation. Instead they consider that the political realm derives from social and economic processes that apply to all parts of the world. A commitment to a particular form of society or a given process of change tends to condition the understanding of the more general 'nature' of political order. Even when such analysts seek to adhere to the principles of scientific neutrality, they provide a model of development that is in consonance with their political beliefs. The tendency to subsume the vagaries of the real world into the requirements of a given theoretical framework can result in analytical dead ends, or in some extreme cases (as with the Khmers Rouges) to a totalitarian vision of politics.

The proponents of a cultural approach do not partake of this voluntarist, and quasi-essentialist, view of the political sphere as merely the locus of social struggle. They do not assess political action in terms of the ideals that are thought to 'explain' the behaviour of the various protagonists. They prefer to focus on the empirical evidence that emerges from the study of codes, symbols and systems of meaning within their historical and socio-cultural context. For example, anthropologists have shown that, even if the concept of time has universal relevance, the notion of what it means in practice varies widely across societies. Similarly, political scientists ought to investigate the domain of the 'politic' without ideological or normative *a priori*.

Our framework, then, breaks from those analytical traditions that consider the political sphere to be an autonomous whole, limited to an arena within which political actors compete on the basis of established programmes and universal ideals. It also distances itself from the work of those who, perhaps for the best of reasons, are committed to reshaping the world into one more recognisably similar to their own. Such approaches inevitably relegate the realm of the cultural to the more analytically insignificant margins since it does not easily fit the preferred universalist models. For us, the key to comparative analysis is the need to take into account the fact that both the definition of the political sphere and the understanding of political action are to be assessed within the context of the infinite variety of social relations to be found across the world.[4] It is upon such foundations that a 'scientific' approach to political comparison is possible.

Unwarranted historical parallels

One of the major areas of disagreement between the advocates of universalist theories and the proponents of a cultural approach has to do with the justification for establishing parallels between societies across time and space. It is undeniably tempting to propose coherently synthetic comparisons that appear to provide explanations for what is taking place in the world today.[5] Indeed some historically rich comparisons are on the face it immediately enlightening, sometimes even elegant. Yet it is well to be cautious here. Such parallels, like the aphorisms they often resemble, flatter the better to deceive. How deep are the insights thus generated?

We, for our part, are dubious of these historical parallels. There is certainly merit in teasing out the possible comparisons between societies at different periods in their history, if only to set our work within an appropriate general context. But it cannot be assumed that this will necessarily provide reliable foundations for the interpretation of current events and processes, and even less for the comparison of Western and non-Western societies. The dangers are many. The search for such parallels can all too easily induce researchers to neglect that which does not fit into the expected mould. There is no incentive for trying to assess politics within its own setting, that is, uncovering what makes sense locally. Graver yet would be the artificial reduction of complex social processes to broad historical trends. Such methods can ultimately lead to the illusion that the 'local is the universal without the walls'.[6]

From St Paul to Karl Marx, Western intellectual history is replete with writers who—for religious, philosophical or ideological reasons—have nourished the burning ambition of doing away with what separates, or differentiates, men. For such thinkers, who reason

---

[4] See here our three case studies in Chapters 9 and 10.

[5] A culturally sensitive observer, however, would point out that the need for coherence is not equally admired everywhere.

[6] To paraphrase the title of a book by the Portuguese writer Miguel Torga: 1986, *L'universel, c'est le local moins les murs.*

in terms of 'citizens of the world', 'proletarians from all countries' or other such universal categories, cultural differences appear derisory and of little consequence. In the same way those nations that have seen themselves as a beacon of humanity are loath to admit to the limits of their influence. Since 1776 the United States has held that its own societal model is the world's best or most advanced. Partly for this reason American political scientists, although they often use highly sophisticated research and analytical techniques, tend to operate on the basis of their own concept of democracy. As a result they find it difficult to provide convincing interpretations of political dynamics in the Third World other than from the perspective of 'dysfunction' or pathology.[7] In France, likewise, the legacy of the universalist ideals that issued from the Enlightenment and the 1789 Revolution makes it hard to take account of the political implication of particularistic dynamics. When reference is made to culture, it is usually conceived as 'humanity's common capital'.[8]

From our viewpoint, the key question is the analyst's ability to enter different systems of meaning. Comparativists who hold on to a single, external model of the polity fail sufficiently to take into account the specificities of the societies in which they are interested. It would be wrong to think that the research quandary is limited to a choice between what Weber called a 'comprehensive' approach and a more distanced analysis.[9] Without doubt it is important for the researcher to show 'empathy' towards the people in whom he/she is interested. However, the danger for the analyst here lies in what might be called excessive 'sympathy'—that is, confining interpre-

---

[7] On the other hand, the researcher who works without preconceived notions, asks open questions and remains sensitive to local representation, will eventually uncover deeper political factors that matter greatly. See, for instance, J.-P. Daloz, 1997, '"Can we eat Democracy?" Perceptions de la "démocratisation" zambienne dans un quartier populaire de Lusaka' in J.-P. Daloz and P. Quantin (eds), *Transitions démocratiques africaines: dynamiques et contraintes.*

[8] Ultimately, therefore, culture is used in the singular and refers to a limited definition in terms of 'what is thought to be best'. Similarly, when American development theorists, like S. Lipset, posit links between level of education, rationality and democratic culture, they also privilege a narrow view, as opposed to that broader one *(that complex whole)* favoured by many anthropologists.

[9] It is well to remember that for Weber the 'comprehensive' approach consisted in stressing what made sense for the actors concerned.

tation to the local viewpoint. Some scholars become so involved with their 'subjects' that they begin to see the world only from their point of view. They have 'gone native'. Such an attitude is as detrimental to comparative analysis as the universalising *prêt-à-penser* mentioned above. We hold firmly to the view that a cultural approach involves both research empathy and a detached scientific perspective. In order to compare societies it is imperative to maintain intellectual neutrality.

It is of course true that the study of other polities or other periods may often evoke a sense of familiarity, an intellectual *déjà vu*. Could it be that the first stirrings of democracy in Europe bear a resemblance to current events in developing countries? Is it not true to say that the condition of the 'peasant'—hungry, devoid of resources, prey to the weather, harassed by real or imaginary fears—is universal? Superficially, perhaps. Yet the comparativist ought to maintain the utmost caution in the face of such obvious similarities, for they seldom provide illuminating insights. Indeed, the claim that certain political processes are 'everywhere to be found' is one that proponents of a cultural perspective would shun. It misleads more frequently than it enlightens.

Teleology unbound

With few exceptions, the founding fathers of social sciences were evolutionists. Marx, Tönnies, Durkheim and Weber all postulated that society was moving in a recognisable direction. Theories based on notions of a singular and universal type of modernisation are ubiquitous today, even if the criteria used for identifying it are not all the same. Most comparative political scientists share these assumptions and, accordingly, consider that their work should primarily be concerned with the study of the processes whereby societies move in the direction of modernisation as experienced historically in the West—that is, Westernisation. However, such a teleological bias leads all too easily to the use, or abuse, of theory for political or ideological purposes.

A cultural approach avoids such historical reductionism and shies away from the ambition to uncover grand theories of evolution, since the quest for such universal synthesis is invariably at the expense of insight. At the same time it avoids the pitfall of incommensurability—

or the argument that because each case is unique there is no possibility of comparison—since such a standpoint makes social sciences redundant. For us, the study of historical processes is justified when it enables the analyst to identify configurations of meaning in the *longue durée*, based on the actual experience of political actors studies over generations.

Those who subscribe to the essentialist or voluntarist framework discussed above face the difficult question of acculturation. When the model does not fit local reality, it is too easily explained on the grounds that this is because of indigenous 'mentalities'. At times this extends to labelling what appears to be different as being 'archaic'. The assumption is that since the people concerned seem unable to cast a critical vision on their own social and political 'shortcomings', they need to be educated (or 're-educated!') into the necessary changes.

Such an viewpoint raises a number of issues in comparative analysis. One concerns the very definition of politics. Anthropologists are sometimes prone to taking a very broad view of the question, equating politics with any form of social integration. Our discipline, on the other hand, is liable to restrict itself to an excessively narrow characterisation. It readily casts away into the world of 'infra-politics' that which does not appear to fit a preconceived political or ideological mould[10]—such as the logics of unequal exchange, particularistic inter-relations and communal solidarity, all areas that are analytically distinct from the more standard study of the State, citizenship or democracy, which are our discipline's standard fare. But why should political expression be limited to those (constitutional, partisan or elective) modalities that are the preserve of the dominant polities? The world's political history is replete with instances of cultural resistance or syncretism, which matter for politics. Finally, political dynamics are more often the result of complex mechanisms that political actors do not master than the deliberate outcome of the exercise of political (or prophetic) will.

---

[10] This form of reasoning can lead scholars to consider that some more distant societies are simply impossible to compare. For a polemical approach focusing on the debate between anthropologists and historians, see M. Detienne, 2000, *Comparer l'incomparable*.

In general, then, a perspectivist[11] framework remains analytically sceptical of such rather naïve evolutionist interpretations.

RED HERRINGS

A cultural approach, because it frequently questions current modes of thoughts and challenges standard comparative political analysis, is often rebuked in the most vigorous terms. There is a panoply of arguments adduced against those who advocate an interpretativist framework, ranging from the charge of culturalism to that of cultural relativism, essentialism or even 'scientism' (that is, undue 'detachment'). Although this entire book is in effect a rebuttal against such allegations, the following three sections will look in greater detail at the most widely cited shortcomings of cultural approaches to politics.

Cultural relativism

As has already been explained, a cultural approach requires of the researcher both the ability to become immersed in the environment under study and the capacity to maintain a neutral analytical perspective. Mannheim's injunction was to lay down competing ideologies side by side and examine them 'from above', as though hovering over the battleground. Similarly our methodology aims to identify the enduring social dynamics of a given grouping and to study how they make sense to the peoples concerned. Such a line of attack is not congenial to those political scientists, or sundry intellectuals, who deny that it is possible to be scientifically neutral.[12] It is also criticised by some on the grounds that an interest in culture is implicitly relativist.

Those critiques rest on the widespread assumption that politics is about the upholding of key values and the quest for the 'better' system of government. Therefore, to those who hold such views, it is difficult to accept that there may be distinct models of 'good' governance, each in harmony with a given historical and socio-cultural

---

[11] We use 'perspectivist', 'interpretativist' and 'interpretive framework' as synonyms for a cultural approach.

[12] In France, where the generalist intellectual is more highly prized than the scientist (liable to display an elitist disposition), this attitude is particularly common. To cite M. de Certeau's famous quip, 'One always speaks from a particular vantage point.'

environment. Hence for us it is less important to define what would be an 'ideal' type of political organisation than to understand why it is that a large number of peoples use 'culture' as a means of refusing to submit to the templates offered to, or imposed upon, them.[13] The attention we give to what may appear to be obdurate parochial 'particularisms' is not an argument against the admittedly admirable universalist injunction that man should free himself from the shackles of 'enslaving' traditions. It is merely recognition that understanding the political logics of those who are different from us entails an understanding of what makes sense to them.

Others argue that students of politics should proceed analytically from 'first' principles—justice, equality, fraternity, so to speak. We hold instead that they should move away from abstract theoretical debates about political philosophy and start from the empirical reality with which they are confronted (as we show in Chapters 9 and 10). In fact, the limits of Western theories of politics are swiftly exposed when studying settings far removed from those from which those theories derive, and to which they may well apply. Ironically, non-Western intellectuals often have recourse to these selfsame categories simply because they were educated, socialised, or politicised within that dominant ideology. One example is an approach in terms of political economy, a discipline elaborated to account for the dynamics of the rise of capitalism in Europe. Clearly this approach is not always relevant to non-Western polities. There it may be more rewarding to reason in terms of moral economy or economy of affection, concepts that have been applied to Southeast Asia and Sub-Saharan Africa respectively as a result of the empirical observation of actual political practices.[14]

It is sometimes alleged that the proponents of a cultural approach are themselves conceptually doctrinaire on the grounds that they are obsessed with local particularisms. But this is not the case. To ap-

---

[13] A. Finkelkrault, 1987, *La défaite de la pensée.*

[14] See J. Scott, 1976, *The Moral Economy of the Peasant*; G. Hyden, 1980, *Beyond Ujamaa in Tanzania.* The notion of moral economy, which is drawn from E. P. Thomson's work on the English working class, refers to a deeply embedded ethic of collective responsibility (for example, in respect of water use) in Burma or Vietnam. Yet Scott's analysis rests on a notion of 'value' that we do not share. Hyden's economy of affection denotes the supremacy of a communitarian ethos, of particularistic loyalty to local bosses, whose protection is required in order to survive. This approach goes against a purely liberal interpretation of economics.

proach different environments with a single theoretical or conceptual apparatus is not the same as studying cultures in their own terms. It may be that in a given number of cases some general social or political theory is relevant and applicable. However, there is a far greater range of instances where observable reality does not fit into rigid pre-existing analytical moulds. To force the evidence to fit a particular model is, from our viewpoint, the opposite of a scientific approach— as we will explain in greater detail at the end of the book.

There are, it is true, a number of scholars who have advocated a radical form of relativism, but most of those are structuralists and not adherents of an interpretative method. For instance, Lévi-Strauss argued against any notion of hierarchy between so-called primitive and modern societies. Foucault, for his part, went as far as to claim that it was pointless to study the evolution of knowledge since it was merely the outcome of a series of successive discourses ('*epistémés*').[15] To ensure clarity we prefer to use the concept of cultural 'perspectivism' rather than cultural 'relativism' since the former is normatively neutral.[16] Indeed, to understand culture in its appropriate context is a far cry from claiming that since cultures differ it is impossible to assess what they mean.

Westerners who study non-Western societies are often confronted with attitudes and forms of behaviour that appear to them irrational. Some Indian peasants refuse to vaccinate the animals from their herd not yet afflicted by a deadly disease, preferring to sacrifice them to a divinity liable to offer protection. In the suburbs of Harare men believe that intercourse with virgin girls will rid them of AIDS. Arab villagers, whose only source of water is infected with typhoid, reject the offer of a pump that would provide a safe alternative. Anthropology enables us to understand the socio-cultural and religious circumstances of such behaviour by explaining how the people concerned relate to the notion of, respectively, cattle, virginity and water. It is clear in those cases that from a medical or scientific viewpoint these attitudes are archaic as well as counter-productive.[17] But is it that simple in all spheres of life?

[15] See, for example, C. Lévi-Strauss, 1962, *La pensée sauvage*; Foucault, M., 1969, *L'archéologie du savoir.*

[16] As Mannheim well understood. For a discussion, see I. M. Zeiltin, 1990 (4th edn), *Ideology and the Development of Social Theory*, Chapter 19.

[17] Nevertheless, it is clear that similar 'irrational' beliefs thrive in the West as well.

As concerns politics, most would agree that it is salutary to live in societies free of fear and arbitrary violence. Many argue that in this respect democracy is by far the least 'bad' of all political systems. But which democracy? That practised in Washington, where money talks loudest, and where marketing and lobbying are the key instruments of influence? That in vogue in Paris, with its implacable majoritarian logic and its tendency towards confrontation? That which prevails in Stockholm, where consensus and morality are the two pillars of politics? Or that which holds sway in Black Africa, based as it is on palaver and cooptation. The point is clear: whereas in the realm of medicine, it is possible to demonstrate, though not always to convince others of, the superiority of some forms of treatment, this is simply not the case in politics. And political scientists, who are trained to study such questions, ought to know that politics is not just about general principles.

To offer another illustration we refer to the experience of non-Western emigrants to Europe. Coming as they often do from societies with a strong sense of communitarian solidarity, they suffer from the effects of what appear to them as cold and distant social relations. In the West it might be thought that processes of individuation, citizenship and human rights protection lift immigrants out of the constraints of particularistic obligation from which they suffered in their countries of origin, so that the overcoming of ascriptive responsibilities makes it possible to avoid inter-communal conflicts and even genocide. But to the immigrant communities such atomistic social behaviour makes impossible the forms of mutual help that offer the best guarantees of social peace and protection. For them a forced process of individual independence can be seen as a new form of compulsion within a society in which they feel vulnerable.

As comparativists concerned with cultural cleavages, it is less relevant for us to debate the respective merit of these two positions than it is to reveal how they make sense within their respective milieu and to analyse their political implications for both individuals and groups. Such a scholarly posture can only be construed as 'relativist' by those who conceive culture in terms of values, beliefs and ideals—

Witness the place of astrology in our magazines, the use of 'clairvoyants' by politicians and the fact that many Americans claim to believe in miracles and angels.

the study of which undoubtedly has its place in philosophical, ideological or even electoral debates but not, as we shall see below, in comparative political analysis. Our argument is that culture, as we understand it, refers only to systems of meaning, which a cultural approach seeks to uncover. Political science can only be 'scientific' if it eschews axiology. An analysis based on values cannot avoid the normative pitfall, and perhaps not even ethnocentrism.[18]

Our aim is to examine cultural differences as they impinge on political thought and action in diverse polities. We seek to provide plausible interpretations of the phenomena we observe, not to pass judgement on their merits. This deliberately neutral—or above the fray—attitude is sometimes considered reprehensible, or even irresponsible.[19] Nevertheless, given the importance we place upon empirical fieldwork, ours is certainly not an ivory tower posture. For us, the mark of a 'scientific' activity is the degree to which the researcher is able to separate analysis from personal considerations, however morally worthy these may otherwise be. A cultural approach, therefore, is not one that favours relativism but one that proceeds from the systematic study of the evidence by means of a scientifically detached perspective.

Essentialism

One of the most common critiques of those who take culture seriously is that they tend to reify it, and in this way to reinforce existing stereotypes. They are charged with providing lazy explanations such as 'French politics works in this way because that's just how the French are'.[20] As there will be ample opportunity to show later, it is in fact those who consider culture a supernumerary, or residual, category who end up making such facile statements. However, it is important to give this critique due consideration.

[18] As we discuss in greater detail in Chapter 3.

[19] Our previous book was subjected to criticism for making such claims of 'scientific' neutrality. See the reviews by J.-F. Médard in *Revue française de science politique*, vol. 50/4–5 (August–October 2000), pp. 849–54,) and G. Prunier in *Afrique contemporaine*, (no. 191, 3rd trimester 1999). We reply to these critiques in P. Chabal and J.-P. Daloz, 'How does *Africa Works* Work? Retour sur une lecture hétérodoxe du politique en Afrique noire', *Annali*, 2004.

[20] M. C. Needler, 1991, *The Concepts of Comparative Politics*, Chapter 7, gives a caricatural view of cultural analysis.

Many scholars consider that the quest for a social or political 'science' must do away with such vague and evanescent notions as culture. What matters to them is to explain differences in more solid terms, such as structural logics or other significant socio-economic variables. Equally, they harbour a deep-seated desire to do away with cultural stereotypes, which habitually simplify identities, assert superiority and are manipulated by political opportunists. Because such typecasts are durable, endlessly repeated, easily exploited and contagious, they are easily taken to be 'common sense'. Intellectuals rightly stand against such social discrimination. But is that a reason for rejecting a cultural approach?

Although stereotypes are crude simplifications of complex realities, the best way to undermine them is to take them seriously. To this end, it is necessary to understand their genesis and to make sense of the historical, social and cultural logics underpinning them. When the inhabitants of one country deplore that people from another country are 'lazy', the most common response among students of that latter society is to denounce the slur. A cultural approach would want to ascertain how the notions of 'work' and 'industry' are perceived in these two settings, whether these concepts themselves are ethnocentric, and if so why? It could be that in the first country labour has become highly praised in the national imaginary (and that, for example, DIY is seen as a worthwhile hobby) whereas in the other it is seen as 'dishonourable' to work with one's hands (status being confirmed by soft and pristine fingers). The point here is not to argue that typecasting can ever be acceptable, but that it is analytically profitable to understand why it arises in the first place.

More generally, therefore, the charge that a cultural framework amounts to an 'essentialist' approach does not stand up to scrutiny. The most cursory reading of the anthropological classics would reveal that the discipline's founders never indulged in such reification.[21] The proponents of the Culture and Personality school, principally Margaret Mead and Ruth Benedict, always rejected a notion of culture beyond human agency. The main interpretativist scholar, Clifford Geertz, also refused a conception of culture as an intangible 'given'. Arguing against a biological underpinning of the notion, he

---

[21] Only Kroeber conceived of culture as being dependent on specific, singular and autonomous historical realities.

saw culture as belonging squarely to the social sphere and thus susceptible to change—as is made clear in his famous definition drawn from Weber: 'Man is an animal suspended in webs of significance he himself has spun.'[22]

However, social reality is infinitely more complex than a crude concept of culture would allow. It is true that human beings are born, grow up and are educated into certain notions, upon which they can undoubtedly have an influence: no-one is a prisoner of his or her culture. At the same time, it would be far too simple to suggest that cultural symbols, beliefs, or myths are merely objects of manipulation. A careful study of this issue reveals that there are in all societies a number of cultural building blocks, as it were, that change so slowly as to appear immutable.[23] Therefore, within the scope of the individual's lifetime such cultural 'codes' are deeply and robustly significant. For this reason alone they bear close scrutiny.

One influential approach here is that of cultural *métissage* or hybridity. Students working on diffusion and acculturation have drawn attention to the processes whereby the modern world brings together and mixes cultures from all parts. These, it is argued, bring about a widespread blurring of cultural boundaries. To them, this would invalidate the study of individual 'cultures', which in any event are influenced by outside forces such as imperialism.[24] Another strand of scholarship has suggested that it may be more useful to think in terms of the superimposition of enduringly distinct registers[25]—a cohabitation of different cultural 'wholes' or 'universes', as it were—rather than in terms of a melting pot or hybridity. Here it becomes crucial to study the ways in which outside cultural influences are juxtaposed with indigenous ones. From this viewpoint it repays analytical dividends to identify the main components of what might be called the hard cultural core—as we sought to do in our previous book *Africa Works*.

Political scientists rightly fear that a focus on culture can result in an ontological approach to tradition. Yet when researchers are con-

---

[22] C. Geertz, 1973, 'Thick Description: toward an interpretive theory of culture' in C. Geertz, *The Interpretation of Cultures*, p. 5.

[23] As we shall discuss in detail in Chapter 6.

[24] See E. Said, 1993, *Culture and Imperialism*.

[25] We refer here to the work of R. Bastide on Afro-Brazilians; see, for instance, 1970, 'Mémoire collective et sociologie du bricolage', *L'Année sociologique*.

fronted with what are clearly vital cultural fundaments, evolved and legitimised over centuries, it is incumbent upon them both to take them seriously and to provide an account of their significance in a contextually meaningful fashion.

Changelessness

The recognition that there are in all societies long lasting cultural foundations sits uneasily with teleological approaches. Scholars, intellectuals, politicians and activists all worry that such an admission could be taken to mean that some parts of the world would be confined to continued 'under-development', or that their peoples would for ever be seen as 'backward'. Laudable as such concerns undoubtedly are, social scientists cannot avert their eyes from what they observe empirically. Yet there is a more insidious reason for rejecting the notion of distinct cultural 'cores': the assumption held by universalist theories that all societies develop along similar lines. This presupposition implies that what today may appear as cultural 'invariants' are the characteristics of society that are bound to wither as it modernises: their apparent distinction is in this way merely 'banal'.[26]

Such reasoning leads to the charge that cultural approaches are guilty of offering interpretations, which assume that cultures are fixed, or unchanging. This critique too is gratuitous. If it is true that interpretativists are particularly attuned to the *longue durée*, and thus to the resilience of cultural traits, they are equally interested in the dynamics of historical change. In point of fact it is the structuralist or system analyst of social change who is markedly a-historical. Even if a cultural approach is partial to synchronic analysis this does not imply that it denies time, or seeks to abolish it; it merely suspends it for the purpose of achieving the thick description on which it rests.

A cultural approach favours, though it is not beholden to, the study of change within continuity. It is wary of saltationist illusions but this in no way means that it subscribes to a 'timeless' notion of society. Thus our interpretation is not necessarily predicated on the idea that some cultural configurations are more resistant to transformation than others. Whether they are or not, and during which periods of

---

[26] There is a French school of thought that is keen to stress the 'banality' of Sub-Saharan societies.

history, is entirely an empirical question. In this respect it is useful to refer to the concept of involution, borrowed by Geertz from Goldenweisser, for it makes it possible to account for cultural patterns that keep evolving—neither entirely stable nor ever entirely new.[27]

In his work on Indonesia Geertz coined the notion of 'permanently transitional society', by which he meant a society that is no longer 'traditional' as such, but is not evolving into a recognisable 'modernity' either.[28] Based on extensive (field and historical) research, most notably on the Dutch and Japanese occupations, he argued that an especially constraining cultural environment had limited the scope for change. This led him to question the conclusions of both liberal and Marxist economists, whom he found guilty of neglecting to take seriously enough the cultural aspects of a singularly complex Indonesian society. As is shown in Chapter 6, our approach is not intended to highlight what Braudel called 'the prisons of the *longue durée*'— that is to imply that some societies, or human groupings, are less able than others to escape the 'shackles' of tradition. It is merely to stress how important it is for comparative analysis to take into account such cultural codes as may be relevant to the ways in which people behave and communities evolve.

Such 'turning points', useful as the identification of key moments in a society's time-line, are often a hindrance to the analysis of the nature of historical change. Even in the case of the apparently most radical revolutions—1789 France or 1917 Russia, for instance—is it not imperative to take into account the myriad continuities with, respectively, the *Ancien Régime* and Tsarist Russia, in order plausibly to make sense of what occurs after the overthrow of the old administration? More generally, therefore, researchers attuned to culture are indeed aware that change consists of cautious attempts to adapt. If such reforms are adopted, it is usually as complement to, rather than replacement of, the previous order. And this too is the outcome of cultural cleavage.

---

[27] See the article, A. Goldenweisser, 1936, 'Loose Ends of a Theory on Individual Patterns and Involution in Primitive Society' in R. Lowie (ed.), *Essays Presented to A. L. Kroeber*, in which Goldenweisser used the metaphor of artistic traditions that could innovate, but only with a given canvas.

[28] See C. Geertz, 1963, *Agricultural Involution* and 1965, *The Social History of an Indonesian Town*.

From a cultural viewpoint it is clear that political doctrines are in many ways akin to religion. They seek to convert the rest of the world; their proselytes aim for absolute victory. Although the twentieth century, with its extremes of totalitarian politics, has tempered somewhat the naïve faith in progress and 'civilisation', political activists as well as social scientists continue to believe in the superiority of a given (future) type of society. However, just as religion has broken down into multiple forms of spirituality, politics also is now revealed in all its multi-cultural complexity. Our approach, therefore, is critical of all homogenising frameworks of analysis. It does not project a single beam that casts all reality into the same light, but attempts instead to illuminate its diversity through a multi-angle perspective.

The claim that our approach is antithetical to an 'intellectualist' one could prompt some to argue that we are prone to similar extremes. Yet, as we demonstrate in the book, our 'extremism' is radically different in that it aims to be anti-dogmatic and open. A perspectivist stance eschews dogmatic and teleological assumptions and advocates a healthy dose of scepticism vis-à-vis general theories in the social sciences. Such an approach is necessary since it has become clear that there is less reason than ever to anticipate the return of grand theory.

2

WORKING ASSUMPTIONS

All scientific undertakings necessarily rest on a given combination of axioms and assumptions. Therefore, those of us working in the social sciences need to make clear our epistemological premises. Because the notion of culture is both controversial and difficult to conceptualise, there is particular need to be systematic in our discussion of the framework within which we are working.

Thus the object of this chapter is to explain our standpoint, not just within the broad ambit of comparative politics but particularly in respect of those theories that include a cultural dimension. Defining culture is not simple but, in our view, the intricacy arises principally from the fact that in most instances an attempt is made to insert it within what are considered to be (other) more 'fundamental' socioeconomic aspects of human agency. The key questions to be examined here, then, concern, on the one hand, the nature and putative 'independence' of the cultural 'variable' and, on the other, its heuristic value to comparative politics.

THE IMPLICATIONS OF DIVERSITY

There are two broad approaches to the relevance of culture. The first considers that, however marked, cultural differences between societies are superficial and merely mask similarities between all human beings. The second asserts that such cleavages are so deep they put into question the very concept of 'human nature'. Starting from an anthropological discussion of this contrast, we extend our reflection to politics and, ultimately, to comparative analysis, providing thereby a clear framework for our methodology.

Unlimited differentiation

It has been customary in anthropology to make a distinction between invariant factors and adventitious cultural characteristics. Kluckhohn, for example, adopted a dualist approach and sought to identify universal features transcending cultural diversity, which he saw merely as the outcome of 'historical accidents'. Structuralism, for its part, is equally universalising, favouring as it does the quest for the general grammar underpinning human agency. When Lévi-Strauss uses the notion of culture, it is merely to refer to those unconscious categories of the human mind from which the respective 'fragments of humanity' have drawn their respective models. What matters is the search for what is universal, in myth or kinship. The study of cultural diversity, taken to be a surface phenomenon, is merely concerned with the examination of a finite number of combinations of cards.[1]

Various anthropologists have thus reduced the range of human civilisations to a limited number of given types. Warning against the dangers of accepting that the world is made up of numerous discrete universes, they approach the study of society with a given interpretative framework aimed at uncovering the 'unconscious universal' within the diversity of cultural practices. Here the 'other' is seen simply as the local expression of a common universe and in this way acts as a mirror. This, in a nutshell, is the ambition of 'fundamental' anthropology.

However, other anthropologists argue that human development has led to an infinite socio-cultural arborescence, with ever multiplying branches.[2] This has made possible countless cultural expressions, an unbounded number of potentialities and motivations, which are important to understand each within their own milieu. From this point of view the number of 'cards', and thus of combinations, would be unlimited[3] within societies that have long been separated and in

---

[1] To evoke the famous metaphor in C. Lévi-Strauss, 1958, *Anthropologie structurale*— a classic in anthropology, which ought to be consulted by those who want further clarification.

[2] To use Warnier's formulation see J.-P. Warnier, 1999, *La mondialisation de la culture*, p. 22.

[3] This, for instance, is Ruth Benedict's perspective. She suggests an analysis in terms of free selection, *absolute choice*, even if her 'patterns' point to the notion of coherent styles within the same culture. See R. Benedict, 1934, *Patterns of Culture*.

which all manners of particularisms have flowered. Interpretativists, for example, prescribe in-depth field study, or 'thick description', of a given community. Geertz writes in this respect, 'Men unmodified by the customs of particular places do not in fact exist, have never existed, and most important, could not in the very nature of the case exist.'[4]

The debate between these various schools of thought turns around the question of meaning. Foucault wrote in 1966: 'The turning point occurred when Lévi-Strauss writing on society and Lacan on the unconscious showed that meaning was merely a surface phenomenon, a reflection, froth, but that which ordered us, that which preceded us, and that which upheld us in time and space, was the system.'[5] However, for the adherents of a cultural approach, such as is offered in this book, it is precisely the study of meaning, of what makes sense to the people concerned, that is of interest. We remain wary of the universalist bias exhibited by structuralism and other similar schools of thought.

Arguments of this type are to be found in all social sciences. In economics, various theories start from the premise that all human beings have similar basic needs, thereby putting forward a kind of universal materialism. Marxists stress the causal significance of modes and relations of production, rejecting out of hand cultural interpretations on the ground that they are not rooted in material life. Conversely, those who take culture seriously argue that material production takes place within a symbolic context, a bundle of meanings, which gives it significance. In the end the notion of a distinction between 'beings' and 'things' is predicated upon intellectual dichotomies that are alien to many so-called traditional societies.[6]

The main question here is clearly that of causal precedence: which comes first, socio-economic relations or culture? Against a vision of man as *homo economicus*, some anthropologists argue that, within many

---

[4] C. Geertz, 1973, 'The Impact of the Concept of Culture on the Concept of Man' in C. Geertz, *The Interpretation of Cultures*, p. 35.

[5] *Le Magazine littéraire*, May 1966, quoted in F. Dosse, 1992, *Histoire du structuralisme*, vol. I, *Le champ du signe, 1945–1966*, p. 386. Our translation.

[6] Prestigious objects were often perceived as an extension of the eminence of the person who owned them. In many settings dignitaries were buried with their possessions. In many others seizing an adversary's belongings was symbolically important in a way that we cannot understand today. It is only when objects became mass-produced that they became reified.

societies, the 'economy' was such an integral part of social relations that it could not be considered separately. To do so was an unjusti-fiable theoretical imposition, which derived from ethnocentrism. Sahlins, in particular, has evidenced the primacy of culture over economic processes and has criticised the universal pretensions of Western economic thought based purely on practical or utilitarian reason. For him, the study of so-called primitive societies exposes the limits of historical materialism. Equally he dismisses the Marxist charge of 'idealism' since the study of meaning within real societies cannot be reduced to the invention of artificial intellectual con-structions.[7]

....what does it mean for politics?

The same is true of the political realm, which it is simply not possible to insulate from a society's cultural environment. How autonomous the sphere of politics becomes and how clearly differentiated it is from its socio-cultural setting are themselves specifically historical, and not abstract, questions. As soon as we seek to uncover systems of meaning it is plain that the notion of the 'politic' changes according to context.[8] The very assumption that there is an analytically separate domain of politics is, therefore, eminently ethnocentric.

A semiotic approach of the type we favour is rare in political science, if only because its methodology is predicated on a very ambitious programme of research.[9] It requires a type of in-depth study that is onerous, especially when it is comparative—since it becomes nec-essary to acquire specialist knowledge of several polities.[10] However, we would argue that this is the only method to make it possible plausibly to contrast vastly dissimilar political systems in very distinct, and differently organised, parts of the world. Because such systems

[7] See here M. Sahlins, 1976, *Culture and Practical Reason*. On overcoming the oppo-sition between materialism and idealism in cultural analysis, see also C. Geertz, 1973, 'Religion as a Cultural System' in C. Geertz, *The Interpretation of Cultures.*
[8] Geertz writes: 'As moral imaginations differ, so do political.' C. Geertz, 1983, *Local Knowledge*, pp. 129–30.
[9] On what a semiotic approach means for us see Chapter 8.
[10] There are, however, a number of single country studies that are sensitive to the cultural question. On the Soviet Union see for instance R. Tucker, 1973, 'Cul-ture, Political Culture and Communist Society', *Political Science Quarterly*, 88.

rest on differing notions of power, norm, order, authority, regulation, representation and government, meaningful comparison depends on detailed local knowledge.

However, critiques of this approach are not just uncomfortable with the research methodology needed to understand indigenous political logics on their own terms. They also argue that a 'science' of politics must aim to subject such data to a rigorously 'objective' critique, so as to uncover the more subterranean realities underlying political processes. Otherwise, comparative analysis merely touches the subjective surface of the phenomena concerned. A number of political scientists thus study cultural variations within a structuralist framework, thereby reducing the number of *configurations* into which political systems fit.

Such, for example, is the Cultural Theory approach, derived from the work of the anthropologist Mary Douglas, who offers a tight grid-group typology. These scholars are sensitive to the importance of the study of political preferences. They agree that interests are culturally rooted and not simply 'given'. They are also fiercely critical of rational choice theory. Nevertheless, they provide a model that reduces cultural combinations to four: egalitarian, hierarchical, individualistic and fatalistic.[11] Their schema, which they believe to be applicable to political science, drastically limits the range of possible cases, even if it avoids one-dimensional universalism.[12] The same is true of other approaches, which seek to bring out significant structural social continuities, such as, for instance, the lasting notion of the 'sacred'. The argument here is that this concept has endured through the ages, even in ostensibly secular societies, where politics, as it were, fulfils the role previously assumed by religion.[13]

Yet, it is worth pointing out that cultural settings are rarely similar and that it is dubious whether their systems of meaning are 'equivalent'. From our point of view, the question is not to determine whether man always reasons within a notion of the 'sacred' and whether the recourse to liturgy is both unavoidable and universal.[14]

[11] M. Thompson, R. Ellis and A. Wildavski, 1990, *Cultural Theory.*

[12] M. Thompson, G. Grendstad and P. Selle (eds), 1999, *Cultural Theory as Political Science.*

[13] See, for example, P. Legendre, 1976, *Jouir du pouvoir.*

[14] See here C. Rivière, 1988, *Les liturgies politiques.*

Rather, it is to reveal the complexity and richness of such forms of moral expression and to cast some light on their comparative implications. Such an approach holds just as well for political analysis, where insights into modes of governance and socio-political agency are drawn from empirical observation and not from the quest for perennial 'structures'.

Indeed, structuralist methods are liable to result in a vision of man merely as *homo politicus*, confronted with a limited range of options, for instance in terms of political systems. It is of course necessary to be able to distinguish between, say, totalitarian and authoritarian regimes and between these two types and a democratic dispensation. But the really interesting question is to compare, for instance, how Soviet, Nazi and Chinese forms of totalitarianism differed in terms of the perceptions of rulers and ruled. Similarly it is useful to be able to tease out why and in which ways numerous political systems exhibit a combination of democratic and authoritarian features. Comparative insight then stems from the ability to make sense of the singularities of each system, rather than from the capacity either to slot them into pre-determined boxes or to place them on a continuum.

Finally, it is well to signal the dangers of assuming that it is always possible to identify given structures, even when there is no evidence of their reality. It may simply be that they do not exist in the cases under study. Thus instead of searching systematically for 'leadership' or 'rationality' it could well be far more comparatively rewarding to ask whether these concepts, at least in the sense in which they are usually used in political science, really do make sense in some settings.

On comparative analysis

Clearly, the difference in approach between those who recognise man's 'infinite cultural plasticity' and those who deem that there are 'hard' characteristics that all human beings share, is consequential for comparative analysis.[15] The latter are prone to considering cultures merely as 'superstructures', which can be transformed by human agency. Many thinkers have acknowledged cultural diversity whilst

[15] See here Geertz's appreciation of Lévi-Strauss' approach: C. Geertz, 1973, 'The Cerebral Savage: on the work of Claude Lévi-Strauss' in C. Geertz, *The Interpretation of Cultures*, and 1988, 'The World in a Text: how to read "Tristes Tropiques"' in C. Geertz, *Works and Lives: the anthropologist as author.*

arguing that there were in fact given paths to man's 'fulfilment'. Athenians living in the 4th century BC, Christian theologians in the Middle Ages, humanists in the 16th century, communists in the 20th century, all believed, and present day liberals continue to believe, that there is but one way to human progress. The problem is that those who do not share their views have always been cast as morally wrong, or simply barbarians. In the name of a given 'moral monism'[16] such visions of the world impose a model of how human potential is best achieved. Because this approach is rooted in a singular view of 'human nature', it necessarily rejects any other conception.

Hence it seems to be necessary for such schools of thought to take for granted the transcultural character of 'human nature'. From this viewpoint, what defines human beings is their similarity. Differences are secondary, when not altogether redundant. But such a viewpoint is fundamentally a-historical, assuming as it does that man has always been what he is, endowed with 'innate' and unchanging features. This is to deny the role that human groupings have had in changing the very conditions of their lives. To illustrate: man's attitude to death, sexuality or decency has been drastically different over space and time. It is the strength of a cultural approach to enable us to understand the huge distinctions between, say, Buddhist Zen thinking and the Western Promethean mind. In the end it is far from simple to define humankind.

To continue a discussion initiated in the Introduction, is it 'natural' to die for one's fatherland or to become a suicide bomber? Is pacifism a higher form of human morality than violence? An interpretative approach abstains from answering these questions from a normative point of view because it casts doubt on the assumption that there are a-cultural and a-historical human 'invariants' that would have been the strict preserve of man since time immemorial. The assumption, for instance, that violence is conceptually distinct from other forms of human behaviour, which is now widely held in the West, did not in the past make sense in many other settings, where it was perceived as an inherent part of other social processes. Indeed, it might not have made sense in the West a few centuries back. The very notion of violence and the rejection of it that is familiar to us are themselves the products of particular historical and cultural circumstances.

---

[16] Cf. Parekh, B., 2000, *Cultural Diversity and Political Theory.*

Consequently a cultural comparative approach does not merely seek out what makes sense to people but it also enquires about why certain notions may be unintelligible within certain settings or what may or may not be readily understood. Similarly it is concerned to show that man's relation with nature is culturally contextual. It is not to be slotted into a few preconceived alternatives. The aim is to insert such interaction with nature within the general environment in which real human beings live. Whatever our case studies, we cannot afford to forget that to the people concerned the world is their world—not necessarily the only world they know, but undoubtedly the one that ultimately matters most to them.

Returning to the central argument of this book, it is perilous to assume that 'politics is an unchanging play of natural passions, which particular institutions of domination are but so many devices for exploiting.'[17] Such presumption might easily lead to the belief that Shakespeare or Machiavelli provided us with insights that apply across continents and centuries. But this is absurd, as Geertz shows, since 'the passions are as cultural as the [political] devices'.[18] In the political realm, as in all others, '[...] the knowable world is incomplete if seen from any point of view, incoherent if seen from all points of view at once, and empty if seen from "nowhere in particular".'[19] A cultural approach, therefore, avoids ethnocentrism by taking cultural disparities seriously. It also steers clear of abstract forms of reasoning, which apply either to no particular context or to a single one.

From the mid-twentieth century American political science has claimed to transcend cultural differences by means of a general method of analysis (inherited from Talcott Parsons) centred on three key concepts: system, structure and function.[20] Here, it was argued, the political system regulates itself as it responds to national and international stimuli and discharges a number of fundamental functions within a given organisational structure. The proponents of this method averred

[17] C. Geertz, 1980, *Negara: the theatre State in nineteenth-century Bali*, p. 124.
[18] *Ibid.*
[19] R. Shweder, 2000, 'Moral Maps, "First World" Conceits and the New Evangelists' in L. Harrisson and S. Huntington (eds), *Culture Matters*, p. 164. In Chapter 3 we show in more detail how we differ from the approach of the above book—Shweder accepted—which although eclectic, often presents arguments that are utterly different from ours.
[20] G. Almond and G. Powell (eds), 1988, *Comparative Politics Today*, Chapter 1.

that such an approach made it possible to overcome the pitfalls of cultural diversity and to uncover identical or analogous processes. This resulted in a research agenda geared to identifying what were called functional equivalents: different structures could, for instance, fulfil the same function in different settings or, alternatively, the same structures could fulfil different functions.[21] This method was not just seen as an advance on previous ones. It was also taken to lay down the foundations for a true 'science' of comparative analysis.

It will be immediately obvious why, from a cultural perspective, such an approach is eminently hazardous. Again we are bound to ask whether the quest for 'functional substitutes' (to use Merton's language[22]) is not an exceedingly ethnocentric enterprise. For example, is it really the case that modern ideologies are the 'functional equivalent' of traditional myths? Furthermore, as Sartori has argued, the conceptual 'stretching' of key analytical categories that is required in order to apply them to the most diverse research terrain is theoretically dubious.[23] Concepts such as participation or mobilisation, which political scientists use to account for certain situations, make little sense in other settings. Their general use obscures more than it reveals. The pretension to explain completely distinct processes by means of a few apparently universal 'functions', or to reduce myriad political logics by means of a few 'operational' categories may be tempting but it is unlikely to offer much analytical insight.[24]

AGAINST REDUCTIONISM

Social scientists habitually seek to uncover causality. If no-one seriously claims that culture is, or ever could be, considered the single causal root of any phenomenon, there are vast differences of ana-

---

[21] See examples of this in M. Dogan, and D. Pelassy, 1981, *Sociologie politique comparative*, Chapter 5.

[22] R. Merton, 1968, *Social Theory and Social Structure*.

[23] G. Sartori, 1970, 'Concept Misformation in Comparative Politics', *American Political Science Review*, 64, pp. 1033–53.

[24] We advocate an approach that is more empirical than is common in our field but we work within a perspective that seeks above all to be comparative—that is, to be of relevance to those who are not familiar with the specificities of the case studies.

lytical opinion regarding the extent to which it can be seen as an independent variable. This section, therefore, discusses the various approaches to this question and in particular those, more reductionist ones, that relegate culture to a residual or subsidiary position.

Is culture an independent variable?

The question here is whether culture is to be seen primarily as a dependent or independent variable. On this point there is in the field a wide array of opinions. They range from the assumption of cultural preponderance over other determinants of human action, to the claim for the primacy of psychological or socio-economic factors, by way of complex systems of explanation in which culture is more or less causally significant. Among social theorists with an interest in culture there are clearly three main positions: those who consider that culture has strong societal effects; those who see culture as the outcome of other, more important historical or socio-economic dynamics; and those who consider it merely of residual explanatory relevance, *faute de mieux* as it were.

Some among early-twentieth-century anthropologists, particularly those associated with the Culture and Personality School, stressed the *psychological*. Mead referred to 'cultural temperaments' in her famous comparative study of sexual behaviour in three different Papua New Guinea communities.[25] Benedict divided cultures between those that tended toward the 'Apollonian' and those that were more 'dionysiac'.[26] Linton spoke of 'basic personalities'[27] while the psychiatrist Kardiner believed that man projected onto a cultural imaginary those tensions that came from family education.[28]

In political science there were a number of American studies that followed in the footsteps of such anthropological approaches. They focused on the relationship between socialisation, personality and political behaviour. They did, however, take into account a number of criticisms that had been made—for instance about Benedict's work on Japan[29]—as regards the underestimation of political change or the significance of social cleavages. Of these, two stand out:

[25] M. Mead, 1935, *Sex and Temperament in Three Primitive Societies*.
[26] R. Benedict, 1934, *Patterns of Culture*.
[27] R. Linton, 1936, *The Study of Man*.
[28] A. Kardiner, 1939, *The Individual and his Society*.
[29] R. Benedict, 1946, *The Chrysanthemum and the Sword*.

Banfield's study of Italian 'amoral familism'[30] and Pye's monograph on Burma.[31]

The next generation of anthropologists, most notably the interpretativists, whilst acknowledging their debt to their illustrious predecessors, moved away from the argument that culture was rooted in psychology. Their work, and that of the following fifty years, showed that the dividing line between cultural and psychological factors, though blurred, was still of paramount importance. No one today believes in the Freudian notion of the 'invariant psyche'. Similarly a more cultural approach puts in their proper perspective such notions as the incest taboo or the Œdipus complex. It also casts a greater degree of contextual relevance upon various types of madness. Although the debate still continues, there is certainly a greater measure of scepticism about the putative psychological basis of culture.

As was suggested in the previous chapter, our approach rejects all forms of essentialism, by which is meant the reification of culture, or cultural characteristics. At the same time, we hold that culture is not merely to be 'defined' as a by-product of more fundamental psychological, sociological or economic dynamics. In point of fact only ecological, geographical or historical factors could be said to have a determining effect over culture. But even here it is well to tread cautiously since there is clearly evidence of reciprocal influence.

Landscape, climate, the ease of movement, the availability of resources, all have impinged on cultural codes. It is possible, for instance, to interpret some shamanic cults as rites designed to help people living in particularly hostile (hot or cold) climates to come to terms with their environment. They transmute the harshness of their surroundings into a positive force so that the symbolic world makes it easier to live in the real one. However, such approaches are sometimes derided. For instance, some dispute the argument that Dutch society is especially consensual, and its inhabitants markedly modest primarily because of the long history of mutual aid that a harsh polder environment required. Nevertheless, there is merit in those studies that seek to connect what might be called a 'mental geography' with observable cultural habits that have political significance.[32]

---

[30] E. Banfield, 1958, *The Moral Basis of a Backward Society.*
[31] L. Pye, 1962, *Politics, Personality and Nation-Building.*
[32] On the Low Countries after the Reformation, see S. Schama, 1987, *The Embarrassment of Riches.*

At the same time it is well to remember, once again, that there can be no single causal factor in the evolution of culture. Climate and the environment are important but they do not condition men mechanically. Similar conditions may induce different attitudes. Eastern Siberians keep warm with a single thick fur coat. Their Japanese neighbours favour the accumulation of thinner cotton kimonos, attire that also has strong cultural resonance. More generally, man's relationship with nature has evolved considerably over the ages. The construction of cities is perhaps the most critical step in this respect. The transition to urban life has created entirely new mentalities, even if the old ones have survived in mutated forms, that have changed human interaction fundamentally. The domestication of the environment, in this case by way of urbanisation, has in turn contributed to change the cultural dynamics of city dwellers.

The same is true in respect of politics. As is suggested throughout the book, we do not consider it plausible to consider the realm of the 'politic' as a pristine independent variable and 'political cultures' as dependent variables. Such a view leads to the notion that these 'political cultures' are malleable, that they are responsible for the absence of certain developments or, alternatively, can be manipulated to stimulate other types of evolution or even sustain regime change.[33] Nor, on the other hand, do we believe that culture determines politics, in the sense in which some argue that modes of production do.

Admittedly we do see culture as a relatively 'independent' variable, but with the following key provisos. First, the concern is with cultures, in the plural, and not with a putative and vague concept of Culture, or Civilisation. Each culture must be understood on its own terms. Second, individuals can be simultaneously the product of a given culture and the artisans of cultural change.[34] In this sense the relationship is dialectical. For this reason a cultural approach is less concerned with establishing the primacy (or independence) of the cultural variable[35] than it is with understanding how culture shapes the practice of politics in specific settings.

---

[33] Witness the notion that democracy can be 'inculcated' in Iraq.

[34] As we show in detail in Chapter 10 when we discuss the case of Sweden.

[35] The quest for 'independent' or 'dependent' variables is of dubious relevance from a cultural perspective, as we show in Part III and the Conclusion.

Macro-cultural cleavages and social relations

The proponents of an interpretativist framework are often charged with neglecting internal social cleavages. Clearly as societies become more differentiated there emerge new cultural distinctions that are important. Individuals who belong to different classes or other social categories begin to behave and think differently. In such cases it is obviously pertinent to conceptualise society in terms of a number of sub-cultures, as it were. This raises the question of cultural straddling and, methodologically, points to the question of the relevant analytical perspective, as will be discussed in Chapter 5.[36]

A number of social scientists, especially those interested in class struggles or social strife, tend to reduce the question of culture to that of ideological struggle. They discount any reference to horizons wider than socio-economic factors.[37] In their view culture is nothing more than the arena in which contests for domination and resistance take place. They adopt a (frequently Gramscian) notion of hegemony to analyse social norms and deviance.

Within the Marxist and structuralist traditions, culture is taken to be the 'outcome' of the interplay of social relations. It is conceptualised as the (symbolic) instrument of domination, which is enforced upon more or less alienated social agents.[38] On the other hand, Weber, who also analysed relations between social groups and cultural ethos, was far less deterministic—sensitive as he was to what he called 'elective affinities'.[39] For their part, proponents

---

[36] Even if we do not partake of Lévi-Strauss' postulate that there are only a limited number of possible combinations, we would agree that to talk of culture implies the existence of 'significant differences' from one human group to the other. See C. Lévi-Strauss, 1958, *Anthropologie structurale*, pp. 351–2.

[37] A common criticism of anthropologists is that they fail to take into account the range of possible behaviour within a given culture.

[38] See R. Hoggart, 1957, *The Uses of Literacy* or M. de Certeau, 1993 (1974), *La culture au pluriel*, from which one can conceive the relative autonomy of dominated culture vis-à-vis the dominant one.

[39] Weber evidenced the tension between the dogma of predestination and the primitive accumulation of capital. What is important in his argument is that the symbolic system had practical consequences wholly unintended by its creators. Weber was concerned not so much to uncover the 'cause' of the development of capitalism, but to show how a particular world of meanings (and of values) favoured the emergence of attitudes and practices that were congenial to both accumulation and re-investment.

of the primacy of culture conceptualise the semiotic worlds with which they are concerned as largely autonomous and self-regulating languages.

We, in turn, hold that culture must be understood as 'deep' context, and not merely as 'reflecting', 'expressing', 'corresponding', 'emerging from' or 'conditioned by' interest-based social cleavages.[40] In this respect we follow in the footsteps of Mannheim's approach in terms of worldviews and are in harmony with the concept of 'mentality' used by a number of historians,[41] who picture the various cultural universes in which we live as 'large wholes' affecting every individual. Of course we are aware that culture is liable to be manipulated or to act as a 'filter' on reality.[42] We know too that it is illusory to assume that culture can be studied as a 'neutral' system of meanings. However, we think it important to reject the view that culture is merely the product of cynical and interest-driven manipulation.

This debate is not only a theoretical issue. We need to demonstrate the pertinence of the cultural dimension in our empirical work. Drawing on our research in Africa, we are critical of the 'politics from below' approach.[43] Based on substantial fieldwork in Nigeria, one of us has shown that relations between rulers and ruled must be understood within the context of a culture of unequal reciprocity between élites and populace, which they all share.[44] We will develop this example further in the chapter on political representation.

---

[40] See here C. Geertz, 1973, 'Ideology as a Cultural System' in C. Geertz, *The Interpretation of Cultures* where the author criticises both classical Marxist conceptions of ideology and constructivist theories of social reality.

[41] We refer here to the French school of *histoire des mentalités*. On the one hand, we admire their empirical commitment and their determination not to reduce causality to the 'material'. On the other, their approach sometimes results in relatively simplistic normative aggregates (focusing on beliefs and values) inserted within particular theoretical frameworks—which sometimes border on the structuralist concern with domination.

[42] See here, among others, V. Turner, 1967, *The Forest of Symbols.*

[43] See Bayart, J.-F. et al., 1992, *Le politique par le bas en Afrique noire.* This approach, which considers social and political issues within the intellectualist perspective of 'resistance' leads to the usage of surprising analytical mixtures in the discussion of the political uses of cultural symbols and a wholesale rejection of any cultural framework. See J.-F. Bayart, 1996, *L'illusion identitaire.*

[44] See J.-P. Daloz, 2002, *Élites et représentations politiques.*

We are also dubious about those theories that reduce the social world to mechanisms of 'symbolic violence'[45] by the élites upon the populace, which results in the devaluing of 'popular culture'.[46] There is evidence that the reverse might be equally true. For instance, in France domestic servants, who came for the most part from a rural milieu, were instrumental in the dissemination of outdated notions of hygiene (concerning, for example, the potential dangers of nail cuttings or of fallen teeth) into the nineteenth-century urban bourgeois world in which they worked.[47] More generally, we would point to the limits of Bourdieu's model of social distinction, according to which the élites' symbols of prestige, their tastes and habits, become hegemonic societal norms, whereas 'popular culture' is usually disfavoured.[48]

There are countless examples that testify to the influence of 'popular culture' over the dominant social classes. Music is perhaps the prime example: jazz, reggae, rap have all now become mainstream. Dances such as polka or tango, originally perceived merely as 'lower class' entertainment, also made their way into the conventional repertoire. The ordinary man's full-length trousers displaced the aristocrats' *culottes*. More recently the American workingmen's blue jeans were adopted not just by rebellious adolescents but also by the élites, who see them as the epitome of casual wear. The same attitude also holds true in art and painting.[49]

---

[45] See here Bourdieu's structuralist-constructivist approach: P. Bourdieu, 1989, 'Social Space and Symbolic Power', *Sociological Theory*, 7.

[46] For a Foucauldian interpretation, see R. Muchembled, 1978, *Culture populaire et culture des élites dans la France moderne (XVè–XVIIIè siècle)*. We could also mention research on the perceptions of colonised, the dominated or feminist studies aiming to show that women have different cultural conceptions. Such work usually results in an analysis in terms of 'self conscious differentiation', resistance and emancipation.

[47] A. Corbin, 1999, 'Coulisses' in M. Perrot (ed.), *Histoire de la vie privée*, vol. IV: *De la Révolution à la Grande Guerre*, p. 403.

[48] P. Bourdieu, 1979, *La distinction*.

[49] Bourdieu started from a critique of the Kantian notion of the '*beau en soi*'. He tried to show how the dominant classes appropriate art, which then becomes a symbol of their position and an instrument of their reproduction. However, empirical work demonstrates that abstract modern art only interests a small section of the higher classes in the United States. Furthermore, it can be shown that members of the middle or even lower classes can also have appreciation for

Clearly there is a dynamic in the social genesis of needs that is driven by a process of subjective comparison within and between social groups. If it is true that the dominant public norms are likely to reflect the standards of the élite, these may well have been (deeply) influenced by 'popular culture', conceived broadly. In other words, the apparent superiority of higher-class social distinction may conceal its more diverse origins, including from the 'lower orders'. It is for this reason that an excessive emphasis on the apparent cultural domination of the élite may well obscure the complex circulation of norms and codes, thus leading to an unjustified reading of the 'bottom' of society from the narrow perspective of the 'top'.

We will return to this question when we discuss the pitfalls of comparisons between Western and non-Western societies. However, even within our own countries it is clear that the cultural impact of what is called 'post-modernity' has seriously undermined the putative hegemony of élite culture—which no longer is, if it ever was, the dominant societal point of reference.[50] There is now creative confusion of lifestyles, a fluidity of identity, in which symbols of high and low culture merrily combine. It is more and more difficult to preserve social status by means of cultural symbols. Not because the so-called post-modern society has become more egalitarian but, rather, because the symbolic expressions of social superiority are becoming increasingly confused. There is now a profusion of cultural 'systems' living side-by-side, interacting little, and it is thus difficult to assess their comparative 'value'.[51]

We also take issue with 'constructivist' approaches, according to which the ability to express reality is constructed socially. Indeed, this 'sociology of knowledge' has come to consider culture as a product of socially constructed institutions that are controlled by the dominant classes.[52] A cultural approach rejects such a pretension to reduce the perception of the world to such a simple matrix. Nor do we find

---

such artistic expression. See M. Lamont and M. Fournier (eds), 1992, *Cultivating Differences*.

[50] See J. Baudrillard, 1970, *La société de consommation*.

[51] See, *inter alia*, P. Blumberg, 1974, 'The Decline and Fall of the Status Symbol: some thoughts on status in post-industrial society', *Social Problems*, 21, and M. Featherstone, 1991, *Consumer Culture and Post-Modernism*.

[52] P. Berger and T. Luckmann, 1967, *The Social Construction of Reality*.

affinity with a 'sociology of knowledge' that explains social reality in institutional terms. We hold instead to Manheim's notion of 'relationism', which calls for a neutral analysis of the totality of the different worlds of meanings within the context of their complex interaction.

In simple terms, the question is whether culture is the product of human agency. Our answer, which eschews both essentialism and sociologising, is clear if cautious. It is plainly necessary to take into account mechanisms of socialisation and of the diffusion of cultural norms. Equally it is imperative to reject the notion that societies are merely the products of the actions of its dominant actors—for they too are subject to the cultural constraints that legitimise their social or political prominence.

This point is crucial for political analysis. If we assume that a society's cultural norms are determined only by the interplay of social forces and politics as the means for the dominated classes to emancipate themselves, then we will tend to regard such norms simply as the outcome of political competition. If, on the other hand, we accept that cultural perceptions are linked to various logics of meaning, deeply embedded in society, then we will proceed to a much more variegated and complex analysis of politics, as the rest of the book will seek to demonstrate.

Context, interests, choice

The notion of rationality has frequently led to reductionist theories, which have been influential and need, therefore, to be discussed in some detail. We can all agree that human beings are possessed of reason. The problem, from our point of view, is that they reason differently in distinct settings. If some make a sharp separation between reason and emotion, others would not conceive of such a distinction. Equally for many the contrast between theoretical and practical reason does not make sense.

There is a huge, some would say immeasurable, gap between the Cartesian *cogito* and the *buddhi*, a Sanskrit term that designates intelligence within the Brahman tradition. Without going into unnecessary detail, the *buddhi*, which comes from sudden revelation, is a 'bridge' between the material aspect of humanity and the principle of the absolute that arises from man's intimate position as a–being–in–

the-centre-of-the-universe. The very first meaning of *buddhi* is the ability to 'awaken'—hence the name Buddha (that is, awakened or delivered) is given to those who have obtained such knowledge.

Within a cultural perspective it is obvious that the study of the question of the relationship between conscience and rationality forces recognition that the significance of the mind's exertion, as it were, is approached from a large number of angles across the world. So what is rationality? What is a rational man? Social scientists need to move away from general philosophical considerations and to take into consideration what may arise from the subconscious or issue from biology.[53] Rationality, at least in its concrete manifestations, is culturally contextual and it is for this reason that utilitarian or rational choice approaches to social and political action are inherently reductionist. The motivations and interests that drive men in one milieu are often incomprehensible to those of another. It is simply not plausible to assume that all human groupings react in the same way to similar situations (insofar as those can be said to exist). Our method, which derives from empirical observation, does not deny the possible use of the concepts of interest and rationality. It merely places them in context and considers their relevance along with that of the other 'logics' that impinge on men's actions.

Even if we take for granted that human beings always weigh carefully the consequences of their actions, we need to accept that the realm of possible choices is constrained by the prevalent universe of meaning within which they live. For example, we may believe it is illogical for subsistence farmers to walk long distances in order to cultivate desperately poor ancestral land when there are newly irrigated fields near their abode. And in some ways it is. Yet 'irrational'

---

[53] For example, to consider that sexuality is merely the outcome of universal biological needs or that it is always the same old story between the sexes is to fail to enter the world of its meaningful significance. A psychologist might focus on the idealisation of the other as reflected in the self. A sociologist might stress deviance from social norms or the importance of matrimonial alliances. An anthropologist might work on matrimonial exchange. A historian might study the invention of courtly love, seen as sublimation of the sexual urge. The interpretativist, however, would argue that what matters is to understand what is valued, or forbidden, within a concrete social environment. As Malinowski pointed out, between the urge and the action there is culture. For us, then, it is crucial to identify the representation of sexuality with the social imaginary and to take into account the mentalities that affect the satisfaction of the libido.

behaviour of this type can be culturally 'logical'. And it is for social scientists to explain why. We would all like to believe that it is easy to transcend the limitations of our own culture and to make sense of that of the 'others'. In reality this is an exercise that requires lengthy training and is never fully completed.

Let us illustrate what this means for politics with reference to our previous work on Africa.[54] The Nigerian Big Man is at once politician and entrepreneur. An outside observer would be surprised to see that he blithely uses the proceeds from his economic activities without concern for the impact that such largesse may have on the viability of his business. His behaviour, therefore, is in some sense irrational. However, a cultural analysis would reveal that his political prominence requires of him that he spend ever more generously both on the conspicuous display of wealth and on redistribution to his clients. His political standing comes at this price. Within such an environment, therefore, the rationality of production is subordinated to that of the search for political standing.[55]

To take another example, most of us would argue that sustainable development is the most rational course of action for the future of our world. But even here it is interesting to note that this notion is understood differently in different countries. In the United States this amounts to the search for an equation that links profit (the top priority), planet (virtually understood as a 'person') and people. In France, on the other hand, the emphasis is on the economy (rather than profit), social concerns (reflecting wider societal issues) and environment (an anthropocentric term that fits well the Cartesian tradition). Here, as in so many other areas, the understanding of what is a universal aspiration is strongly coloured by the cultural context.[56]

Many aim to develop a form of scientific rationality that transcends cultural cleavages; others would like to evolve a form of supracultural political rationality. But such a quest is illusory. It is true that

---

[54] P. Chabal and J.-P. Daloz, 1999, *Africa Works*.

[55] J.-P. Daloz, 2002, 'Big Men in Sub-Saharan Africa: how élites accumulate positions and resources', *Comparative Sociology*, 2/1, pp. 271–85. On the other hand, we must admit that rational choice perspectives are sometimes based on sophisticated, if not entirely convincing, field research. See for instance, S. L. Popkin, 1979, *The Rational Peasant: the political economy of rural society in Vietnam*.

[56] As has been apparent in the debate concerning the Kyoto Protocol, for example.

the impact of globalisation, discussed later, has conspired both to disseminate Western culture worldwide and to create a sort of transnational way of life. It is also true that non-Western countries are increasingly confronted with social models that are alien to them. This may well lead to the development of forms of 'cultural syncretism', as we shall discuss later.

However, when contradictory cultural logics meet, the interpretativist is compelled to ask which will prevail 'in the last instance'.[57]

---

[57] To borrow from the Marxists the notion that 'in the last instance' it is the economic structure that matters most.

3

ANALYTICAL FOUNDATIONS

One of the most common charges levelled against those who stress cultural distinctions is that of excessive empiricism, a posture making it impossible to provide credible generalisations. The question raised here is that of the standard epistemological contrast between the search for the identification of universal recurrences and the quest for the understanding of the distinguishing features of given processes. Both, clearly, are equally valid. As Seiler, the comparativist political scientist writes: '[T]hese two perceptions of reality [are] equally scientific. The former is the norm in the natural sciences while the latter characterises the cultural sciences'.[1] However, the results achieved by the social sciences are more uncertain since they deal with realities that are far more elusive than in the natural sciences.

On this we would concur with Boas, the pioneer anthropologist, who noted that the empirical study of particularisms in human societies is not compatible with the models of the natural sciences. For us, a 'scientific' approach consists in the rigorous and systematic exposition of heterogeneity and not in the often theoretically artificial attempts to systematise more and more events with less and less theory. We would also eschew all normative approaches. This chapter explains why we steer clear of those conceptual frameworks, common in comparative politics, which are based on the analysis of values, political culture or the exaltation of differences.

UNDERSTANDING DIFFERENCES

The aim of this section is to respond systematically to those who argue that the scientific nature of our discipline must derive from the

[1] D. Seiler, 1985, *Comportement politique comparé*, p. 13.

application of general theories that avoid cultural 'atomism'. We will show that attention to cultural diversity is fully compatible with a comparative undertaking. Indeed, it is our contention that it is not just possible but also desirable to conceive of comparative politics as a non-positivist, yet entirely scientific, enterprise. One of the book's main arguments is that a 'scientific' method in political science ought not to seek to replicate the criteria of verifiability and predictability, and the search for 'iron laws', which apply to the natural sciences. As will be shown later, it must instead meet a different test of 'scientificity'.

The fruitless search for the lowest common denominator

Numerous social scientists assume—for philosophical, ideological or even, like Parsons, for theoretical reasons—that it is incumbent upon them to emulate the so-called hard sciences and provide universal laws. Others are aware of the significance of cultural diversity but neglect it for fear that their analysis might suffer a crippling relativistic bias. The case of the anthropologist Ruth Benedict is in this respect quite instructive. It appears that early on in her career she was aware of the ontological diversity of her research case studies while at the same time became concerned about the hazards of the quest for ever more precise factual descriptions. Her methodological solution was to offer a classification in terms of identifiable coherent 'patterns' to account conceptually for the types of behaviour uncovered in her fieldwork. According to her each culture is defined not primarily by the juxtaposition of characteristics but by they way in which they combine.[2] Clear as that scheme is, Benedict may well have over-emphasised the need for consistency, which has been vastly inflated among a number of structuralists and functionalists.[3]

---

[2] R. Benedict, 1934, *Patterns of Culture.*

[3] The obsession with coherence is itself culturally bound. It is in this respect interesting to read again Lévy-Bruhl—*La mentalité primitive* (1922)—a scholar whose arguments against unilinear evolutionism have often been misunderstood or distorted. He shows clearly how certain 'mentalities' are more comfortable with contradiction than others. In Sub-Saharan Africa we have often noticed how political actors were able constantly to operate on different registers—that is 'to live with contradictions'—which from our own European viewpoint would appear to be incompatible.

A number of political scientists advocate a 'middle range' analytical position: neither excessively empirical nor dogmatically universal. As was discussed in the previous chapter, this position may consist in confining diversity to a limited number of systemic configurations. However, from our point of view this search for the lowest common denominator is rather 'a-scientific'. The problem is not so much that it is difficult to find evidence of common processes but that this appreciation rests on the use of excessively wide and vague criteria, which can easily lead to a neglect of empirical reality. The heuristic merit of comparative description, which obviously cannot be an end in itself, is to use the analysis of what makes sense locally to construct comparative explanations.

By way of illustration we discuss briefly the issue of corruption—the comparative study of which has made great strides in the recent past. A 'gradualist' approach would deem that it is a general phenomenon, more or less salient in different parts of the world.[4] Some of our Third World colleagues might argue that corruption is indeed universal and that calling attention to its acuteness in the non-Western world is a way of deflecting attention from what happens in Western societies. A more systematic comparativist, however, would seek to assess the relevance of different types of corruption—for instance, between business and political élite, as in France, or between all social strata, as in Sub-Saharan Africa.

Our approach would favour an analysis rooted in the *longue durée* and would highlight the important dissimilarities between perceptions of corruption across the world.[5] It would also question the usefulness of what is largely an ethnocentric concept in settings where there is ambiguity about the illegality of the practice—condoned in certain (clientelistic) situations and condemned in others for blatantly political reasons. It is clear, therefore, that an approach in terms of values, which is discussed below, would be an impediment to the understanding of the local webs of meaning that influence practices

---

[4] By 'gradualist' we refer to Sartori's usage, which concerns those scholars who privilege the search for 'degrees' within a universalist continuum, and thus seem to avoid reference to any dichotomies. See G. Sartori, 1994, 'Bien comparer, mal comparer', *Revue Internationale de Politique Comparée*, 1/1 (April), p. 26.

[5] See, for instance, J.-P. Daloz and M. H. Heo, 1997, 'La corruption en Corée du Sud et au Nigeria: quelques pistes de recherche comparatives', *Revue Internationale de Politique Comparée*, 4/2 (September).

sometimes all too easily assimilated with corruption. Again a 'scientific' approach, as we see it, would reject both ethnocentrism and universalism in this respect.

Consequently the cultural perspective is not easily compatible with those approaches, which aim to go beyond appearances, context and empirical experiences in order to reveal the underlying structures of the phenomena in question. Geertz, who was here heavily influenced by Wittgenstein's writings on the 'publicity of meaning', once said: 'culture is public because meaning is'.[6] Culture may be symbolic but it is intelligible to those who can master its deeper codes. For us, then, the notion of analytical depth has more to do with the link between phenomenon and interpretation than with a reference to the subterranean.

Therefore, we do not accept that it is impossible to 'decipher' culture because it refers to the world of the invisible, even of the unconscious. Difficult as it may be to enter this world, a properly trained scholar, with the right approach and sufficient time, ought to be able to make sense of the evidence. It is true that most of us lack perspective on our own culture, principally because it makes implicit sense to us. Equally we are liable to be deceived by the more visible aspect of socio-cultural reality, as the metaphor of the iceberg suggests.[7] Nevertheless, as will be shown in Part III, there is nothing mysterious or intricate in the application of a cultural methodology.

It certainly does not involve a structuralist and deterministic 'Semiotic science' designed to explicate the connotation of signs—which can go as far as repudiating the relevance of the historical context within which actors speak and act, on the ground of its parochial contingency.[8] Such a formalist standpoint only buttresses the theoretical illusions generated by the will to ape the natural sciences. Under the guise of linguistics, perhaps the 'hardest' of all the

---

[6] C. Geertz, 1973, 'Thick Description: toward an interpretive theory of culture' in C. Geertz, *The Interpretation of Cultures*, p. 12. See here the discussion on 'eye blinking' (drawn from G. Ryle) in what is perhaps Geertz's most famous piece.

[7] The well-worn and ubiquitous metaphor of the tip of the iceberg reflects the commonsensical but ultimately hollow observation that the visible, or public, aspect of social behaviour amounts to role-playing, whereas its 'real' significance lies in what is hidden.

[8] Our method for the analysis of what people say and do will be found in Chapter 8, Section 1.

human sciences, or of impressive looking mathematical equations, these methodologies offer a pseudo-science of the social world, which obscures far more than it enlightens. They also reveal an unjustified inferiority complex with respect to the natural and physical sciences.

Beyond the complex of generalisation

It has often been claimed, among others perhaps most insistently by Norbert Elias, that the social sciences ought to aim for large-scale theoretical synthesis. Raymond Aron, for his part, advocated the highest possible level of conceptualisation: '[in a later] stage of theoretical abstraction, we will perhaps discover the essential functions of all political order.'[9]

However, are there in political science culturally free principles, let alone 'iron laws', such as Michels claimed in his study of oligarchy? Many scholars are prone to derive sociological generalisations from their research on specific case studies. Michels averred that all organisations, even ostensibly democratic ones (in which all members were deemed equal), would *necessarily* evolve into oligarchies, *because* of their inherent characteristics. His analysis of (largely German) socialist parties in the period before the First World War is undoubtedly rigorous.[10] In his book he maintains scientific analytical neutrality and refrains from passing judgement on the implications of his conclusions. The problem arises when he seeks to draw a universal principle from his study. Examples of similar extrapolations abound: the principle of class struggle, the processes of individualisation or of the rationalisation of human agency. The point here is not to deny the soundness of the analysis provided by Michels, Marx or Weber. It is simply to suggest that the validity of their conclusions may be limited in time and space.[11]

Admittedly the acceptance of cultural plurality goes against the classical systems of causality, as they developed from the nineteenth century. If the world is infinitely complex, and subject to myriad interpretations, how can we generalise? However, this caveat does not in our view invalidate the quest for objective knowledge. We reject

[9] As quoted in F. Dosse, 1992, *Histoire du structuralisme*, vol. I, p. 210.
[10] R. Michels, 1971 (1915), *Les partis politiques.*
[11] We develop this point more fully in the book's Conclusion.

approaches that relegate culture to the background whereas its effects are clearly (and sometimes causally) relevant to the politics that we aim to understand. A cultural perspective is one that enjoins the analyst to study word and deed within the appropriate context. This is not to claim, as an essentialist might, that culture 'determines' thinking and agency, or that our analysis is confined to the cultural 'enclave'. As we have already stressed, we want to move away from simplistic causality. To say that culture matters, is not to say that only *it* matters.

However, positivists often charge the interpretative school with being excessively allusive.[12] Whatever the merit of such a general critique, we shall show in the chapters that follow why we consider that our approach is indeed scientific—even if our understanding of what that means in the human and social sciences differs from the norm. For us a scientific method is not one that attains the highest level of abstract generalisation but one that takes into account the divergent webs of meaning to be found across the world. There are indeed very contrasted political realities in different parts of the globe and it is the work of the comparativist to explain why, and how, this is significant.[13]

From case study to comparative analysis

If we reject a notion of political 'science' built around a single formal and deductive logic, we do not believe either that an interpretative framework is confined to the compilation of case-study monographs. Admittedly a cultural approach requires a high level of local knowledge and it is not easily feasible for a single scholar to accumulate such data from a large number of distinct environments. However, that is not what is at stake. Comparativists can use judiciously the

---

[12] See here the critique in P. Shankman, 1984, 'The Thick and the Thin: on the interpretive paradigm of Clifford Geertz', *Current Anthropology*, 25/3.

[13] As we tried to do in *Africa Works*, where we discussed the processes of political informalisation. This led us to offer an analysis of the nature of the 'State' in that part of the world, which explained why it was not differentiated from society. We were careful to note that not all States on the continent were similar—there are huge differences between Senegal and Somalia, for example—but we argued that general patterns could be observed by means of comparative analysis. We develop this discussion further in Chapter 9.

material garnered by those scholars who have specialist local knowledge. They can also work in collaboration or collectively.

Of course we are mindful of the hazards of an overly impressionistic vision of different polities across the world. We recognise too
that it would not be desirable merely to limit enquiry to a detailed list
of the distinctions between these diverse settings. Such would provide at best a fragmented and incoherent picture. However, we believe the injunction to maximise local knowledge is in fact an asset to
political analysis. The key to achieving comparative insight, as will be
explained later, is to focus research on a clearly defined and heuristically relevant topic. However erudite one might be, it is better to
avoid the claim to take 'everything' into consideration.

Furthermore there is nothing wrong with the ambition to add a
political angle to the existing 'thick description' mosaic. The comparativist does not aim to acquire 'exhaustive' knowledge but merely
to search far and wide for those cultural factors that impinge on the
exercise of political power. We are not on the quest for a 'fundamental' political anthropology. The aspiration is not to ensure that the
evidence gathered is all-inclusive, but merely to ensure that it is sufficient to sustain the assessment of the cultural dimension at stake.
Modest as this is, it is probably more useful than the production of
general 'models' based on vague or unconvincing variables, which
merely result in the emergence of competing schools of thought.

To many political scientists comparative analysis requires above all
a degree of conceptual and theoretical abstraction—which, from our
standpoint, is both a condition and an obstacle to the undertaking.
The charge is that those who study 'other' cultures eventually come
to internalise their logics, but may then find it difficult to transmit
that knowledge to those without any acquaintance with the specificities of the settings in question. This is why our method aims to
present conclusions in a way that renders them widely intelligible,
including to specialists working in other areas.

For example, the question of the State—discussed in detail in
Chapter 9—often raises the issue of the nature of comparison. When
is a State a State? The query itself brings forth issues of disciplines,
conceptualisations and competing hypotheses. One can opt for a
limited approach, using ideal types, and confine analysis to the
question of whether the observed political entities conform to the

schema. But this forces comparison along the evolutionist lines of an historical continuum: how 'developed' or 'backward' are the States in question? Or one can adopt the broadest and inclusive sweep, identifying as states all manners of political congeries—thereby losing the concept's analytical sharpness.

Our method, detailed in Part III, offers instead an epistemology of singularity. In this respect, we follow in the footsteps of historical sociology, which pays especial attention to differences in historical trajectories.[14] It may be that such an approach is more intricate than some of the others on offer, but we hold that it is infinitely more rewarding, as we will endeavour to demonstrate in Part IV.

DEAD ENDS

In this final section, we explain why we dissociate ourselves from a number of standard political science approaches to the question of culture. Our primary aim here is not so much to demonstrate the limits of those methods, though this may well be one the outcomes of the discussion, as to explain why they fail to meet the scientific criteria we propose for comparative analysis. We discuss in turn the question of 'values', the notion of political culture and the issue of multi-culturalism.

The search for values

A large number of scholars, from various disciplines, equate culture with systems of beliefs, customs and those habits that affect social behaviour. At the heart of all these definitions lies the notion of 'values', which refers to that 'conception of the desirable' commonly shared within a given social grouping.[15] From this viewpoint, 'values' ensure integration, by means of socialisation, and give coherence to

---

[14] One key difference, however, is that we focus more on the synchronic rather than the grand dynamics often privileged by historical sociology, which have often resulted in rather unpersuasive structuralist interpretations. There is no space here for a critique of the work of B. Moore, T. Skocpol, S. Rokkan or C. Tilly. For a general discussion of these issues, see Y. Déloye, 1997, *Sociologie historique du politique*.

[15] See here C. Kluckhohn, 1951, 'Values and Value-orientation on the Theory of Action' in T. Parsons and E. Shils (eds), *Toward a General Theory of Action*.

perceptions of identity (of the self and others). If it is arguable that such an approach is useful as concerns 'traditional' communities, it is less likely that it can offer insights in respect of 'modern' polities, with a high degree of social differentiation, and even less of 'post-modern' societies, in which normative conventions have long shattered.

The interpretative approach—which some trace back to de Tocqueville and Weber,[16] but which was most systematically developed by Geertz—is both broader and deeper in that it concentrates attention on 'meaning'. To use a modern metaphor, culture is here conceptualised as 'software', which provides codes, rules and instructions. This may appear to be a very constraining notion but it offers instead a heuristically creative analytical system. Human beings inherit cultural codes from birth, which remain relevant throughout their lifetime. They are passed on to their descendants. Without them man would be confined to the realm of instincts and senses. A semiotic approach (see Chapter 8) makes it possible to decipher these codes, or 'webs of meaning'. As Geertz wrote, it is not 'an experimental science in search of law but an interpretive one in search of meaning.'[17]

Of course ours is not a philosophical quest for the general connotation of 'meaning' but only an investigation of what makes sense to the people concerned within their own historical and cultural context. Laughter may be a characteristic of humankind, as Rabelais said in the preface to *Gargantua*, but what matters is how forms and perceptions of laughter may differ. A sardonic laugh, for instance, is eminently cultural. The point here is to suggest that it is impossible to derive social significance from any physiological expression outside a real (as opposed to imagined) social setting. In the Far East, for example, it is desirable to laugh at oneself when one is embarrassed, or ridiculous. Consequently those present will also be expected to laugh. Westerners, however, are well advised not to follow suit, lest they offend the person in question.[18]

---

[16] Although Tocqueville reflected on what made sense in America, he did stress the links between values and political regime. Weber too wrote much on the importance of taking into account what made sense to political actors, but he also gave pride of place to values, or ethos. Whilst suspicious of general theories, he remained an evolutionist and doubted that it was possible to understand the world without reference to values.

[17] C. Geertz, 1973, *The Interpretation of Cultures*, p. 5.

[18] See note 6 above.

A comparative approach in terms of 'values' is bound to encounter serious epistemological difficulties.[19] In the first instance, it is far from clear that there is a normative consensus on the question within any contemporary society. Second, there are immense analytical hurdles involved in working out the extent to which such 'values' have been internalised, inculcated, or forced upon various segments of society. Third, it is not clear what method to use in order to achieve an 'objective' survey of a given community's 'values. Confronted by a foreign researcher, a Swede, for instance, will be far less inclined to criticise his/her country's 'values' than an Italian. Does this not matter? Finally, there is the question of the researcher's axiological neutrality, a consideration that is neglected in large swathes of social sciences. To us, therefore, only an approach in terms of 'meaning' offers a neutral analytical framework.

Despite the limitations outlined above, comparative approaches in terms of 'values' continue to hold sway in comparative politics. Indeed, they predominate in the quantitative studies of public opinion and in those presently fashionable studies of social capital.[20] They are also at the core of present debates about globalisation, the end of history, the 'clash of civilisations' or the notion that under-development is a 'state of mind'.[21] A number of neo-development-alists take culture seriously, and even suggest the need for a return to a cultural paradigm—by which they mean, however, the study of those 'values' that promote human progress. To them, clearly, some 'values' are obstacles to development.[22]

Again this raises the question of whether culture is an independent variable (discussed in Chapter 2) liable so instrumentally to affect socio-economic and political development either positively or nega-tively. It is a question without answer, since it is quite simply im-possible to demonstrate singular causality of this type. As individuals we may all have an opinion about genital mutilation, abortion, hunting, shopping on Sunday or nudist beaches. But how is the social

[19] See here B. Badie, 1983, *Culture et politique*, Chapter 3.
[20] R. Putnam, 1993, *Making Democracy Work*. For a critique, see E. Ritaine, 2001, 'Cherche capital social, désespérément', *Critique internationale*, 12 (July).
[21] F. Fukuyama, 1995, *Trust*.
[22] See the chapters by the two editors in L. Harrison and S. Huntington (eds), 2000, *Culture Matters*.

scientist claiming axiological neutrality able to pronounce against or in favour of such behaviour?

Therefore an approach in terms of 'values' cannot avoid largely sterile debates. It is a recipe for a clash of opinions on almost any topic selected for comparative research. A semiotic analysis, on the other hand, makes it possible not just to understand culture generally but also to allow for disagreements about 'values' within any given culture. Indeed, once we accept that culture is not a concatenation of normative standpoints but the *language* that makes understanding possible, it becomes easier to explain why individuals who live within the same cultural setting can hold antagonistic convictions, based on different 'values'. As is immediately apparent, this is of utmost relevance to the field of comparative politics.

Political culture

We would also distance ourselves from the concept of political culture, which is widely used in our discipline. Whether of behaviouralist of institutionalist pedigree this notion cannot but be normative. Frequently it also is functionalist, since some values are considered to be more 'functional', or 'dysfunctional', in respect of those political dynamics that are deemed most desirable.[23] The importance of this concept in American political science is such that it has spawned a whole separate area of research, frequently devoted exclusively to the theme of democratic values[24] or development.[25] This approach has been heavily criticised, not just by those who reject such simplistic causality but also by other comparativists;[26] by some who are concerned to refine this perspective;[27] and by a few who have slightly recast their earlier theories.[28]

---

[23] For example, a fatalistic conception of the world is not favourable to democratic change—and vice versa.

[24] G. Almond and S. Verba, 1963, *The Civic Culture.* The work of historians does not usually suffer from such normative tendencies. See, for instance, M. Baker (ed.), 1987, *The Political Culture of the Old Regime,* vol. I.

[25] As is obvious right from the publication of G. Almond and J. Coleman (eds.), *The Politics of Developing Areas,* 1960 (and its reference to the ancient notion of 'cultural lag'). The authors consider developing countries only from the point of view of their having to 'catch up'.

[26] M. Dogan and D. Pelassy, 1981, *Sociologie politique comparative.*

[27] R. Inglehart, 1990, *Culture Shift in Advanced Industrial Society,* Chapter 1.

[28] G. Almond and S. Verba (eds), 1980, *The Civic Culture Revisited.*

However, our critique is different. It concerns the argument implicit in all these approaches that there can develop a *political* culture autonomous from the rest of a society's cultural codes. This is at the very least questionable. In the first instance, it is well to remember 'that not all human societies experience political control; in some social control is enough.'[29] Furthermore in the less 'complex' societies that anthropologists habitually study, 'culture cannot be political because it is global'.[30]

Consequently comparativists who examine non-Western societies are unlikely to be able to identify a discrete *political* culture variable, operational in an area of human existence distinct from, say, the *economic* or *religious*. Such a behaviouralist approach, therefore, is guilty of neglecting all relevant anthropological knowledge about the relationships between cultural codes and social action, which shed useful light on the exercise of power. Or, as has been pithily stated by a French scholar: 'le politique ne renvoie plus finalement qu'au politique.'[31]

Within an interpretativist perspective the notion of culture refers to a far wider semiotic framework within which its influence over political, economic and religious activities is eminently *indirect*.[32] A political culture approach, which reduces the concept to an inventory of beliefs and 'values' likely to bring about or sustain a democratic political order, leads to a superficial and a-historical analysis of attitudes. Although some of our colleagues readily concede this point in principle, they appear not to see its relevance to comparative politics. To us it is fundamental.

In the 1970s a large proportion of the literature on political culture centred on communist countries; that is, societies where political change had been brutal rather than gradual.[33] This work had the merit of asking questions about the disjuncture between the newly imposed 'revolutionary' ethos and pre-existing cultures.[34] However, it tended to continue to consider *political* culture in isolation.

[29] D. Seiler, 1985, *Comportement politique comparé*, p. 153.
[30] Y. Schemeil, 1985, 'Les cultures politiques' in M. Grawitz and J. Leca (eds), *Traité de science politique*, vol. III, p. 238.
[31] 'Politics only refers to the political.' B. Badie, 1983, *Culture et Politique*, p. 44.
[32] See M. H. Ross, 1997, 'Culture and Identity in Comparative Political Analysis' in M. Lichbach and A. Zuckerman (eds), *Comparative Politics*, pp. 46 ff.
[33] S. Welsh, 1993, *The Concept of Political Culture*.
[34] See A. Brown and J. Gray (eds), 1977, *Political Culture and Political Change in Com-*

A scholar like Inglehart, for his part, sought to address some of the shortcomings of the political culture approach by pointing out in his book that, in advanced societies, cultural differences may be 'enduring' if not 'immutable'.[35] Yet his research was primarily based on large-scale inter-cultural quantitative surveys of 'values' and attitudes, which interpretativists view with some scepticism since they pay no attention to the semiotic dimension. Are there not questions 'that make sense in England or Scandinavia but shock the Japanese or cannot even be translated into Arabic?'[36] These are the very concerns that raise the serious methodological issues that will be discussed in Part III.

After a relative lull there was in the 1980s a resurgence of interest in political culture, now moving away from a 'civic' culture perspective. The objective was to link political change with culture. Eckstein, for instance, tried to answer the criticism that the notion of culture was conceptually vague by making a conceptual distinction between attitudes and 'cultural orientations'.[37] Others have worked on the relationship between social and political identities.[38] Some have sought to show the relevance of political culture as against the currently fashionable approaches in terms of rational choice.[39] Yet others have tried to reconcile in-depth anthropological research with the frequently used constructivist framework of contemporary political science.[40]

---

munist States; White, S., 1979, *Political Culture and Soviet Politics*; and A. Brown (ed.), 1984, *Political Culture and Communist Studies*.

[35] R. Inglehart, 1990, *Culture Shift in Advanced Industrial Society*.

[36] M. Dogan and D. Pelassy, 1981, *Sociologie politique comparative*, p. 15. See also M. Dogan, 1994, 'L'analyse quantitative en science politique', *Revue Internationale de Politique Comparée*, 1/1 (April).

[37] H. Eckstein, 1982, 'A Culturalist Theory of Political Change', *American Political Science Review*, 82, pp. 789–804.

[38] D.-C. Martin, 1989, 'A la recherche des cultures politiques: de certaines tendances récentes de la politologie française', *Cahiers Internationaux de Sociologie*, LXXXVII, pp. 223–48.

[39] R. Eatwell (ed.), 1997, *European Political Cultures*.

[40] W. Mishler and D. Pollack, 2003, 'On Culture, Thick and Thin: toward a neo cultural synthesis' in Pollack, D. et al. (eds), *Political Culture in Post Communist Europe*. Finally one might also refer here to the work on 'very advanced' countries, where it is deemed that political competition is no longer related to social

If these scholars, sometimes dubbed 'neo-cultural', undoubtedly moved the discussion forward, they remained hampered in our view by the normative nature of their research framework. Indeed, their work is primarily concerned with issues such as the advent of democracy or the access to citizenship (both in the Third World and in Eastern Europe), which differs little from their predecessors' interests. Their reference to the interpretativist approach, and even more to Geertz, is often gratuitous, token or even incoherent, since their notion of political 'science' is one he always denounced. They still cannot envisage that the study of politics requires attention to the deep local systems of meaning and that, in some settings, for example, the notion of 'general interest' simply does not make any sense.[41]

From a comparative perspective, it could be argued that the notion of *political* culture is relevant to countries where the political sphere is very strongly differentiated from society. There it may refer to mechanisms of legitimacy that are not reducible to concrete social modalities: for example, the doctrine of civic universalism or of equality of rights in France since the Revolution. But how vast is the domain of political culture? Still in France, should we refer to political culture, or cultures—the latter often applied to various currents within different political parties? Does this mean, therefore, that there are left, right, Gaullist, liberal, socialist and communist political *cultures*?[42] For us, such a usage of the notion refers primarily to ideological differences. Beyond the antagonistic visions of the 'ideal' society they hold, what is of interest to an interpretativist approach is that all these factions operate within systems of meaning (or a 'complex whole') they share. We will show in Part IV how a cultural approach is in this respect able to reveal a greater depth of comparative political understanding than the study of 'political culture'.

---

cleavage but only to specific issues, which politicians seek to exploit instrumentally. See here T. Clark and V. Hoffmann-Martinot (eds), 1998, *The New Political Culture.*

[41] For an example of what this means in relation to an important theme in political science, see Geertz's 2003 Sidney Mintz Lecture: 'What is a State if it is not a Sovereign? Reflections on Politics in Complicated Places', *Current Anthropology,* forthcoming. See also C. Geertz, 1963, *Old Societies and New States.*

[42] S. Bernstein (ed.), 1999, *Les cultures politiques en France.*

Post-modernism and the exaltation of diversity

If the first half of the twentieth century was the time of political ideology, the second seems to have been characterised by 'cultural' politics. Much of what is written about culture today is part of a post-modernist current primarily concerned with multiculturalism. Adherents to this approach celebrate cultural differences, which they want contemporary societies (mostly in the 'white' West) to acknowledge. They call into question the claims of cultural superiority derived from the imperial past. The right to be different has led to the claim for different rights.

If the challenge to the Western sense of its own superiority has now gained full momentum, such post-modernist movements have yet to come to terms with the fact that others, and not just in the past, have made similar claims. Westerners are far from the only ones to have asserted pre-eminence. The Chinese have always believed that they were the very centre of the universe. Arabs have no doubt that their language ought to be the only Islamic language and they have expected all other Muslims across the world to acknowledge the prominence of their own sacred sites.

Therefore, the problem with such post-modernist approaches is that they too end up being ideological. Although in principle they encourage 'absolute relativism', on the basis that all cultures are equally worthwhile, in practice they tend to lionise the cultures of the 'colonised', the 'oppressed', or the 'minorities'.[43] Not infrequently they appear to be interested in 'revenge' rather than insight or giving voice to the oppressed, for which they even claim 'cathartic' cultural virtues. Our view is not that these efforts are not justified, but simply that they contribute little to the understanding of culture in the semiotic sense we use.

It seems to us important to develop a cultural approach that is distinct from what are, quite clearly, 'a-scientific' standpoints. It is interesting to note here that a number of post-modernists agree with the interpretativists in respect of the importance of cultural cleavages. But they criticise them for not following through on the analysis

---

[43] This is not a new tendency. Witness Lévi-Strauss' ostensibly relativist position, which nevertheless endowed 'primitive' peoples with virtues unknown in the West. He also considered that the Orient was centuries ahead of the West in some critical respects.

with a call for multiculturalism—a militant posture we believe ought to be kept separate from 'scientific' research. The question for us is not so much how extensive multiculturalism might be, but what it actually means to identifiable groups of people in concrete societies.[44]

More generally, then, we view this post-modernist controversy more as an ethical or philosophical debate than as a method for comparative analysis. For example, the key question of 'assimilation' in France and Britain turns on whether it is better to try to integrate minorities or to recognise their diversities. In both countries the argument rapidly harks to a definition of what is or is not essential to the cultural 'practices' of such minorities. There can be no agreement, sometimes not even understanding, since each views the other from the standpoint of its own moral code and values, not to say superiority.[45]

In sum, then, this first part of our volume ought to make it plain why a cultural approach, such as we favour, avoids the normative perspectives that are so central to the practice of political science.

---

[44] We address the tricky question of identity in the next chapter.

[45] Others claim that there is a 'third way', which involves inter-cultural dialogue within a minimal agreement on what might be called the universal desiderata of modern societies—an option that seems on the face of it unpractical.

Part II. APPROACH

A cultural approach to politics is neither an attempt to reduce politics to culture nor a desire to cast agency into a relativist mould. It is, as was explained in Part I, a framework that makes it possible to understand the exercise of power in its relevant context. What this means is that there is no obvious mechanism by which it would be possible to explain the politics of a particular setting without making sense of the cultural factors that affect power and induce individuals, as well as groups, to behave as they do. To assume there is a transparent way of interpreting political events that relies solely on the tried and trusted theory of self-interest and utilitarian rationality is always possible. *Ex post facto* explanations often 'demonstrate' that the logic of apparently complex situations can be assimilated to the pursuit of clearly identifiable goals. However, attempts to forecast what might happen in the future clearly show how feeble such narrow approaches can be. Politics is not just about interests.

To illustrate we can do no better than examine briefly some aspects of the war in Iraq. Before the conflict outside observers (not least of whom 'academic' policy advisers) took a fairly simple view of the likely course of events. Since Saddam Hussein was a bloody tyrant, there necessarily was massive opposition to his regime and it was expected that, undermined from within, it would quickly collapse once hostilities had begun in earnest. Similarly the country appeared to be split into a straightforward tripartite division: hostile Kurds, an oppressed Shiite majority and the ruling Sunni (Tikrit) minority. Again Kurds and Shias would quickly rise in defiance of the dictator. Other than a simplistic division of society between ethnic and religious groups, there was little concern about other historical or socio-economic factors. As for the future, the coalition would endeavour to put in place an 'all-inclusive' political framework that would allow the establishment of a new democratic political order. Admittedly the US administration did not speak with a single voice

94

on the matter, but its campaign plan was in the end very largely predicated on such assumptions.

What happened once the conflict started revealed how simple minded this a-cultural approach was. What different Iraqis did when confronted with a full-scale military invasion of their country was not straightforwardly determined by fear or narrow interest. It was in large measure conditioned by what made sense to them at any particular moment and such an attitude hinged on a series of complex assessments, which can only be fully understood within their appropriate historical and cultural settings. Shias, who in any event were far from forming a single bloc, did not merely behave in terms of a simple opposition to a regime that had hounded them. They were more than 'religious beings'. They could also be Iraqis, Arabs, southerners, urban, educated, poor, pro-Iranian etc. In brief, their religious identity was only one of many facets, which became differently salient as the situation evolved, during and especially after the war. Similarly Kurds could also be Iraqi nationalists or part of a particular local faction, and their interests went in different directions. They were more than 'ethnic beings'. A large number also envisaged their future within a federal Iraq. Finally there were many different Sunni viewpoints, not all former supporters of Saddam Hussein.

The conflict revealed many other contradictions, which also require attention. The weight of over thirty years of an authoritarian, avowedly secular and 'socialist' Baath party impinged on individuals and communities in ways that affected the manner in which they responded to the takeover of their country by an outside military force. Equally Saddam Hussein's belated resort to an 'Islamic' ideology showed that, regardless of his previous secular viewpoint, he could not fail ultimately to rely on the religious 'culture' of his people and of his neighbours in the Middle East. Finally the fact that a large section of the population could consider Saddam Hussein the legitimate defender of the country suggests that factors of history were, unsurprisingly, paramount. Iraqis, or at least some of those who are today Iraqis, have a long, and proud, 'national' past during which they have always rallied to the defender of the homeland who stands up to foreign invasion. Myths too matter, but understanding how requires a culturally sensitive analysis.

The aim of this second section is not to provide a definition of culture that would aim to make it possible for political scientists to factor in the 'cultural variable' in their analysis.[1] An approach that would conceptualise culture in more formal terms than those suggested in our Introduction would, again, fall prey to the idea that there is a single notion of the concept that applies to all situations, regardless of their historical or socio-political environment. Such would indeed be a 'culturalist' method. Our hope, therefore, is to explain how cultural factors are relevant to some of the fundamental questions of political analysis. What those factors are and how they are to be interpreted must, of course, be determined by the circumstances of the cases under study. To explain what happened to the Shias of Basra in the first half of 2003 it is probably helpful to understand that, as the British forces sought to persuade them they were being liberated and some of their Iranian religious brethrens to convince them they were being violated, their political stance evolved over time according to the historical memory their culture conveyed about deliverance and subjugation—and about the British, for that matter.

Part II seeks to explain how culture is pertinent to three key issues of political analysis: identity, order and change. These are by no means the only areas of interest to political science, but we would argue that they ought to form the backbone of any comparative framework, for they represent the three central axes of the political arena. If, in other words, we are to appreciate how questions about politics can illuminate the understanding of the exercise of power, we must study how culture matters to political identity, how it helps configure the political order and how it affects political change over time. The issue of identity conditions individual and collective behaviour. The matter of order determines the context within which power is sustained. The question of change makes it possible to give a meaningful, diachronic, analysis of what happens over time and not just a superficial snapshot of events. Taken together these three topics force the analyst to furnish a deeper, and thus more plausible, comparative account of political events across the globe. A brief discussion of the Iraqi case makes plain how the three questions, taken up in the three chapters that follow, do matter.

An appraisal of the nature of political identity in that country clearly demands an appreciation of the many ways in which individ-

---

[1] As explained in Chapter 2 above.

uals see themselves and perceive others. How does religion affect behaviour politically among the different sections of the Shiite population? Is 'Kurdishness' an ethnic or a national quality? The question of culture and political order is even more obviously relevant for here we focus on the two central issues of how power is understood in its local context and how culture is used politically. The polity that Saddam Hussein erected imposed a rigid overall framework of control, but it had to rely on age-old networks of power in which clan and religion were paramount. Will the 'national' myths, which he created, continue to embody the national sovereignty of the Iraqi nation? Finally there is little doubt that culture will influence greatly the future of Iraq. Just as the Baath party sought to reinvent an ideology to justify a form of modernity both secular and 'egalitarian', relegating in the process religion and ethnicity to the dustbin of history, so the new rulers of the country will have to make sense of the composite culture they have inherited. Will Saddam Hussein's attempt at frogmarching the country into modernity or the shock of the Western military invasion favour a 'return' to the so-called traditional culture of the region?

The point here is not only to present a framework for the comparison of Iraq with other similar countries but to suggest what a cultural approach to comparative political analysis can offer by means of this particular example. It is of course true that cultural factors have not always been neglected in political science but they have most often been considered supernumerary, or residual. They are brought in when other variables seemingly fail to provide sufficiently enlightening (or sometimes sufficiently convenient) explanations. What we want to suggest here is that it is imperative to approach the comparative study of politics by means of a properly grounded understanding of culture, taken in its broadest sense, as a system of meanings, which demands sustained scholarly interpretation—and not merely *ad hoc* reference.

4

CULTURE AND POLITICAL IDENTITY

Comparative political theory is built on an implicit notion of how identities form and how they matter. With some variation that notion is drawn primarily from the experience of the modern Western 'man'. Not surprisingly, but perhaps a trifle unwisely, the bulk of present day comparative analysis has, therefore, developed a theoretical construct in which the basic unit is the individual as it is conceived to be in our own societies. Political scientists operate very largely on the assumption that modernisation is unidirectional and results in due course in a variant of Westernisation. This view holds as true that development brings about the transformation of 'traditional' society, in which communal factors predominate, into a society of individuals pursuing their own self-interests and behaving politically as discrete citizens.

This seems a very old fashioned critique

Our contention, however, is that analysts ought not to make any such suppositions about the nature of political identity. Instead they should probe into the societies they claim to study in order to determine how perceptions and representations of identity shape the behaviour of individuals and the communities within which they live. It may be that, at a general level, comparisons between North Americans and Northern Europeans can be based on common assumptions about how individuals view themselves and their fellow citizens. However, the vast bulk of the world's population lives in societies where the relations between self and other, or individual and community, are by no means as straightforward as development theory assumes they have become in the West. Hence an understanding of their politics and, even more, a comparison between them, does require a more systematic exploration of the link between culture and political identity.

98

Because the notion of identity is complex, drawing as it does on a wide range of disciplines (including sociology, anthropology, economics, psychology and even philosophy), the aim of this chapter needs to be explained more clearly.[1] We are here interested in discussing how groups and individuals think of their own political 'identity'. What this means will of course differ markedly in different settings and it would be impossible sensibly to explain the range of issues that may be relevant to the formation of such political identity in all parts of the world. Our aim, therefore, is more limited. In the first part we want merely to suggest how culture impinges on the ways in which individuals' notions of self and group shape their views of political identity. In the second we examine in more detail the political relevance of some key cultural constructs—ethnicity, religion and nationality—which are clearly salient today in the political behaviour of groups across the globe. The overall objective is to discuss the relevance of culture, and the merit of a cultural approach, not to provide an overview of the literature on political identity.

HOW WHO WE ARE MATTERS TO WHAT WE BELIEVE....

Issues of identity are notoriously deceptive. They appear to be easily susceptible to the insights of common sense. Is it not evident that who we are conditions what we believe? Perhaps, but the really meaningful question is how? As soon as we confront this challenge, we become aware of the complexity of the answer. Indeed, if we are to hold to common sense, we immediately face a contradiction. Whilst we would in the main reject a simplistic causal link between our own identity and what we believe, we are used to applying it, if not wholesale than at least as a shortcut explanation, to 'others'. We are rational; the other is superstitious. We are modern; the other is traditional. Stated in this stark way such a formulation might generate outcry: it is no longer politically correct to make such assumptions

[1] As the bibliography on such topics is immense we have deliberately avoided burdening the text with references to the major works in the various disciplines to which we have turned for a better understanding of the question of (political) identity. Readers will find in the Bibliography some indication of the sources that have been most useful to us.

about those who are different from us. Yet this standpoint itself is as ethnocentric as its opposite, for it implies a relativist view that is intimately bound to our own, Western centred, notion of the 'equality' of cultures. Therefore, the relationship between culture and political identity cannot be taken for granted. It must be elucidated in its appropriate historical context.

Notions of self: what is an individual?

Moving beyond common sense, we must start at the very beginning and consider how notions of self are related to what we are as individuals and how we behave politically.[2] Our ambition here is modest in that we do not intend to address the issue of the self from a general standpoint but merely in respect of its relevance to politics. We are concerned with the way in which it is possible to appraise the significance of culture for political identity. The notions of self with which we deal are those that impinge on relations of power, not those that condition other areas of human behaviour. Of course it is true that in real life the political 'sphere' cannot be so easily dissociated from the others. Equally all aspects of the notion of self have some political implications.

Political theory, like the economic theory on which it increasingly models itself, is predicated upon the principle that, for the purpose of analysis there is a single universal notion of what an individual is, however divergent its genesis may have been.[3] So, for example, it is commonly held (in political science textbooks) that human behaviour is primarily to be understood as the outcome of private decisions made by single persons surveying the range of options open to them. Political acts follow from the exercise of utilitarian and rational calculations in which one's own well being is measured in relation to that of other, equally discrete, individuals. If game theory is perhaps at one extreme of such a conceptual outlook, reducing action to a series of chess-like moves, there is nevertheless at the core of our discipline an axiomatic belief in the uniform nature of the notion of self that is

[2] For a psychological approach see I. Burkitt, 1991, *Social Selves*.
[3] For a clear and comprehensive introduction to standard political theory, which is virtually silent about cultural approaches, see D. Marsh and G. Stoker, 1995, *Theory and Methods in Political Science*.

embodied in the singular political actor, most commonly defined as 'citizen'.[4]

It is not our intention to suggest that comparativists ought in every case to initiate their research with a study of the ideas of the self in the societies they examine. There may well be instances where this issue is not consequential. However, we would argue that in cases where comparisons are essayed between vastly different parts of the world, it is necessary to ensure that analysis is based on a systematic survey of the question of the meaning of the individual. Although the study of the perception of the self is commonly the preserve of psychology, that of political action falls squarely within the ambit of our discipline. The question is thus how to link an understanding of the self with a study of political behaviour.

The task is not esoteric, for what is required is not a 'psychological profile' of individuals but merely an investigation of what makes sense to the people concerned. Therefore, this does not presuppose research into the individual 'psyche', but an examination of the terms in which people explain political behaviour. On the other hand, the task is not simple, since the appreciation of other cultures is not achieved lightly. It requires at the very least a realisation that it is a central area of concern for the analyst. It thus demands a suspension of judgement, an open mind, about the hypotheses and models that may be applicable to the case studies.[5] Instead of starting research with a preconceived idea of the self that guides the behaviour of individuals in a particular setting, comparativists would need to accept that differing notions in this respect might have significant effect on the comparisons undertaken.

Two examples will illustrate what we mean here. The first is drawn, perhaps inevitably, from Geertz's work—as presented in his well-known essay, 'Person, Time and Conduct in Bali'.[6] Here the anthropologist explains how perceptions of self are contingent on the names individuals receive. These names are intended to locate the person within a long chain of genealogically classified relatives, and not to confer upon the individual any distinctive, or even unique, characteristics. Because, as Geertz explains, the notion of time is

---

[4] On game theory, see *inter alia* H. Gintis, 2000, *Game Theory Evolving.*
[5] Part IV is devoted to a systematic discussion of these methodological issues.
[6] In C. Geertz, 1973, *The Interpretation of Cultures,* pp. 360–411.

cyclical, there is a sense in which individuals simply fit into their allotted slot within a repeated pattern of successive generations. It follows from this, naturally, that political action is circumscribed by the place allocated to the individual within this recurrent model. That place is very largely made plain by the name attached to the person. This analysis does not imply, of course, that such a state of affairs will always hold fast. It is, however, deeply relevant to an understanding of (chiefly local) politics in Bali during the period under study.

The second example concerns the notion of the self held by those who believe in reincarnation, and particularly caste.[7] Although it may seem that such a personal belief is of little consequence to political analysis, there is little doubt that it has important consequences for the political life of those who harbour such conviction, both at the individual and collective levels. Whatever reincarnation means, and that does of course vary widely, it implies minimally that people see themselves as having 'inherited' some of the attributes of those from whom they have issued—person or animal. This is likely to give them a very specific perception of the circumstances in which they live, indeed of life itself. It might, for example, induce in them a degree of fatalism that could not easily be explained otherwise. It might equally lead to widespread political passivity within the groups that share such views. At the very least it is a key part of their culture, which fully deserves to be taken into consideration when attempting comparative work.[8]

Locating the community: gender, family, kinship, network, nation and beyond

Discussions of self cannot, of course, be dissociated from those of community, or grouping, for the very notion of the individual, however focused on the single person, is tied to that of the society of which it is a part. Examining self and community separately is only a methodological device. The key here is to consider the importance of analysing individual political actions within their social context. In practical terms this means that comparing events and behaviour in

[7] On caste, see L. Dumont, 1970 [1967], *Homo hierarchicus.*
[8] See for example, S. Bayly, 1999, *Caste, Society and Politics in India.*

different polities requires a differentiated focus, which is appropriate to the setting in question. For instance, important as political parties are to the conduct of politics in the West, it may well be that their study is not appropriate to the understanding of political competition in some areas. Explaining patterns of (political) leadership in countries where parties are important and in those where they are not would then demand a focus on different political groupings. Finally, as we shall see in the next section, most of us are members of many circles of identity, so that political action is rarely explained by one type of belonging only.

Locating the relevant grouping does not merely involve casting a gaze at the people one intends to study, in the manner of the scientist investigating a sample under the microscope. It necessitates an understanding of the webs of meaning woven by collections of individuals and an analysis of their social interaction. This is turn calls for an appreciation of the many ways in which people engage others both within what may appear to be their own 'natural', geographical, community and beyond. Comparing local politics in the south of France, in rural Morocco and the American Midwest suburbs, for example, would call for a series of anthropologically sensitive studies of the people from these areas. The point of such surveys would be to determine how best to identify the sub-groupings that affect local political life most profoundly. In southern France one would stress the importance of locality, religion and party affiliation. In rural Morocco factors such as gender, religious affiliation and language would be critical. In the suburban Midwest social standing, race and education would matter greatly.

Hence, locating the 'community' means avoiding making *a priori* assumptions on how individuals relate to the groupings of which they are a part. It is a question of assessing the cultural factors that can clarify the relevant links between the comparative project at hand, such as explaining local politics, and the political behaviour under examination. There is no single way of tackling that problem. A cultural approach entails the ability to adjust method to the evidence generated by the appraisal of the types of groupings that are most relevant. This may well mean that when it comes to assessing what matters most to local politics in a particular society, the relevant unit of analysis will be the ethnic group, whilst in another it will be the village, the local brotherhood, the social club or the political network.

However, a study of the selfsame people concerned with a different comparative question might well suggest that different factors apply. To continue with the above example, an enquiry into political militancy in the south of France, rural central Morocco and suburban Midwest, would lead to an examination of different types of groupings. In the first the historical tradition of opposition to the central state would be found to provide one of the keys in this respect. In the second affiliation to Berber brotherhoods would probably matter greatly. In the third gender- or issue-based activism would likely define the relevant political community. Obvious as these examples appear to be, they are intended merely to illustrate how the political significance of the links between individuals and community can only be gauged by means of a culturally contextual comparative framework.

More generally, therefore, our method points to the fallacy of assuming that a collection of individuals formed in fairly well defined communities that are congenial to comparative political analysis—such as class, party, church, trade union, neighbourhood etc.—can be taken to act politically in the same way across the globe. The point here is not merely to state the obvious: people do not behave mechanically on the basis of their affiliation to a particular grouping. It is to explain that the very notion of community itself is contingent on the question being asked.

People's identities are multiple, complex and fluid. Individuals are possessed of different facets, not all of them equally obvious or salient at all times. How and under what conditions these become important politically is only partly conditioned by the immediate grouping within which they live. Other than in very circumscribed and relatively undifferentiated societies, such as are perhaps still to be found in the remoter reaches of Papua New Guinea or the Amazon, most people are tied to a range of social units with which they engage at various levels. How they behave, and more importantly why they do so, is thus the result of the nature of their interaction with these different groupings. To understand politics in such a situation demands an appreciation of the culture within which this interaction occurs.[9]

[9] For one appreciation of one aspect of this question, see A. Maalouf, 1998, *Les*

Our discussion of community thus far has been limited to the more obvious geographical, ascriptive or social groupings. However, when comparing societies diverging widely in terms of social differentiation it is important to consider a more expansive notion of the concept. Here there are three important areas. The first has to do with what might be termed acquired group identities, whether religious, political or professional. The second concerns the relevance of those processes of modernisation that are taken, to use German sociological language, to lead from *Gemeinschaft* (community) to *Gesellschaft* (society).[10] The third relates to the extent to which economic development brings about a process of social individualisation. All three obviously affect the ways in which individuals behave politically, but a cultural approach would caution against overly simple assumptions of political causality in this respect. Nor would it be wise to assume that 'modern' group identities are created necessarily at the expense of more 'traditional' ones. The two may quite happily marry, and co-exist differently, within very similar individuals. This too is a matter for empirical research.

Consequently, the main danger in comparative politics is that the (unavoidably limited and recurrent) questions being asked in the field run the risk of forcing an artificial analysis of the historical and cultural context. For instance, there is a highly developed field of our discipline that studies electoral behaviour comparatively.[11] Normally contrasts are made between relatively similar polities: for instance, Western Europe, the United States and the former White Dominions.[12] Most of the detailed empirical studies about voting behaviour are relatively enlightening because they compare polities that are culturally not too distinct—even if there are limits to how useful it is to assume similar political posturing in northern and southern Europe, for example. However, the study of societies that share a large

---

Identités meurtrières, a study by the well-known francophone Lebanese novelist on how identity links to violence.

[10] A distinction originally made by Tönnies. See F. Tönnies, 1955 (1887), *Community and Association*.

[11] See *inter alia* A. Kornberg and H. Clarke, 1992, *Citizens and Community.*

[12] For the classic work in this respect, see S. M. Lipset and S. Rokkan (eds), 1967, *Party Systems and Voter Alignment.* For a more recent approach, see, for instance, I. Crew and D. Denver, 1985, *Electoral Change in Western Democracies.*

number of historical, social, economic and geographic traits does not warrant making similar assumptions about the comparative analysis of political parties in other, very different, settings.

Contrasting parties and electoral behaviour in various countries of the world, then, entails a study of political behaviour in respect of political preference and affiliation that could obscure two key issues of political life in a given society. The first is that party politics may well be of secondary significance and studying that aspect of political life could mislead the observer. It could also force attention on events and processes that make it more, rather than less, difficult to understand other crucial political dynamics, which determine election results. Such is quite clearly the case in postcolonial Africa, as we have shown in our previous book.[13] The second is that it pre-determines the type of grouping to be studied—in this instance, members or sympathisers of a party—regardless of its true significance to the people concerned. Whether the assemblage formed around parties or to support party coalitions is significant in the life of particular societies is an empirical, not an *a priori*, question. In Northern Ireland, for example, party politics are conditioned by the historical, cultural and religious context within which people are born, and remain locked, within given political groupings.

The methodological concern to locate the community is thus not trivial. It calls for a difficult balancing act between the application of a research agenda driving the questions to be asked and a solid grasp of the cultural texture of the setting under study. The claim that it is not possible, or even desirable, for political scientists to acquire the in-depth local knowledge gained by anthropologists is not, in our view, a valid objection to the contextual demands required of comparative analysis. What is needed is not the systematic acquisition of knowledge about a particular community, or grouping, with a view to present an exhaustive account of their 'way of life'. It is, more prosaically, a comprehension of the cultural matrix within which politics are conducted and power is exercised.

Circles of identity: multiple layers, overlaps and shifting registers
A focus on identity and community, though methodologically necessary, might easily lead to a reification of these two concepts, or

[13] P. Chabal and J.-P. Daloz, 1999, *Africa Works*.

to what many might construe as a culturalist position.[14] Indeed, the injunction to study the cultural context—so as to identify the relevant notions of the self and to locate the more significant groupings—could be misconstrued as an attempt to classify people into pre-set categories. The reverse is the case, as we have already made clear, since our aim is to derive an appreciation of what these categories mean in practice from the observation of what makes sense to the persons in question. Nevertheless, it could still be argued that what makes sense to people—or the ways in which they make sense of their political environment—is itself based on essentialist notions. This is a fair point, which warrants further discussion.

An understanding of the types of identity and forms of community that are relevant to political action need not necessarily be conditioned by what the actors themselves officially profess. What is of importance for analysis is an exploration of how they explain to themselves what they do. The need to heed how people justify their action is obviously not the same as taking what they say at face value. A cultural approach does not rely on the postulate that what makes sense to people furnishes the explanation of their behaviour. Instead it extracts from the assessment of this subjective data the material that will require further examination. It means, therefore, that by paying attention to what people say, we lay down the basis for an interpretation that will avoid the twin perils of either accepting uncritically the rationalisation they give or dismissing it as, for example, 'false consciousness'. Thus the charge that a culturally sensitive methodology falls prey to the fallacy of identity-driven politics is very wide of the mark.

Because this misapprehension is so widespread—particularly in France, where the Republican ideal brooks no dissent from the notion that all individuals are equal citizens—it is worth explaining in greater detail why a cultural approach cannot be beholden to the illusion of identity.[15] The argument that a concern for questions of

---

[14] The charge of 'culturalism', particularly in the minds of those who use the term as a critique, is that of cultural determinism: the notion that one's identity (that is cultural origins, background or attributes) provides the key 'explanation' to behaviour or, in this instance, political action.

[15] To echo the title of a book by a French political scientist that charges vigorously at the culturalist windmill. See J.-F. Bayart, 1996, *L'illusion identitaire*.

identity will necessarily result in a culturalist interpretation is ill-advised. It derives from the assumption, itself most definitely culturally bound, that politics is merely about the clash of ideas and interests that issues of identity are used to conceal. There is here a stark difference of approach between the British and the French. The former readily conceive of the notion of ethnic minority whereas the latter can only admit to immigrants or foreigners. But, as this example makes clear, the words used to describe what are in effect groupings of foreign people, or people of foreign origins, who have settled in Western Europe, do not, at least in our eyes, provide an explanation as to why they behave politically as they do.

The debate about the relevance of identity to politics often turns on a sterile dispute about causality. Those who believe that issues of identity are the driving force of politics tend in most instances to conceive of that notion in a fairly static and immutable fashion. A particular aspect of one's idea of self can all too easily become a *deus ex machina*. Their opponents argue that identities do not exist *per se*, outside of a given historical and political context, and it is illusory to reason as though they were 'essential' in this way. It is politicians who manipulate these issues out of self-interested ambition. The fault in such dichotomised discussion lies in that it engages in intellectual shadow boxing, covering up entrenched ideological positions: either that identity 'causes' given political actions or, alternatively, that it is 'manipulated' by political actors with ulterior motives. The reality, however, is not so simple.

Our method privileges a more open and more dynamic slant. Notions of self or feelings of belonging are not straightforward. Above all, they are neither singular nor unchanging. Even in what are still sometimes quaintly described as 'primitive' societies, individuals do not see themselves, nor do they see others, only as members of the small-scale grouping of which they are a part. Distinctions of gender, age, occupation, status or kinship combine to make up a fairly distinct profile for each individual. A female spirit medium, a hunter, a craftsman or a herdsman all make sense of their own world in slightly different ways, even if they share much within their kin group. In other, more modern, societies the situation is more complex. African-Americans, French *beurs* or British Caribbeans are not simply members of their ethnic groups—even if this is a convenient peg for political lobbying. Such a cultural designation is but one of myriad others, which are differently relevant according to circumstances.

Accordingly we prefer to employ the concept of 'circles of identity',[16] using it as a convenient pictorial representation of what happens in real life, regardless of the level of complexity of the societies we study. This makes it possible to explore the most relevant aspects of identity and community, as derived from an analysis of what makes sense to the people concerned, with a view to assessing their significance for politics in specific and concrete situations. Moreover, we deploy this notion in a dynamic fashion, within the appropriate historical context. Circles of identity do not merely exist, floating artificially in mid-air, as it were. They are in constant flux, incessantly interacting with each other over time in ways that need to be examined, not taken for granted. Hence what counts for comparative analysis is not so much the identification of the ostensibly more salient contemporary forms of identity as the investigation of how such circles combine under differing historical conditions.

Our emphasis is on the multiple layering and overlaps that impinge on the notions of the self and of the 'other'. It is in this way the converse of a culturalist position, which holds that there are fixed 'cultural' characteristics. The key to our approach is the unpacking of the cultural matrix within which these different circles of identity are activated. In Pakistan, for example, Islamic parties have had a limited audience since independence. Confined in the main to the 'tribal' areas of the Northwest Frontier Province and Baluchistan, they had until recently failed to attract much support in the urban centres of Punjab and Sindh. The events linked with the war in Afghanistan, the rise and fall of the Taliban regime, the actions of Osama Bin Laden, and the conflict in Iraq have combined greatly to enhance the salience of the circle of identity linked to religion in Pakistani politics. This is not to say that Pakistanis were not Muslims before, or that they favour today a fundamentalist reform in the country. It is to show that under such circumstances as they have recently experienced, many more have felt compelled actively to demonstrate their religious allegiance.[17]

---

[16] A circle of identity might be conceptualised in the way that an 'ensemble' is in mathematics.

[17] See O. Bennett-Jones, 2002, *Pakistan*.

Finally we would also propose the concept of 'register', by which we mean the bundle of circles of identity that is most active at a particular moment in time. Here there are two central issues at stake. The first is that, even when one particular notion of the self or conception of the community is predominant among a given group of people (as is that of the *umma* for many Pakistanis), there are still several other active registers that are of importance to their lives. Human beings, other than zealots, are very rarely conditioned by a single attribute. They function *continuously* according to the demands of various registers, which may not always be in harmony. Some of the 11 September 2001 Al Qaeda suicide pilots were seen to enjoy alcoholic drink and female company in American nightclubs before they unleashed fire on their country of residence.

The second is that it is quite common, especially at times of socio-economic and political stress, or large cultural disparities, for people to operate *simultaneously* on different, and sometimes contradictory, registers. This is true, for instance, in areas of the world such as postcolonial Africa where the political élite can at the same time behave in full conformity with technological modernity whilst otherwise relying on the occult. But it is even true in our own Western societies, where there are frequent cases of people who are concurrently utterly rational and wholly irrational, according to the norms of the country in which they live: witness the debate about evolution theory in the United States.

....BUT DO WE DO WHAT WE ARE?

One of the central weaknesses of our discipline lies in the way in which it constructs models of causality. Admittedly the age of grand theory is over and few today would, for example, explain events on the basis of a simple Marxist model of development. There is indeed a new sensitivity to a range of factors in key areas of our social and political lives, such as gender, environment or heritage, that were barely discussed twenty years ago. Nevertheless, there is still a strong instrumentalist assumption in political science when it comes to contrasting what happens across the world. Political scientists are prone to construct models and in doing so they tend to divide between two distinct, and largely incompatible, camps. The first holds that socio-economic and political factors condition culture, and explain how cultural beliefs are used politically: people deploy identity as a cover-up for other, more covert, interests. The other favours an analysis that assumes a fairly straightforward correlation between identity and political action: people, usually far away, behave as they do because of who they are. For this reason it is not enough to establish that the matter of identity is multifaceted, as we have done above. It is essential to tackle directly the issue of the relevance of identity to what we do politically.

We will not here address what is perhaps the dominant strand in the study of political identity, at least in the Western world: the relevance of socio-economic factors for political action. There is indeed an immense body of comparative political sociology that studies the significance of, say, class, occupation or status, for electoral choice.[18] Equally there is now substantial work on the relation between gender and politics.[19] These are areas of comparative politics, with a focus on Western societies, which lie at the core of our discipline. They are self-evidently important to the understanding of how these polities have evolved in the modern past. Our concern lies with how such comparative questions have been extended to the non-Western world and here we would make two remarks. One, there has been a tendency to extend the comparative sociology that has evolved from the study of Western societies to the rest of the world: for instance, to assume the universal relevance of class to politics. Two, there is a dearth of theory that arises from the in-depth study of non-Western societies: to return to an earlier example, how the occult can affect political action.

For this reason the remainder of this chapter examines more particularly those areas of identity that are especially critical in non-Western societies (even if they are also relevant to Western polities). Of all the possible attributes employed today to explain political behaviour, three stand out: ethnicity, religion and nationality. Not only do they lie at the core of the politics of most 'developing'

---

[18] See, for example, S. Bartolini and P. Mair, 1990, *Identity, Competition and Electoral Availability*.

[19] R. Connell, 1987, *Gender and Power*; N. Fraser, 1989, *Unruly Practices*; E. Frazer (ed.), 1993, *The Politics of Community*; K. Jones and A. Jonasdottir (eds), 1988, *The Political Interests of Gender*; V. Randall and G. Waylen (eds), 1998, *Gender, Politics and the State*; J. Squires, 1999, *Gender in Political Theory*.

countries, but they have become salient again in post-communist Eastern Europe and Central Asia as well as in our own Western societies (ranging from the Basque region to Belgium, by way of the United States).[20] Furthermore these are political 'variables' on which current comparative politics finds it difficult to establish causality, mired as it is in assumptions of development and definitions of culture that make analytical progress difficult.[21]

Ethnicity

Ethnicity is one of the most widely cited causes of political action, but one of the most difficult concepts to define precisely.[22] Once seen as a more sophisticated notion than tribalism, forever associated with the colonial period, the term is nevertheless as unclear as its use is widespread. Branded as a major source of political agency in both the most and least economically developed countries, from the United States to Rwanda, it seems readily to be taken as an instrumentally fundamental aspect of human nature. More important, within the perspective of our discussion it is a concept that has been at the centre of the comparative analysis of Western and non-Western societies since the mid-twentieth century, surviving virtually unscathed in the canon at a time when most other so-called cultural factors were subjected to rigorous scrutiny.[23] Perhaps this is due to its perennial relevance in the United States, where it has now become an accepted modern political category.[24] Perhaps it is due to the increase in ethnic violence in Africa and other parts of the world.

The compelling force of the concept of ethnicity derives from the perception that it provides a singularly tight fit between identity and

---

[20] Of course, we do not claim that these are the 'central' issues of political identity in Western countries, merely that they are still at the heart of some of the other, more focused, questions concerning identity that are relevant—such as regionalism, language policy, violence, education, immigration, integration.

[21] Which is best illustrated in our view in L. Harrison and S. Huntington, 2000, *Culture Matters*, a volume whose very disparate nature demonstrates, as we have mentioned already, at once the renewed interest in culture and the limitations of the present notion of the concept for comparative analysis.

[22] For an early attempt at clarification, see F. Barth (ed.), 1969, *Ethnic Groups and Boundaries*.

[23] P. van den Berghe, 1981, *The Ethnic Phenomenon*.

[24] For a discussion of this point, see D. Hollinger, 1995, *Postethnic America*.

community. Most definitions stress those factors which explain why individuals are shaped by the bonds they share with the group to which they feel they belong. An ethnic identity is thus thought to combine considerations of origin, kinship, race, language, history and culture with a strong sense of distinction from other, equally well-delineated, groupings.[25] Hence the notion is predicated on two fundamental assumptions. The first is that it is possible to identify clearly those characteristics that distinguish one ethnic group from another. The other is that such features are of primary, or determinant, significance for members of these groups. Both need re-examination if we are to make clear how a cultural approach differs from the somewhat mechanistic conception of ethnicity still prevalent in political science.

The defect in the present notion of ethnicity is that it denotes a single mode of belonging based on a fairly narrow view of what it means to be a member of a community.[26] Seen from present day modern and economically advanced countries, where the notion of self and the relation between individual and society are construed as 'private', this sense of belonging can all too easily be reified. *In* the West it is viewed primarily as an emotional attachment to a community of origin or, more pragmatically, as a basis for lobbying. *From* the West, however, ethnicity in less economically advanced, or simply culturally different, settings is perceived more as a primordial sentiment, a quality of being which is overwhelming—that is, over which people have little control. Although the same term is used in both instances, in reality the one is the reverse side of the other. Westerners, who see themselves as emancipated from ascriptive considerations but 'choose' to remain ethnic, project onto the 'other' the emotional charge it has acquired in their own society. If we, though 'developed', still feel ethnicity, how much more others, who are not yet so 'advanced', must be prey to its embrace?

Such an approach, therefore, reveals the extent to which the notion we employ is fundamentally rooted in an implicit theory of evolution, at least in two important respects. The first is the expectation that human development inevitably results in a similar form of individualisation, a process in which people become discrete individuals, increasingly detached from their 'communal' origins. The

[25] See, for instance M. Banton, 1997, *Ethnic and Racial Consciousness.*
[26] See B. Anderson, 1991, *Imagined Communities.*

second is that development brings about a more 'objective' basis for political agency—that is, one drawing less on ascriptive, inherited and collective considerations and more on utilitarian, or 'rational', grounds. As our approach makes clear, there is no reason to make such categorical assumptions. Indeed, proper attention to culture, most particularly our own, would indicate that our suppositions about the personal and collective changes that take place in respect of ethnicity are an intricate part of the way we make sense of the world in which we live. In other words, it is our perception of the gradual disappearance of ascriptive factors that provides the basis for our claim that development changes the purchase of ethnicity on our lives from determinant to freely chosen.

Of course the modernisation of society does bring about important changes in our notion of self and our perception of community. However, the point is to move away from a teleological view of such mutation, away from evolutionary theory, and to accept that the instrumental quality of ethnicity is both historically and culturally bound, whatever the setting. Furthermore a contextually sensitive analysis of the role of ethnicity in those societies where it is supposed to be most politically significant shows that it is neither as clear-cut nor as causal as it is blithely assumed to be.[27] Let us examine both questions in turn using Africa as our main case study.

The idea that ethnicity is easily identified is very largely a myth, in part due to the colonial method of classifying 'natives'.[28] Most colonised subjects viewed themselves at the intersection of a number of circles of identity, of which ethnicity was only one. Moreover what came to be defined as ethnic encompassed a wide range of features, such as religious beliefs or links with the world of the dead, which were often invisible to the Western eye. Many of these characteristics were shared with other groups. A careful examination of the pre-colonial era in Africa shows that ethnicity was an eminently fluid and malleable characteristic. Individuals, and even whole groups, could easily change ethnic identity, or entertain several, or, alternatively, consider themselves part of extended religious and occupational

[27] For a more general discussion, see G. Delannoi and P.-A. Taguieff (eds), 1991, *Théories du nationalisme*.

[28] Here we draw from P. Chabal and J.-P. Daloz, 1999, *Africa Works*, Chapter 4.

groups, such as the Dyulas, which the colonial officials, for their part, also deemed to be ethnic.

At the same time ethnicity need not automatically be politically consequential.[29] The fact that it became especially salient during the colonial period had to do with specific historical and political factors, which combined to invite 'native' self-identification along a single, simplified, 'communal' identity chart. The colonial state measured its dispensations along these lines, so it was beneficial for Africans to present themselves as distinct members of particular groups.[30] Similarly today's recurrent ethnic conflicts in Africa are not principally the result of inherent ethnic hostility.[31] They are the outcome of the increasingly acute competition for power in an increasingly deficient clientelistic political order, where the control of resources is a measure of the ability to exercise power.[32] The violence that racks central Africa today, channelled along apparently clear ethnic lines, is in reality a contest for the control of the enormous riches available in the region. As Lonsdale has argued persuasively (based on the study of Kenya), it is imperative to distinguish between political tribalism, or the instrumental (ab)use of communal distinction for political gain, from moral ethnicity, which provides the ethical framework for the life of a particular community.[33]

Religion

A similar, though not quite as intractable, problem arises with the assessment of the significance of religious identity for politics. There is a large body of literature on the effect of beliefs on individual norms and behaviour.[34] There is also considerable comparative interest in the role of religious institutions. Finally, there is research on the influence of religious values on politics, ranging from the impact of

[29] For a general discussion of the link between ethnicity and nation, see A. Smith, 1992, *The Ethnic Origins of Nations.*

[30] For a general discussion of the relations between ethnicity and politics, see P. Brass (ed.), 1985, *Ethnic Groups and the State.*

[31] T. Ranger and R. Werbner (eds), 1996, *Postcolonial Identities in Africa.*

[32] B. Berman, 1998, 'Ethnicity, Patronage, and the African State', *African Affairs,* 97 (389).

[33] Lonsdale, 1996. 'Ethnicité morale et tribalisme politique', *Politique Africaine,* 61 (March).

[34] See here, for instance, E. Gellner, 1992, *Postmodernism, Reason and Religion.*

(Christian or Islamic) fundamentalism to the political inclinations of Christian democratic or Muslim reformist parties.[35] However, for all that there is little consensus on the significance of faith on political action. As is the case for ethnicity, political scientists often make assumptions about putative differences between the ways in which religion is experienced, or lived, in Western and non-Western societies.

A common distinction made in socio-political analysis is that ethnicity is concerned with identity and religion with belief. We are born with a particular notion of who we are, but religion is something we are taught. We could, for instance, imagine converting to another faith whereas we cannot alter our ethnic origins. This appears superficially to be true, but again it is a very ethnocentric view which fits in with the ways we make sense of the modern, Western, economically advanced and socially fragmented world in which we live. It is undoubtedly culture bound. Far from being a universally useful distinction, it is one with little analytical value in large swathes of the globe. As we have already seen, ethnicity itself is the result of a number of circles of identities, some of which can be discarded or changed. Conversely a very large number of people (such as the majority of Muslims) would consider that religion is God-given, and not to be renounced under any circumstances.[36]

Furthermore in many societies faith and ethnicity are part of the same core bundle of attributes that marks out the contours of a dominant sense of identity. It is simply impossible to dissociate one from the other. Not only are many ethnic groups defined primarily on the basis of religion, in many instances faith is the key characteristic that distinguishes one community from the next. Ethnic divisions in West Africa are often delineated according to whether a grouping is Muslim or not.[37] Insofar as the distinctions in Northern Ireland are ethnic, they are certainly based on an exacting notion of what faith means.[38] It is difficult to consider that a Unionist militant

---

[35] For some relevant discussion of religion and politics in different parts of the world, see G. Wills, 1990, *Under God*; J.-P. Chrétien, 1993, *L'invention religieuse en Afrique*; P. Sugar, 1999, *East European Nationalism, Politics and Religion*; and, of continued interest, M. Weber, 1951, *The Religion of China*.

[36] For a relevant comparison, see B. Badie, 1986, *Les deux Etats*.

[37] C. Coulon, 1983, *Les musulmans et le pouvoir en Afrique noire*.

[38] J. Ruane and J. Todd, 1996, *The Dynamics of Conflict in Northern Ireland*.

would consider converting to Catholicism.[39] Equally the Jews' sense
of identity undoubtedly rests on their faith. Even secular Jews would
not deny that their religion, if only as culture, is a core attribute of
how they define themselves in the world. Thus not only are religion
and ethnic identity related but they are difficult to understand outside
of their proper historical environment.

Nor is it always clear what religion actually means. We in the West
are comfortable with the main, established, world faiths—Islam,
Christianity, Buddhism etc.—and familiar with most of their subdi-
visions—Sunni and Shiite; Catholic and Protestant; and so on. Yet we
do not know as much about other, minority or more subterranean,
groups: Ahmediyyas, Zoroastrians, Mormons, Jehovah's Witnesses
etc. Are these to be considered religions or merely sects? What is the
significance of the difference between the two? Finally we are poorly
placed to assess the nature and role of a vast array of systems of belief,
which may often appear in the West more akin to sociological categories or 'pagan' rituals. How, for example, do we interpret the caste
system in India? Do the Inuit people have a religion? What is a
central African animist creed?

The point here is not so much to offer evidence of the diversity
and range of creeds but to show that it is impossible to provide a
meaningful definition of religion outside its relevant cultural context.
Although the main world religions possess fairly well defined dogmas
and sacraments, they too are strongly conditioned by their surroundings. There is debate about what the 'correct' beliefs and rituals
of each religion are supposed to be. World religions, which have
spawned many local variants, are often racked by divisions. Some
would even argue that some forms of Christianity in African, South
American or Caribbean societies are simply outside the pale. Equally
a number of Islamic states deny that Ahmadis are Muslim.[40] And
some Jews have denied that their Ethiopian co-religionists belonged
to the same faith. Nor is it plausible to assess the significance of
religious factors in politics other than in the context of a properly
identified historical period. Muslims in the area of what is now
Afghanistan were not always 'fundamentalist'. Calvinists in the south

[39] See, for example, S. Bruce, 1994, *The Edge of the Union.*
[40] See Y. Friedmann, 1989, *Prophecy Continuous.*

of France were once enemies of the state; they are today part of its élite.

A cultural approach to the political significance of religious identity, therefore, favours an analysis in terms of how faith matters in a specific, contextually bound setting. Drawing in part on the method used by Max Weber in the *Protestant Ethic and the Spirit of Capitalism*, our work seeks above all to achieve two aims.[41] The first is to understand what religion means to the groups concerned, what relation there is between faith, on the one hand, and social, economic and political activities, on the other. The war in Iraq appears to have set Islamic resistance against US imperialism. Yet the situation may be more confused. Perhaps Saddam Hussein's manipulation of religious sentiment was far less politically significant in Iraq than the Bush administration's belief in the United States that it was fighting a 'just' war, in the religious sense. The second is to identify those aspects of faith that are most relevant to the political issues under study. As Weber argued, it was the Protestants' belief that their fate was predetermined which induced them to seek success in this world rather than accept 'fulfilment' in the next. Similarly could the Untouchables' acceptance of caste have contributed to keeping them from achieving more fully the human rights to which they are entitled under the Indian Constitution?

The final example, from Africa this time, will show how intricate the relation between faith and identity may be. On the continent the political legitimacy of putative political élites is bound up with a clear notion of representation: to be representative of a group one needs to share its 'identity', including religion.[42] At the same time, however, both élites and populace remain susceptible to the occult. Political leaders cannot afford to allow witchcraft in their region of origin to cast a spell over their legitimacy, hence the need to maintain proper munificence vis-à-vis their own community.[43] Nonetheless, most politicians have national ambitions, and cannot be seen to oppose

---

[41] What we draw from Weber's method in this instance is the attempt systematically to work out what the influence of religion may have been on a distinct group of individuals in respect of business.

[42] The question of the analysis of representation within a cultural approach is discussed in detail in Chapter 10.

[43] P. Geschiere, 1997, *The Modernity of Witchcraft*.

other faiths or neglect other forms of religious power. They are thus constantly juggling demands, and influences, both from overt religious groups and covert forces. In some instances political decisions are directly, or indirectly, the outcome of a belief in the occult, which political élites claim does not exist.[44] In such cases an analysis of the exercise of power cannot hope to identify the significant political factors without taking into account matters of belief.

Nationality

Of the three attributes of identity we discuss here nationality is ostensibly the most clear-cut, probably because it is the one with which we, in the West, are most familiar. Nationality is supposed to be the foundation of our modern states.[45] We all know instinctively what it means to be Welsh, Czech, Malay or Ukrainian. Yet a moment's reflection shows that our understanding of the concept is both historically and contextually defined. If most countries appear to have one dominant 'national' core, they are also comprised of a number of other groups whose origins are different. Moreover the principal community, which has given the country its 'national' identity, is itself often composite, sometimes only recently formed. Very few are the present nation-states that derive from a single, easily identified, culturally homogenous and historically discrete collection of individuals linked together by ethnicity, language, culture and history. Most countries, regardless of how they explain their origins, are not straightforwardly modern embodiments of a given nationality.

At the same time it is clear that many nationalities do not find expression in the present configuration of nation-states. Recent events have highlighted the plight of the Kurds, perhaps one of the largest groups not to possess its own sovereign territory. Yet there are

---

[44] See S. Ellis and G. Ter Haar, 2004, *Worlds of Power.*

[45] The literature on nation, nationality and nationalism is immense. Reference can be made to only some of the key texts: B. Anderson, 1991, *Imagined Communities*; P. Birnbaum (ed.), 1997, *Sociologie des nationalismes*; E. Gellner, 1983, *Nations and Nationalism*; G. Hermet, 1996, *Histoire des nations et du nationalisme en Europe*; E. Hobsbawm, 1991, *Nations and Nationalism since 1780*; E. Kamenka, 1992, *Nationalism: the nature and evolution of an idea*; E. Kedourie, 1960, *Nationalism*; H. Kohn, 1960, *Nationalism*; H. Seton-Watson, 1977, *Nations and States*; A. Smith, 1971, *Theories of Nationalism* and 1992, *The Ethnic Origins of Nations.*

many other communities that consider themselves distinct from the country in which they find themselves—the Basques in Spain, the Chechens in Russia and the Tibetans in China. Of course this is because the current constellation of independent countries is a recent development, which occurred chiefly during the last two centuries. Not every nationality could achieve its own independence within the newly emerging international state system.[46] But it is also a consequence of the fact that 'national' sentiments are not as limpid as they sometimes appear to be. Despite its ready acceptance as a politically relevant concept in the West, the notion of national identity is far from being unproblematic.

The common view in our discipline is that nationality is a politically consistent variable, both amenable to proper characterisation and susceptible to being measured, and even quantified. There is a belief that it consists of a number of universally valid factors—among which ethnicity, language, culture and territory are deemed to be crucial—that come together to provide a 'subjective' sense of belonging based on unambiguously 'objective' criteria. It is also assumed that human beings, at least in the modern period, are *ipso facto* endowed with a 'sense' of nationality and that such is one of the primary attributes of any political identity.[47] Where nation-states are almost wholly of multiple origins—as in Germany, Italy and, above all, the United States—the sense of nationality is inculcated through myth, education and culture. Nevertheless, the most widely shared assumption in comparative analysis is that all people have a clear feeling of nationality. From such a supposition is easily derived the conviction that this political attribute can reliably be contrasted across the globe.

Here, however, a cultural methodology would suggest much greater caution, for at least two reasons. First, it is far from obvious that there is a generally analogous conception of nationality across time and space, even in the contemporary period. Second, it is even more debatable whether notions of national belonging have meaningfully comparable political consequences. If the cases of the Vietnamese, Khmers, Hungarians, Kurds and Basques suggest that some

[46] See J. Mayall, 1990, *Nationalism and International Society.*
[47] For a classic argument about the relationship between modernity and nationalism, see E. Gellner, 1997, *Nationalism.*

nationalities are centuries old, there are a greater number of instances where national sentiment is a recent invention. It has been argued that what contributed most to the transformation of a sense feeling of nationality into 'popular' nationalism was the widespread use by literate élites of the written word, made possible by the expansion of the printing press.[48] However, what has been identified as nationalism in Europe can be seen as ethnicity in Africa.[49] Thus there is little *a priori* reason to consider that the concept of nationality is any more transparent or any more politically consequential than that of ethnicity.

Our approach suggests that nationality ought also to be conceptualised as one circle of identity, as complex in its making and as variegated in its usage as any of the others, which may seem in the West to be much less concrete. An assessment of the texture of that aspect of individual and collective identity calls for an analysis of the webs of meaning of which it is an aggregate. These differ according to context and circumstances. What may have been taken for ethnicity, tribalism, regionalism or even religious irredentism can in a specific historical situation become an awareness of nationality. In any event the inference that such is the case can only be made *a posteriori*. The fact that nationality seems today to be such an essential attribute of political identity is due less to its inherent significance than to the present importance of the nation-state, as it has evolved in the last two centuries.

Thus, to return to our earlier example, it is plain that the Kurds' claim for an independent homeland is more historically justified than that of many other 'nationalities' in the region—certainly more deeply rooted in history than the creation of Iraq, an entirely artificial postcolonial construct. Yet given present historical constraints it is unlikely that Turkey, Iran and the newly reconstructed Iraq would allow the creation of an independent Kurdish state—a move that the international community would also fail to endorse. This does not make the present salience of Kurdish identity any less. Nor does it mean that in the distant future their aspiration for a homeland may not be satisfied. However, it is not possible to deduce from this observation that the Kurds possess a keener sense of nationality than other

[48] B. Anderson, 1991, *Imagined Communities.*
[49] J. Lonsdale, 1994, 'Moral Ethnicity and Political Tribalism' in P. Kaarsholm and J. Hultin (eds), *Inventions and Boundaries.*

communities. Its present acuteness is largely a result of current circumstances.

In sum, our approach suggests three important conclusions. First, the relationship between notions of self and perceptions of community need to be studied within their appropriate historical and cultural setting. Second, relevant aspects of existing individual political characteristics must be conceived as the resultant of the intersecting and overlapping of a large number of circles of identity and should never be taken as a 'given'. Third, the political significance of any such cluster of circles can only be measured empirically and then only in terms that make sense to the people concerned.

5

CULTURE AND POLITICAL ORDER

One of the central objects of political science is to explain how individuals and communities organise themselves politically. The search for what may be common between diverse groups of people is predicated on the ability to contrast the polities within which they live. However, the very notion of political order is problematic. In this respect standard theories of comparative politics make two fundamental assumptions that condition the way in which analysts proceed. One, there is an evolution in the 'ordering' of politics over time, ranging from simple and 'traditional' communities (*Gemeinschaft*) to highly complex and evolved modern societies (*Gesellschaft*).[1] Two, political order is the outcome of human agency: it is people who construct the framework of the polity they desire.[2] Both of these suppositions are, on the face of it, eminently reasonable. Yet we would argue that they imply a relationship between politics and culture that is not warranted. We discuss both in turn.

Although it is broadly true that there has been a move from simpler to more complex social groupings, culminating today in highly diffuse yet relatively cohesive societies, it is by no means clear that such evolution has been univocal. There are today modern societies of vastly different political character. Both Japan and Finland are democracies, but their apparently similar political order conceals myriad differences, which it is necessary to understand in order to explain their politics credibly. Furthermore it is a vast over-simplification to argue that modern political systems are the deliberate and

[1] For a return to the sociological origins, see M. Weber, 1978 (1968), *Economy and Society*. For a critical analysis, see R. Schroeder, 1992, *Max Weber and the Sociology of Culture* and R. Collins, 1986, *Weberian Sociological Theory*.

[2] For a classic statement of the classic comparative view, see S. Huntington, 1968, *Political Order in Changing Societies*.

self-conscious creations of those who have worked to establish more effective and more accountable order. Both their travails and the workings of the systems that have come to stay have been conditioned by very specific historical and cultural factors, many of which well beyond the scope of human agency.

Consequently, this chapter attempts to investigate the intricacy of the link between culture and the political order.[3] Although we intend to touch on a number of key aspects of this vexed question, we want in particular to explain why the two most common approaches to this issue are analytically limited, and limiting. The first consists in considering that culture is used as an ideology by manipulating élites, who seek to exploit it in order to gain, and hold, power. We will show that such manipulation itself takes place within a cultural context, within which the élites have to work. The second consists in arguing that in some (usually distant) societies, cultural constraints are so strong that they condition political agency: political élites are here seen as the handmaidens of an all-powerful culture (or religion, or civilisation). The sections that follow will demonstrate that such an interpretation is predicated on an excessively instrumentalised idea of culture.

WHAT POWER MEANS IN ITS LOCAL CONTEXT

Our assumption is that an analysis of the political order requires an understanding of power at the local level. By local we do not refer simply to the smallest relevant geographical or territorial unit but, much more important, to the socially most significant context.[4] In many cases this will be found within a small-scale community, perhaps family- or kin-based. Conversely for large numbers of people the most relevant grouping might be widely scattered. Here local context may thus mean a village in a particular case and a worldwide diaspora in another. Or it may even mean both, as it does, for instance,

[3] See here M. Archer, 1996, *Culture and Agency*; J. Bowen and R. Petersen, 1999, *Critical Comparisons in Politics and Culture*; D. Cuche, 1998, *La notion de culture dans les sciences sociales*; N. Dirks, G. Eley and S. Ortner (eds), 1994, *Culture, Power, History*.

[4] We use the notion of local here in much the same way that Geertz does in C. Geertz, 1983, *Local Knowledge*.

for networks of African traders, Italian mafias, Chinese businessmen, who operate throughout the world but who continue to define themselves primarily in terms of their belonging to one particular family, ethnic or regional grouping. The point here is less to locate with precision the group's home physical boundaries than it is to identify the 'local' roots of the system of political order within which the logic of politics makes most sense to the people concerned.

Units of analysis

The very first hurdle is thus quite clearly to define the appropriate unit of analysis. As has already been indicated, identifying the local is not merely a matter of focusing attention on what might be construed as the smallest relevant political unit: ward, parish, hamlet, village, *quartier, barrio,* neighbourhood etc. It is, rather, a question of understanding how people define themselves in relation to the various communities with which they interact within the circles of identity that matter most to them. In formerly colonised areas it may be that people are simultaneously part of overlapping 'traditional' and 'modern' groupings and relate to each in apparently contradictory fashion. In Western societies, on the other hand, it is probably necessary to look into the ways in which individuals are atomised and disconnected, linked to others more by virtual means ('music fraternities', chat rooms) than through face-to-face contacts.

Whatever the case, such a notion of the local as we seek to use undermines the most common criteria of comparative politics, and this for three main reasons. First, it stresses that it is not possible to ascertain, *a priori,* which are the most relevant units of analysis. This is a matter for empirical analysis. Second, it makes allowance for the fact that the significance of such local units may well change over time, or under altered circumstances. There is in this respect no fixed 'traditional' or 'modern': we are all linked to myriad units, the significance of which is contextually determined. Third, it starts from the premise that it is not always possible to compare apparently similar local units. Meaningful comparison must be demonstrated, not assumed.

The distinctive aspect of our approach (as is shown systematically in Part III) is the emphasis on the relevance of culture to the identification of the consequential units of analysis. It is not enough to take at face value the official complexion of a political system. We need to

appreciate how such a structure makes sense to the people concerned. If, for instance, we are interested in the ways in which local
would-be politicians enter the public arena, it may be that in some
countries we have to look at professional associations, religious
organisations, or sport and social clubs whilst in other cases we need
to study secret societies, age groups or trade union activities. The
point here is not so much to explain that politics in all societies is
widely diffused, which it obviously is. It is to show that identifying
the most politically significant units of analysis requires an in-depth
knowledge of the relevant historical and socio-cultural context.

Far less obvious, however, is the damage caused by ostensibly
plausible, but in fact deceptive, comparisons. It is generally assumed,
for instance, that individuals vote for the political party that is most
likely to meet their 'rational' (utilitarian) self-interest, however that
may be defined. It is further presumed that since such choice can only
be exercised within a multiparty system, an individual's self-interest
will *ipso facto* incline her to vote for a party committed to democracy.
Such an approach, though perhaps broadly true in the West today, is
patently incorrect when it comes to a number of contemporary
Muslim societies. How, otherwise, can one account for the fact that a
majority of Algerians voted in 1991 for a party dedicated to the abo-
lition of democracy—at least as it is understood in the West. Indeed,
for a follower of the *Front Islamique du Salut* (FIS) in early-1990s
Algeria, rational political self-interest meant one-party Islamic rule, as
it does in many Muslim countries today.[5]

A cultural approach operates on the basis that comparisons cannot
be decreed *a priori*, but only set up once the question being investigated has been related to the appropriate level of analysis within the
relevant context. In this instance, an assessment of party politics in
Muslim and non-Muslim societies requires an analytical framework
that would enable a comparison of notions of representation rather
than party competition.[6] Equally the validity of any party system is
tied to the concepts of legitimacy held by people at the local level.

[5] The purpose here is not to assert that Islam and democracy are incompatible but
merely to suggest that a comparative analysis of party systems in Muslim and non-
Muslim countries may not be a valid way of assessing divergences in political
opinions within those two groups of societies.

[6] As we discuss at length in Chapter 10.

If, as is the case in the Languedoc region of France, some villagers vote for the Communist Party because they feel it is their natural political 'home', then it matters little to them how many other left-wing parties solicit their votes. If, as is the case in West Africa, villagers vote for the party founded by their own 'Big Man', then there is no chance that they will cast their ballot for anyone else, regardless of the fact that their leader may have no realistic chance of winning the national elections.

The more general argument here is that significant comparisons can only be made on the basis of a historically and culturally grounded sensitivity to the key local units of political analysis. Even a contrast between relatively similar countries, such as Britain and France, is a perilous business. Take the role of village or town councils. In France they exercise enormous influence and control wide areas of social, economic and cultural activities. So in this context mayors are powerful figures who wield real power at the local level. They validate building permits and issue planning permission. In Britain such councils have limited powers and mayors (other than in London) are figureheads rather than executive politicians. For this reason an appreciation of the main locus of power and of the ways in which local financial decisions are made demands local knowledge.

More generally, therefore, the parameters of comparative enquiry need to be defined in harmony with the particulars of the case studies and not from any theoretical *a priori*. Of course it is inevitable that the questions we seek to answer are themselves culturally based, and in this way not 'objective'—in the sense that they may not be seen to be equally relevant to all. No doubt a focus on political parties, for example, is a peculiarly Western obsession. But we need to be clear as to why we choose particular units of analysis. More important, we need to be able to demonstrate that a comparison between such units is both feasible and enlightening.

Social relations

Making sense of any given political order involves understanding the social relations that underpin it. Here too, standard political analysis is based on an implicit theory of the link between the social and political realms, and a strong sense of causality, which determine the parameters of the research agenda. The chief assumption is that

economic development drives social change in very specific, scientifically observable directions that are common to all modernising
societies. In turn, social change fashions the evolution of politics.

Such a model postulates, for example, that processes of modernisation and individualisation bring about the advent of *homo economicus*, that rational person who lies at the core of micro-economic
theory. It follows, therefore, that modern man behaves economically
in particular ways, based on specific configurations of social bonds,
which can be identified precisely. Similarly it is taken for granted that
economic development induces transformations in social relations,
which are critically important for the evolution of political processes.
As the grip of 'tradition' is eroded, individuals behave increasingly as
politically 'responsible' citizens, entrusting their political fate to identifiable actors, organised in parties and competing on the basis of
clearly distinct programmes of action.

This vision of development conflates modernisation and Westernisation and in this way fails to consider that there might be divergent
historical experiences resulting in dissimilar forms of social relations.
It is today evident that the trajectory of countries, particularly in East
Asia, which are now as economically advanced as those of the West,
suggests that modernisation is not concomitant with a single model
of the development of social relations. Nor, for all the suppositions
made about the democratisation of the globe, is there good evidence
that modernisation induces similar forms of politically accountable
systems in all economically dynamic societies. Such correlations can
no longer be taken for granted. The two key questions of, on the one
hand, the evolution of social relations and, on the other, the links
between social and political change thus need to be studied with as
few preconceptions as possible.

It is common in comparative politics to make allowances for differences in the nature of social relations in, respectively, 'modern' and
'traditional' societies. The former are conceptualised as polities where
professional, associational or activity-based horizontal relations are
predominant; the latter as communities where ascriptive, parochial,
patrimonial or vertically rooted relations are the norm. There is thus
in our discipline a recognition of the different nature of social
relations in differently developed countries. The problem lies in the
assumption of neat dichotomies between the two and in the presumed

evolution from the one to the other. The aim here is not so much to summarise the literature on the social base of politics but to reflect on the constraints that present-day generalisations impose on comparative analysis.

Let us discuss the limitations of an approach based on the dichotomy between 'modern' and 'traditional'. In the first place any analysis based on such distinction is unable to take into account the mixed, or hybrid, nature of all societies. Even in the most economically complex countries the realm of the 'traditional' is not without relevance to politics. Today a large number of Americans do not believe in the scientific foundation of evolution theory and this view unquestionably colours their perception of politics. Conversely some of the most economically backward societies are informed by concepts of 'modernity' that impinge strongly on their social reality, which in turn influences politics. In many African countries Rambo is seen as a role model for an alienated, atomised and disenfranchised youth that seeks a political role. Their model of politics is not so distant from that found on those of the council estates in Britain or *banlieues* in France.

Secondly, there is every reason to question the supposition that some forms of social relations are more politically significant than others, regardless of context. Of course it can be stated with certainty that in all polities there are some key aspects of social organisation that have a strong bearing on politics. We know that in some settings old-school networks, or semi-secret groupings (like Free masonry), are important whilst in others ethnic bonds or religious associations (like Muslim Brotherhoods) are paramount. Understanding the relevance of these various social configurations is of the utmost importance but the question of comparing their political significance is even more complex.

Because the assumptions that are found at the core of our discipline are drawn from the experience of Western societies, most comparative exercises are constructed on the notion of the primacy of a certain number of hypotheses. Of these the most important is undoubtedly that which links class with politics. To pursue our previous example, almost all discussions of the role of political parties are predicated on some variant of this sociological variable. Here there are two conjectures. The first is that as societies become more socially complex, they evolve into distinct classes, which then seek political representation. The second is that over time politics becomes less ideological and the link between class and party dissolves, ushering in a new age of issue-based multiparty competition. As ever this is broadly true in the West, but even here there is a need for strong qualifications: in parts of Europe party affiliation may well continue to be dictated by family tradition or regional points of view. Elsewhere it may not be the same: in Japan and Taiwan, for instance, other factors impinge on politics and parties are not only the expression of class interests.

Finally a cultural approach stresses the importance of taking a dynamic, historically based view of social relations. For example, Western Europe is today confronted with the consequences of the failure to integrate racial/ethnic minorities. The assumption that national economic posperity would erode divisions based on racial/ ethnic origins has turned out to be wrong. True, it is difficult to disentangle causalities in this respect since such minorities are often economically disadvantaged. Nevertheless, the fact that many supporters of al-Qaeda in the West are drawn from second- or third-generation immigrants from comfortable socio-economic backgrounds does raise difficult questions of interpretation.[7] At the very least we need to investigate how issues of identity evolve in multi-cultural societies.

More generally, the political import of race relations in different Western countries requires proper understanding of the cultural issues that influence people to become racist or to combat racism. For example, it is clear that attitudes to race in Sweden, the Netherlands, Denmark and Norway have been changing since the 1990s because of the recent incidence of acts of racist violence. These four countries have had to come to terms with the possibility that their efforts at 'integration' have been less than wholly successful. Yet their reaction to this undesirable state of affairs has been conditioned by differences in the appreciation of the origins of racism: is it primarily due to xenophobia or to socio-economic factors?[8] As is obvious from the debates

---

[7] See here the very convincing argument developed by Olivier Roy. O. Roy, 2004, *Globalised Islam*, particularly Chapter 7.

[8] The recent conservative government in Norway has been willing to debate the issues of racism as they relate to the concentration of immigrants in the country's cities. The same has happened in Denmark, where the conservatives are also in

taking place in all four countries, there are perceptible cultural divergences to the issue of multiculturalism and racism.

Political actors

Understanding power in its local context means, finally, identifying the relevant political actors.[9] Such an undertaking is not quite as simple as existing politics textbooks suggest, for the political relevance of particular individuals, or groupings, is not a 'given'. Although it may appear that in each society there are a limited number of persons, or bodies, that discharge well-identified political functions, the realities of power are usually more complex than any official model suggests. It is usually possible without undue trouble to detect those who matter formally, such as elected politicians in the West, or chiefs in chiefly societies. Plainly, making sense of the authoritative hierarchical structure is a necessary first step. However, this is far from sufficient since such an official view of politics is rarely a true reflection of the way power is actually being exercised. We know that individuals with no sanctioned position do possess (sometimes considerable) political sway over others.

What is at stake is the appreciation of the variegated ways in which power, authority, control and influence impinge on the workings of the politics that really affect people's lives. The difficulty here lies in identifying such webs of power and in finding means of advancing comparative analysis. While anthropology affords in-depth knowledge of how power is organised in particular societies, there is no obvious means to contrast individual case studies. Structuralism and functionalism propose methods to conceptualise the workings of politics across countries. The former stresses the need to pay attention to the manner in which different structures execute similar political tasks—the implication being that particular processes give

---

power. In Sweden and the Netherlands, however, the topic is far more sensitive and there seems to be a higher degree of reluctance to enter into such discussions of racism—although this changed in 2005 in the Netherlands, following the killing of the film maker Theo van Gogh by a Muslim man. This may be due to differences between political parties but it could also have to do with the questions of 'national' self-image and of culture.

[9] Power here refers to overt and covert, formal and informal, politics.

rise to comparable structures. The latter suggests instead that what matters is the function performed by various political entities, or actors. The proposition here is that, whatever the structures, all political systems have to perform a certain number of functions, which are identifiable. It is thus a matter of uncovering the 'black box'.

The aim here, as we explained in Part I, is not to deny the possible merits of structuralist or functionalist methods, both of which provide suggestive roadmaps for comparative analysis, but to explain why such approaches are not compatible with the ones we advocate.[10] Put quite simply, the fundamental problem with both of these paradigms is the assumption that either structure or function can meaningfully be compared. From our point of view, such an assumption is rarely straightforwardly true. Again it is clear that political systems with relatively similar historical roots, in countries with relatively similar cultures, are relatively plausibly candidates for some variant of a structuralist or functionalist framework. However, even here we would argue that divorced from a cultural approach they would only provide limited insights. What matters is not so much an *a priori* position on the most appropriate methodology but the willingness to recognise that the aims of comparative politics are not best served by a pre-set theoretical agenda. The choice of conceptual framework must fit the case study.

A cultural approach makes possible the identification of important political actors in two ways. First, it proposes to make explicit the systems of meaning that validate authority in society. It seeks to unravel the historical, symbolic and socio-culturally contingent factors that most affect the way in which power is perceived and the manner in which it is exercised. Second, it recognises that significant political agency is to be found in both the formal and informal sectors of political life—two areas that need equal research attention.[11] It thus attempts to devise a methodology that makes it possible to understand how the informal, or invisible, works and, more crucial, how it impinges on the role of political actors who are usually ignored by comparative analysis. It also calls attention to the unofficial aspects

---

[10] See Chapter 2.
[11] As we will show empirically in Chapter 9, which provides a discussion of the State in Sweden, France and Nigeria.

of the political role of official politicians. Finally, it provides a means of studying the increasingly salient role of non-state actors in international relations.[12]

How then do we identify the key political actors? Crucial to our approach is the recognition that relevance is largely contextual. Starting at the top, the official function of official politicians is itself subject to the vagaries of any given historical situation. The position of a president, prime minister, or minister of defence varies greatly when a country is at war. Parliament also operates differently in such circumstances. Less obvious is the fact that all official politicians are involved in non-official activities, some of which have strong political resonance: witness the importance of the business connections that most American elected officials enjoy.[13] Also relevant is the political influence of non-politicians. Here examples abound, from the pronouncements of influential religious figures to the actions of key representatives from civil society, such as union leaders, NGO activists, intellectuals, artists or scientists. To give only one example, the role of *Médecins sans Frontières* in forcing onto the international political agenda the notion of humanitarian intervention in countries where human rights are massively violated, demonstrates the political influence of non-official actors.[14]

More significant from our point of view is the realm of the informal. In all polities official politicians also have non-official influence. Politics is about power and office holders use their power informally, in ways that only a culturally attuned analysis can identify properly. However, our main concern is with the political role of informal political actors, more particularly in the large number of non-Western societies where official State structures are plainly not suitably congruent with the realities of political identity and the constraints of social relations.[15] Here standard political theory is quite simply bereft of operational analytical tools, and comparisons between political actors become difficult, if not impossible. How, indeed, does

[12] See here the work on what are called 'new wars', such as M. Duffield, 2001, *Global Governance and the New Wars.*

[13] As is undoubtedly well illustrated by the links between Vice-President Dick Cheney and the business consortium Halliburton, which has benefited from the contracts awarded for activity in Iraq.

[14] See R. Jackson, 1990, *Quasi-states.*

[15] We discuss the issue of the 'informal' in Chapter 9.

one account for the importance of, say, spirit mediums in contemporary Africa and how does one assess their political role in a comparative study of African, Latin American and East Asian democratic transitions?[16]

Even more intriguing is the question of the simultaneous recourses to formal and informal registers, by which we mean the reciprocal influence that such factors might have on political actors. Perhaps the most obvious instance of such a phenomenon is, to follow from the previous example, the weight of religious belief.[17] It is an acknowledged fact that interpreters of the faith may have unofficial, though not covert, functions in many countries. But it is less readily accepted that they might in fact exercise real power over large numbers of people, regardless of their official position. The heads of the Mouride Brotherhoods, for example, have always played a very important role in Senegalese politics: they command the votes of their followers and are actively cultivated by politicians.[18] Voodoo priests in Benin are often to be found at the heart of the political establishment, even if this is repeatedly denied in official circles.[19] Finally, and more controversial, witchcraft continues to exercise real influence over political agency in contemporary Africa.[20]

THE POLITICAL USES OF CULTURE

If our approach allows us to cast a fresh look at the ways in which the political systems concerned actually function, it also affords us insights into the political uses of culture. In the first part of this chapter

---

[16] A superficial outlook would dismiss their influence on democratisation, but a more acute enquiry into the realities of power at the local level would show that they might in fact have decisive impact on the perceptions of rural dwellers about multiparty elections. For two useful Africa volumes on this issue, see H. Behrend and U. Luig (eds), 1999, *Spirit Possession* and J.-G. Deutsch, P. Probst and H. Schmidt (eds), 2002, *African Modernities.*

[17] See S. Ellis and G. Ter Haar, 2004. *Worlds of Power: religious thought and political practice in Africa.*

[18] See J. Copans, 1989, *Les marabouts de l'arachide*; C. Coulon, 1981, *Le marabout et le prince*; and D. Cruise O'Brien, 1971, *The Mourides of Senegal.*

[19] On this issue one will read with profit an important novel by one of Africa's foremost writers. See A. Kourouma, 1998, *En attendant le vote des bêtes sauvages.*

[20] A topic discussed in detail, in respect of Africa, in our previous book, *Africa Works*, Chapter 5.

we discussed how best to locate, identify and analyse some of the relevant socio-political variables and the nature of political agency. Here we want to cast a comparative glance at how culture is deployed politically. Therefore, we are interested in the processes whereby political actors both understand and exploit their culture for their own ends. This is important in two ways. First, because we want to investigate whether, as critics of culturalism assert, the political use of culture is merely instrumental, cynical or manipulative. Second, because we seek to uncover how it is possible to develop a comparative analysis of such political uses that is not itself culture bound, even less culturalist.

Inventing rationality

The first and most significant political function of culture in all societies is to provide a framework for the enunciation of rationality.[21] The aim of political anthropology is to research, and make sense of, the criteria that govern public life. No matter how small or remote the group under study, it is understood that only an appreciation of culture can enable the analyst to grasp the 'moral' parameters of political action.[22] The reason for this is quite simple: in order to apprehend the workings of a polity it is necessary to work out its rationality. This entails working out its two distinct aspects: the first concerns the 'logics' of a political system; the second involves understanding how actors explain what they do. It is our argument that the best means of achieving such insight is to use a cultural approach in the sense in which we have defined it: that is, an interpretation of the webs of meanings within which political rationality is situated.

However clear the notion of rationality may seem in political anthropology, it is more difficult to explain how useful it is to the discipline of comparative politics. Political scientists do not dispute that micro-studies can uncover specific forms of rationality at the local

[21] See here our discussion in Chapter 2, pp. 74–77, and Conclusion, p. 313.
[22] If anthropologists sometimes place excessive emphasis on the cultural symbols and artefacts deployed in political rituals, there is no gainsaying their conclusion that an analysis of the political realm does indeed rest on a comprehension of the culture that underpins it. For a discussion of these issues, see J. Gledhill, 2000, *Power and its Disguises.*

level, which help to understand why actors behave as they do in specific circumstances. However, the theory to which they most readily subscribe is that 'modern' *homo politicus* operates on the basis of a universal form of political logic, most clearly defined in rational choice theory.[23] Whatever regional variations may be found, it is argued, human beings everywhere behave according to the same criteria of individual, utilitarian reasoning. We have already explained why we think such an assumption is wrong-headed. We want here to suggest that it is the opposite approach, the cultural perspective, which can best contribute to an enlightening comparative analysis.

Our argument is that what is universal is the process by which a society's political rationality, or logic, is born and evolves. Politics is always rooted in culture, everywhere. To say that a given political rationality is a product of the local culture is merely to make a statement about its genesis, not about its complexity, even less its worth. Furthermore it is emphatically not to suggest that there are societies in which political actors behave 'rationally' and others in which they behave 'irrationally'.[24] It is, however, to make clear that political logic is always constructed, contextually, within the culture of which it is a part. Thus the aim of a cultural approach is to seek to understand how such logics emerge, or are 'invented', how groups of people come to agree, even if only implicitly, on what rational political behaviour is.

It is precisely because all political actors claim to act rationally, even when, to outside observers, they appear not to do so, that it is important to give ourselves the means to seek to elucidate whether they do. Clearly not everyone behaves logically at all times, even on their own terms. Nor is there an unchanging consensus in society as to what a rational political action is. These are the questions needing investigation, since failure to answer them may induce the political analyst either to dismiss the reasons given for an action or to make assumptions that may not be validated within the context in question.

---

[23] For a clear exposition of the parallel between rational choice theory and economic rationality, see P. Dunleavy, 1991, *Democracy, Bureaucracy and Public Choice.* For a review of such an approach, see K. Monroe (ed.), 1991, *The Economic Approach to Politics.*

[24] A critique all too readily made of *Africa Works* by those who misunderstood our discussion of the rationality of the belief in the occult within the modern African political context.

It is generally taken for granted, for instance, that integrity is an asset for any politician. And in a very broad sense this is probably true. Therefore, it would seem 'rational' for political actors to behave with probity. At the same time there is a widespread perception that politicians are not entirely honest, or at the very least that they readily distort the facts to serve their own purposes. Furthermore there are many successful politicians in a number of countries who are known to be dishonest, and sometimes to be utterly crooked, but who do not seem to be penalised by their constituents for it. Why? A simplistic explanation would consist in arguing that they manage to 'get away with it'. However, a cultural approach would seek to understand what the meaning of political 'integrity' entails in its appropriate context.

The point here is to move away from the utterly superficial view that some 'cultures' are partial to corruption. To do this we need to re-examine our own postulates. As soon as we genuinely try to explain what is a paradox—'dishonesty pays'—we make cultural assumptions. Either we believe, as do many cultural relativists, that we are simply not in a position to judge what other people do and hence to measure what appears fraudulent.[25] Or we believe that such political behaviour is the sign of a lack of political 'maturity', of the absence of political modernisation. Interestingly both sets of explanation fail to deal with the question of what is or is not rational for the people concerned because they continue to make simple assumptions about the notion of political rationality.

A cultural approach, on the other hand, would encourage the analyst to try to understand such political behaviour from the point of view of the local actors, both rulers and ruled. Do the people concerned consider that it is dishonest? Why? Is it possible that what appears to us a single, coherent, illegal deed is understood locally as being composed of a number of different acts, some of which are legitimate and others not? Can an ostensibly fraudulent action ever be acceptable? When is illegality illicit? Two examples can illustrate the difficulty of comparative assessment in this respect.

In East Asian countries (like South Korea and Taiwan, for example), it is generally accepted there might be corruption between business and political élites.[26] However, it is expected that the former

---

[25] For our views of cultural relativism, see Chapter 1, pp. 48–52.
[26] Tu Wei-ming (ed.), 1996, *Confucian Traditions in East Asian Modernity.*

can be directed by the latter to invest in economic areas that are as yet unprofitable but are consensually adjudged of national importance. Perhaps this behaviour is considered rational because there is an over-whelming culture of economic 'nationalism' shared by all. In Africa, on the other hand, as some Africans themselves have suggested, em-bezzling the state is acceptable, but stealing from one's community is improper.[27] What we want to suggest here is that only a methodology attuned to culture will make it possible to assess both what duplicity means to the local actors and whether such behaviour as we observe is, or is not, politically rational.[28]

Creating myths

Political scientists do not readily discuss myths, which are often seen as the preserve of anthropologists, historians or, perhaps, students of (especially early) literature. Social scientists prefer to see themselves as concerned with the hard facts of socio-political life, not its imaginary constructs. Nevertheless, comparativists have come to realise that a particular category of belief serves a specific function in political systems: those linked to what we might call myths of origin.[29] The process of investigating other societies has brought about a realisation that peoples' own sense of their 'native' roots, of their history (how-ever implausible some of the claims appear at times to the outside observer), is a key factor in what is often described generically as 'po-litical culture'.[30] De Tocqueville was perhaps the greatest of the early such scholars, the pioneer comparativist, offering an analysis of the United States that took fully into account its people's own sense of destiny.[31]

Nevertheless, the bulk of contemporary political analysts, partic-ularly (and paradoxically) in the United States, tend now to consider

[27] See K. Saro-Wiwa, 1991, *Similia*, in which he commented on this aspect of local politics.
[28] The fact that in Southeast Asia illegality works to stimulate economic devel-opment whereas in Africa it does the opposite is also a question about which a cultural approach would have much to say.
[29] See the by now classic explanation of the origins of nationalism: B. Anderson, 1991, *Imagined Communities*. [Revised edition].
[30] For an applied discussion by the same author, see B. Anderson, 1990, *Language and Power*.
[31] A. de Tocqueville, 1968 [1835–40], *De la démocratie en Amérique*.

that myths of origin primarily concern newly independent countries or less developed societies, in which such notions are at the centre of political identities that are still fragile.[32] It is seen merely as research that might help to explain how national myths condition political behaviour, such as 'age old' hostilities. Of course such a narrow view of 'political culture' leaves little place either for a different understanding of culture or a distinct appreciation of the political relevance of myths. The study of myths is fitted into an analytical scheme which views all beliefs either within an ideological (or religious) perspective or in instrumental terms—that is, merely as 'explanation' of, or 'justification' for, certain types of political action.

We approach the question very differently, since we are concerned with the interpretation of meaning and not with the nature of belief. What matters is less the ability to distinguish political myths from other types than the capacity to make sense of this type of credence in its appropriate socio-historical context. Historians naturally concentrate their attention on the accounts given by different groupings of their genesis, if only because they serve as convenient platforms for 'nationalist' ideologies of all hues. However, a cultural viewpoint considers that it would be wrong to assume that there are no myths other than those of origin, which are relevant to politics—and not just in non-Western, or less developed, countries. Taking myths seriously is the first step towards understanding how they affect notions of identity and influence political action.

We stress two important points. The first has to do with the process by which myths emerge, or are created. The second is concerned to link their historical sedimentation with the political uses to which they may be put. Hence it is not sufficient for comparative analysis to identify in different societies myths that appear to have similar political 'functions', such as the notion that one's country is innately blessed by God or derives from the great deeds of an ancient warrior. We can take it for granted that all societies have such rationale. However, we cannot assume that all myths, however alike they may seem,

---

[32] For an example of the political role of myth in Northern Ireland, by one of a few American political scientists interested in a cultural approach, see M. H. Ross, 2001, 'Psychocultural Interpretations and Drams: identity dynamics in ethnic conflicts', *Political Psychology,* 22 (1). See also I. McBride, 1997, *The Siege of Derry in Ulster Protestant Mythology.*

materialise in similar fashion and even less that the ways in which they so materialise are equally consequential.

In Africa, for instance, all ethnic groups have relatively analogous narratives of origin, which most commonly link their identity with the arrival of a god-like ancestor in the particular area in which the self-proclaimed group now resides—as the tragic history of Rwanda reminds us. The Serbs of Bosnia affirm now, as strongly as they did when Turks actually threatened their 'independence', that their sense of identity is rooted in a long history of resistance to Muslims. Similarly, Sri Lankan Sinhalese have in the recent past asserted their autochthony against the alleged foreign origins of their Tamil neighbours. However, what is of interest is the specific historical context in which cultural claims of this type are made. In all three cases these issues have arisen, or become more salient, in specific socio-economic circumstances. In other words, 'national' myths of this type become politically significant under conditions of historical 'stress', which needs to be understood in their appropriate setting.

Therefore, it is clear that a standard feature of all myths is that they are actually the opposite of what they are taken to be by those who believe in them. They are claimed to be inherent, intrinsic, or given features that mark out a particular society. However, they are usually a response either to the necessity of constructing a clearly defined sense of identity or to meet a perceived threat from other groups. Myths are thus the material from which communities are 'imagined'.[33] Whether such 'imaginings' are plausible is, of course, a matter for infinite discussion since there is ultimately no way objectively to corroborate the historical claims made on their behalf by the believers, or the converts. What matters is not whether the Serbs have a valid claim to sovereignty or whether the Hutus and Sinhalese completely misrepresent their own history. It is the fact that myths of this ilk make possible large-scale political violence.

The process whereby myths are created is thus embedded in a society's culture. Debating their validity is beyond the remit of political analysis. How they contribute to the local political order, on the other hand, is of greater comparative consequence. Here a cultural approach is essential, for the task is to tease out the relevance of myths to politics, to explain how they impinge on a political 'language'

[33] B. Anderson, 1991, *Imagined Communities*.

shared by all. The English hold that they are 'fair', the French that they are 'rational', the Scandinavians that they are 'egalitarian' and the Americans that they are 'efficient'. It would not be difficult to provide an historically grounded exegesis of such notions. Equally it would be possible to argue that these myths are merely gratuitous generalisations. More interesting, however, is how they affect the ways in which the citizens of these respective societies come to share such an idea of the business of politics.

It is indeed in the appreciation of how the people concerned explain, justify, defend, or exalt their own prized customs that the key to a culturally sensitive comparative study is to be found.[34] Much as we would like to believe that it is possible to construct a comparative method that need not rely on such elusive notions, the reality is that we need a means both to conceptualise these beliefs and to integrate them into our investigation. Part IV will show how our method makes such analysis possible. Here we merely want to stress how short-sighted it would be either to assume that myths are irrelevant or that they can be relegated to a realm of personal subjectivity that has no place in scientific enquiry. The only way to evolve meaningful contrasts is to build into the analysis a way of overcoming the inherent ethnocentric nature of any discussion of belief, value, norm, or even legend.

Legitimating conflict

Of all the putative political uses of culture it is that of justifying conflict that is most frequently discussed by political scientists and the public at large. The explanation commonly offered to explain discord, hostility or war is that cultures are perceived to be not easily 'compatible', when not altogether unable to coexist. Huntington's clash of civilisations should in this respect be seen as only the latest in a long tradition of such lines of reasoning.[35] It may be that in the post-

---

[34] 'Prized customs' should not be equated with 'values'. The former refers to reference points in a group's mythology, from which a certain notion of identity derives. The latter means the local 'moral justification' for a particular belief. Although the two may appear synonymous, they differ in that values are defined in terms of their relevance to behaviour whereas customs stand as reminders of who we are, like historical monuments.

[35] S. Huntington, 1996, *The Clash of Civilizations and the Remaking of World Order*. Although Huntington's idea of civilisation is broader than that of culture, what it

Cold War period a focus on cultural differences appears fresh, but in truth it merely harks back to a perennial theme in the analysis of the relations between peoples, nations and countries. It is at the heart of international relations.[36] The issue of the link between culture and conflict is thus a difficult question since it touches on widespread prejudices about the 'other'.[37] It is also an area in which common sense is misleading, as we shall see below.

There are two inter-connected arguments here that are not always clearly demarcated, but that need to be distinguished for analytical purposes. The first, and most widespread, is that the roots of conflict are to be found in the political incompatibilities induced by cultural differences. The second is that political actors perennially manipulate cultural symbols, highlighting their compelling distinctiveness, in order to cloak their instrumental intent in locally validated terms.[38] We discuss them in turn.

The assumption that it is possible to distinguish distinct and permanent 'political cultures' is deeply rooted in our discipline, as has already been indicated. The very notion of 'political culture' presupposes a belief in the analyst's ability to identify given political characteristics derived from specific cultural traits *and* that such attributes have clear political consequences. To take only one of the earliest examples in the field, it has been argued, for example, that the 'amoral' political complexion of southern Italian politics is derived from the culture of the family in that region.[39] It is a logical, but fateful, short step from such supposition to that which consists in arguing, as Huntington does with some force, that some 'civilisations' are not compatible. To be sure, the notion that Islam is a culture in the same sense as the practices of southern Italian rural dwellers raises concern

shares with the proponents of the notion of 'political culture' is that what matters most are values. It is in this respect, therefore, quite different from our own understanding of the concept.

[36] For a recent discussion of the changing nature of the international arena, see D. Held *et al.* (eds), 1999, *Global Transformations.*

[37] M. H. Ross, 1993, *The Culture of Conflict.*

[38] For an important debate on the manipulation of Muslim culture in the Indian context, see F. Robinson, "Nation Formation: the Brass thesis and Muslim separatism" and P. Brass, "A Reply", *Journal of Commonwealth and Comparative Politics,* 15, 3 (1977), pp. 215–34.

[39] E. Banfield, 1958, *The Moral Basis of a Backward Society.*

about levels of conceptualisation, and would certainly deserve more careful attention.[40] Nevertheless, the point is clear: (political) cultures are different and such differences may result in hostility and even armed clashes.

The second line of argument is also familiar in political science.[41] It is the preserve of those who consider culture to be synonymous with identity. They do not accept that there are fixed and given political identities, which might lead to conflict. For them identities are always socially and historically constructed, fluid and liable to change. It is thus not the supposed incompatibilities between different political 'cultures' that are the causes of discord. Clashes occur because self-interested political actors exploit such differences of identity as are assumed to exist in order to mobilise support. In so doing they sharpen and make more visible certain aspects of 'identity', setting off in the process a greater degree of antagonism between different groups. This is, typically, one of the arguments developed in respect of Africa: ethnic violence on the continent, it is argued, is thus the outcome of political manipulation by political élites.

Although it is not to be denied that political actors often justify conflict on the basis of cultural differences, the analysis of the causal relation between the two is not best advanced by means of the lines of attack outlined above. This is because both operate on the assumption that it is possible to 'define' culture in terms of real, or invented, values. Our approach, which rests on the premise that culture is an historically and contextually produced system of meanings, rather than of 'values', offers one way of moving away from simple dichotomies and reductive causalities. We are less concerned to explain why conflicts are commonly legitimised by reference to cultural 'differences' than to study the political context within which a particular cultural justification of that nature is thought to be appropriate, and effective.

For their part, rational choice theorists claim that violence breaks out when it is in the 'interests' of political actors to unleash it and that cultural factors are only invoked as a justification, or as ideology. This may well be true but is of little explanatory value, since the key

[40] On whether there is such a thing as an Islamic 'culture', see O. Roy, 2004. *Globalised Islam: the search for a new 'ummah'.*
[41] See, *inter alia*, J.-F. Bayart, 1996, *L'illusion identitaire.*

question is not how violence is justified but why it makes sense for people to employ it when they do. Here rational choice is helpless simply because its examination of self-interest is always made *ex post facto*. In other words, the explanation is tautological: conflict occurred because it was in the interests of the actors concerned to engage in violence.[42]

A cultural approach to the study of the legitimation of conflict is self-evidently not the same as a culturalist explanation of conflict. Ours is an attempt to explain why the only way plausibly to understand such processes is to study what makes sense to the actors involved in hostility. In other words, we need to unravel the historical and cultural context within which political actors seek to justify violence by reference to clashes in values. On one, very superficial, level the answer is clear: hostility towards others requires a belief that the 'other' is intrinsically different, when not inferior, so that violence can be justified. However, this obviously is no serious explanation as to why such 'difference' suddenly becomes so acute as to merit hostility. Why do national competitors or individual neighbours turn on each other when they do?

To take a recent example, it is not credible to claim that Serbs assaulted Bosnia's Muslims because of incompatibilities in 'culture', or even 'civilisation'. We need to identify why Milošević's nationalist discourse could resonate in the minds of Bosnian Serbs in this way. One can thus point out that the salience of an 'ethnic' sense of identity at that time, though later legitimised by reference to a history of resistance to Islam, was merely the outcome of the exploitation by Karadzić and his supporters of a conveniently instrumental notion of culture. Such ethnic legitimation only made sense in the context of Yugoslavia's post-communist break up and Milošević's dream of a Greater Serbia.

Similarly the attempted genocide of the Tutsis in Rwanda can in no way be explained merely by a supposed age-old 'ethnic' hostility between them and the Hutus, such as a culturalist approach would claim. This abominable event must be put in the context of long-standing economic hardship, shortage of land, and intense political

---

[42] For one compendium of the limits of rational choice, see D. Green, and I. Shapiro, 1994, *Pathologies of Rational Choice Theory.*

rivalry within a weakening patrimonial political system in which political accountability had virtually ceased to exist. However, the notion of a sense of 'Hutu-ness' constructed on hostility to the Tutsi 'outsider' had powerful historical resonance in the social imaginary. The fact that ethnic violence is now endemic in Rwanda, Burundi and most of central Africa is unfortunately the result of decades of ethnically 'justified' violence. Here, as perhaps in the Balkans, recent events will have allowed politicians to legitimate violence on the basis of supposed cultural differences.

The political use of culture to legitimate conflict is thus the outcome of two distinct processes. The first is that the ideology of violence requires rational cause, which is most easily provided by reference to notions of differences rooted in culture. Such logic is implacable: because we are different we cannot resolve our problems peacefully. The second is that we need to protect that which makes us distinct, or unique, which is our culture. Any sign of hostility towards us is, *ipso facto*, an attack on that culture.

The conflation of these two processes has led political scientists to suppose that culture could be the 'cause' of conflict, whereas in reality it is only the language in which it is expressed. If this is true, then it can be argued that ideology is in large part the political exploitation of culture.[43] Paradoxically, therefore, making sense of this all too familiar pattern of self-justification requires a cultural approach, such as we advocate, for only it can illuminate the systems of meanings within which such exploitation can take place.

The question of political order is central to comparative political analysis. We have shown how a cultural approach makes it possible both to sharpen our understanding of the local arena within which power is exercised and to cast a fresh look at the ways in which political actors use, or abuse, culture instrumentally. We have in the process explained how such an approach is the very opposite of culturalism, in at least two fundamental respects. First, it predicates analysis on the search for the contextually meaningful idiom—that is

---

[43] For two contrasting views of the uses of ideology, see D. Donham, 1990, *History, Power, Ideology*; T. Eagleton, 1991, *Ideology*.

in terms of what makes sense to the people concerned. Second, it seeks to explain, rather than take for granted, the political uses of culture. We have also emphasised the need for comparativists to consider the evolution of political order in its local context within the perspective of the long-term—an issue to which we now turn.

6

CULTURE AND POLITICAL CHANGE

One of the charges levelled against the use of culture in social theory is that it gives an account of human action based on an implicit notion of society as unchanging.[1] This critique was first mooted in respect of early anthropology, whose pioneers were prone to consider that the rationality of the groupings they studied was largely to be explained on the basis of 'a' culture—an 'ur'-complex of norms and values. Behind this approach lay an assumption about the workings of what was then called 'primitive' society—that is, communities believed to exhibit the characteristics of a different way of live, contrasting sharply with our modern one. Quite naturally, and not unfairly, one of the questions most often asked was whether a 'primitive' society could become 'modern'. Although anthropologists claimed that their primary interest was merely to describe communities different from ours, the question of change would not go away: how indeed do societies mutate?[2]

Theories of social (and political) change, on the other hand, identify factors, or variables, which purport to explain the transformation of all societies. These usually stress economic, social or environmental roots—most often relating them causally—implying thereby that the triggers for change are universal. Almost always culture is considered to be a secondary factor, a dependent variable as it were, evolving as a result of deeper socio-economic and political mutation. There are of course exceptions to such approaches, of which the work of Max Weber is perhaps the most notable.[3] The task he set

[1] We discuss the criticisms levelled at a cultural approach in Chapter 1.
[2] For a useful introduction to anthropology, which touches on many of the issues in Part II of this book, see H. T. Eriksen, 2001, *Small Places, Large Issues.*
[3] See here his attempt to provide a comparatively grounded understanding of China: M. Weber, 1951, *The Religion of China.*

himself, that of making sense of the many and complex ways in which culture affects social and political change, is, we would argue, one that is as relevant today as it was when he was writing. For us, certainly, one of the keys to a comparative approach is to identify the nature of the relationship between cultural and political change.

THE MYTH OF TIMELESSNESS

Perhaps the most acute critique faced by those who work within the cultural perspective in the social sciences is that they use a method constructed upon a complete fiction: the assumption that culture is ageless. This assessment derives from the view that a cultural approach presupposes a notion of culture that is based on a given number of attributes (norms, values, customs, beliefs etc.) that are taken to be, and forever to remain, the main characteristic of a particular group of people. If this is sometimes how some social theorists define culture—whereupon, the charge may be valid—we have already explained that our approach is completely different. We see culture not in terms of its intrinsic identity but as the symbolic system that enables people to share meaning. That system evolves over time. Hence, our methodology rests on the very idea that social and political transformations are culturally grounded.

What is tradition?

Comparative politics tends to view tradition primarily as that bundle of practices and conventions within which political actors operate.[4] Within the discipline, therefore, culture and tradition are, for practical purposes, synonymous.[5] Tradition is seen merely as the backdrop to politics, the décor behind the political stage.[6] What this means is that it is relegated to the status of a residual category. It matters only in two ways. First, it may help to set the study of the main variables within their relevant context: for instance, an age-old hostility between two

---

[4] See how tradition is (or is not) incorporated in what is a fairly standard survey of the literature: R. Chilcote, 1994. *Theories of Comparative Politics.*

[5] As is apparent in all Comparative Politics textbooks.

[6] For a much more systematic and enlightening discussion of tradition see, for instance, L. Rudolph and S. Rudolph, 1967, *The Modernity of Tradition* and J. Heesterman, 1985, *The Inner Conflict of Traditions.*

nations is obviously a factor that has nourished political attitudes and must be taken into account. Second, it is believed that it may affect politics in a particular way—it is a bias (as scientists would say) that must be incorporated into the analysis: for example, a long period of resistance in certain peripheral regions of a particular country against the central state is likely to affect political action over the contemporary period.

Some students of Cultural Studies,[7] on the other hand, make much of traditions, often seeing them as the crucible for individual and collective (political) action. For them it is custom that informs agency. Here understanding how people's 'culture' differs from, and is resistant to, dominant 'cultures' is paramount.[8] For others tradition means a culture of origin. In large measure present day 'ethnic studies' rest on the assumption that people's ways, and by-ways, are very determined by their 'traditions'—even if that is not often defined specifically. Thus Indian-Americans or Mexican-Americans are believed by the proponents of such views to have inherited certain identifiable beliefs, or customs, that directly affect their notion of their place in the world and, more important, their idea of change: for example, it is sometimes claimed that in such a context community solidarity matters more than individual advancement.[9]

Leaving aside Cultural Studies, there is in the West today a tendency to consider tradition in a number of set ways. Often tradition is assumed to be either akin to culture or it incorporates large aspects of it. It is defined as a collection of habits, customs, values, norms, experiences etc., which are 'given' and relatively homogeneous—in any event amenable to explicit, and even exhaustive, description. Furthermore its significance is deemed to be relatively straightforward. Finally and perhaps most crucial, tradition is more often than not

---

[7] There is of course a plurality of view in Cultural Studies. For an overview of the field, see especially, S. Hall, 1996, 'Cultural Studies: two paradigms' in John Storey (ed.), *What is Cultural Studies? A Reader.* See also S. During (ed.), 2000, *The Cultural Studies Reader,* 2nd expanded edition, and S. Hall, D. Morley and K.-H. Chen (eds), 1996, *Critical Dialogues in Cultural Studies.*

[8] For a discussion of sociological approaches to culture and of culture as resistance, see Chapter 2.

[9] For a critical review of the relationship between Cultural Studies and the study of 'political culture', see A. Dörner, 1999, 'Politische Kulturforschung und Cultural Studies' in O. Haberl and T. Korenke (eds), *Politische Deutungskulturen,* pp. 93–110.

seen as timeless, since there seems to be no explanation of how it may evolve over time. But does 'ethnicity', for instance, always affect individuals in the same way or is it possible that the very reality of what it actually means changes and that such transformation matters?

Hence the key impediment to the use of tradition as an analytical category is that it is presumed to be an identifiable (or bounded) combination of local characteristics, which are both somehow rooted in the past and possessed of an ageless existence—as though at some stage in the evolution of history they had spontaneously coalesced into a cluster of factors that are now taken to be 'the' tradition. Such a conception is widespread. It is the basis for common sense,[10] sayings, proverbs or what passes for popular culture. It is, in other words, an integral part of the way we perceive the world. Not surprisingly it is a notion that fits in with the dichotomous way we (in the West at least) tend to perceive social and cultural reality. What is traditional is not, and cannot be, modern. What is modern is not, and cannot be, traditional. The two are opposites—by definition, as it were.

This type of reasoning is often extended to imply that that which is modern is, *ipso facto*, 'modernity'. In other words, such a view is congenial to a hierarchical sense of modernity, one that is based on an implied concept of evolution, culminating in Westernisation. Paradoxically, those who denounce such hierarchy often fall prey to the same form of (Western) reasoning, except that they value 'tradition' more highly than 'modernity'. What both sides find difficult, or impossible, to accept is that there is no inherent theoretical or historical reason why tradition and modernity should stand in such dichotomous relationship.[11] Our approach moves away from this tyranny of dichotomies because it is based on an analysis of meanings, rather than on a definition of tradition confined to clear (chrono-

---

[10] We cannot resist citing Geertz's formulation here: '... [C]ommon sense [is] a cultural system; a loosely connected body of belief and judgement, rather than just what anybody properly put together cannot help but think... Common sense is not a fortunate faculty, like perfect pitch; it is a special frame of mind, like piety or legalism. And like piety or legalism (or ethics or cosmology) it both differs from one place to the next and takes, nevertheless, a characteristic form.' C. Geertz, 1983, 'Introduction' in C. Geertz, *Local Knowledge*, pp. 10–11.

[11] For an interesting discussion of the nature of the dichotomy between modernity and tradition by a scholar of Islam and other religions, see T. Asad, 1993, *Genealogies of Religion*.

logical or spatial) boundaries. It enables us to avoid the trap of viewing traditions as 'timeless'.

For us, tradition is not 'a' body of customs and values, the specialist knowledge of which would somehow provide the key to the political behaviour of a particular society, or grouping. It is instead the ways in which specific groups of people construe and deploy past and present symbols. Of significance is not the symbol (or custom, or habit) *per se* but its current meaning for the people concerned. Thus there is no 'single' interpretation of beliefs or values. What matters is how such 'traditions'—whether long-standing, recent or invented—are deployed to specific ends. It is in this way no longer necessary to trace the genesis of given customs or to invest certain values with a virtually sacrosanct quality. It is enough to tease out the webs of meaning underneath the discourse.

Therefore, the cultural perspective dispenses with the dichotomies that have crippled social science in that their use has forced research into the dead-end of identifying in which ways some traditions may be more significant than others. It does away with the need either to define tradition explicitly or to classify societies according to their degree of modernity—both of which ambitions are, in our view, without hope of success. Instead it makes it possible to pay proper attention to what particular communities hold to be traditional and how they perceive such traditions to be relevant to their current political and social lives. Tradition is best seen as one particular cluster of meanings, which provides a way of understanding and adapting to change. All traditions are rooted in our perception of the past, but they are expressed in contemporary idiom.[12] All traditions are relevant to modernity.

Cultures change tectonically

If an understanding of culture is, in our view, necessary to the analysis of social and political change, the question arises as to how culture itself changes over time. It is not enough to reject, as we do, the common sense idea that traditions are, or ever can be, 'timeless'. We need here to explain how our approach accounts for the evolution of

[12] See here a by now classic approach to this question: E. Hobsbawm and T. Ranger (eds), 1983, *The Invention of Tradition*. For a different approach, see W. Griswold, 1994, *Culture and Societies in a Changing World*.

the system of symbols by which people make sense of their lives and environment. Again what counts here is not so much the identification of the 'drivers of change'—largely a futile quest in our view, since all 'variables' are interconnected—but an elucidation of the ways in which people's views upon, and uses of, culture alter. This apparently simple question turns out in fact to be not just complex but also consequential for social theory, for it impinges on the understanding of the dynamics of change within any given society.

There are two familiar approaches to the question of how culture evolves.[13] The first holds that it changes incrementally, altering continuously in myriad ways as it responds to the stimuli of socio-economic dynamics. Here the argument is that the factors ('tradition', values, norms, beliefs etc.) that make up a culture are constantly evolving in order to adapt to the demands of everyday life. Thus, for example, the primacy of family life for Bengalis in Britain or Moroccans in France is slowly, but surely, being eroded as immigrants settle and have children in their adopted country. The second considers that there is a cultural 'core' that remains central to people's identity and continues to affect their beliefs and behaviour however much the surface of social life may change. From this point of view Bengalis in Britain or Moroccans in France continue to hold dear a notion of their 'native' culture by which they regulate their lives regardless of how long they have lived in their country of adoption. Moreover, it is argued, even second or third generations immigrants remain attached to that cultural kernel, even if they re-interpret it to suit their new circumstances.[14]

Both views are valid and they are not necessarily mutually exclusive. They respond to two distinct aspects of what passes for culture in our own societies, which are, it must also be said, singularly obsessed by the question of change. The first addresses the issue of the apparent seamless transition that takes place, so that no one is able to say, with any degree of certainty, when a particular aspect of a given culture has actually changed.[15] And indeed it is the case that such evolution can

[13] For one possible general discussion, see M. de. Certeau, 1980, *La culture au pluriel*.

[14] For a more sociological approach to these, and other issues, see D. Crane (ed.), 1994, *The Sociology of Culture*; and from a point of view that differs from ours: M. Ferguson and P. Golding (eds), 1997, *Culture Studies in Question*.

[15] For another approach, See J. Kahn, 1995, *Culture, Multiculture, Postculture*.

never be properly dated. At best it might be suggested that it occurred within a relatively vague period, such as a decade or a generation. We know, for instance, that 'free love' boomed in the late 1960s and early 1970s—and no doubt in part because of the contraceptive pill—but we do not know precisely when our sense of the sexual permissible advanced in such a way as to make that possible.

The second points to the equally valid observation that culture seems to act as the keeper of what people hold dear and in this sense appears to be a bulwark against change.[16] It is that which remains steadfast when all around is engulfed in rapid mutation. It is the beacon that enables people to continue to find their way in what is now always referred to as 'rapidly moving times'. When there is a change—and looking at the question over periods much longer than an individual's lifetime it is quite clear that there is an evolution—it is not one that any person readily appreciates since it would require specialist knowledge of key cultural markers over historically long stretches.[17] Thus it stands to reason that immigrants should hold onto what they believe to have been their forefathers' 'values'—even if that conviction is exposed as illusory when, after a lifetime abroad, they return to their village of origin.[18]

Our approach, on the other hand, does not employ a notion of culture based on an unambiguous definition of its constituent parts but rests on a method that seeks to relate the use of symbols with the interpretation of meaning. Therefore, the question of change acquires a different complexion. What needs to be explained is the way in which that relationship alters over time. If the need to 'make sense' of reality and 'communicate' with others remains the same—at least within a relevant unit of measurement, such as an individual's lifetime—it matters little whether the symbolic repertoire and the lexicon of meanings change, or even why they alter.[19] We are primarily interested in identifying, understanding and discussing the ways in which the people concerned make sense of the changes they witness or undergo; how they explain what they do, in the ways in

[16] See J. Alexander and S. Seidman (eds), 1991, *Culture and Society* and, from a very different angle, G. Bauman, 1997, *Contesting Culture.*

[17] And would it be possible to agree on 'objective' markers?

[18] For one study of how 'values' are held tenaciously in an emigrant community, see P. Werbner, 2002, *Imagined Diasporas among Manchester Muslims.*

[19] See R. Shweder, 1991, *Thinking Through Cultures.*

which they do it.[20] It is that aspect of perception, as it were, which requires analysis, for it is that which provides an insight into their (individual as well as collective) behaviour.[21]

From this standpoint we would argue that culture changes *tectonically*—meaning that the process is marked by three characteristics: it is perceived by us to be subterranean, unpredictable and to proceed in unequal quantum jumps. As is the case with the geological phenomenon in question, the consequences of such invisible changes are usually only revealed to us when they coalesce into 'extra-ordinary' events, as earthquakes are in physical terms. The point of the analogy, however, is not to suggest any clear, and measurable parallel between the movement of tectonic plates and the evolution of culture. It is merely to propose an image that may help to understand the manner in which we conceptualise cultural change. We do not of course imply that such change is catastrophic, but that it only becomes obvious when it brings about a radical, often sudden and permanent change.[22]

We would stress two key points here. The first is that it is not possible easily to measure cultural change unless there is in fact such a rapid, ostensibly sudden and dramatic break. Only then does it become clear that the way in which we interpret reality has indeed radically mutated. One such recent example was the acceptance in Western armies that women could go into combat. Although this decision was the outcome of a long and gradual process of emancipation in the armed forces as well as of the struggle for gender equality in Western societies at large, it took the abrupt realisation that women killed and were killed in armed conflict to force us to measure the distance travelled from what had seemed to be a cultural 'invariant': the symbol of the woman as the giver and nurturer of life.

The second is that culture does not change in a unilinear, or progressive manner, as is often believed. Following our tectonic analogy, it leads to unexpected movements. True there has been a convergence of some cultural aspects between societies. No one today

---

[20] For a highly structuralist approach, to which we do not subscribe, see B. Berger, 1995, *An Essay on Culture*.

[21] For a different, more sociological approach, see M. Archer, 1996, *Culture and Agency*.

[22] For a classic treatment of the question from an anthropological viewpoint, see B. Malinowski, 1945, *The Dynamics of Culture Change*.

believes, for instance, that cameras actually 'capture' the soul of those who are photographed and, more generally, everyone incorporates some knowledge of science in any explanation of natural catastrophes. But the situation is complex in that it is difficult to speak of progress *per se*. From our viewpoint as comparativists what is noteworthy is that people still resort to an admixture of factual and fictional explanations when they seek to explain to themselves what is happening to them.[23] Witness the spread of New Age ideas in Western societies or the fact that 'culture gurus' now lecture to multinational businesses about achieving more 'meaningful' success.

The point then is that it is difficult to explain cultural changes in objective terms—that is, terms that are not themselves associated with our own symbolic world, our own manner of thinking. It is usually only possible to observe a notable evolution in the way in which individuals within a given society make sense of its predicament *a posteriori*. For this reason we think it more useful to leave aside any attempt to define cultural change as such and to focus attention on the impact of such evolution as may be occurring in those areas of political life that matter for comparative analysis. Why, to return to the case of Africa, is the 'tradition' of witchcraft so significant in 'modern' Africa? For us then the question of change is eminently practical: what matters is how political meanings evolve and why. The rest is speculation. Culture is not an abstract concept but the code we use to make sense of our lives.

Culture affects politics in the 'longue durée'

Our aim is not so much to explain how culture evolves as to make clearer the way in which it shapes politics. Comparative analysts, who by trade deal with different societies (and different types of development) across the globe, find themselves in the thorny situation of having to deal with vastly different cultural contexts. Whether they recognise it or not they have to make assumptions about how, and to what extent, cultural factors affect the questions they study. In most instances, as we have shown, they elect to relegate culture to the backdrop or to consider it as residual.[24] Equally their work habitually

---

[23] See here W. Booth *et al.* (eds), 1993, *Politics and Rationality.*
[24] For a notable exception here, see B. Badie, 1983, *Culture et Politique.*

confines itself to a synchronic analysis, making less necessary the study of how these factors may turn out to be a relevant part of the understanding of the political contrasts they seek to elucidate. Nevertheless, the plausibility of comparative analysis must in the end be linked to its capacity to evaluate (political) change over time. Otherwise it is little more than a snapshot of present habits.

It is indeed because comparative politics is primarily concerned to contrast contemporaneous situations that its practitioners find it so difficult to integrate cultural factors into their analysis. Seen from a synchronic viewpoint culture may well appear to be a 'given', an invariant, which can easily be confined to context. Since political change is frequently rapid, or at least not so sluggish as to escape the attention of the actors involved, it may well appear that a succession of synchronic pictures can furnish a reasonable account of political change over short periods (meaning no more than a generation). This is probably true but, to pursue the photographic analogy, a sequence of snapshots offers an infinitely less convincing rendering of reality than a motion picture. Similarly, therefore, comparative analysis would be much enriched by an account of change that provided an interpretation of the evolution of meanings and not just of events.[25] From our point of view comparative work ought to be able to offer a diachronic explanation of the contrasts between distinct forms of political change in different settings.

The difficulty here is that there is an immeasurable gap in scale between political and cultural change: the former is, in historical times, swift; the latter is, as we explained, tectonic and thus more obscure. Without doubt it is difficult to make plain how culture has affected the evolution of politics in a single country. It is clearly even more arduous to do so across geographical borders. However, our approach does not attempt to identify and factor in 'a' cultural variable for purposes of comparative analysis. What we want to understand is how an assessment of the ways in which distinct groupings explain the political environment in which they live can be made analytically richer by incorporating an account of how the dynamics of cultural change matter. For instance, a study of why second-generation immigrants from Muslim countries should consider becoming

[25] For a historical, though structuralist, approach that is relevant to our viewpoint, see the work of F. Braudel.

al-Qaeda supporters today would require us to understand how their notion of religion has been influenced by the modern (or even postmodern) filters through which they perceive culture in a Western environment.[26]

Therefore, the key to a cultural approach is to set comparative analysis within a sufficiently long historical timeframe—or, to use the expression coined by the *Annales* School, within the 'longue durée'.[27] This is different from a conventional historical method, which contrasts different settings within a common period: for example, the Middle Ages or the 'long' nineteenth century. What matters is not so much to recognise differences within a given epoch as to identify both the age and the factors which bring about a shift in the way in which culture affects politics.

For instance, it is clear that one of the most significant processes in the history of Europe is the move from religion-based to secular politics.[28] We know that such a change had a profound impact on the development of the modern State, even if that differed in each individual European country. Gradual change resulted in the very (tectonic) emergence of secular politics.[29] However, a proper appreciation of this momentous political evolution must rest upon an understanding of how cultural shifts made possible, induced or triggered, such an evolution. The argument here is not, as we have had cause to show before, that culture 'explains' such a transition, but simply that a full explanation as to why it took place cannot neglect the cultural factors involved. The strength of the method we advocate is that it requires of comparative analysis an evaluation of the timeframe that is relevant to a meaningfully heuristic contrast in the evolution of different political environments.

To continue with the example given above, how would our approach seek to study the actual, or putative evolution of politics from being religion-based to secular? It would certainly not do so from the viewpoint that such a shift is historically 'inevitable', and that a com-

---

[26] For two recent, and illuminating, discussions of this question, see O. Roy, 2004, *Globalised Islam* and G. Kepel, 2004, *The War for Muslim Minds.*

[27] See P. Burke, 1990, *The French Historical Revolution.*

[28] Which Max Weber studied systematically.

[29] For a useful comparison between European and Muslim states in this respect, see B. Badie, 1986, *Les deux Etats* and O. Carré (ed.), 1982, *L'Islam et l'Etat dans le monde d'aujourd'hui.*

parison between societies where it has or has not occurred should be informed by a sense of 'historical' sequence. Instead it would seek to provide an analysis that incorporated factors of sufficiently 'longue durée' in order to explain the reasons why in some settings this transition has taken place and in others not. In this respect what matters, for example, is not why Islamic societies have not 'yet' become secular, but the cultural reasons invoked by Muslims in specific communities as to why a society can be at once modern and religious.[30] Or to put it another way, we would want to understand why it is 'self-evident' to members of, respectively, secular Western and religiously based Middle Eastern societies that 'their' conception of the common political good should be as it is.[31]

The issue raised above about Islam, merely as an illustration, also makes plain how a cultural approach provides a greater analytical cutting edge. Indeed the acutely sensitive issue of the 'integration' of Muslim minorities into ostensibly secular Western European societies is better approached by a method that allows us to compare how these different viewpoints make sense to the people concerned than by simple (minded) assumptions about the 'reluctance' of Muslims to assimilate into 'modern' pluralist, and lay, societies.[32] An understanding of the tensions between secular and religious tendencies within Muslim societies over time would also reveal that the current presupposition that secularism is inherently impossible in Islam is questionable.[33] In any event, an understanding of the complexities of the contemporary situation requires at the very least an examination of the many paths Islam has taken since its inception and the concomitantly multifaceted ways such 'culture' as affected politics in Muslim and non-Muslim societies over time.

[30] See here, *inter alia*, J. Schacht, 1966, *An Introduction to Islamic Law*; G. E. von Grunebaum, 1962, *Modern Islam*; and J. Chelhod, 1958, *Introduction à la sociologie de l'Islam*.

[31] On the concept of the political good in Islam, see F. Rahman, 1979, *Islam*.

[32] See here T. Ramadan, 1999. *To Be a European Muslim* and T. Ramadan, 2001. *Islam, the West and the Challenge of Modernity*. The legislative debate about the wearing of headscarves in French state schools brought into the open the difficulties of reconciling individual rights and secularism with the notion that some Muslims hold of their religious 'duties'. An interesting comparison in this respect would be between France and Turkey.

[33] See O. Carré, 1993, *L'islam laïque ou le retour. La grande tradition*.

THE FURY OF MODERNITY

Here we turn our attention to the putative effects of cultural change upon modern societies. The question is how the slow, but accelerating, meeting of cultures from different parts of the world influences both how we think of ourselves and the manner in which we conceptualise socio-political relations. Theories have advanced in two (broad) directions. The first follows in the footsteps of Edward Said in casting a critical gaze upon the complex ways in which relations of power across the world impact on notions of cultural worth.[34] The second examines how modern cultures everywhere emerge out of a process of hybridity, or creolisation—that is, the formation of modes of thought and patterns of values that grow out of the meeting, and blending, of the mix of aesthetic viewpoints and tastes which globalisation and the accelerating speed of communications make possible.[35] As comparative political scientists our concern is not so much to provide a critique of such theories as to discuss how these influential arguments may be relevant to our approach.

The illusion of dichotomies

One of the most relevant insights offered by students of culture today is that it is meaningless to seek out clear boundaries between different cultural settings across the globe. If there was ever a time when some societies were completely cut off from the rest of the world then Europe's imperial sweep, culminating in the colonisation of vast expanses of the planet in the nineteenth century, brought most of world's peoples into contact. Indeed it can scarcely be denied that even those societies, such as Japan, which sought actively to resist Western influence, were only able to do so by assimilating their 'modernity'. In other words, imperial domination brought with it the systematic influence of Western culture upon local communities. As a result the furthest reaches of the world became infused by a host of

[34] E. Said, 1978, *Orientalism*. For one view of the opposite process, see J. Carrier, 1995, *Occidentalism*.

[35] See, *inter alia*, R. Young, 1990, *Colonial Desire* and U. Hannerz, 1996, *Transnational Connections*. For our part, we prefer the notion of register to that of hybridity, as we discuss in Chapter 1. We offer a critique of theories of hybridity in Chapter 9. Edward Said himself criticised approaches in terms of cultural hybridity in *Culture and Imperialism*.

values, norms, beliefs, originating from the West. Education, science, technology and the arts all came under the influence of the imperial centres of power.

At the same time the imperialist project made possible the propagation of 'native', or exotic, cultures to the centres of power. As is perhaps best known in respect of the influence of 'primitive art' on early-twentieth-century painters, but is equally true of other areas of creative activities (extending to cuisine and clothing), Western cultures were, and still are, deeply influenced by the peoples they conquered. Equally the culture of those colonised areas such as Brazil is deeply creolised—meaning only that the apparently straightforward transplantation of European civilisation into the Latin American setting has in fact resulted in a local 'civilisation', which issues as much from the influence of the Indians or the Africans who were brought there as slaves.[36] Hence, it is argued, even if there are countries, and societies, that are ostensibly more politically powerful than others, the contemporary world is one in which we now all are cultural mestiço.[37]

Although there is a plurality of voices in Cultural Studies,[38] a strong case has been made for the view that there is today a reciprocal assimilation of the cultures of the so-called traditional and modern societies, wherever they may be in the world. At the same time what marks the hierarchy of cultures is dictated by relations of power, between the centre and periphery—both across the globe but also within the West, where the values of the élites conspire to belittle those of the 'other' (whether a local minority or immigrants).[39] Power then, rather than merit, is what distinguishes 'high' from 'low' culture in the West as well as in the Rest.[40] We draw from Cultural Studies the useful insight that the boundary between the 'traditional' and 'modern' is largely an artificial construct, which derives from the established

---

[36] For one of the earliest discussions of such 'hybridity', here in the case of Brazilian culture, see G. Freyre, *Casa Grande e Senzala*. For an argument in terms of register, which we favour, see the work of the French Brazilianist: R. Bastide, 1970, *Le prochain et le lointain* and 1971, *Anthropologie appliquée*.

[37] For one view of the question, see M. di Leonardo, 1998, *Exotics at Home*.

[38] See note 7.

[39] See H. Bhabha, 1994, *The Location of Culture*.

[40] See P. Chatterjee, 1993, *The Nation and its Fragments*.

social sciences. However, we would argue that the whole field is based on a very problematic notion of culture, which is largely concerned with the respective social (and political) 'standing' of various aspects of human activity deemed in this way to constitute culture.[41]

As we explained at the outset, we take culture to be the symbolic world that gives meaning to our lives. Today's European youth is steeped in a culture drawn from the cultural universe of the immigrant or the Third World.[42] There is a distinct blending of cultural artefacts, such as music and sartorial style, which points to new forms of more hybrid youth identity. Conversely, in Africa alienated youth engaged in violence readily portray themselves as modern 'Rambos' and see themselves as thoroughly 'Westernised'.[43] But what do such comparisons of youth across the Western world, Africa, or even beyond. The sharing of a number of cultural attributes is not, in this instance, a necessarily reliable pointer to the political worldview, and even less of the political behaviour, of young people in different countries. Put bluntly, people who like the same music (often for reasons of fashion), the same films or the same clothes do not necessarily hold the same political views—even less do they behave politically in similar ways.

For this reason we need to approach the question of the dichotomy between 'tradition' and 'modernity' differently. For us this issue raises the far more important subject of change, which is evidently at the heart of all social and political theory. One school of Cultural Studies provides a way of conceptualising change—in this instance by means of an argument in favour of subverting the standard notions of the 'traditional' and 'modern'—by stressing the importance of cultural hybridisation. A comparative cultural approach such as we employ stresses the artificiality of the dichotomy between 'tradition' and 'modern', as of all analogous contrasts, for a different set of reasons. What is at issue here is not so much the implied relations of power—

[41] As well as with the normative injunction that 'subaltern' cultures should resist dominant ones.

[42] Or one might also point to the fact that working class 'culture' in Britain today includes attributes, such as earrings, which have had widely divergent connotations—for instance, of shame or distinction—over the years but which today span different socio-economic groupings.

[43] For a discussion of the case of Sierra Leone, see P. Richard, 1996. *Fighting for the Rain Forest.*

domination and subordination—that such concepts may imply, even if those are relevant, but the theoretical assumptions that underpin the use of such dichotomies in our discipline.

The contextually relevant conception of change that informs such a perception of cultural, as well as socio-political, dichotomies is that of the theory of evolution as applied to the social sciences.[44] It is only possible to speak of 'tradition' and 'modernity' in dichotomous terms because of the supposition that there is a fairly straightforward path to development. This postulate derives, implicitly or explicitly, from the world of the hard sciences where it has been demonstrated (though even here there is no absolute consensus on the matter) that biological or technological evolution advances in one direction. In those areas there is some obvious merit in identifying an earlier (traditional) from a later (modern) stage in a recognisable evolutionary process. Here it can be shown that the later stage is more advanced than the earlier both in terms of complexity and of achievement. Whatever value one attaches to such a hierarchy of progress, there is at least the possibility of comparing like with like.

Such is not the case in the social sciences. Of course it can be argued that there is a gradual move towards more complex and more sophisticated societies in which individuals can achieve more diverse and autonomous goals. But it is simply not possible to claim with any degree of certainty that such social progress is either irreversible or unidirectional.[45] Other than in purely normative terms it is also difficult to argue that one particular form of contemporary social arrangement is 'better', or more 'efficient', than another. For instance, is the Japanese or the Swedish variant of a system combining liberal democracy and capitalism superior? The response hinges on the type of question asked: superior in terms of economic growth or social protection? The point is clear: that the notion of a 'tradition' or 'modernity', such as is defined in the physical sciences, is quite simply of no real value in the social sciences, at least from the comparative

---

[44] Here we leave aside discussion of theories of post-modernity, which (though interesting in themselves) are less relevant to political science than they are to sociology or cultural anthropology. In any event a proper account of this large field would require more space than can be warranted in this chapter.

[45] For one discussion of such implied teleology, see D. C. Tipps, 1973, 'Modernisation Theory and the Comparative Study of Societies', *Comparative Studies in Society and History*, 15.

viewpoint. A society's 'tradition' (such as, for instance, Confucianism), invoked by many as an asset in the modern world, can easily be perceived by others as a hindrance to 'modernity'.[46]

Therefore, we conclude that the analytical value of dichotomies in the field of comparative politics is negligible, or nil. The useful exercise is not to establish a scale of evolution, from 'tradition' to 'modernity', but to assess how different societies deem tradition to be important to their modernity. Therefore, what ought to be compared is not the 'tradition' in itself but its role within a given socio-political setting. A cultural approach to the comparative study of elections, for example, would ask why is it important for Americans to persist with a complicated, and in many ways unfair, presidential electoral system—not whether such an arrangement is 'modern' or not. Similarly it would study why modesty is deemed a political asset in The Netherlands and Japan but a handicap in Italy or Nigeria.

How cultures modernise and why it makes a difference

We discussed above how cultures change tectonically and why it is difficult to measure the ways in which they are transformed. We now need to tackle the question of how cultures modernise—not, as is clear from the above section, because there is merit in establishing the 'modern' credentials of different traditions, but because it is important analytically to work out what modernity may mean in this context. The reference in the social sciences to the process of modernisation is ubiquitous and yet it is by no means clear. In part it is a deeply engrained notion within our own Western world: the cult of the superiority of the 'new' over the 'old'. In part it is a reflection of the extent to which our economic system operates on the assumption of constant forward motion: progress is measured by the endless search for more efficient production. In part it stems from the belief in the West that human (particularly political) agency can fashion culture(s) in a more 'progressive' way. In part, finally, it is a measure of the power exercised in the world by those countries that are seen to have developed most successfully.[47]

---

[46] Tu Wei-ming (ed.), 1996, *Confucian Traditions in East Asian Modernity.*
[47] For an approach that illustrates these views, see F. Fukuyama, 1992, *The End of History and the Last Man.*

For all that, there is precious little consensus on what modernisation actually entails. Nor is there much clarity on the question of what causal relationship there may be between 'modernisation' and culture.[48] It is often asserted that a certain outlook or 'mentality' is a pre-requisite to the constitution of a modern society—by which is usually meant a society able to adapt to rapid change. It is held to be self-evident that 'traditional' communities are those that are least able to transform and adjust to the challenges thrown up by a constantly evolving world. Modernisation in this view is, then, simply the ability to make best instrumental use of social, economic and technological innovation. This of course is a circular argument since the very definition of modernisation derives from the observation that modern societies possess the (cultural?) properties that made it possible for them to become socially, politically, economically and technologically 'advanced' in the first place.

In practical terms, therefore, modernisation is a code word for Westernisation—that process by which the West acquired its present socio-economic complexion. Of course the West is not homogenous either culturally or politically. Democracy means very different things in different countries. Equally it might be argued that some societies are now politically post-modern, in that ideology matters little and policy differences between various parties are marginal. Nevertheless, there are general features of Western polities, which are readily taken to define the foundations of the 'modern' political world.

This fairly general, though often implicit, notion has three consequences for comparative analysis. The first is that a modern culture is taken to be a Westernised culture, however vague a notion that is. In other words, the cultures of other parts of the world are measured against that which is seen to represent modernity because it is economically most advanced. By implication, what is not Western is not modern. The second is the assumption that modernisation is only possible where a society's 'culture' evolves in ways that are compatible with Westernisation. This entails not just the talent to establish and make efficient a capitalist economy, but also the ability to ensure that

---

[48] For a sample of what assumptions are made in this respect, see L. Harrison and S. Huntington (eds), 2000, *Culture Matters.*

'political culture' is not a drag on the social evolution that is required to underpin such a process of development. In other words, a modern culture is one that facilitates Westernisation. Other cultures are valued for their 'authenticity' or 'exoticism', rarely as effective agents of modernisation. The third is the belief that political actors can change cultural 'codes'—that is, re-fashion culture for particular political goals. Paradoxically, therefore, it is the West that holds most strongly that revolutionaries are able to provoke cultural ruptures, when the evidence (as in Russia or China) is that this is not the case.[49]

Here, as ever, our concern is not to define modernity in the abstract but to evolve an idea of modernisation that enables us to make meaningful comparisons. Our starting point is simple, though it may appear iconoclastic within the common perspective of the social sciences: modernisation is simply the process by which socio-economic change takes place, whatever its nature. Or to put it another way, modernisation is that process by which societies initiate, resist or adapt to change. Since no change is wholly indigenous, such a process is necessarily a reflection of the ways in which societies relate to the outside world, economically as well as culturally.

A first point then is that we take modernisation to be neutral rather than synonymous with Westernisation, since there is an infinite number of ways in which individuals and groupings can be 'modern'—that is, cope with change. A second is that we think it possible that there may be forms of modernisation that are not suited to, or even compatible with, the existing socio-economic models of the advanced economies. What this means is that we take seriously the possibility that all societies modernise, even when they are not economically or technologically 'successful' and in this way appear, at face value, to remain 'traditional'.[50]

What matters for us then is how cultures modernise, not whether they are 'modern'. What this means is that we are interested in the individual and collective methods employed to engage with change and not whether such engagement is compatible with, or conducive to, Westernisation. To return to an example given earlier, we consider that the present adaptation of witchcraft in contemporary Africa is a

[49] For an interesting study of the culture of Russia, see O. Figes, 2002, *Natasha's Dance*.
[50] This was one of the main findings of our previous book, *Africa Works*, Part II.

form of cultural modernisation.[51] It is a rational response to the pressures applied upon societies facing the twin challenges of greater global (economic, social and technological) flows and more acute poverty. Although in terms of a simple view of social evolution witchcraft may be considered 'traditional', or backward, its use today must be understood as part of the process whereby African culture responds to modernity as it is experienced on the continent at the moment.

Of general interest to us then is the manner in which apparently 'traditional' forms of cultural expression—such as the wearing of *hijab* by second or third generation Muslim women in Western countries—mutate in order to provide a symbolic framework for making sense of the modern world as it is experienced by the peoples concerned. Without entering into a debate about this particularly contentious issue of the display of Muslim 'identity' in the modern world, it is clear that what this dress codes means is complex. At the very least it blurs the boundaries of the 'modern' and 'traditional'. More significant, it is the outcome of a particular path of Western Islamic cultural modernisation and most definitely not the expression of a 'tradition' frozen in time.[52]

Hence cultures modernise in ways that are congruent with existing traditions. There may sometimes occur radical breaks, or ruptures, in cultural mutations—due to catastrophic events, such as invasion, disease, or population displacement. However, on the whole the process of change fails to live up to the dramatic notion that modernity and tradition are in opposition, or incompatible. The idea that culture is either a crucible or an obstacle to the acquisition of modernity is fanciful. Some forms of modernisation have historically resulted in spectacular (technological or economic) progress. Others have proved to be more congenial to the slower evolution of society into a form of modernity different from that of the West. Others still are today refractory to the discipline of the modern world, at least as we know it in the West. In all these instances culture is an integral part of the process of modernisation: neither merely cause or hindrance

---

[51] See here P. Geschiere, 1997, *The Modernity of Witchcraft* and H. Moore and T. Sanders (eds), 2001, *Magical Interpretations, Material Realities.*
[52] See here O. Roy, 2004, *Globalised Islam* and G. Kepel, 2004, *The War for Muslim Minds.*

but, rather, the symbolic language used to anchor change into the foundations of society.

Development, globalisation and all that jazz

Current perceptions of the putative role of culture in modernisation are heavily influenced by our views of the twin pillars of the contemporary world system: development and globalisation. Notions of political change today are very largely conditioned by the widespread belief that there is a sweeping movement across the globe resulting in the consolidation of capitalism and liberal democracy. There is at the same time a pervasive conviction that this process of globalisation is both new and radical: for the first time in history the force of socio-political ideology (here, liberalism) is underpinned by a vigorous and universal economic practice (here, capitalism) making use of instantaneous worldwide communications. Both supporters and opponents of this process of globalisation hold that it is indeed the major agent of economic, socio-political and cultural change today.[53]

It is not our intention here to debate the merits of theories of globalisation. We wish merely to explore the extent to which this idea of the contemporary world affects the cultural approach to comparative politics we advocate. An enquiry into the genesis of the concept of globalisation reveals that its origins are not as new as they are often taken to be.[54] There are of course immediate and proximate reasons for such a point of view, of which two are paramount: the end of the bipolar world and the spectacular improvement in telecommunications. The former, neatly encapsulated in the highly ideological, but apposite, formulation of 'the end of history', is but the conceptual projection of the supposedly unchallenged hegemony of the values most fully embodied in the United States.[55] The latter, though the outcome of a slow process of technological innovation, is perceived as a sudden and far-reaching change in the practice of communication that has dramatically altered the realities of time

---

[53] See, *inter alia*, A. Hoogvelt, 1997, *Globalisation and the Postcolonial World*. For the argument that claims a 'third way'—that is neither pro nor contra—see the overly ambitious J.-F. Bayart, 2004, *Le gouvernement du monde*.

[54] A. Scott (ed.), 1997, *The Limits of Globalization*.

[55] F. Fukuyama, 1992, *The End of History and the Last Man*.

and space. The result is the prevalent belief that globalisation has unleashed a full-scale economic, political and cultural revolution.[56]

This of course not the first time in history that a successful hegemon considers it is both the model for mankind and the centre of the universe. To take but the most obvious examples, the Chinese at their imperial prime saw themselves as the undisputed champions of their own type of global supremacy and considered the rest of the world as uncivilised, or barbarian. Similarly the British had cause to think in the nineteenth century that their brand of imperialism had forever changed the world. Yet there is a sense today that globalisation as we are now experiencing it really is of a different hue, both because of the reach of the global economy and because of the ubiquitous influence of the social and cultural baggage it conveys.[57] All that can be said at this stage is that it is likely that those who lived through earlier episodes of imperial domination probably felt the same. The perception of the sweep and sway of hegemonic supremacy is of necessity congruent with the ideological context.

However, a more historically informed view of present day globalisation would show that it is rooted in two distinct, though interrelated, aspects of the West's process of modernisation: economic development and expansion. We have already discussed how the theory of comparative politics is imbued with a clear sense of development that reflects the Western experience. As a consequence, analysis is implicitly or explicitly concerned with the business of assessing the extent to which the economic and political evolution of other parts of the world conforms to that of the West. A brief examination of the concept of globalisation shows that it too is taken with the view that the effect of this alleged worldwide revolution is to accelerate the mutation of the rest of the world into the Western mould. Both those who welcome and deplore such transformations share the conviction that globalisation is uniquely powerful in making such homogenisation possible. In that sense they both share the assumption that imperial ascendancy brings about similar socio-

[56] For a review of the arguments from a viewpoint that differs from ours, see M. Featherstone (ed.), 1990, *Global Culture*.

[57] For one discussion of these issues from a structuralist point of view we do not espouse, see J. Friedman, 1994, *Cultural Identity and Global Process*.

cultural and political outcomes. But that is far from clear, as is illustrated by the strength of local, regional, parochial and religious reactions to globalisation.[58]

The point here is not to expose globalisation theories as facile, Western-based, conceptual simplifications of what is both a less unique and less all-encompassing process than both fans and foes contrive to believe.[59] It is to make plain that whatever the present version of globalisation may in retrospect turn out to be, it ought not divert us from the complex task of developing a cultural approach able to account for the political changes that we can observe concretely in the real world. The Coca-Cola sign may be truly ubiquitous but this does not make it easier to understand how, for instance, South Asian or African societies make sense of the impact that global pressures apply upon them. The echoes of the latest political ideologies purveyed by television, film or the Internet may have influenced the stuff of local politics in those two parts of the world. However, it is highly improbable that the import of caste on Indian rural social relations or of clientelism on rulership in Africa has been significantly altered by the consolidation of capitalism and the spread of high-speed communications worldwide.[60]

The understanding of the relationship between culture and political change requires an analysis that does not reify notions of modernity. We have argued that a cultural approach to comparative politics must include three central planks. The first provides a framework for studying cultural change. What matters is not the identification of the mutation of any given culture, since this is usually only possible *a posteriori*, but the examination of how change is explained, or exploited, within a given cultural setting. The second is that an appreciation of such change requires a cultivation of the long-term, diachronic perspective, where the key lies in those aspects that trigger sudden, and sometimes unpredictable, shifts in political consciousness. Finally modernisation must be analysed not so much in terms of the extent

[58] B. Meyer and P. Geschiere (eds), 1999, *Globalization and Identity.*
[59] See R. Robertson, 1992, *Globalization.*
[60] D. Miller (ed.), 1995, *Worlds Apart.*

to which change conforms to Westernisation but rather in terms of the many various possible paths to political development. Globalisation does not make such diversity any less likely. And it is this diversity that comparative analysis must seek to assess.

Part III. METHOD

As we see it the aim of comparative politics is to explain why and how the exercise of power differs in distinct settings—and not to try to fit the experience of various polities within the single mould of a given type of socio-political 'modernisation'. Therefore, the cultural approach we advocate is attuned to that ambition: we seek to devise a method able both to account for singular experiences and to provide a means of contrasting their evolution. This is no simple matter, for these two goals are not instinctively compatible.[1] The first requires an in-depth and diachronic historical enquiry, intended to provide the longer-term perspective needed to explain the development of a given case on its own terms. The second demands the deployment of instruments suited to the analysis of the factors that are best able to make clear the contrasts and similarities of these polities at a particular time in their evolution—a more synchronic line of attack.

The view that an interpretive framework is particularly appropriate to comparing polities does not rest on the claim that culture is the most significant variable, even less the only one susceptible to explain variation. It does not presume that that there are cultural 'givens', providing the keys to existing differences. That is why it is worth re-stating plainly what has hitherto been merely implicit: *a cultural approach is not culturalist*. Our reasoning is not predicated on culturalist premises—that is, the assumption that differences in political behaviour originate in differences in cultural characteristics. Quite the contrary: we plead instead for an analysis that makes clear why political processes need to be explained on their own terms *before* they can usefully be compared. Our aim, therefore, is to provide the most compelling explanation of political singularity as a prelude to engaging in the infinitely more perilous exercise of comparing distinct cases.

[1] See our discussion in Chapter 3.

To us then the most convincing manner of discharging such a comparative brief is to devise a method suited to the task at hand—namely, one that reconciles the nature and the sequence of the two requirements outlined above. However, we do not believe that it is possible to achieve comparative insights simply by juxtaposing these two different types of analysis—the in-depth case study and the examination of the contrasts between different cases. It would not do merely to draw on two or three anthropological accounts of politics from different parts of the world and to deduce from them that there are strong functional similarities in the ways in which power is exercised. This is not just because these discrete studies would have had distinct, and possibly incompatible, analytical ambitions but also because they would in all probability have given only a snapshot of politics at a particular point in time. This could not provide adequate data for a satisfactory comparative exercise since this would require asking similar questions about different settings.

Hence it is necessary to devise a methodology making it possible to pursue these two types of investigation concurrently. Our standpoint, based as it is on the study of a large number of discrete polities across the world, is that a cultural approach to comparative politics entails thinking *inductively* and *semiotically*. We shall explain in the next two chapters how this is to be done. We want here to make clear, and if possible to put in plain words, what this means—but also what it does not mean. Let us right away confront the issue of origins. Our use of these notions is not a reference to any scientific, or pseudo-scientific, school of thought, either in the physical or social sciences. Mindful as we are that these epistemological frameworks have been used with varying degrees of success for different theoretical purposes, we intend here only to draw on them insofar as they reflect the method we advocate. We recognise that it is perilous to resort to concepts central to other disciplines. At the same time we hold firm to the view that, provided we can explain why and how we employ them, it is entirely legitimate to do so.

Let us now move to the problem of definition. By thinking *inductively* we mean only to express the fact that our approach consists in employing the concepts and theories that are most relevant both to the questions being asked and the cases being studied. In other words, we aim to build an analysis that is congruent with the material generated by the comparative research undertaken. We do not, as it were, set out the comparative framework by means of a pre-existing conceptual approach, but erect the analytical structure that is best suited to the examination of the comparative questions in which we are interested. It is in this sense, and in this sense only, that we proceed in a way that qualifies as *inductive*. Our use of concepts, theories and analytical structures depends not just on the questions asked but also on the conclusions we draw from the preliminary examination of the material that relates to the areas of enquiry on which we concentrate. As we shall show later, many comparisons are simply not appropriate even if they readily suggest themselves to the comparativist in search of material.

Our method, secondly, is built upon what we term thinking *semiotically*. Understandably such a notion might readily evoke an already existing discipline, Semiotics, and a school of thought within the social sciences that constructs the explanation of reality upon the study of utterances or signs. If there is no gainsaying this inference, we want to make it clear from the outset that our method does not in any way derive from such theories.[2] Instead when we use the concept of 'semiotic' we refer only to the definition given by Geertz, which we cited in the Introduction to this volume, and in which he explained that the analysis of culture consisted in the interpretation of meaning, that is, the understanding of actions and symbols in their appropriate context.[3] Stated in its simplest form, thinking *semiotically* refers to the decoding of what makes sense to the actors concerned by means of an historically and culturally based study of the ways in which they formulate an explanation of the logics of their politics. What we advocate then is the 'translation' of such local political accounts into a

---

[2] Nor does it have anything in common with what are broadly called post-modern approaches, which are grounded in strongly relativist premises. See here Chapters 1 and 3.

[3] For ease of reference, we cite this quote in full again: 'The concept of culture I espouse... is essentially a semiotic one. Believing, with Max Weber, that man is an animal suspended in webs of significance he himself has spun, I take culture to be those webs, and the analysis of it to be therefore not an experimental science in search of law but an interpretive one in search of meaning. It is explication I am after, construing social expressions on their surface enigmatical.' C. Geertz, 1973, 'Thick Description: toward an interpretive theory of culture' in C. Geertz, *The Interpretation of Cultures*, p. 5.

language that is amenable to comparison with other cases. It is of course true that we cannot hope to provide such interpretation as though we were removed from our own context. Yet we maintain that by making explicit our method of 'translation' we provide the standpoint for the assessment of our approach.

Let us, to conclude, give one example, which we shall develop at length in Chapter 10. The question of political representation is central to our discipline. The common comparative approach consists in providing a working definition of that notion and examining the role of those who are seen as representatives. We, for our part, would start instead with an examination of how different communities conceive of what we mean by representation, for the term as it is typically used makes assumptions about the type and mechanism of representation that reflect our own experience. We would then focus on how individual representation is achieved. If, for instance, we found out that in one community it meant 'ascriptively to be similar to' and in another 'to convey the views of', then we would seek to use a conceptual framework that allowed a fruitful comparison between these two forms of representation. The ultimate aim would not be to compare the ways in which, say, elections allowed 'proper' representation. Rather it would be to provide an insight into the extent to which representation was possible, and effective, in the different cases under study. By such means it would become possible, for instance, to draw enlightening inferences from the contrast between multi- and single- or no-party political systems.

7

THINKING INDUCTIVELY

The admonition to think inductively may at first appear to go against the scientific grain.[1] As previously discussed, the methodology generally used in comparative politics is ostensibly based on that applied in the 'hard' sciences, which consists in setting up hypotheses and testing them.[2] These hypotheses are derived from the systematic observation of phenomena, which are thought to be similar, and for which the analyst is trying to establish causal relations.[3] The same set of circumstances is supposed to result in the same processes; the same causes have the same effects.

The difficulty with this approach, as has already been explained, is that the key to the scientific method rests on the ability to keep the variables constant and to replicate testing—so as to validate or invalidate hypotheses.[4] However, in the world of the social sciences—that is, the world of human beings and societies—it is impossible to

---

[1] For a useful overview, see A. Rosenberg, 1995, *Philosophy of Social Science*. Although this is a fundamental issue in Social Science, we shall not in Part III engage in a debate about epistemology, useful as that would be, but will only focus on method in comparative politics, and more particularly on the difficulties of constructing meaningful comparisons between Western and non-Western polities. For an introduction to the epistemological framework of our discipline, see A. Zuckerman, 1991, *Doing Political Science*.

[2] See General Introduction and Chapter 3.

[3] For an overview of the foundations of the discipline, see P. Merkl, 1970, *Modern Comparative Politics* and R. Merritt, 1971, *Systematic Approaches to Comparative Politics*. For a more recent, and more critical, view, see L. Mayer, 1989, *Comparative Political Enquiry*.

[4] If in some sciences like chemistry testing involves setting up experiments, in others like astronomy it means testing hypotheses about observations made. What links the two within a scientific approach is the possibility of identifying regular, or replicable, variables that will explain causality.

control the variables and to replicate testing.[5] There is no way to test them 'scientifically'.[6] Furthermore, since such hypotheses are on the whole derived from the experience of our own societies, it is not necessarily the case that they apply to other settings. The end result is, from our viewpoint, very 'unscientific': we postulate correlations for phenomena, which we observe in a context different from ours, but which are based on the inferences we draw from our own circumstances.[7]

Our argument, therefore, is that for the social sciences to seek to ape the method used in the physical sciences is illusory.[8] What is important is not to attempt to meet the test of predictability or falsifiability but to meet the test of *plausibility*—the only realistic yardstick in our disciplines. From this standpoint we hold that a cultural approach to comparative politics can offer a scientific method with which to meet the challenge of providing credible accounts of contrasting processes in different parts of the world.

By 'scientific' we mean here simply a systematic methodology that can be applied to widely divergent cases, in different areas, and which enables the analyst to offer plausible explanations of singularities and commonalities. It is within this context that we advocate a method based on thinking inductively, rather than deductively.[9] As will be obvious from the discussion below, the merit of such an approach lies in its practical utility, and not in its intrinsic theoretical superiority.

---

[5] For a discussion of some of these issues related to causal and interpretative approaches, see M. Martin and L. McIntyre (eds), 1994, *Readings in the Philosophy of Social Science.*

[6] And even less to apply the test of 'falsifiability'. On this key issue, see K. Popper, 1965, *Conjectures and Refutations.*

[7] For example, the supposition that urbanisation in and of itself reduces ascriptive ties, based on the experience of the industrialised West, turns out to be wrong in Africa.

[8] See here Z. Bauman, 1978, *Hermeneutics and Social Science.*

[9] There is of course a substantial body of work debating the merits of inductive and deductive methods in the social sciences, to which we cannot refer here. Most of this debate took place in the United States in the 1950s and cannot be dissociated from the political context of the time—that is the trauma of totalitarianism in Europe and the ambition to create a 'scientific' (anti-Marxist) social science. For a classic statement against 'inductivism'—conceived in the narrowest possible form—see C. Hempel 1966, *Philosophy of Natural Science*, pp. 11–12. For a useful survey of some of the important issues related to this debate, see M. Hammerseley, 1992, *Social Research.*

However, it is a method that seeks to uphold the standards of scientific enquiry whilst accommodating the fact that the world of human action is not amenable to simple testable replication.[10]

THE TERRAIN

The primary, and perhaps most difficult, task of the comparativist is to identify what we call the terrain of research.[11] The choice of questions and case studies must be appropriate. Only meaningful comparisons can yield meaningful insights. For this reason we would argue that the very first requirement of an inductive method is to verify systematically the plausibility of the comparisons being envisaged. We explain in the sections that follow how this can be done in practice. We want here to stress that the only credible justification for comparison ought to be pragmatic: that is, to enable us to understand better what is happening in the world in which we live—and not to demonstrate the pre-eminence of one theory, or school of thought, over another.

Asking real questions in the real world

The first step—asking real questions in the real world—is simply stated, and may even appear facetious, but is in fact not so easily put into practice, and this for three main reasons. The first is that the questions that will most naturally occur are those with which analysts are confronted most directly in their own environment. These are obviously issues that are relevant to the societies in which they live but which may not be so elsewhere. Above and beyond the general, and mostly useless, claim that all problems are in and of themselves important, it is clear that both their salience and implication are contextual. For example, the fact that the issue of 'identity' is presently politically significant in the United States is no indication that such an issue is perceived in the same 'individualist' manner in Calcutta as it is in California.[12] The point is clear: there are no neutral

---

[10] Although we are not in this book offering a systematic account of the meaning of 'scientific' in the social sciences, we are suggesting some of the important features of what such an account would mean for comparative politics.

[11] This section builds on Chapter 5 (i).

[12] See J. Hunter, 1991, *Culture Wars*; W. Michaels, 1995, *Our America*; and M. di Leonardo, 1998, *Exotics at Home*.

questions, but only questions that are more or less germane to the cases under study.

The second is that our expectations of causality, or correlation, are also contextually bound. We are likely to set up a comparison on the basis of an assumed, and sometimes unacknowledged, notion of causation. We often simply take for granted causal relationships, which would need to be examined, or at the very least questioned. Following on from the example given above, we might infer from the situation in the United States that the issue of 'ethnic' identity is associated with social division, especially if we presume that the consequences of ethnicity in Africa, for instance, are similar to those found across the Atlantic.[13] Such supposition would, in our view, simply invalidate any comparison between the two because the contexts are so different as to make a simple contrast devoid of plausible utility. Ethnicity may be a factor in the United States and in Africa, but a cursory examination of the different settings would suggest that what it means is tied to the cultural setting.[14]

The third is that social scientists in the West are prone to what we would call asking pseudo-questions, by which we mean questions with little heuristic pertinence or negligible importance in the real world. It has been suggested, for example, that there is merit in examining the childhood psychological foundations of major revolutionary leaders as a means of ascertaining whether there is a certain psychic predisposition to the act of engaging in subversive activity.[15] Now it may well be that all recognised revolutionaries experienced childhood traumas, but it does not follow from such a banal observation that there is any value in constructing a theory of revolutionary 'animus' on the basis of such subjective and insubstantial speculation.[16] In respect of what a comparative study of revolutions ought to be able to make more transparent, the focus on childhood

[13] On these issues, see Chapter 4.
[14] As this suggests, the very concept of ethnicity is likely to be devoid of analytical value unless it is set within the right historical context. For two contrasting views on this, see J. Lonsdale, 1996, 'Ethnicité morale et tribalisme politique', *Politique Africaine*, 61 (March) and D. Hollinger, 1995, *Postethnic America*.
[15] See here H. Lasswell, 1948, *Power and Personality*; V. Wolfenstein, 1967, *The Revolutionary Personality*; and B. Mazlish, 1976, *The Revolutionary Ascetic*.
[16] See I. Feierband *et al.*, 1972, *Anger, Violence and Politics* and T. Gurr, 1970, *Why Men Rebel*.

psychology (even assuming it could be researched properly) is of little consequence.[17]

Therefore, our injunction to ask real questions in the real world is not in jest. It is a pre-condition to worthwhile comparison. Not all questions are worth asking, especially when the reason for doing so is ideological—as it often was during the Cold War—or intellectualist, that is merely to assert the heuristic superiority of a particular school of thought. For example, the search for a class-based confirmation of a particular phenomenon, such as rural political mobilisation in India and Africa, may or may not be relevant to the problem in question. The approach would need to justify its merit in the specific case studies.[18]

It can safely be said, for instance, that in the case of Africa there has been very little gained, and a great deal obscured, by the application of Marxist, or neo-Marxist, theories to the question of communal polities.[19] For example, there were undoubtedly economic dynamics that contributed to communal conflict in Rwanda, but these were not played out along recognisable class lines. The situation was infinitely more complex and can only be elucidated by taking into account a large number of historical, sociological and cultural—not just economic—factors.[20]

Asking real questions also means focusing attention on credible comparisons, which entails identifying the issues that are significant at the local level. This may appear a blindingly obvious point to make but it is of no little importance. Even a hasty glance at the output produced in the field of comparative politics would show that a vast number of publications are concerned with processes that are of little weight to the people whose behaviour is being investigated. For instance, the present post-modern anxiety about the effects of cultural globalisation is in all likelihood an irrelevance to the nomadic

[17] The best and most convincing such studies of politics and personality from that period are probably E. Erikson, 1958, *Young Man's Luther* and 1969, *Gandhi's Truth.*

[18] For an example of a contextually justified comparison, see P. Hill, 1982, *Dry Grain Farming Families.*

[19] In contrast to what is a sophisticated use of socio-economic theory in B. Berman and J. Lonsdale, 1992, *Unhappy Valley.*

[20] On Rwanda see, *inter alia*, G. Prunier, 1996, *Rwanda 1959–1996.*

peoples of Central Asia who chance to view television.[21] A genuine
desire to understand what they make of the 'culture' conveyed by sat-
ellite would be better fulfilled by studying the many and complex
ways they view a film like *E. T.* or interpret a display of cheerleaders at
an American football game. Whatever it means to them, it is unlikely
to be immediately apparent to, say, a cultural theorist sitting in an Ivy
League campus and working on urban alienation.[22]

Finally, attending to the real world is a reminder to comparativists
that their work is influenced by, and may in turn influence, perceptions and attitudes vis-à-vis other peoples, communities and countries. The scientific ambition, which political scientists entertain, can
easily extend to the belief that they are able to be objective, to detach
themselves from the circumstances in which they find themselves.
But this is illusory. A cultural approach is one that is also predicated
on the need to explain how our work makes sense in our own environment. The outcome of our travails can only meet the test of plausibility within the perspective of the here and now. It is what best
explains a comparative investigation in the circumstances within
which the work is presented to the wider public.

For example, Fukuyama's *The End of History and the Last Man* and
Huntington's *The Clash of Civilizations and the Remaking of World
Order* are self-evidently products of the post-Cold War American
perceptions of the world. The one argues that the age of liberal
electoral democracy has now finally arrived. The other has come to
the conclusion that what most threatens world order is the rise of
fundamentalist Islam. At the same time such books obviously
impinge on the way Americans, and others for that matter, may now
perceive international relations, with palpable consequences for the
ways in which Western policy makers will envision the conduct of
foreign policy in the years to come.[23]

---

[21] For a useful discussion, see P. Rosenau, 1992, *Post-Modernism and the Social
Sciences*.
[22] For an influential post-modern view on these questions, which differs from ours,
see A. Appadurai, 1997, *Modernity at Large*.
[23] Equally Huntington's latest volume, on immigration into the United States,
responds to a real question but at the same time will inevitably help to re-set the
agenda. See S. Huntington, 2004, *Who are We? The challenges to America's National
Identity*.

Understanding the appropriate contexts

Once real questions have been identified, and the choice of applicable cases made, much preliminary work still remains to be done before any comparative scrutiny can be undertaken. Indeed, the most potent hazards in our discipline—above and beyond the widespread resort to theoretical *a priori*—is to seek out 'data' in haste.[24] As discussed, comparativists tend drastically to narrow the range of evidence they consider, on the grounds that it must be analogous across borders. Accordingly there is a tendency to underestimate the difficulty of gathering material that will serve to answer the questions asked. This has less to do with the dearth of data available than with the more complex issue of which facts it is relevant to examine and why.[25] Are statistics, for instance, to be relied upon in a comparison of the political impact of taxation in countries like Norway, Angola and Pakistan? Probably not, as in the last two countries, taxation is too contentious an issue and the statistical service too feeble to provide any kind of reliable guide on this question.

Furthermore it is not merely the question of data that is at stake.[26] Our argument is that the quality of comparative analysis depends on the extent to which the questions asked have, in each case, been formulated within a framework of research that will most likely yield enlightening results.[27] This is more complex than merely translating a standard questionnaire into the local language. At the very least it requires the systematic assessment of the validity of the proposed analytical enquiry in light of the information available about the particular polities under study. This may well result in quite considerable changes to the original research plan, which could involve recasting the questions asked. So, to continue the above example, it may well be that achieving insight into the relationship between taxation and politics in Angola and Pakistan requires an approach that deliberately eschews any overt reference to that link.

[24] On this question, see C. Marsh, 1988, *Exploring Data* and D. Silverman, 1993, *Interpreting Qualitative Data.*

[25] For a summary of the pitfalls of comparative methods, see D. Marsh and G. Stoker, 1995, *Theory and Methods in Political Science*, Chapter 12.

[26] For a systematic survey of research methods, see here E. Scarbrough and E. Tannenbaum (eds), 1998, *Research Strategies in the Social Sciences.*

[27] For a standard treatment of comparative methods, see R. Hague *et al.*, 1998, *Comparative Government and Politics.*

Consequently, such cautious reappraisal of the relevance of the research questions to the terrain depends on an acute understanding of the appropriate settings within which the analysis is to be deployed. A cultural approach to comparative politics, therefore, advocates a two-step research methodology. The first—asking real questions—must go hand in hand with an in-depth study of the individual cases selected for examination. Although it would be unrealistic to think that comparativists could ever be in a position to undertake the type of local investigation achieved by anthropologists, we would still contend that what is required does involve a large amount of historical and anthropological type research. To limit enquiry to narrowly defined political questions is artificially to erect a barrier between a realm of human agency that, in practice, can never be dissociated from the others—as is obvious to us once we start reflecting on the intricacies of our own milieu, which we understand 'instinctively'.

Political scientists may be resistant to this approach, if only because they often aim to emulate the 'hard' sciences, where investigative progress is very largely predicated upon the ability to narrow down the research terrain and to limit as much as possible the number of variables under study.[28] However, in our field a 'scientific' approach entails the opposite, as it were, that is the need to widen the scope of research in order to establish the relevant links between a large number of putative variables, many of which outside the narrow confines of politics. In other words, being a good political scientist demands an approach that is distinct from that of the physical scientist. Although this may appear paradoxical to some of our colleagues, we would argue that being 'scientific' is in reality (as opposed to myth) to adapt methodology to the requirements of the research terrain with which one is confronted.[29]

It is of course true that political scientists cannot be expected to acquire systematic knowledge of a large number of countries before they undertake comparisons. However, that is not what is demanded. What is needed is the ability to understand the appropriate contexts—meaning here to explore a wide range of possible causal links

---

[28] For a good introduction to research methods in this respect, see here F. Devine and S. Heath, 1999, *Sociological Research Methods in Context*.

[29] See here Chapter 3.

across society, so as better to shed light on political questions[30] or even to cease seeking causality if it should be at the expense of analytical clarity. A cultural approach would stipulate in this regard that the researcher must acquire such information as is necessary in order to begin to understand how the peoples concerned make sense of the issues under study.

This requirement—testing our 'hunches' against what the people concerned think matters most—is the key to explaining how an inductive approach need not be the endless quest for all relevant facts, as critics of this method would argue. Hence, from our point of view, it is patently useless to seek to assess the relevance of particular 'variables' within a given setting before appreciating what their significance might be within the context in which the research is taking place. For instance, research into the link between religion and politics in Germany and Afghanistan would be meaningless if confined, for instance, to 'religious parties', for the simple reason that to compare a European Christian democratic party and an Afghani Islamist party is quite simply not to compare like with like—as becomes immediately obvious when the question is set within what we call the appropriate context.

The point here is not that the comparativist needs simultaneously to take into account the widest possible range of information— although a good appreciation of history is strongly advisable. It is that she must take the trouble to explore the contexts within which it is plausible to ask the questions being addressed. Such an approach is not mysterious. It entails nothing more than the study of those aspects of society that are most relevant to the enquiry and a willingness to reconsider the original questions, should the material so uncovered cast doubts about the feasibility or modalities of the research agenda. To conclude our example, then, a study of religious parties in Germany and Afghanistan would in fact be quite arduous for a West European specialist, for the simple reason that it would entail a good understanding of Islam and of the recent evolution of Islamism in South and Central Asia, the Middle East as well as Western Europe. It would also require a very keen ability to assess the main causes of political change, and stagnation, in these different parts

---

[30] For some relevant considerations here on what an 'anthropological' method entails, see M. Abélès and H.-P. Jendy (eds), 1997, *Anthropologie du politique*.

of the world—in which, at a minimum, the meaning of religious virtue and political sagacity are in no way similar.

Marking out the significant boundaries

Once questions are identified and contexts clarified it becomes essential to identify boundaries—by which we mean both to circumscribe the questions under study and ascertain the contours of the comparative investigation. This often appears misleadingly simple, though it always turns out to be critical. The topology of the topic selected for research is not a mere piece of information. The mapping out of the research terrain and the outlining of its edges are integral features of the analytical process. Artificially narrowing down the reach of a question or, alternatively, leaving vague its critical limits are 'scientific' choices that impact directly on the quality and significance of the research outcome. Marking out analytical boundaries is thus an integral part of any methodology, even when it is not acknowledged, or only done by default.[31]

What appears merely to be a somewhat technical issue turns out to be a consequential methodological question, which deserves serious consideration. Practitioners of comparative politics often operate on the basis of (largely unrecognised) assumptions in this respect—a bias that seriously mars the validity of the conclusions they reach. In this instance, as ever, the failure to make clear the analytical postulates reflects a lack of awareness of the extent to which social science methodology is influenced by the historical, intellectual and cultural environment in which we live. We must be aware of how present circumstances may influence us. For instance, it is undoubtedly the case that the type of research carried out today into Islam is driven by concerns about fundamentalism, both in the West and elsewhere, rather than by an interest in, say, comparative theology.

A cultural approach pays especial attention to this question because it involves a complex methodological reflection on the factors that may affect the plausibility of comparative inferences. It entails an explicit consideration both of the cultural parameters of the framework used by the analyst and of the cultural constraints placed

---

[31] For a sophisticated and systematic discussion of comparative politics in this respect, see B. Badie and G. Hermet, 1990, *Politique comparée.*

on research. For instance, and returning yet again to issues of identity, it would be important to note whether an Africanist engaged in the study of ethnicity in Africa came to this question either from the standpoint of being an African-American or of being particularly interested in, say, Diaspora Studies. This would help to make clear why the boundaries of the terrain—here ethnicity—might have been extended to include concern with the questions of identity, region and race well beyond the confines of the African continent. Clearly such methodological issues are of relevance to the analytical merit of comparative research on race and/or ethnicity.[32]

More broadly, therefore, our methodology demands that comparativists spell out clearly the limits of their areas of investigation, explaining in the process what are their primary analytical concerns. It is important to give reasons for the choices made, and to show that these are in consonance with the overall aim of the comparative ambition: to pursue an example discussed above, why privilege the study of the explicit dogma of religious organisations (say, 'Jihad') over the examination of the membership of political parties that are influenced by a religious 'ideology'. Or, to take another example already discussed, it might appear obvious that political scientists should concern themselves with the studies of elections. However, as hinted before, there may well be cases in which a focus on elections would be at the expense of understanding, for instance, the actual (as opposed to supposed) source of the legitimacy of African political élites.

On the other hand, it is equally important to delineate the analytical boundaries—that is, account for the choice of the investigative instruments being used. Here there is a need to justify the critical angle(s) selected in order to achieve the comparative objectives of the proposed research. Why go for a sociological survey rather than participant observation? Why assume economic rationality in political calculations? Why privilege an approach based on extensive questionnaires rather than the study of 'grey' literature? Such questions are at the heart of any comparative analysis. The 'scientific' obligations of our work demand of us that we account explicitly for the congruence between our analytical tools and the terrain as we have demarcated it. Such tools are in no way neutral and their use imparts analytical constraints on the comparison we seek to make.

[32] See here M. Banton, 1997, *Ethnic and Racial Consciousness.*

Our argument, which will be recast at the end of the volume, is that the fruitful practice of our discipline requires the aptitude to be eclectic in the selection of the conceptual frameworks that are best suited to the comparative agenda. It is the choice of the questions, the understanding of the contexts and the marking out of the analytical boundaries—rather than any ideological or disciplinary imperative—that ought to determine our work's theoretical underpinning. This conclusion does in some sense undermine the very basis of comparative politics, as it has developed since its inception in the 1950s, bound as it was with a certain notion of what a political 'science' should be. However, leaving aside any nostalgia for things past, we would argue that a more scientific approach to comparative analysis should follow a harder calculation of the heuristic value of the various theories available to our discipline.[33]

THE ANALYSIS

For expository purposes, we have in this chapter separated out the discussion of terrain and analysis. However, in reality they ought to be approached simultaneously, the one informing the other. Indeed, a key feature of our method is that terrain and theory must, as it were, be in harmony. Nevertheless, in practice comparativists carry out research first and analyse their data at a later stage. So that, whilst meaningful fieldwork is only feasible when the analytical framework is clear, the two stages are usually distinct, both in nature and in time sequence. Furthermore some comparativists may be skilled in one and not the other. The aim of this section is to discuss in some detail what comparative analysis entails, if it is to achieve its scientific ambition—that is, meet the test of plausibility, of which the primary characteristic is that it ought to advance our understanding of the differences and similarities between the cases under study.[34]

In this respect perhaps the single most important feature of analysis within a cultural approach is the manner in which the validity of concepts and theories is constantly tested against the limits of reality.

---

[33] This entails a more catholic attitude to what constitutes a valid methodology—an attitude that is the core of our cultural approach.

[34] For a useful overview of some of these issues, see A. Stepan, 2001, *Arguing Comparative Politics*.

In other words, it is not enough to declare, once and for all, that the selected conceptual framework is the most appropriate. It is also essential to question at every step of the analytical process whether the use of the chosen concepts and the deployment of the preferred theories are heuristically valuable.[35] Again, terrain drives analysis. In the physical sciences the confirmation of a theory's primacy is crucial as it provides the instrument with which to advance research. In the social sciences, however, the situation is different, since there patently cannot be a 'single' theory of human agency.

Deploying relevant concepts

The conceptual armoury in comparative politics is vast, but it draws principally from two types of sources.[36] The first derives from social and economic theories; that is, from the attempt to hypothesise the world around us, which is most developed in sociology and economics. The second stems from the empirical observation of society, past and present, which is best represented by the disciplines of history and anthropology.[37] The former seeks to advance a general theory of human behaviour, either in the social or economic sphere, and endeavours to refine the concepts that will most convincingly account for observable facts. The latter tries above all to report what it deems to be observable reality, either today or in earlier periods. Here the emphasis is primarily on clarity of exposition, even if all empirical statements are of necessity based on some conceptual notion of what reality is/was like.

Although the contrast between the two can easily be overdrawn, there are real differences within our discipline between those who favour one approach over the other. The first maintain that it is crucial to define clear and operational concepts, which can be applied to a wide range of case studies. Only in this way is it possible to develop an 'objective' comparative framework, enabling us to assess

[35] A scientific approach does not entail the consistent application of a single theoretical framework, as it inevitably does in the physical sciences, but the recourse to the concepts and theories that are most likely to shed light on the comparative questions.

[36] For an alternative view, see M. Needler, 1991, *The Concepts of Comparative Politics.*

[37] Of course, there is some degree of overlapping between these two genealogies, but on the whole it is possible to discern a clear distinction between their efforts at conceptualisation.

the relevant differences between various settings.[38] For such scholars concepts derive from theories of socio-political agency and change, which hold true regardless of the particulars of the local circumstances: an election is an election, wherever and whenever.

The second consider that local specificities can only be meaningfully expressed by means of notions that are sensitive to the particular milieu. Drawn primarily from area or period specialists, such scholars seek above all to be accurate in their description and faithful in the rendering of the dynamics they study. For them it may mean providing a new or distinct concept that can satisfactorily explain what they observe locally. For example, an election in an Islamic community is not a poll—that is the mathematical aggregation of votes cast—but an expression of the will of the *umma*, that is, a way of expressing affiliation to a particular community.[39]

The choice of approach obviously has a direct impact on the type of analysis offered. In the first case there is indeed a certain consistency of explanation, since the different case studies are all examined by means of the same conceptual tools. On the other hand, there is very little sense of how local dynamics influence the processes under examination. In a multiparty election individuals express a party preference and hence register a political opinion. Yet it is not clear why they do so and, especially, what it means to them. In the second there is evidently greater discrimination in the explanation provided of individual situations. Here we are provided with an explanation of the local perception of a multiparty poll, offering an account of the electoral choices made. But it could be argued that we are left with fewer means to assess whether multiparty elections mark the 'democratisation' of the polity in question.[40]

---

[38] For a classic statement of the dilemmas involved, see G. Myrdal, 1970, *Objectivity in Social Science*.

[39] The notion of the will of the *umma* is somewhat similar, though not identical to, Rousseau's *general will*. For a useful comparison between early and modern Islamic political concepts, see E. Rosenthal, 1958, *Political Thought in Medieval Islam* and H. Enayet, 1982, *Modern Islamic Political Thought*. On the concept of the *umma* in relation to the General Will, see F. Shaikh, 1989, *Community and Consensus in Islam*, pp. 13–23.

[40] See the example of Africa here: L. Diamond and F. Plattner (eds), 1999, *Democratization in Africa*.

The cultural approach we propose provides a way out of this dicho-tomous, not to say schizophrenic, heritage. Our argument is that we need not, indeed ought not, choose between the two, but that we should find a way of reconciling their rationale. As intimated, a sci-entific method in comparative politics entails selecting wisely between concepts and theories, so as to advance the understanding of the empirical reality with which we are concerned. We shall discuss theories in the next section. We want here to come to grips with the thorny issue of concept use in comparison and to explain how an inductive process can help refine analysis. This is crucial since without an adequate deployment of concepts it is impossible to evolve a com-parison that generates added value, above and beyond the in-depth study of sundry cases. Concepts provide the common lexicon, with which the comparativist analyst can make a meaningful statement about political agency and processes.[41]

The key to our approach lies in the quality of the 'fit' between the universal connotations of a political concept and the unique local texture of the question being investigated. The closeness of this 'fit' is conditioned by three factors. One, the concept must be 'first-order', by which is meant that it refers to the most general characterisation of a given phenomenon. Two, the concept must be shown, rather than assumed, to be relevant to the cases selected for comparison. Three, the concept ought to be used flexibly, or creatively, so that it is adapted to the local circumstances: used as an instrument to reveal the logic of a given process in its own specific setting, rather than forced into a preconceived mould. We discuss each in turn.

A 'first-order' concept is one that is applicable to the largest possi-ble range of cases, including our own society. It excludes, therefore, all *sui generis* or particularistic notions that claim to reflect the distinc-tiveness of a given environment. But it also excludes what is some-times called 'conceptual stretching', which results in such broad notions as to make them analytically meaningless.[42] There is no need for the invention of concepts to reflect the supposed uniqueness of a

---

[41] This is why concepts are both useful and limited. For an appreciation of this question, see the Conclusion.

[42] On 'conceptual stretching' see G. Sartori, 1970, 'Concept Misinformation in Comparative Politics', *American Political Science Review*, 64 (December). For a discussion of how the concept of the State has been unduly 'stretched', see Chapter 9.

particular terrain. Such, indeed, are not concepts in a heuristically meaningful sense, since they merely act as paraphrases. On the other hand, as clearly no concept in the social sciences can have consistently homogeneous universal application, the identification of 'first-order' notions is not an endless quest for some kind of conceptual 'holy Grail'. We are not interested in conceptual purity for its own sake. A 'first-order' notion—such as power or legitimacy—is one that can help to explain how the people concerned make sense of politics *and* can plausibly be applied to most cases, ranging from advanced industrial societies to isolated rural communities in remote areas of the world. The point here is not to suggest that there is a hierarchy of such concepts, but simply that analysts should make clear how the notions they use are first-order, in the sense defined above.

The second factor follows quite logically from the first: concepts must be shown to be relevant. This means that comparative analysts must provide a justification for the use of particular notions, explaining the basis upon which they have made their choice. The important aspect of our method in this respect is that there can be no *a priori* stance, no general position, when it comes to the selection of concepts. Here the only test is whether they serve a valuable explanatory service; otherwise they are surplus to requirement. To return to an earlier example, the use of the notion of 'democracy' in the present circumstances of Africa is more likely to confuse than clarify our understanding of either the ways in which power is actually exercised or of the contemporary configuration of politics on the continent.[43] Comparative analysis is best served, therefore, by a resolutely pragmatic approach to conceptualisation.

The final feature of our method requires that concepts be deployed creatively. Whilst we naturally advocate the clearest possible definition of the notions used, we urge flexibility in the analysis. Here it is simplest to explain what we mean with reference to an example. It is relatively easy to provide a general characterization of political legitimacy. The difficulty lies in the application of the concept to particular cases. The form in which people articulate their understanding of that notion may be difficult to reconcile with the view we form of what it means, at least in our own societies. We may need to widen the scope of our research, to deepen our interpretation of

---

[43] See M. Bratton and N. Van de Walle, 1997, *Democratic Experiments in Africa*.

what makes sense locally, in order to come to terms with the way(s) in which legitimacy is expressed or embodied. This is where we need to be creatively open to the analysis of the local material. The quality of insight we can generate will ultimately depend on our capacity to translate the indigenous notion of legitimacy into one that can usefully be compared across borders.

Applying pertinent theories

Comparative politics attempts not merely to describe but also to explain.[44] The merit of interpretation hinges on the plausibility of the correlations, or causalities, revealed in the analysis.[45] In this respect deploying relevant concepts is merely a first step. The quality of the insights ultimately depends on the application of theory, since it is indeed theory that binds together the way(s) in which concepts are employed and advances comprehension of the significance of the comparisons in question. Scrutiny rests on concepts. Analysis, for its part, derives from the adroit handling of theory, or theories.

We gave reasons in Part I for the view that there is no longer any place in political science for grand theory.[46] Indeed, few comparativists today, with the major exception of rational choice theorists and Marxists, would subscribe to a single analytical framework encompassing the political evolution of all societies. Yet our discipline is still largely premised on the assumption that a 'scientific' approach requires an overarching theoretical architecture, a systemic explanatory grid binding the various socio-economic and political dynamics that characterise a given polity. By now it will be clear that we reject this vision of a 'hard' political science and advocate instead an approach that is sensitively attuned to the material with which we work: that is, human beings.

A cultural approach to comparative politics holds that the scientific test of plausibility is best met by what we call theoretical eclecticism.[47] Thinking inductively, as we see it, means anchoring analysis

---

[44] For a standard introduction to the question of explanation, see G. Peters, 1998, *Comparative Politics*.

[45] For one particular view of the comparative exercise, see C. Ragin, 1987, *The Comparative Method*.

[46] See Chapter 1.

[47] We present a systematic defence of this method in the Conclusion, pp. 317 ff.

in relevant theories—that is, making judicious choices as to which theory is applicable to which comparative research question. Such a contention is often unpalatable to political scientists, who tend to consider theoretical consistency as an asset. For this reason it is essential at this stage to bring together the strands of our argument in respect of what we consider to be a scientific method in our discipline.[48] Building on what we have argued so far, we would suggest that theory in the social sciences should be treated nimbly, lest it overdetermine analysis. By nimbly, we mean that theoretical preference should at all times be informed by empirical reality, since analytical insight is enhanced, rather than diminished, by theoretical eclecticism.

The idea that theoretical inclination should depend on observed facts may at first seem odd. This is because we, in the social sciences, are still prone to thinking in terms of grand(ish) theory.[49] In the physical sciences, which to many practitioners of our discipline continue to represent a model, such a claim would hardly raise any controversy. Scientists as a rule resort to the theory that is most convincingly relevant to the empirical observation they make. The difference is that they tend to work on micro-problems—at least in comparison with social scientists—*and* that they would expect the model they employ to be consistent with an overarching general theory of the physical, chemical or biological world.[50] In the physical world heuristic sharpness requires the ever tighter narrowing down of research focus, whereas in the world of social beings, it demands investigative breadth.

Since insight into human society and social agency depends on making wide-ranging connections, comparativists are compelled to deal with a very large number of complex socio-political, economic and cultural issues. Accordingly they perforce need to have recourse to a variety of theories, if only to address the discrete questions that need elucidation for comparative purposes. The key to theoretical eclecticism is twofold: making clear why, concretely, a particular theory is preferred to another *and* providing an explanation as to how

---

[48] For a contrasting view, see H. Weisberg (ed.), 1986, *Political Science.*

[49] For a useful historical background, see Q. Skinner (ed.), 1985, *The Return of Grand Theory.*

[50] Until such time as the working theory is undermined or overturned. See here T. Kuhn, 1962, *Structure of Scientific Revolution.*

to link the various theories employed. A cultural approach, therefore, is not one that privileges a culturalist theory of social agency and change. On the contrary, it is one that remains open as to which theory might make most analytical sense. Ours is thus not a method that is theoretically prescriptive, as would be an essentialist interpretation of the world. It is instead one that is theoretically open ended—with one aim only: to use comparative analysis as a means of providing explanatory added value.

We shall offer in Part IV a systematic application of such an approach. Here, and by way of illustration, we should like to show how we applied this method in our previous study on Africa. The project aimed to explain how power is exercised and how politics function on the continent. The conclusion we drew from our empirical research in a number of countries was that most existing conceptual frameworks were ill suited to the analysis of what was actually happening in these societies, and this for two main reasons. The first was that they applied theories that were not appropriate to the terrain. The second was that they failed to use analytical instruments that were relevant to contemporary African political realities.

Having redefined the terrain of enquiry so as to encompass a large number of ostensibly non-political actors and processes, we drew up a list of 'first-order' concepts with which to develop an analysis of power in Africa. We also realised that the only way of elucidating political questions on the continent was to bring to bear on our work evidence from other social and human sciences—such as history, sociology, anthropology, economics as well as the study of literature and religious beliefs. The book was thus composed of three parts: one each on political, social and economic issues. Each centred on what empirical observation suggested were the key issues affecting the complexion and conduct of politics on the continent. In each section we had recourse to a number of distinct, though related, theories in order to elucidate specific questions, the import of which had been impressed upon us by their salience in the real world.

The discussion on belief, entitled 'The Taming of the Irrational', alluded to theories on religion and development as well as to the anthropology of the occult, in order to explain why it is that today on the continent the world of the 'invisible', which we in the West wrongly construe as 'irrational', continues to have such decisive political influence.[51] The debate on Africa's economic weakness, entitled 'The Bounties of Dependence', had recourse to theories of economic rationality and of political calculus (or game theory), to account for the evident paradox that the political élite have hitherto sought ways of maintaining dependence rather than encouraging economic development.[52] In both instances our choice was guided by the power of the evidence and the search for the conceptual framework that would most plausibly elucidate the political issues thrown up so vividly by our comparative study of postcolonial Black Africa. The book ended by bringing together the theories employed in the nine chapters to suggest a new paradigm of politics in Africa.

Developing comparative insights

An inductive method is for us a means of overcoming one of the most crippling limitations of politics as it is currently practiced: the commitment to the notion that a 'scientific' method can only derive insight from the rigorous testing of hypotheses. The problem with this argument is not just with the concept of testing, as was discussed before. It is also with the idea that it is possible to evolve hypotheses to apply across the board to Western and non-Western countries drawn simply from the experience of our own industrially advanced societies. From our viewpoint this is not just impossible but also undesirable, as it is based on the premise of a single form of social and human development that cannot be sustained. The setting up of comparisons between widely divergent polities can only generate genuine insight if the methodology itself is able to take into account their distinct history and their wide socio-economic and cultural differences without forcing them into an artificial, and ultimately heuristically sterile, mould.

The merit of thinking inductively is that it makes it possible to build up comparative analysis cumulatively, as it were.[53] A cultural approach suggests that the best technique to develop comparative insight is to evolve a methodology that relates the larger explanatory

---

[51] P. Chabal and J.-P. Daloz, 1999, *Africa Works*, Chapter 5.

[52] Ibid., Chapter 8.

[53] In the conclusion of *Africa Works*, we proposed a general account of politics in Africa as a way of combining the separate strands of the analysis developed in the various chapters.

picture with the resolution of analytically 'intermediate' problems. What this means is that in this respect 'induction' entails what might be called a 'piecemeal' approach to comparison, one that adds layer upon layer of insight, with a view to make better sense of the similarities and singularities uncovered by the research. The fitting of the various explanatory pieces of the overall comparative question, unlike that of a puzzle, is not pre-determined or unique. There are more or less plausible ways of bringing together the diverse elements under comparison into one suggestive explication.[54]

Developing comparative insights in political science is thus not akin to what is seen as 'paradigm shift' in the history of the physical sciences—that is, the sudden quantum leap from one type of theoretical framework to another wholly distinct one.[55] The injunction to think inductively is meant precisely to tailor analysis to the realities of the terrains with which political comparativists deal. Elucidation here entails merely a more plausible explanation than those hitherto available, not an entirely new way of tackling the question. It also means, and that is a critical aspect of social science generally, evolving an account that makes sense within the contemporary context in which we live. Just as there can be no 'definitive' account of a given historical event, there can be no 'definitive' analysis of a particular political phenomenon or process. The best that the historian or the social scientist can aim to offer is an interpretation that is meaningful to the contemporary audience for which they write.[56] Whilst this point is now generally accepted in respect of history, there is still great reluctance to recognise that it applies equally well to the social sciences—and this, as we have pointed out, is very largely due to the 'scientific' pretensions of its practitioners.[57]

But if the testing of hypotheses is not the measure of the achievement of comparative politics, how are we to know when we have developed comparative insights? Without an objective criterion with which to assess the validity of analysis, is there not a risk that a cultural

---

[54] See here R. Chilcote, 1994, *Theories of Comparative Politics*.

[55] On paradigm and paradigmatic shift, see T. Kuhn, 1962, *Structure of Scientific Revolution* and G. Gutting (ed.), 1980, *Paradigms and Revolutions*.

[56] For a useful discussion of how history is informed by theory, see P. Burke, 1992, *History and Social Theory*.

[57] On one approach to history, see R. Collingwood, 1993, *The Idea of History*.

approach will make spurious causal connections? How can the test of plausibility be met merely by the accretion of knowledge brought about by an inductive method? The question is pertinent and merits attention. The charge levelled against the use of culture in the social sciences is that explanation is dependent on the analyst's perception of factors, which to all intents and purposes are subjective. This critique of a cultural approach is valid within the narrow confines of a theory that aims to apply in the social sciences the methodology of the physical sciences—for which there is indeed a single answer to the hypothesis and a ready means of testing its validity.

However, a cultural approach is one that seeks to advance understanding by making plain at every stage of the analysis why the question under study is handled, conceptually and theoretically, as it is. Let us illustrate with reference to an earlier example. When comparing Western and Muslim societies comparativists often propose two broad interpretations. The first is to state that Islam is, as Christianity was in the West, only relevant to politics so long as society has not developed sufficiently to become secular. In this view the reason why Muslim polities are so resolutely hostile to democracy is that they are still politically 'under-developed'. The second is to suggest, as Huntington most recently did, and as assorted fundamentalists believe, that faith in Islam constitutes a separate 'civilisation', an entire way of life distinct from that of the West. No matter how economically advanced such societies are they will continue to operate on the basis of socio-political norms that are, and will forever be, divergent from those of present day democracies. The difficulty, which some specialists of Islam have tackled successfully, is to provide an account of contemporary Muslim politics that eschews such artificial dichotomy.[58]

A cultural method would consist in setting up a plausible means of comparing Muslim and non-Muslim societies. Rather than juxtaposing polities merely on the grounds of religion, we would want to examine various aspects of political agency between countries that are in other respects relatively similar: West African Muslim, or Middle Eastern, or Gulf, or Central Asian countries. There are obviously vast differences between these polities both within a single group and across regions. As a result it would only be possible to build up a picture of what an 'Islamic society' entails, or even whether there is

[58] One such approach is B. Badie, 1983, *Culture et Politique* and 1986, *Les deux Etats*.

such a thing, by exploring comparatively a series of intermediate, or middle level, questions on various aspects of social, economic and cultural life.

Such an exercise would likely reveal that it is simply not possible to speak of a single Muslim way of life; and that questions about the exercise of power in these societies hinge on a wide range of other factors, most of which can only be understood historically and within the relevant cultural context. An explanation in terms of 'civilisation' would, for example, fail to account for the trajectory of a country like Turkey—at once Muslim and secular. Nor would it illuminate the question of Muslim politics in Western countries, where reference to religion has often more to do with issues of identity than with faith.[59] In sum, attempts at testing hypotheses about Muslim societies based on the recent experience of those countries where fundamentalism has made inroads would merely narrow down the range of issues which an understanding of the political inclinations of different Muslims in different settings would bring to light.

Thinking inductively is not a single key to a simple problem. Nor is it a method set in stone, waiting to be applied, mechanically, to comparative analysis. Rather it is a way of breaking down the work involved in putting together the various strands of any comparison. By linking terrain to analysis in the ways suggested above it becomes possible to fit together a series of explanations, which help to make sense of the processes under examination. The core of our approach in this respect is to apply the test of plausibility at every stage of the exercise—whether in asking questions, understanding contexts or applying theories. Piecemeal as this method undoubtedly is, it is in fact the only scientifically plausible way to deal with the complexities and inconsistencies of the world of humans and societies across the globe.

[59] See O. Roy, 2004, *Globalised Islam*.

8

THINKING SEMIOTICALLY

A cultural approach to comparative politics, such as we favour, ultimately rests on what Geertz called the interpretation of meaning—that is, an explanatory method that draws from the study of what makes sense locally. Of course this type of analysis is not one with which the discipline is familiar, even less comfortable, since it points to an uncommon kind of investigative activity. Thus there is disquiet in the field with research that relies on the discussion of such elusive material as symbols, codes, words or even utterances.[1] The norm is to handle 'harder', if possible statistical or quantitative, data or at least evidence that is not excessively dependent on what might be seen as the researcher's 'subjective', or personal, reading. The idea here—and this attitude has had a very strong influence on our discipline—is to be able to compare like with like, by means of *standardised* procedures of enquiry, such as questionnaires and surveys.

As suggested before, the interpretation of meaning—that is thinking semiotically[2]—implies in practice the 'art of translation', a pursuit more commonly associated with literature and literary theory than with the social sciences. And yet we would argue that it has its place at the heart of comparative politics, since that activity hinges on the ability to make sense of the dynamics of polities with distinct histories and evolving according to processes that demand discrete elu-

---

[1] There is of course a long tradition of political anthropology in which such research is carried out—tradition from which we have learned a great deal. See here, for an introduction to the field, J. Gledhill, 2000, *Power and its Disguises* and, for an older (and rather universalising) approach, G. Balandier, 1967, *Anthropologie politique*.

[2] We stress again that when we use the concept 'semiotic' we do not mean the structuralist theory of signs as it is applied to linguistics but the analysis of meanings within given societies.

cidation. Our understanding of what translation denotes draws on Geertz' stylish formulation, which it is worth citing here again in full:

'Translation'... is not a simple recasting of others' ways of putting things in terms of our own ways of putting them (that is the kind in which things get lost), but displaying the *logic* of their ways of putting them in the locutions of ours; a conception which again brings it rather closer to what a critic does to illumine a poem than what an astronomer does to account for a star.[3]

The key to the method, as should be immediately apparent, consists in being able to 'display the logic' of what others do within our own 'system of meaning'—a clear statement of what is required; and evidence, if evidence were needed, that such an approach is the opposite of what is usually construed as 'culturalism' by those who decry a cultural approach in politics.[4] Translation in this sense is a systematic attempt to avoid the unthinking imposition of our own assumptions upon the material generated by comparative research. Therefore, the interpretation of meaning involves a dual method, as developed below: learning how to read the evidence and developing a method for 'translating' it. In reality the two ought to happen in consonance but are here separated for clarity of exposition.

READING THE EVIDENCE

The question here concerns how to gather and handle the evidence required for comparative analysis. Following on from the previous chapter we would argue that in large measure that aspect of research proceeds inductively in two important ways. The first is that there should be no *a priori* restraint about the type of data gathered. This will depend on local circumstances and will be determined by the appropriate context(s). The second is that the research agenda needs constantly to be revised in light of the preliminary conclusions drawn from the analysis of the data previously gathered. In other words, the search for further evidence is itself influenced by the interpretation of the material already collected.[5] The three sections that follow

---

[3] C. Geertz, 1983, 'Introduction' in C. Geertz, *Local Knowledge*, p. 10 (emphasis added).

[4] Of which one example, within a French tradition of political science that is generally hostile to cultural analysis, is J.-F. Bayart, 1996, *L'illusion identitaire*.

[5] Although this may appear an exceedingly *ad hoc*, or unsystematic method—and

attempt to make clear how to employ this method in respect of the observation of what people say and do.

The connotations of meaning: making sense of what people say

The foundation of an interpretive approach consists in the translation of meaning, as defined above.[6] Studying what people say involves much more than merely recording words, statements, speeches and publications. There is of course a place for this basic type of work, which in any event should form part of the preliminary investigative background.[7] However, a cultural approach endeavours to consider the meaning of utterances much more systematically, and this from two distinct viewpoints.[8] The first relates to the variety of sources used, which could range from overtly political speeches to the use of myths in the national imaginary or the influence of religious symbols. The second has to do with the socio-cultural framework within which such evidence is analysed—meaning here both that different sources must be assessed within their appropriate context and that their elucidation may also require different theoretical approaches. We discuss both in turn.

Our claim in respect of the range of sources is not primarily an argument about extending the type of political evidence—although that remains a sound injunction: the wider the sources, the more sophisticated the research is likely to be. Rather, it is a plea for the examination of the kind of evidence that is politically relevant but does not fall within the ambit of recognisable 'political data'. It might of course be objected that it is a little incautious to ask of political scientists that they give attention to an infinite range of possible data.

---

seen from the standpoint of the approach used in the physical sciences, it could well be—we would argue that it is in fact the only realistically 'scientific' one that can be adopted in an area where the analyst needs above all to be sensitively attuned to the specificities of the polities (s)he seeks to compare.

[6] For one introduction to the problem of translation, the differences between description and analysis as well as the perennially thorny question of the 'emic' versus 'etic' debate in social anthropology, see T. H. Eriksen, 2001, *Small Places Large Issues*, pp. 34–6.

[7] For a presentation of methods in anthropology, see R. Bernard, 1994, *Research Methods in Anthropology*.

[8] For one very influential school of thought on the interpretation of utterances, which we do not apply to our method, see R. Barthes, 1964, *Eléments de Sémiologie*.

Such is plainly not what we imply here. What we have in mind is more straightforward and more practical: comparative analysis ought to be concerned with any material that has some significant bearing on the particular issue(s) being investigated. For instance, as will be shown later, what clothes politicians wear, or the means of transport they use, may be of relevance to the understanding of political representation.[9] Similarly astrology may be a pertinent factor for certain political actors—as is known to be the case in India, where it often has a bearing on important decisions.

This approach involves the acceptance that the analyst is likely to have to consult a different type and range of sources for each separate polity, or society. This may appear problematic to comparative politics theories for two reasons. On the one hand, it strikes at the heart of its methodology, which stresses that valid comparison depends upon the use of similar, or at least comparable, evidence. On the other, it goes against the belief that the 'scientific' validity of the conclusions reached is derived from the fact that comparative analysis is based on the systematic gathering of a given, and pre-established, type of evidence. We acknowledge the challenge that our approach throws at the foundations of our discipline, but we hold to the view that a genuinely 'scientific' comparative study is only possible if every effort has been made to identify the relevant local evidence.[10] And this, we would argue, entails a flexible method when it comes to the consideration of appropriate data.

This can be illustrated with a discussion of a very focused question: how do 'advisers' influence politicians in the United States and Africa. A standard approach to this question would identify those individuals within the close policy circle who matter most, compare the ways in which they seek (directly or indirectly) to counsel their political masters, and attempt to uncover how they do so. A comparison of that nature would be limited. Because the notion of 'political adviser' is derived from one setting—broadly the West—its application to another part of the world would in all likelihood yield results that pointed to a (tautological) convergence in their practice and influence. And indeed, such people are today ubiquitous, performing apparently very similar tasks. From such limited observation

[9] See Chapter 10.
[10] On the meaning of the 'local' here, see Chapter 5, pp. 124 ff.

it might then be concluded that their widespread presence is an indication that political leadership throughout the world is becoming more similar. Which is probably true as far as it goes but is not particularly enlightening. A narrow comparative framework delivers a narrow, and somewhat self-serving, conclusion.

A cultural approach, on the other hand, would start from a broader question, that of influence, and would seek to identify both what 'political advice' entails and what the main sources of political influence were in the different settings under study. Therefore, the key preliminary issue would be to uncover the relevant factors that underpin what is called advice—a concept that carries very different connotations in different societies. We would then want to know how the widest possible range of 'advisers', or 'experts', operated within their own environment. This would reveal that in Africa, for instance, there is a vast array of so-called 'invisible forces'—many of which have to be mediated by those who have access to the occult—which may well have a greater bearing on policy decisions than the besuited and bespectacled masters of spin who surround the president. Hence the relevant comparison for the purpose of assessing the political behaviour of political leaders in these two parts of the world might be, as a sharp-witted anthropologist recently suggested, between the spin-doctors and the witch doctors![11]

Our second line of reasoning is that evidence has to be assessed differently according to context, and that this may well entail the use of different theoretical approaches. This again is anathema to the keepers of orthodoxy in politics and even more particularly to those who work within the perspective of rational choice theory.[12] For them it

---

[11] P. Geschiere, 2003, 'On Witch Doctors and Spin Doctors: the role of 'Experts' in African and American Politics' in P. Pels and B. Meyer, *Magic and Modernity*.

[12] Here we subscribe to what Sahlins says: '[A]s an explanatory account of *culture*, of the specific attributes of cultural phenomena, rational choice economism is the weakest epistemologically and the least substantial—for the same reason that it is the most general and irrefutable. Neoclassical rationality is the absolute zero of cultural theories because it has to give itself the culture, assume as a priori the local system of meanings and values, in order to demonstrate people's rationality. Otherwise how would one know why it is rational for a Trobriander to save his yams for his sister's husband or a Kwakiutl chief to spend everything on a potlatch? As anthropology, rational economizing is tautology.' M. Sahlins, 2000, 'Introduction to Part One' in M. Sahlins, *Culture in Practice*, p. 39.

matters little what people say; what matters is what people do.[13] Even if we assume, as we must, that all people behave 'rationally', the difficult question is to make sense of what rationality means in its local context. To that end it is essential to explain the 'logics' underlying what people do. This requires an understanding of the socio-cultural language they use by means of the appropriate 'translation'.[14] The point here is that such translation is only possible if the utterances concerned are considered within their specific historical and cultural setting. Because the relevant context is bound to be different in each society that task can only be accomplished by means of locally contextualised analysis.[15]

It may appear that such method opens the door to a theoretically incoherent framework, one that consists of an arbitrary mix of conjectures with very little to bind them and no conceivable means of refutation.[16] However, this charge is only valid within a very narrow, and essentially sterile, conception of science. As we have argued, the role of theory is to provide an approach to a research question that is more, rather than less, likely to yield a 'valid' answer. The 'validity' of that answer ought only to be measured by the extent to which it can explain the phenomenon under scrutiny. In comparative politics the test is whether a theoretical/conceptual approach manages both to account for individual cases and to advance our understanding of the political processes at work. We illustrate this point by returning to an example cited in Part II.

We have discussed already why it is unwise to consider statements about 'ethnicity' outside the specific context within which they are uttered. We have also suggested that, because of this, it is simply unre-

[13] The central problem of rational choice approaches is that they only work *ex post facto*: people have done what they have done because it was 'rational' to do so. When the theory is tested in real life, and in real time conditions, it becomes fuzzy: asked before the event what is likely to happen in a given situation the adepts of this theory can usually provide at best tautology—people will do what they will do because it is rational—or vague guesswork.

[14] Understanding in this sense should make it possible to assess why people say things that are not in agreement with what they do.

[15] Description and analysis, as has already been noted, are quite different. To understand utterances within their appropriate context is *not the same* as explaining what these utterances refer to according to the logic underpinning them. Thus the charge that our method means 'going native' does not hold.

[16] Reference here is of course to K. Popper, 1965, *Conjectures and Refutations*.

alistic to suppose that there could be a 'single' theory of ethnicity—
one that could account for the experience of 'group belonging' in all
parts of the world, at all times.[17] Nor is it possible to employ a 'single'
model of how ethnicity may be used politically. Since the very notion
of what we conceptualise as ethnicity is itself open to debate, it stands
to reason that only a culturally informed approach can hope to make
sense of what people say in respect of their sense of identity. Hence, it
may be appropriate to resort to a theory of group psychology and
individualism to explain ethnicity in the United States.[18] At the same
time, it may well be that in Africa, the key to understanding ethnicity
is to approach the question from the more anthropological angle of
notions of self, community morality and the more economic perspective of reciprocity.[19] Hence, the use of contextually relevant
theories helps us to understand not just what is happening in the
United States and Africa but also in which way(s) it is meaningful to
make comparisons about ethnicity.

The intricacies of behaviour: making sense of what people do

Reading the evidence involves more than translating what people say.
What ultimately matters for politics is what people do or, to be more
precise, how power is exercised in reality. On the surface it may
appear simpler to make sense of what people do than what they say.
But this is misleading. Of course acts are superficially more 'readable'
than utterances in the (common sense) way that it seems simple
enough to describe them. However, a moment's reflection makes it
plain that this is not the case: such accounts are in fact eminently subjective, reliant as they are on the origin, bias, skill and interest of the
observer. Observation is not a neutral process; it is contextually
bound.[20]

How would a French political scientist explain a Latino march in
Los Angeles claiming equal rights for Spanish speakers? How would
a Brazilian sociologist describe the annual gathering of Hindus on
the shores of the Ganges? How would a Congolese electoral analyst

---

[17] And in this respect it is debatable how useful the concept is. See the discussion in
Chapter 4, pp. 112.
[18] See D. Hollinger, 1995, *Postethnic America*.
[19] See here P. Chabal and J.-P. Daloz, 1999, *Africa Works*, Chapter 4.
[20] See J. Lofland and L. Lofland, 1985, *Analysing Social Settings*.

account for the writing of graffiti in a Paris 'dormitory' town? All these are significant 'acts', which impinge more or less strongly on the socio-political situation in the countries concerned. And all of them could easily be used to buttress or undermine a particular theory of what politics means in these, and other, settings. For this reason making sense of what people do also entails the interpretation of meaning.

Behaviours, like utterances, are not easily contrasted. It is arduous enough to provide a coherent elucidation of single events, within identifiable polities. It is infinitely more difficult to offer insightful comparisons, even of what may (often superficially) appear to be similar, or equivalent, actions in distinct settings. The point here is not to argue that comparison is impossible, which is the common standpoint of the area specialist, but simply that there is great danger in supposing that it is straightforward. This warning of the complexity of the undertaking is salutary since it helps to focus attention on the perils of over-simplification, not just for comparative analysis, but also for policy making. As we know, the advice offered by political scientists on the basis of crude comparative reasoning can be fateful. Many of the worst errors committed by those countries that, for better or worse, intervene in the domestic affairs of other societies derive from analytical misjudgements. These failings are usually due to an excessively (or wilfully) naïve interpretation of what 'other' people do.

Let us take one seemingly uncomplicated example: a crowd marching and waving banners against the intervention forces in Iraq in August 2003 is, on the face of it, easily understood.[21] As some American commentators see it, Iraqis, who ought to be grateful to the 'coalition of the willing' for their overthrow of Saddam Hussein, are being manipulated by 'foreign elements'. Yet this 'biased' view of what has happened is at the expense of a more searching, and politically more acute, analysis. Is it important to note that the crowds are waving such banners in Najaf, not Kerbala, and that they have been organised by a group supporting a particular Shiite ayatollah, who

---

[21] For one interesting interpretation of the historical background to the errors committed in relation to the post-2003 Iraq crisis, see T. Dodge, 2003, *Inventing Iraq*. For an analysis of recent events in Iraq see T. Dodge and S. Simon (eds), 2003, *Iraq at the Crossroads*.

happens to oppose the Interim Administration set up in Baghdad? Is the point of the march, then, less to protest against the foreign 'infidels' than to give a hint to the would-be political rulers of Iraq that they will have to count with this particular ayatollah? A worthwhile interpretation of this event would at a minimum have to include an assessment of rivalry among Shiites in the Najaf/Kerbala region, an analysis of the key 'religious' edicts issued by respective ayatollahs, a sense of the degree to which they 'represent' the political views of some of the poorest and most disenfranchised urban dwellers, a study in Iraq-Iran relations, and an estimate of the chances that the future Iraqi government will be Islamic, as decreed by Shiite ayatollahs.

What this example shows is that a serious attempt to understand a political event, which could otherwise be neatly fitted into a preconceived notion of 'protest', entails recourse to a number of theoretical viewpoints. In this particular instance there is obviously a need to understand the history of Shiite Islam in the Iran-Iraq region, the background to ayatollah rivalry in the Najaf/Kerbala area, the political ambitions of local leaders, the impact of the Saddam Hussein regime upon Islam, as well as the sociology of poverty and politics in these two important Shiite cities.[22] Only then would it be possible to suggest that there are strong similarities between these events and those that lay behind the Iranian revolution or, perhaps, the political success of Islamist groups in Algeria in 1991. The mere fact that poor and disenfranchised urban dwellers are marching behind the banners of a local ayatollah does not otherwise provide evidence enough that a comparison between Iraq, Iran and Algeria is apposite. Even less would it warrant an interpretation of current Iraqi politics as part of a pan-Islamic movement in the region.

On a different register, people in some European Union countries demonstrate against joining the Euro currency. Why? On the face of it, they would seem to be unconvinced, or worried, about the economic effects of losing control over monetary policy. They worry about the European Central Bank. They think that their standard of living will fall. Yet a more discriminating study of the reasons for such

---

[22] For one useful historical survey of the recent past, see M. Farouk-Sluglett and P. Sluglett, 1990, *Iraq Since 1958*. For an account of the earlier period, see Haj, S., 1997, *The Making of Iraq, 1900–1963*. For a more complete history, see C. Tripp, 2000, *A History of Iraq*.

behaviour would quickly reveal a large number of other, decidedly non-economic, factors ranging from history to psychology. In Denmark these derive in part from suspicion about German power and influence. In Sweden they have to do with a deep sense of the uniqueness of the Swedish model of social democracy, which many think would be threatened by European economic policies. In Britain there is longstanding opposition to the concept of European integration, deep suspicion of France's role in the EU and a widespread notion that relinquishing Sterling would constitute a blow to national identity. Popular behaviour, by way of voting and protesting against the EU currency, can only be properly interpreted by taking into account the extent to which local factors affect assumptions about how people assess the supposed 'economic' merit of further monetary integration.

The point is clear: making sense of what people do is intricate. Acts do not speak; they have to be interpreted. Translating what they mean into a language that enables comparison is only possible if great care is taken to explain their actions in terms that make sense to those who perform them. It is for the comparativists to adapt their theoretical framework to that requirement and not for the facts to be fitted into a pre-set conceptual approach designed to make comparative analysis easier. An assessment of apparently similar, or seemingly equivalent, political acts is only valid if the interpretation of each of those discrete acts meets the test of plausibility. This entails making good sense of the evidence.

The complexities of observation: making sense of the evidence

The third area of interpretation that matters has to do with the actual reading of the data. It is, as we have suggested, necessary to explain what people say and do in terms that take account of the appropriate context, that is to explain utterances and acts in ways that make sense to those concerned. To that end, the analyst needs to eschew any explanation based on what has often been referred to as 'false consciousness', by which it is usually meant that individuals may be thinking thoughts or doing things they do not understand but for which there is a good explanation, which significant outside observers are able to provide. This analytical, or rather political, stance is antithetical to a cultural approach, such as ours, which seeks to build explanation on the basis of how those involved account for their own lives. In the same vein, therefore, we believe that the interpretation of the evidence is a far more complicated task than is usually credited by political scientists, who are prone to thinking that their professional training enables them readily to explicate what others think or do.

Political scientists and sociologists use data collection techniques—such as statistics, polls and surveys—which they consider reliable because they are quantitative and replicable. Social anthropologists, on the other hand, resort largely to participant observation, from which they draw much of their evidence, because they believe that only immersion into a particular society will yield the contextual information they require. Historians, for their part, favour written over oral sources, since they believe those to be both more objective and more easily subject to cross checking.[23] In all these instances, the practitioners of the disciplines concerned rely on what they consider to be safe, tried and tested, research instruments. However, a cultural approach makes greater demands in that it considers that no method used to gather evidence is *ipso facto* reliable in all cases. Making sense of the data entails substantiating the use of particular research methodology and technique. There can be no single framework for the interpretation of comparative political evidence. Interpretative instruments need to be both sensitive and congruent with the nature of the evidence.

This can be illustrated by discussing a relatively complex (policy) issue, which turns out to be surprisingly political: how best to alleviate poverty in Third World countries?[24] A standard comparative analysis would offer some objective criteria for assessing poverty (such as the UN Human Development Index) and seek to identify what might be called the 'drivers of change'—that is, those agents and processes most likely to work to reduce poverty in these countries. It might also compare the ways in which poverty had been lessened in those parts of the world that are presently economically more advanced. It would, finally, try to frame the analysis within the

---

[23] A good summary of the relevance of social theory to historians will be found in P. Burke, 1992, *History and Social Theory*.

[24] This section is based on an extensive analysis by one of the authors of the documentation on poverty reduction produced by the British, Dutch and Swedish ministries for cooperation and development aid.

context of aid policy: what can the West do to help? Therefore, the answer to the original question involves three separate analytical steps: assessing poverty, identifying 'drivers of change', and offering policy advice. But are these compatible? Can comparative analysis in this case meet the test of plausibility? Let us examine these three in turn.

The most problematical part of the comparative study here is undoubtedly the first: evaluating poverty. Although it is clear that there are absolute limits in this respect below which human beings simply cannot survive, it is otherwise debatable whether there can be a single measure of what it means to be 'poor'.[25] Above that threshold, poverty is of necessity a relative concept and it is unlikely that it can be properly assessed outside its proper context. Being poor has connotations that go far beyond the possession of material objects and these can only be understood with reference to the appropriate historical and socio-cultural environment. In some settings someone who has no cattle considers himself poor, regardless of other economic assets.[26] For others poverty turns on the absence of education. In yet other cases poverty is understood as relative deprivation—that is, the inability to acquire certain goods (ranging from bicycle to television, by way of washing machine).

Identifying drivers of change is also comparatively tricky. It rests on the assumption that the lessons of the history of those societies in which poverty has been reduced imply that such was achieved deliberately, by means of the effort of philanthropists and enlightened politicians. Now it is true that the amelioration of the plight of the poor in the West benefited from the devotion of many compassionate individuals and benevolent societies.[27] However, on the whole it was the result of bitter political struggles between the élite and the underprivileged. In any event it occurred within the context of a developing industrial market and strong economic growth, which eventually managed to provide employment for those who were without the means to sustain themselves. Inequalities continued to exist, and in

[25] For one of the most influential recent discussions on poverty, see A. Sen, 1983, *Poverty and Famines*.

[26] See here, for example, D. Anderson and V. Broch-Due (eds), 1999, *The Poor are not Us*.

[27] For a survey of poverty alleviation in Britain in the key period, see M. Rose, 1986, *The Relief of Poverty, 1834–1914*.

many cases widened, but the number of people below the absolute destitution line decreased markedly. Hence history suggests that poverty was reduced through the combined effects of economic development and greater political equality, rather than as a result of deliberate policies. Could the same be true in Third World countries today?

Moreover a careful reading of the comparative evidence of poverty in the non-Western world today suggests that famine, which is its starkest expression, is very largely the outcome of the absence of political accountability in those countries.[28] Consequently it is unlikely that it would be possible to identify 'drivers of change' among the dominant political actors who are responsible for the situation that produced poverty in the first place. If the roots of misery lie in the ways in which power is exercised in some of these countries, where there is limited political responsibility and little or no economic growth, the question as how best to relieve hardship is intimately tied to that of political change. Which brings us to the third issue: aid policy. Whilst the provision of food is imperative where people are starving, it is important to realise that its delivery will in itself have a political impact on the recipient country. Food, or any other aid, must perforce transit through official channels and will therefore strengthen the hand of those who control them. Finally if poverty is largely due to the absence of political accountability, it stands to reason that foreign aid is hardly an appropriate 'driver of change', since it forces recipient governments to account to donors rather than to their own people.

The reason for discussing this example at such length is twofold. First, to show that comparative analysis is not merely an academic exercise. It is readily used for practical purposes—most often, but not always, in policy advice—in ways that expose the limits of the methodology used.[29] Nevertheless, comparativists who simplify excessively, in this instance the question of poverty alleviation, may well influence policy in a direction that turns out to be incompatible with the stated objective. Second, to demonstrate concretely the complexities of observation. Making actual sense of the evidence, here as

---

[28] See here Amartya Sen's arguments: A. Sen, 1999, *Development as Freedom*.

[29] Of course political analysts are not always responsible for the manner in which policy makers exploit their findings unless they themselves have provided policy recommendations—as many are prone to do.

in other respects, implies the ability to deploy interpretive instruments that are congruent with the historical and socio-cultural context from which that evidence is derived. From our viewpoint such skill is one of the virtues of a cultural approach to comparative politics.

TRANSLATION

If the interpretation of political meaning entails the art of translation, as defined above, how then is this done 'scientifically'?[30] Within the perspective of a cultural approach the key aspect of this methodology is the ability to reveal the logic of political dynamics. We need to explain what is happening in terms that make sense locally while at the same time provide an explanation that fits into the types of analysis with which we examine and assess politics in our own societies. This means of course that there can be no 'definitive' conclusion to a comparison between political processes, but only an interpretation that is in consonance with the explanatory schemes most widely used in the contemporary society in which we live. Translation is contextually bound and relative.[31] Clearly there is an accumulation of knowledge over time that is useful for comparative politics, but such data is likely to be reinterpreted, again and again, from one generation to the next.

Historians readily accept that the account they give of a particular event, process, or question evolves over time. The way we assess the French Revolution today, both in Britain and in France, for example, differs markedly from the interpretations given thirty or a hundred years ago. We know that the 'reading' of historical evidence changes not just because we uncover new data but also because we look at the data differently as our own societies evolve. We perceive the past differently and interpret the evidence accordingly. However, in political science there is a marked reluctance to admit to the relative nature of our conclusions. Here again 'scientific' pretensions get in the way of

---

[30] See note 6.

[31] As indeed it is in literature: there can be no 'definitive' rendering into English of a foreign classic such as Proust's *A la recherche du temps perdu* but only one that suits the tastes and outlook of our time. It does not mean that the most recent translation is always better, but it does imply that we feel the need for periodic new translations more in harmony with our times.

realism or, indeed, insight. To conclude the case for a cultural approach we want here to suggest that what makes a methodology scientific[32] is the very degree of sensitivity to the relevance of the socioeconomic and political context in which we, and the peoples we study, live. Let us now explain in more detail how to apply this method to comparative politics.

The rules of the political game(s): decrypting the political matrix

The object of comparative politics is to make useful assessments of the contrasts between the ways power is exercised in different societies. In this respect the primary aim of analysis is the understanding of what we might call the game of politics in each of the individual polities (countries, regions, communities) under examination.[33] Most comparative research agendas ask specific questions about distinct actors or processes. However, we would argue that it is not really possible to provide a satisfactory explanation for such focused enquiries without offering first a credible account of the overall political arenas with which we are concerned. In other words, the usefulness of comparison is predicated on the extent to which comparativists are able to situate their conclusions within the context of the *logics* of the socio-political realm as a whole. Doing comparative politics means in the end decrypting the political matrix of each of the societies, or communities, we study.

This implies that whilst the comparative focus is understandably confined to a limited set of questions, a cultural approach commands that we seek to uncover the overall political picture. It entails deploying a method by which we attempt to understand the *rules* of the political game in the societies we study. We have explained how this is made easier by an inductive approach. We will close the book with a call for theoretical eclecticism.[34] Here we want to show what the translation of the logic of the political system into our own 'locutions' (to use Geertz's word) means in practice. The main question here is that of causality. What are the reasons why the political

---

[32] At least in the sense in which we have defined it: that is, meeting the test of plausibility.

[33] For a discussion of the politics of the 'rules of the game' in relation to the question of the formal and informal, see Chapter 9.

[34] See Conclusion.

'system' works as it does? What has determining influence over what? Why do political actors play the game as they do? What are the consequences of their behaviour for the polity as a whole? How, finally, does the realm of politics relate to the other—social, cultural or economic—spheres of society?

The notion of matrix here is useful because it points both to the arena within which politics is played out and to the multiple connections, causal or otherwise, between the political realm and the other areas of economic and social activity.[35] What we are after is not so much a depiction of the formal features of the political system concerned—useful as that may be—but an explanation of how it actually works. This entails the evaluation of the formal and informal aspects of actual, as opposed to merely official, political dynamics. Decrypting the political matrix, then, involves at least three methodological steps. The first is to decode the workings of the formal political system: understand how it really functions, above and beyond its official architecture and mechanics. The second is to make sense of the informal aspect of power and assess its relevance to the game of politics: that is, explain how the ostensibly non-political may be important. The last is to provide an appraisal of the putative causal significance of the differences and similarities uncovered between different polities.

Working out how a political system operates is not to be confused either with studying constitutions or with explaining how it discharges the functions that are taken to be its preserve.[36] What we advocate is the unravelling of the *logic* of what happens in real life, not how well the systems works as machines. Let us take a seemingly plain example: we may know how different electoral procedures (Proportional Representation, first-past-the-post, Electoral College, two-round elections etc.) work, and even assess their effectiveness in conveying public opinion at the ballot box.[37] Yet we would be remiss in

[35] In mathematics a matrix provides a pictorial representation of quantities or expressions that is treated as a single entity and which can be manipulated according to particular rules.

[36] Both of these exercises have their place in political science, but we would argue that their relevance is more limited when it comes to comparative analysis. The pertinent area of political science here is institutionalism. See J. March and J. Olsen, 1989, *Rediscovering Institutions.*

[37] On the links between elections and representation, see B. Manin, A. Przeworski

our analysis if we did not investigate the practical consequences for
political behaviour of the voting method extant in the countries
where they are used.

Party strategy, selection of candidates, electoral alliances, political
programmes, and the ways in which power is exercised after the
elections, are all strongly affected by the voting system.[38] In point of
fact the very texture of power as it is experienced in everyday life is
coloured by the technicalities of the formal electoral mechanism.
However, the task for the comparativist is not merely to explain the
effects of different voting systems on elections but, more crucial, how
similar electoral mechanisms may have entirely different consequences in different political settings. For instance, in Portugal the election
of the president by universal suffrage does not grant him pre-eminent
executive powers, powers that remain vested in parliament. Power is
thus shared between the head of State and the legislature. In Africa,
however, the reverse is usually the case. Why? Although the reasons
are complex, one key factor is how the population views the role of
the ruler. There can be but one 'chief' and the president is thus perceived to have pre-eminence over the national assembly—regardless
of constitutional standing.

More complex still, but equally important, is the need to bring to
light the informal logic of a given political system. This requirement
may at first appear startling to the student of comparative politics
since it implies a type of research with which the discipline is not so
very familiar. Indeed, it might well be asked how it is possible to
know about what is off the record. Our method should make it clear
that uncovering the unofficial is not a complete mystery, even to the
outside observer, when a cultural approach is applied.[39] By rooting
the search for evidence in what makes sense to the peoples concerned, we are of necessity directed to consider the informal. The
best way to explain how this is done is to suggest that it is revealed
indirectly, by means of probing the limits, the boundaries, the

---

and S. Stokes, 1999, 'Elections and Representation' in A. Przeworski, S. Stokes
and B. Manin (eds), *Democracy, Accountability and Representation*.

[38] For a general discussion of the relationship between representation and democracy, see B. Manin, 1997, *Principles of Representative Government*.

[39] For a concrete application of this method to the comparative politics of Africa,
see P. Chabal and J.-P. Daloz, 1999, *Africa Works*, Chapter 10.

contours and the hidden dynamics, of the formal. Somewhat like a black hole the informal is best assessed by its effects. The difficulty, then, lies in decoding its mechanisms. For example, in Japan it is generally recognised that the kernel of power is in the hands of an informal, or unofficial, coalition of politicians, key businessmen and certain high-ranking civil servants who exercise decisive influence on the executive, legislative and judiciary.[40]

Finally we need to appraise the significance of the comparative analysis of the different polities under study. Here the challenge is to develop an analytical language into which the separate assessment of the respective political matrices can all be translated. Or to put it differently, to identify the code with which it will become possible to reconcile the translations made of the discrete political logics, which research has identified. This is perhaps best explained through the further discussion of the previous example on elections. We may understand the mechanics of the different electoral systems used in our selected countries and we may also have made good progress in teasing out the informal aspects that inform political practices. What we need is to relate these two sets of inferences to a comparative discussion of the political legitimacy of elected officials in those selfsame countries. For example, how important is the voting method to the respect and authority these politicians possess? And how useful is this electoral scheme in enforcing political accountability? Is it possible that, as in Japan, a particular voting mechanism may confer all too easy a victory on a party and that this may work against the legitimacy of elected politicians? Or is it the case that, as in Africa, a first-past-the-post scheme makes coalition government unnecessary and, because in a clientelistic system no politician can afford to be in opposition, it leads in this way to the wholesale discrediting of formal 'democratic' politics of that type?

The passage of time: explaining (r)evolution

The conundrum of political science is that it has failed to evolve a plausible theory of change that could account convincingly for what has taken place worldwide in the recent past. Based as it is on an implicit notion of (economic, social and political) development,

---

[40] A useful background to the culture of politics in Japan is K. van Wolferen, 1990, *The Enigma of Japanese Power.*

which very largely derives from the experience of the Western industrialised countries, it tends to conceptualise change as the *de facto* Westernisation of politics—chiefly liberal democracy. Since it is quite clear that, above and beyond a general process of modernisation, there is a wide range of possible political evolutions, the discipline is left without the means to compare systematically how polities throughout the world are evolving, other than in very broad and general terms. This has major implications, not just for the accuracy of present comparative analysis but also for the future of a field of social science that claims to provide insights into the transformation of political systems over time.

Of course grand theory offered, and for some continues to offer, a vision of coherent socio-political dynamics from which it is deemed to be possible to fashion a framework for the comparative assessment of the progress of present day polities.[41] However, we believe this age is now over.[42] Consequently, the conceptualisation of socio-political change must take into account what has happened since we have begun to understand that societies do not evolve in a single linear fashion. Therefore our argument that a cultural approach is the appropriate way to proceed is not an arbitrary choice. It is a response both to the realisation that general theories are no longer relevant *and* that the only realistic way of making sense of the contemporary world is to employ a conceptual framework that is malleable enough to encompass its manifold diversity and its often-surprising evolution. This means that we can make no cast-iron assumption about the character and direction of political change. Furthermore we must eschew any expectation of causality between economic, social and political transformation. We need to acknowledge the variations in the nature of contemporary modernity and the multiplicity of socio-political experiences to be found across the globe today.

---

[41] The most notorious recent attempt to chart the course of modern political evolution is in fact a contemporary adaptation of a very nineteenth-century unilinear Hegelian notion of progress. See F. Fukuyama, 1992, *The End of History and the Last Man*.

[42] As we know, the age of grand theory in the social sciences was a product of the intellectual and scientific revolution of the long nineteenth century, in which the study of the experience of the industrial revolution, of technological progress and the understanding of biological evolution combined to suggest iron laws of change. For a discussion of this issue, see Chapter 1.

Our approach is based on the systematic attempt to interpret meaning within its appropriate historical and cultural context. Hence the construction of our interpretive framework is derived from the reading of the evidence, such as it is. This is also true of the assessment of political change. Our method, therefore, does not require a 'theory' of change *per se*, since it is based on a concept of 'science' that eschews the test of predictability in favour of that of plausibility. For us the understanding of political change must originate in the understanding of how individuals and societies themselves make sense of what is taking place over time. This does not mean that we account for change merely on the basis of what the peoples concerned think of it but that the material from which we work is that drawn from their perceptions of the transformations to which they are witness. We have already discussed the relation between culture and political change, pointing out in particular that there is no necessary, even less causal or reciprocal, correlation between the transformation of society and the alteration of culture.[43] Let us now illustrate how our approach can cast light on the study of comparative change.

We return to a topic of considerable contemporary relevance: the contrast between the political evolution of Muslim and non-Muslim societies. The two broad models that are currently on offer are both limited. One holds that in due course Muslim polities will also modernise, by which is meant move in the direction of the more advanced liberal democratic countries.[44] The other contends that there is an Islamic culture, which makes it impossible for such an evolution to take place, and deems that such societies will forever remain 'undemocratic'.[45] However, from our standpoint these two approaches fail to consider how Muslims living in Islamic states account for what has happened to their societies in the modern period. A careful reading of the evidence, and in particular a study of the many distinct political opinions to be found in such polities, would reveal that there are two separate issues here. One has to do with the difficulties such states

[43] See Chapter 6, where we seek above all to give an account of how cultures themselves changed over time.

[44] For a proponent of this view, see J. Esposito, 1992, *The Islamic Threat*.

[45] For a sample of the popularising proponents of this view, see B. Lewis, 'Islam and Liberal Democracy', *Atlantic Monthly*, February 1993, and M. Kramer, 'Islam v. Democracy', *Commentary*, January 1993.

have hitherto faced in achieving a balance between economic development and political accountability. The other turns on the failure of most of these countries to confront successfully what might be termed the challenge of Western modernity. The combined impact of these two separate processes has resulted in the advent in some (but by no means all) Muslim polities of political fundamentalism.[46]

The present obsession with the consequences of such fundamentalism for the security of the West, however, has obscured the analysis of the roots of such a phenomenon.[47] A study of the explanations given in Muslim countries for the evolution of their societies since the nineteenth century, and specifically since the end of colonial rule, would make clear that there are complex dynamics at work on many different levels, which are not likely to result in a uniform type of development. Countries with histories, cultures, and socio-economic backgrounds as diverse as Indonesia, Pakistan, Iraq, Morocco and Senegal are experiencing change and adapting to modernity in vastly different ways. A cultural comparative analysis of some of the specific problems they face—such as low economic growth, education, poverty, inequality, regional tension, ethnic conflict etc.—would establish that there is no single Muslim path to development, even less the consolidation of an Islamic 'civilisation' with a dynamic uniquely distinct from that of the West.[48] Which itself begs the question of which West? Some Muslim polities are evolving differently from others, but that evolution is neither unique nor coherent. Furthermore fundamentalism is not the preserve of Islam, as we know.

The trial of comparison: contrasting singularities

A cultural approach to the analysis of change is not an exact science but the most plausible account of why it is that polities have evolved as they have in a specific historical setting. Ultimately comparative politics stands and falls on its ability to provide a 'value added' explanation to our current understanding of the complexion and evolution of real societies in the real world. For this reason we are entitled

---

[46] See here J. Esposito and F. Burgat, 2003, *Modernizing Islam.*

[47] See here O. Roy, 1994, *The Failure of Political Islam*; 2004, *Globalised Islam*; and G. Kepel, *The War for Muslim Minds: Islam and the West.*

[48] On the notion of Islamic civilisation, see S. Huntington, 1996, *The Clash of Civilizations and the Remaking of World Order.*

to assess the merit of a methodology on the basis of the insights it generates. Therefore, it is paradoxical that, faced with the widespread failure to make sense of present events, some political scientists tend to justify their activity on theoretical grounds. For them, studying contrasts between societies is intended primarily to sharpen our conceptual framework.[49] So, for instance, it was thought during the 1990s that a comparative study of Africa and post-communist Eastern Europe would help re-define the general nature of the contemporary relationship between the State and civil society.

However, such an approach was in our view unwarranted, for reasons that illustrate both the relevance and the limits of our discipline. To begin with the assumption that it is possible to compare the link between state and civil society in these two, very distinct parts of the world is not tenable.[50] Ostensibly such a comparison was justified on the grounds that during the period in question there was in these two regions a process of democratisation, ushered in by civil society resistance against authoritarian or totalitarian states. However, to posit a hypothesis about the causal role of civil society merely on the basis of the observation that popular discontent and the advent of multiparty political systems were contemporaneous was to engage in an ill-considered analytical enterprise. The notion that the nature of political change occurring in Sub-Saharan Africa and Eastern Europe was comparable rested on an illusion, and not on the appreciation of what was actually taking place in these two regions. What happened was that the aspiration to conceptualise political protest as the voice of civil society got in the way of observing what was actually unfolding.

Based on an artificially conceived and historically ignorant idea of what civil society was in our own Western polities—an idea that paid little attention to culture—a theory was proposed suggesting that democratisation (whatever that meant in practice, above and beyond multiparty elections) derived from the self-acquired power of civil

---

[49] For a discussion of some of these issues, see A. Zuckerman, 1997, 'Reformulating Explanatory Standards and Advancing Theory in Comparative Politics' in M. Lichbach and A. Zuckerman (eds), 1997, *Comparative Politics.*

[50] This section draws from the thorough discussion of the concept of civil society, its Western origins and its possible application in the non-Western world found in S. Kaviraj and S. Khilnani (eds), 2001, *Civil Society.*

society to check the hegemony of the State.[51] Yet it ought to have been plain that what we in the West understand as civil society was the outcome, and not the cause, of the advent of democratic, that is more accountable, political practices. It is because in Western Europe the State was forced to concede greater and greater political answerability to larger and larger sections of the population that a space emerged for the expression of the political voice of (civil) society. Only then did it become possible for civil society to act as a check against state abuse. Historically, therefore, civil society was consolidated as a means of standing against the pretensions of a relatively strong and effective state. It is the evolution of the State into a modern, bureaucratic and interventionist institution in parallel with the organisation of social interests along horizontal lines that made possible the materialisation of what is now called civil society

In the case of Eastern Europe it was indeed the organised, but politically disenfranchised, sectors of society—trade unions, churches, human rights organisations, civic associations—which exploited the newly available political space, created by Gorbachev's reforms in the Soviet Union, to mobilise against communist rule.[52] The extent to which their action resulted in the advent of genuinely accountable systems, once communist rule had collapsed, was largely conditioned by their pre-communist political and cultural history. Where there were democratic roots—as in Czechoslovakia, Hungary and Poland—democratisation was relatively smooth; where there were no such antecedents—as in Romania, Bulgaria or Albania—the transition has been much more chaotic. A comparison between different East European countries would in this respect have been illuminating, as it would have focused attention of the weight of history and culture on the development of both State and civil society. However, a comparison between Eastern Europe and postcolonial Africa was not illuminating, for the simple reason that in the 1990s the nature of politics south of the Sahara bore no relation to that of Eastern Europe.

As we have shown in our previous book, power in Africa is exercised essentially along personalised patrimonial lines—with stark

---

[51] This argument, as it was thought to apply to Africa, will be found in J.-F. Bayart, 1986, 'Civil Society in Africa' in P. Chabal (ed.), *Political Domination in Africa*.

[52] On post-Marxist theory, see C. Pierson, 1986, *Marxist Theory and Democratic Politics*.

consequences for the State and, in consequence, for the putative formation of civil society.[53] The defining feature of such political 'order' is that socio-economic and political relations are vertical, linking the élites in unequal relations of reciprocity with their clients. In such circumstances the State is not emancipated from society, there is little distinction between the public and private spheres and, however authoritarian the State may on the surface appear to be, it is unable to assert either effective control of government or, even less, hegemony on society. As a result the very notion of civil society does not make sense. The African postcolonial State cannot in any conceivable respect be meaningfully compared to the totalitarian post-War communist State in the former Soviet bloc. The two simply have nothing in common, either organisationally or politically, other than their formal nomenclature.

This example serves to illustrate the need for a cultural approach, since it shows clearly that the validity of comparison lies in the capacity of a conceptual framework to contrast relevant singularities meaningfully. It is our contention that this method conspires to make reasonable comparisons more likely and the outcome of the exercise more fruitful. In the specific instance of the study of civil society in postcolonial Africa, we have shown already that a comparison between sub-Saharan polities does yield worthwhile insight. As suggested above, a similar application of the method to the countries of Eastern Europe in the 1990s would also have resulted in significant findings. However, a contrast between these two parts of the world, though theoretically intriguing, is largely sterile. In other words, it fails to meet the scientific test of plausibility.[54]

Thinking semiotically, or the interpretation of meaning, may appear to be a rather vague method when it comes to the comparative analysis of distinct polities across the world. However, it offers instead a valid framework for the exercise of our discipline, and this for three

---

[53] For a discussion of the State and civil society in Africa, see P. Chabal, and J.-P. Daloz, 1999, *Africa Works*, Chapters 1 and 2.

[54] The same probably applies to current theories of the democratisation of the non-Western world. See here R. Luckham, and G. White, 1996, *Democratisation in the South*.

sets of reasons. It focuses attention on the reality of events and processes as they actually take place *and* as the people concerned perceive them. It places extreme attention on the understanding of political systems as they really function. And it provides a credible way of assessing political change over time.

Part IV. APPLICATION

At this stage in the development of our argument we need to offer concrete illustrations of the practical applications of our method. To this end it would have been possible to provide a wide range of examples, but we have opted instead to demonstrate the merit of our approach by concentrating on two key themes in comparative politics: the State and representation. Therefore, the two chapters that follow are an attempt to apply concretely our method to both of these issues. Each chapter includes a general discussion of the concept from a cultural point of view, followed by its application to three distinct case studies: Nigeria, France and Sweden. Hence the aim of this fourth part is to give a sense of how an analysis based on the interpretation of local meaning can help to provide comparative insights in respect of three quite different settings.

When we read a historical novel, or watch an epic movie, we often wonder whether the past was really as it is portrayed. How is it possible to know what people thought and experienced, why they behaved as they did, several centuries ago. Of course we do have some evidence, but we always run the risk of anachronism, which is a form of ethnocentrism, when attempting to give a representation of the past. This was a pitfall that artists did not always avoid. For instance, European religious painting at the end of the Middle Ages could scarcely conceive how people in the Middle East dressed fifteen centuries earlier. The portrayal of the protagonists and the depiction of the background of the main biblical scenes expose the artists' inability to transcend their own environment. Hollywood's reconstitution of Antiquity suffers from the same defect. The decors, the costumes might appear more realistic but these ostensible reconstitutions of the past tell us more about the time when they were done than about the period being depicted. It is always convenient to present the past in terms of the present, the unknown in terms of the customary.

Similarly much reporting about current events in other countries exudes a reassuring sense of proximity because it is expressed in (shortcut) terms congenial to us. However, more often than not these are distortions of the ways in which these events have been perceived and experienced locally by people different from us. Ironically it is often the local intermediaries, schooled as they have been in the same journalistic techniques as their foreign counterparts and eager as they are to demonstrate their professional command of these practices, who contribute most to this illusory familiarity. The outsider is thus told what he wants to hear in recognisably plausible idiom. However, in order to understand a foreign culture it is also necessary to interpret what the 'native' does not say—either because it is self-evident or because it is embarrassing. Can a roving agnostic Western journalist really make sense of a religion that affects every aspect of everyday life or what it means to live surrounded by spirits, who command what happens in family, professional and personal life?

What obviously impacts on journalists working in foreign lands also (though perhaps less obviously) affects comparativists. It is true that cultural historians, particularly those who study 'mentalities', and anthropologists have long stressed the importance of different forms of representation. We owe them a large debt. Nevertheless, it is well to stress that comparative analysis involves the systematic application of a method that self-consciously aims to interpret not just what people say but also what they do.

The need to 'make sense' is at the heart of political life, if only for politicians to justify their action, to identify their opponents or, simply, to garner support. Yet, from our viewpoint, political scientists fail sufficiently to study how people in other settings relate to their political environment; how they understand it and to what extent they identify with it. Such concerns about the need to interpret variations within distinct settings should be at the very heart of comparative analysis. What matters most in this respect is the attempt to reveal political logics within their own local context—which few comparativists essay.

All too often comparative scholarship comes to this question from a normative standpoint. The approach habitually consists of the application of the latest 'politically fashionable' concept—such as 'good governance' or 'social capital'—to different polities with the avowed ambition to measure their 'performance'. Our discipline is thus intent on assessing the 'development' of political systems on the basis of their ability to change, evolve and mature into what are considered to be more 'advanced' stages. Consequently, the aim is to identify what factors may constitute obstacles to such 'progress'.

Our objective is entirely different. We seek to make sense of local meaning in terms that are congruent with the explanation of reality that indigenous actors provide. Our approach is neutral, if not objective, since we subject our concepts to the test of local plausibility, even if this means (as is the case for the notion of the State) that we are forced to reconsider the assumptions that lie behind the use of such concepts, drawn overwhelmingly from the Western experience.

9

THE MEANINGS OF THE STATE

Thanks in part to the insights provided by historical sociology, it is undoubtedly true that in the last few decades our understanding of the genesis of the State has made remarkable progress. We now know more clearly why it is not *the* 'natural' framework of political activity, as a particular philosophical and juridical tradition would have it, but merely one specific mode of political organisation, which emerged in some European countries after the Middle Ages.

Yet there is still much confusion about the concept. It is frequent for historians or anthropologists to use a broad definition and to apply it to cases where, within the perspective of political science, the notion of the State is not relevant. Furthermore even within our field there are wide divergences. Some scholars consider the State purely as the instrument of the dominant classes for accumulation and violence. Others stress the importance of professional bureaucracies that have overcome patrimonial logic and see it as the vehicle for development and modernisation. Yet others view the State as an impediment to the flowering of the creative 'forces' of society.

The approach we advocate does not pretend to challenge, but rather to build on, the very considerable achievements of historical sociology as applied to politics. We aim to stress another, complementary, angle of attack, which looks in depth at the meaning(s) of the State in contrasted settings. We discuss first the relationships between culture and States. In the second part of the chapter we essay a comparative analysis of three strikingly distinct cases: France, Sweden and Nigeria.

CULTURE AND STATES

In many (ancient or extra-European) polities the notion of an impersonal system of government treating every individual as an 'abstract' citizen, deserving of equal protection and suffering equal legal obligation regardless of considerations of identity, does not make any sense. In these instances the political community is defined less by geographical boundaries than in terms of a sense of collective consciousness going back to ancestral filiations, customs, beliefs or practices. Similarly the idea of formal equality, transcending all communal or religious identities, is incomprehensible in societies where the political realm is conditioned by primordial factors.

In order to set in context the comparative analysis of the empirical cases that follow, we think it useful to re-examine the processes that contributed to the emergence of the State. We then want to cast afresh the debate about how successfully the Western State adapted to non-European conditions. Finally we would like to stress the difficulties of political institutionalisation and the importance of the informal—both of which are crucial to our argument.

Foundations

As many social scientists have pointed out, the State as it emerged and was consolidated in Western Europe over several centuries was the result of complex processes. Right from the outset it is important to emphasise that it was not the outcome of premeditated political action but the product of intertwined social and political dynamics that local actors did not fully control or even comprehend.[1] In other words, this particular form of political organisation did not arise from the deliberate application of specific political theories. It would be more accurate to refer here to fortuitous socio-historical developments, even if they did respond to specific local political logics.[2]

What were the main processes that led to the constitution of the State? First, there was a movement towards *centralisation*. The formation of the State required the end of territorial parcelling and of the juxtaposition of multiple autonomous and competing units. In several European countries it was the ultimate dominance of one particular House over the others that marked the end of the feudal age. However, even in polities that underwent an absolutist phase,

---

[1] N. Elias, 1982 (1939), *The Civilizing Process*, vol. II: *State formation and Civilization*.
[2] C. Tilly, 1975, 'Reflections on the History of European State-Making' in C. Tilly (ed.), *The Formation of National States in Western Europe*.

with the complete domination of one particular dynasty, the process of centralisation was laborious and never fully completed.

Second, it entailed a protracted dynamic of resource concentration and then an attempt at *monopolisation*, in the first instance of military means. Indeed, war—at once mission and a means of gaining resources—had been the business of the aristocracy during the Middle Ages. Then the contending forces were little more than *ad hoc* coalitions, gathered together on the basis of particularistic loyalties rooted in relations of kinship, vassalage or exchange.[3] Over time military confrontation grew to be more large-scale, based on better-organised armies, which had become both the means to achieve, and the symbol of, larger unity. As Weber first noted, the State then succeeded in monopolising legitimate violence both internally and vis-à-vis competing external polities[4].

The process of monopolisation also (and crucially) concerned taxation. In the case of France, for example, royal levies were long considered exceptional and they were contested. However, with the Hundred Years War, which required huge expense, taxation became institutionalised. Fiscal monopoly strengthened the authority of central power and made it possible to plan large-scale and long-term outlays. More generally, it contributed to the progressive monetisation of the economy.

Thirdly, the twin processes of centralisation and monopolisation led to the establishment of a bureaucracy, which constituted the basis of the administrative State system. This involved a dynamic of State *differentiation* and the emergence of a clear distinction between public and private spheres. As Weber made plain, the rise of the State marked the end of patrimonialism—that is, a break with the logic of personal allegiance in which 'patrimonial servants' owed labour and allegiance to their 'patrons'. Such a development only became possible when recruitment to the bureaucracy was based on professional merit and competence, rewarded by commensurate salaries and career prospects independent from the vagaries of politics. These were the conditions required to ensure that civil servants remain neutral, dis-

---

[3] See, for instance, G. Duby, 1973, *Le dimanche de Bouvines.*
[4] By contrast, in some Italian cities a dominant family controlling a neighbourhood was able both to have a militia and a prison.

charging their tasks responsibly and rationally within a clear legal framework.[5]

The last aspect in the development of the State, which can only be discussed briefly here, was *institutionalisation*. This took the form of the written codification of laws applicable to all citizens and entailed legal responsibilities on the part of those who held political or bureaucratic office. Together with centralisation and differentiation this resulted in the creation of pyramidal systems of legality (under-pinned most frequently by a constitution and a supreme court). In parallel, it brought about hierarchical structures of bureaucracy and government resting on the juridical order instituted by the State.

For the sake of clarity of exposition we have limited our remarks to these four fundamental aspects of the emergence of European States. There are of course a number of other considerations that are of importance in terms of refining the concept or studying its his-torical manifestations. Of note would be the relationship between the State, the nation, other territorial entities and different types of political regimes; its role in regulating competing social forces and in imposing order; its links with the élite; and, finally, its economic function, either as actor or regulator or, possibly, as manager of the welfare system. A number of these issues will be touched upon in the three case studies.

From a comparative point of view, therefore, the analysis of the processes that contributed to the formation of European States has led political scientists to reconsider the forms of political organi-sations to be found either in earlier periods or beyond that geo-graphical area. For us the use of the notion in settings where the four processes discussed above have not occurred, or have occurred errat-ically, is a form of 'concept stretching' that is inimical to the proper understanding of the exercise of power.[6]

---

[5] M. Weber, 1946 (more recent edition 1991), *From Max Weber: essays in sociology*, translated and edited by H. Gerth and C. Wright Mills, Chapter 8. The theoretical analysis of differentiation was also advanced by functionalist scholars, of which T. Parsons was one the first. The problem is that they set their analysis within a debatable evolutionary theory, which they claim to be the universal key for mod-ernisation. On these issues see B. Badie and P. Birnbaum, 1979, *Sociologie de l'Etat*.

[6] Of course we understand that many are unhappy with the implication that the 'West' is responsible for the 'invention' of the State and its modern administration. Many of those would want to argue that the Western variant of the State is charac-

Political anthropologists, who deploy a different comparative framework, have sometimes elaborated typologies that distinguished between 'stateless' (segmentary or acephalous) societies and those with
a so-called 'primitive' or 'traditional' State.[7] Using an exceedingly
broad approach, some even define the State as that political system in
which rulers are able to exercise coercive power over a specific population within a given area. This may be a necessary criterion but it is
far from sufficient. We will not touch here on the discussion of 'infra-
State' communities,[8] as defined by anthropologists themselves, except
to warn of the assumption that posits their necessary evolution into
States.[9]

When it comes to the case of 'primitive' States it is important to
stress that they bear almost no resemblance to those which historical
sociology would recognise as such. Not only were they not centralised but also they scarcely had the means of controlling the (often
frontier-less) territories over which they claimed political dominance. Given the importance of the transition from segmentary to
geographically based polities this in itself would militate against the
idea that such political organisations were akin to 'incipient' States.[10]

Although in a number of African and pre-Colombian South American kingdoms there was vast accumulation of riches, this did not
amount to a monopoly over resources. Leaving aside a number of
other relevant considerations in this respect, it is enough to point to
the limits of their taxation systems. This took the form of tribute,

---

terised by a high degree of institutionalisation but that other models are possible in
non-European settings. This would seem justified in view of the fact that the
European States themselves were, by present standards, weak for many centuries.
For methodological reasons that we have already discussed (and to which we
return in the Conclusion) we find it more useful to offer this approach to the formation of States as an introduction to our comparative case studies.

[7] See, among others, M. Fortes and E. Evans-Pritchard, 1940, *African Political
Systems.*

[8] On which there are disagreements between different schools of thought (functionalism, structuralism or cultural analysis) and different disciplines.

[9] This is a widespread assumption in classical anthropology. See, among others,
R. Lowie, 1942, *Social Organisation.*

[10] For instance, even in cases of remarkable large-scale territorial expansion following conquest domination rested primarily on complex and fragile networks
of allegiance and not on systematic 'administration'. The West African kingdoms,
sometimes dubbed 'empires' are clear illustrations of this stuation.

either informal or linked to clientelistic relations, a system in which the intermediaries retained a substantial amount of what was meant to go to the central authorities or the relevant 'patron'. Of course there were huge differences between some of these polities, but none of them had evolved bureaucratic forms of fiscal transfers along the lines of those that characterise contemporary States.[11]

The question of differentiation is critical here and it makes plain why, from the viewpoint of political analysis, it is problematic to speak of a 'traditional' State. The 'primitive' communities, which anthropologists have studied, exhibit no specialised political roles. This does not mean that there were no political activities as such but merely that these (asserting group rules, conflict resolution, the discussion of objectives) were intimately linked to other spheres, most notably the religious.[12] Frequently a diffuse notion of the political, the world of the invisible (whatever the local beliefs) and social relations intermingled, as was obvious from sacred rituals, collective decisions, formal customary decisions or festivals. To separate such activities according to political roles or functions is an excessively ethnocentric enterprise. For example, in such societies there were rarely to be found clearly demarcated executive responsibilities: decisions were implemented by means of communitarian pressure— possibly reinforced by the fear of religious sanction—and seldom by a corps of specialised officials.

Where there were 'governments', or even a proto-administration, they tended to rely on particularistic means of pressure or clientelistic dependence. Such cases can thus be seen to belong to what Weber labelled 'patrimonial rule'. A number of Africanists are anxious to redeem the pre-colonial period and do not accept this point, arguing instead that there were pre-colonial States and bureaucracies.[13] However, as will be explained in greater detail later, these political organisations were not institutionalised and politics in such contexts derived from a straddling of the formal and the informal.

[11] We stress again that this argument is in no way ethnocentric. We merely point out these differences. See note 6 above.

[12] This raises yet again the question of the definition of the 'politic', which anthropologists often relate to processes of integration, regulation and anti-entropy mechanisms.

[13] See, for one instance, M. Balogun, 1983, *Public Administration in Nigeria*.

Equally, if we take into account the characteristics discussed above, it is not helpful to refer, as historians and archaeologists often do, to the States of the Antiquity. Of course the legal procedures developed in Mesopotamia and the norms prevailing in Sumer, Babylon or in Assyria—which go back thousands of years—testify to attempts to set up formal codification. However, similar to the Hebrew laws, such normative regulations remained rooted in the sacred.[14] We could also point to other characteristics—such as the weak differentiation of the 'governmental institutions' or their confused 'administrative' responsibilities—which undermine the notion that these ruling organs constituted a State.

Even in the Greek cities of the Antiquity the political realm was not autonomous either from the religious sphere or from kinship systems. Undoubtedly it is to those cities that we owe the concepts of democracy and citizenship. Yet their *demos* only encompassed a minority of the inhabitants. Furthermore the distribution of authoritative offices (including the top one, that of the *Archon*) by means of a draft/lottery went against the creation of a distinct political sphere. Despite a move towards greater specialisation over the centuries, Ancient Greece never developed institutional structures clearly differentiated from society.

The situation in Rome was not exactly the same. The emergence of a *res publica* evidences a certain distinction between civil society and the political realm. The juridical order rested not just on customary rights but upon more structured dispensations. The concept of citizen extended further than in Greece. Admittedly there also appeared to be greater institutionalisation. However, a number of characteristics of the Roman political order[15] make it problematic to characterise such political structures as a State. The imperial bureaucrats did hail from diverse social origins, enjoyed a special 'professional' status, evolved certain bureaucratic specialisation and began to have access to a real 'career'. On the other hand, the Emperor, who was also the supreme religious leader, was able to dismiss them at will.

[14] For example, even if the most famous of the Mesopotamian codes, that of Hammurapi, is not strictly speaking a religious law, the king is depicted receiving it from the sun God and the God of justice.

[15] Clearly what is designated as the political universe of the Roman period is the outcome of several centuries of change, which from a comparative point of view would need to be studied in their full diversity.

Furthermore Roman magistrates combined judicial, legislative and executive responsibilities. Finally kinship and family ties remained dominant within a world in which the role of the *pater familias* was pre-eminent. Without a doubt much of what we consider today characteristic of the State issues from the Roman political systems, as they were re-constituted between the thirteenth and eighteenth centuries (and especially during the Renaissance). Nevertheless we must remain mindful of their fundamental cultural differences.[16]

Late Antiquity, during which Christianity slowly gathered strength, and the early Middle ages, which suffered the invasions of the 'barbarians', were not favourable to the creation of a State. This was a convoluted period during which the cultural influences from southern and northern Europe clashed and mingled. In the age of the Merovingians the king's authority hardly extended beyond his entourage. The monarch considered his kingdom as his own personal domain, to be parcelled out among his sons, and readily mixed his own wealth with the realm's revenues. Even the Carolingian empire failed to move away from a patrimonial notion of power, since control over territory was based on the princes' loyalty to the suzerain. The period that followed was characterised by extreme political fragmentation, at the polar opposite from a centralised system. The diverse paths that led to the emergence of what we today take for granted as States (but which in truth was only one of many possible political outcomes), issue from a later period, at the end of the feudal age.[17]

Turning now to the non-European world, we would argue that even the most prestigious 'civilisations' (to use a scientifically problematic term[18]) did not evolve States—at least not according to the criteria discussed above. The Chinese Mandarinate (and the bureaucratic systems it spawned in the region) cannot be equated with

[16] See P. Grimal, 1981, *La civilisation romaine.* For example, the notion of the 'law' today differs from the Roman one. Then it was seen as the will of the people and it could apply to very specific areas, which would seem more peripheral today, such as the adoption of a particular child. On the other hand, what is today essential, such as financial legislation or the budget, did not come under the legislative purview in Rome.

[17] In some countries, such as Russia or Japan, the feudal order (itself a debatable notion, which has generated much controversy) did not disappear until very late.

[18] On this subject, see a special issue of *International Sociology,* 16, 3 (September 2001).

Western States. Admittedly the meritocratic recruitment of the higher civil servants was key. But it rested on the acquisition of general knowledge, which had little relevance to their duties. Although theoretically open to all, recruitment was socially biased, since the required education (including the mastering of Mandarin) could only be afforded by the few. In practice most candidates were themselves the offspring of those in place. For this reason, and also because of the venal nature of the official positions, the system became quasi-hereditary. As Weber had already noted, it rested on prebendal practices.[19] If social prominence appeared to derive from bureaucratic rank rather than birthright or wealth, in reality the mandarins were able to accumulate riches and to reproduce themselves socially over time.

In Korea, where (differently from other countries in the region) there was great pride in the Confucian mandarin heritage, which enjoyed traditional prestige, there quite clearly prevailed a non-State system.[20] The King (quasi-independent vassal of the Chinese Emperor and absolute ruler within his realm) relied on educated bureaucrats, or *Yangban*, recruited by exam. Yet candidates could 'buy' the examiners who, because of their key role, occupied a critical social position.[21] Newly appointed *Yangban*, who usually started their career in the provinces, needed to gather the wherewithal to reimburse what their family had invested to secure exam success. Because they were usually transferred after two years—precisely to prevent excessive graft—there was little time to obtain such revenues. They relied on the support of local 'collaborators' who, though not paid, took their share along the way. The higher-level civil servants, who were rarely posted in their region of origin, were thus compelled to rely on auxiliaries with an intimate knowledge of the area and entered in this way into relations of clientelism.[22] In addition these

---

[19] See M. Weber, 1946 (more recent edn 1991), *From Max Weber: essays in sociology*, translated and edited by H. Gerth and C. Wright Mills, Chapter 17. For a more recent study, see O. van der Sprenkel, 1958, *The Chinese Civil Service* and S. van der Sprenkel, 1977, *Legal Institution in Manchu China*.

[20] See here, among others, P. C. Hahm, 1987, *The Korean Tradition and Law.*

[21] On the mechanics of this system, which evolved over the centuries, see for instance K. Lee, 1984, *A New History of Korea.*

[22] According to Hahm those bureaucrats who refused to 'play the game' ran the risk of being accused of corruption since thus 'collaborators' often had ready access to

bureaucrats had to gather the means of 'buying' future promotions and of ensuring for their retirement. This system lasted until the end of the nineteenth century, when it entered into crisis in large part due to intolerable prebendal pressure.[23]

Generally, then, in such systems as were found in the Far East, the political and administrative spheres had achieved little differentiation. The mandarins effectively acted as a roving aristocracy, relying on patrimonial collaborators. The bureaucracy was thus not neutral, nor did it rest on professional competence. Although these administrative organisations were predicated on a common cultural structure, which gave it a semblance of unity, it did not constitute a legal order transcending particularistic arrangements.

When comparativists define the State as that administrative and political organisation that emerged in Western Europe from the end of the Middle Ages, it is not necessarily to set it up as a model. Even less to suggest that other modes of political order, either more ancient or found outside that geographical area, are 'inferior'. It is merely to stress the fundamental differences between these different systems. Since it is clear that the Western State was not the outcome of deliberate political 'planning' and since it was only conceptualised as such *a posteriori*, the argument cannot be normative. In other words, there is no inherent European 'superiority' in the fact that the State emerged in that part of the world. Furthermore it is clear that the evolution of the State has been halting, and easily reversible. In many ways present States are far removed from certain ideal-types, as we will see later.

Nevertheless, there is little doubt that from an analytical standpoint the distinctions made by historical sociology between the different types of 'States' extant have been useful to comparative politics. We, for our part, would like to build on such work by proposing a cultural approach, focusing on a discussion of the extent to which the notion

---

the government through (often occult) networks. See P. C. Hahm, 1987, *The Korean Tradition and Law*, p. 67.

[23] A 1862 report (written by the reforming Gi Jong Jim to the King) states: 'your governors treat the provinces they administer as their personal domain; local officials serve themselves as though they were fishing in their own local pond; the royal emissaries charged with collecting taxes overstep the mark as if they could not resist gulping the local pastries.'

of the State makes sense in different settings. However, before we present our three case studies we should like to return to the thorny question of the extension of the 'State' beyond its Western European heartland.

The transplanted State and the tricks of the mirror

Today the State seems to have become the only legitimate form of government, if only for reasons of credibility at the international level. Nevertheless, analysts need to go beyond the formal appellation. It is understandable why the leaders of the so-called developing world should want to acquire respectability by casting their institutions under this rubric. However, it is incomprehensible why political scientists should conspire in this, particularly when it is obvious that such political structures are lacking some of the major attributes of the State, which were discussed above.

The most extreme such approach is that of international law, which confines identification to the formal structure in place regardless of whether the State has control over the territory it claims or whether it is sufficiently institutionalised to discharge its official functions. Among political scientists there is a tendency to speak of State 'construction', 'formation', or to deploy such (rather ethnocentric) caveats as 'soft', 'weak', hybrid 'unfinished' or 'neo-patrimonial'. This situation illustrates the confusion engendered by such a mix of scientific, normative or dogmatic discourses.

There have been a number of ideologically or intellectually driven phases in the study of the spread of Western style States throughout the world, which have touched on some of the sociological characteristics discussed briefly above. Only those approaches will be mentioned here that either concur with the view that State development is historically a Western process or believe that it is in that part of the world that it has reached it most evolved complexion.

Developmentalist views hold that there is a universal process of State construction that results in due course in the establishment of institutions along the lines of those to be found today in Western Europe, North America and Australasia. Some of these theories are highly sophisticated but they remain irredeemably ethnocentric and teleological. For those who advocate this position the assumption is that no political system in the world can remain immune to the political processes that have marked the evolution of the most 'advanced' nations. They hold, for instance, that the differentiation of the political sphere from society is a readily exportable method for achieving key structural changes instead of acknowledging that it is merely one of the singular outcomes of the historical trajectory of a number of European countries. Nations may be more or less politically 'developed', but it is postulated that, if they apply the 'right' recipes (along with the 'right' policies of social modernisation and economic growth), they will eventually come to acquire a State resembling that of the more 'advanced' countries.

By the 1970s such theories, which had been evolved in respect of the more recently independent countries, had reached their limits. Given the lack of progress, particularly in Africa, their exponents were forced to explain what was happening on the basis of developmental 'delays' or 'dysfunctions'. Analytically, however, such views rapidly lost credibility, since they were clearly unable convincingly to account for what was taking place politically in those countries. Although they were eventually replaced by other approaches, developmentalist theories continue to exercise strong influence. Those who live from the policy advice proffered to Third World countries have a vested interest in continuing to refer to the likely evolution of the State in the Western direction. Equally the rulers of the so-called 'less advanced' nations have a stake in the argument that their governmental institutions are 'catching up' with those of the West.

Marxist and neo-Marxist perspectives obviously do not envisage the Western State as the ultimate stage in political development. For them it is but the embodiment of bourgeois domination and is deemed either to be transcended or to whither. In their own way, however, they mirror the ideological and teleological approaches of development theory. Whether they view the State as a vehicle for accumulation, violence or as the symbol of foreign imperialist domination, their reasoning remains economically deterministic and ignores local historical dynamics and cultural specificities. Dependency theories, though politically hostile to American concepts of development, are in fact the reverse side of a similar approach and like them they were exposed for their heuristic vacuity in the 1970s. However, like them too they continue to exercise influence and have re-emerged recently in the guise of anti-globalisation.

Since the 1980s the trend has been towards more subtle interpretations, many of which based on biological metaphors: hybridity, graft, phagocytosis and cystic or mimetic growth. Greater empirical sophistication has made it obvious that non-Western societies have adapted these systems to their own environment. The question here becomes how the structures of the (Western) State have adjusted to distinct and unfamiliar environments. Such approaches mark a vast improvement over developmental or dependency frameworks of analysis, which considered the evolution of governmental institutions in non-Western countries either as necessary transplantation or as unwelcome intrusion. However, as we explained in our previous book on Africa, they failed to make clear the lack of balance in such transfers: the receiving organ is far more influential than the transplanted constitution.[24] Or, to extend the biological metaphor, the dominant 'genes' issue from the local habitat; the recessive ones from the West.

Some scholars have concluded that the grafting of the State has been rejected and that the successful operation of Western type institutions was only possible in its original environment. Others have developed a sophisticated analysis of the export and import of Western political institutions, giving particular importance to those actors from either side who have been influential in the transfer of such models.[25] Comparisons have also been made between those cases where the State has been imposed (through colonial rule or as result of donor conditionalities), those where it has been willingly embraced as a recipe for development and those where it has been mimetically and mechanically constructed. Finally it is clear that in this respect there is a further distinction between an approach in terms of 'ideal-type' or in terms of the relative 'effectiveness' of the States in question.

Whatever the differences between these schools of thought, most of the work on 'institutional genetics' has continued to concentrate attention on the State. It is as though it had become impossible to study contemporary political systems otherwise, limiting analysis to identifying 'deviations' or dissecting the 'unintended consequences'

[24] P. Chabal, and J.-P. Daloz, 1999, *Africa Works*, Chapter 10.
[25] B. Badie, 1992, *L'Etat importé*.

from the model. This syncretic approach claims to offer a 'middle way' between teleological (especially developmental) dogmatism and 'cultural' extremism.[26] It rejects equally those who argue that non-Western settings are 'soft', thus easily susceptible to foreign models, and those who see them as 'compact blocs', immune to outside influence.

Scholars who are empirically minded know that the importation of foreign models is problematic and usually provokes resistance. For our part we reject the dichotomy thus established between the view that such imports are either salutary or nefarious. At the same time we do not subscribe to those syncretic approaches, which are perennially confined to debating the extent to which the Western State has been adopted, adapted or rejected. These are critical questions, which echo a number of issues discussed in the first two parts of this book. For us a cultural approach is far from being deterministic since it pays suitable attention to the dynamics of change, as well as to the circulation of political models.

As explained in Part III, our method is inductive and centres on the interpretation of meaning. All approaches that draw on the Western model, or experience—whether theoretical, ideological or even empirical—are locked into a deductive practice. Admittedly we all need a frame of reference for comparative analysis, but, as we shall show in the Conclusion, it is possible both to maintain critical distance from the Western perspective and to evolve a scientific analysis of political difference.

To enter into theoretical debates merely on the basis of the political and administrative lexicon of Western theories—also frequently used by non-Western scholars who have been trained in our academies—confers an illusion of analytical familiarity as regards political 'diagnosis' or 'remedies'. Here it is not a matter of technology transfer but of the transfer of the modalities of political order and legitimacy. Even those who claim to be critical of universalist approaches ought to realise that the study of the circulation of such imported models cannot be an end in itself. Comparative analysis needs to dig deeper and seek to uncover the impact of this commerce of (political) meanings at the local level.

[26] See here Y. Mény, 1993, *Les politiques du mimétisme institutionnel.*

The formal and the informal

The political analysis of the State needs to be multifaceted. In this section we shall stress the comparative dimension of institutionalisation and of the formalisation of political rules. However, it will be clear that our reflection on these issues links to other aspects of political analysis.

All cultures are part of a given normative order, which is more or less formal, explicit or rigid. In numerous settings the community's regulating principles are not to be found in written legal codes. They belong to the world of the implicit or tacit—which naturally does not mean that they command any less respect. Yet this raises the question of the institutionalisation of regulations—about which one may take a broad or narrow view. For many scholars, among whom anthropologists, it is legitimate to refer to institutionalisation so long as there are stable and effective norms and rules of conduct. Others restrict the use of the concept to cases where laws have been codified, most often in juridical form—where, therefore, normative legitimacy operates within a relatively differentiated, official, coherent and strictly defined legal framework.[27]

From this viewpoint a comparative examination of the diverse cultures extant throws up interesting cleavages, of which we will mention only a few. Many societies are highly intransigent when it comes to the violation of their (formal or informal) norms. Anthropology is replete with examples of 'traditional' communities whose people believe their very existence requires total obedience to principles and customs that have served them well since the origins of time.[28] The observance of these rules is perceived as the guarantor of collective survival; any deviance is seen as 'unnatural' and potentially lethal. On the other hand, other communities value above all flexibility, compromise and *ad hoc* accommodation: here group survival is linked to the ability to adjust.

Moving on to a second comparative dimension, societies are more or less prone to formalisation. In some countries (as in Germany, for instance), there is an apparent predilection for clearly defined norms,

[27] Such an approach might be based on an implicit ethnocentric hierarchy, which we for our part seek to avoid.

[28] In this respect one could define culture as the conversion by *homo sapiens* of instinctive survival practices into replicable and transmissible knowledge.

preferably in written forms and overseen by official bodies. Such cultures are uncomfortable with fluid, or ambiguous, situations, which tend to engender noticeable social disquiet. In other societies the opposite is true: any attempt at systematic regulation is depreciated and commonly ignored.[29] Many among those who have studied misunderstandings in international trade have pointed to the fact that Westerners seek rapidly to formalise transactions by means of contracts. In the Far East (China, for example) what matters most is the setting up of regular contact, the progressive establishment of informal relations of trust that are ultimately difficult to break. This attitude, which privileges self-discipline, is in harmony with historical experience and cultural context.

The development of long-distance trade over centuries forced Chinese traders to operate outside the family units, which had always constituted their framework of reference. Given the absence of a formal Western-style juridical order legalising commercial transactions they transposed the rules of Confucian ethics that regulated family life to their international networks. Business relied on the creation of ties of loyalty and the need to maintain one's reputation, which was protected from deviance by harsh collective sanctions.[30] We are not here entering into the debate of whether Asian 'values' are more or less conducive to economic development. We are only concerned to point to the existence of different types of 'contractual' logics, both of which both have demonstrated their efficacy.

For us such an analysis of the interpretation of the formal and informal aspects of social behaviour is crucial to the understanding of the State. Whereas in highly formalised societies adherence to written rules is paramount, there is ostensibly far greater room for manoeuvre in informal settings. Of course informality does not mean anomie. In informal contexts the notion of rule is deliberately

---

[29] See E. Hall, 1966, *The Hidden Dimension* in which Hall mentions the case of the Poles, for whom it is socially acceptable to disrupt queueing. Of course it would here be important to assess the extent to which there was a class element in such behaviour, since the disorganisation of established order could also be a form of resistance. See Chapter 3, where we discuss those cultural logics that transcend such social variables.

[30] See D. Perkins, 2000, 'Law, Family Ties and the East Asian Way of Business' in L. Harrison and S. Huntington (eds), *Culture Matters*, who provides and interesting comparative discussion.

vague. Acceptable behaviour derives from a number of general principles, or what might be termed 'an intelligence of circumstances',
rooted in and bounded by orally transmitted traditions. Clearly, it is
difficult to give an account of such a system, even for those who have
been socialised into it, precisely because it is not formalised. In this
way it is like the air we breathe.[31]

As we have detailed in *Africa Works*, such informal socio-political
and economic relations, which appear disorderly, are readily used
instrumentally within what is effectively a patrimonial, or clientelistic, context.[32] Equally a study of African 'bureaucracies' reveals a
system where there are as many unwritten 'rules' as there are em-
ployees and where personal relations largely determine outcomes.
Such particularistic dynamics are difficult to understand for those
who hail from societies in which written regulations are effective.

When it comes to countries where formal legal codes are paramount, the question for analysis is the extent to which those rules
are followed. In some societies respect for written norms derives
from a strong internalisation of their merit: failure to conform is
troubling or even incomprehensible. In other settings, however, it is
the reverse: non-compliance is routine, when not highly prized (if
not officially, at least in private). Yet again it is a matter of uncovering
the local modalities of power and socio-political relations according
to the method suggested in Chapter 4, as we shall aim to do when we
discuss the notion of the State in France and Sweden. We leave phi-
losophers and ideologues to debate whether it is more 'civilised' or
more 'alienating' for a society to have a highly formalised mode of
social control (within a democratic framework), which commands
widespread respect for the law. Our concern here is merely to point
to the importance of such considerations for the understanding of
distinct political systems.

The above discussion is not meant to suggest that comparative
analysts should assume either that there is a sharp dichotomy between
the formal and the informal or, even less, that there is a 'natural' continuum from the one to the other. It is merely intended to stress the

---

[31] In this respect one might mention a standard distinction in anthropology between context 'rich' and 'poor' cultures, in which communication is more or less
implicit.

[32] P. Chabal and J.-P. Daloz, 1999, *Africa Works*.

divergences between those environments where States are based on the rule of law and those where the very notion of such a State does not make any sense. Of course it might be argued that all political systems encompass both 'normative' and 'pragmatic' characteristics and that political success often depends on the ability to take liberty with the former.[33] We know that in the West (regardless of divergences between juridical traditions) lawyers and attorneys often move in a world both of punctilious respect for formal procedures and regulations *and* of recourse to all manners of arrangements that are sometimes of dubious legality. Whatever the case the point here is that such contrasts in actual behaviour—as opposed to formal legislation—are crucial when it comes to making meaningful political comparisons. As argued in Chapter 5, the working of a political order is not merely the outcome of ideological domination. If political actors draw on existing cultural repertoires to assert their legitimacy, they have to do so within the common cultural environment of which they too are a part.

In other words, what matters most here is to stress that playing with the rules may itself be part of the rules of the game. To understand how entails an analysis of actual differences in this respect between various polities. As will be shown in the second, comparative part of this chapter, the behaviour of political actors in the three countries is extremely divergent.

Our research on Africa has revealed that local politicians are exceptionally loath to accept the authority of State institutions over their personal conduct. Within a particularistic political order accountability rests essentially on the rulers' ability to meet the demands of the communities and factions that support them. It is thus essential to demonstrate one's own pre-eminence over the realm of the formal. In this respect a last minute change in the constitution making possible a third presidential mandate is only truly shocking to those who uphold constitutional primacy—not to the leader's supporters.

In France, as we shall see, politicians pay homage to the Republican or European institutions but often find ways of ignoring or bypassing them when it is convenient. In Scandinavia, however, the legitimacy of political actors appears to depend on their subservience

[33] See F. G. Bailey, 1970, *Stratagems and Spoils.*

to State institutions. In the former Soviet Union legislation did not command absolute authority since the Communist Party, underpinned by Marxist-Leninist ideology, remained the ultimate political arbiter.[34] Laws were in practice mere instruments and this raises the question of political differentiation within totalitarian systems.

Beyond these general comparative considerations it is useful to examine the cultural factors that may have impinged on the formation of Western States. Here some analysts have stressed the importance of the separation between the spiritual and temporal realms, which brought about a form of social and political order rooted in this disjunction. They argue that this division between the profane and the religious (and between their respective forms of legitimacy), which became established in some countries, led to the distinction between private and public spheres and thence to the emergence of State institutions differentiated from society. This separation, which is meaningless in many settings (especially in most Islamic countries), has had a deep influence over our conception of power, authority and law.[35]

Yet the situation in the West is not so clear-cut. Comparative analysis reveals significant differences in the political relevance of the relationship between religion and politics in countries such as Italy, the United States, Norway and France. We do not intend here to enter into a debate about the prerequisites to secularisation (or about the fundamental split between what belongs to God and what belongs to Caesar) in the emergence of the modern Western State.[36] Such approaches in terms of dualist or monist cultural codes are probably useful. Yet it is probably more enlightening to go beyond the analysis of discourse in this respect and focus instead on the realities of life, as

[34] See A. Fogelkou, 1987, 'Law as an Ornament of Power' in C. Arvidsson and L. Blomquist (eds), *The Esthetics of Political Legitimation in the Soviet Union and Eastern Europe.*

[35] See *inter alia* B. Badie, 1983, *Culture et politique.*

[36] For Huntington such a distinction is fundamental to the Western path of political development, whereas in the Islamic world 'God is Caesar', in the Confucian tradition 'Caesar is God' and for orthodox Catholicism 'God is Caesar's junior partner'. See S. Huntington, 1996, *The Clash of Civilizations*, p. 70. In the Scandinavian countries, where the State is paramount, the dominant church has been Lutheran. For a discussion on religion and democracy, see here A. Stepan, 2001, *Arguing Comparative Politics*, Chapter 11.

they are actually experienced by the peoples concerned. And it is in this direction that we would want to see the study of States evolve.

STATES IN MIND

Contrary to the standard deductive approach, we do not seek here to gauge how our case studies fit a given abstract definition of the State. As argued in earlier chapters, we do not see comparative analysis in terms of the search for common denominators or as the quest for typological classification. Our method rests on empirical research with strong emphasis on the local perspective—that is, an interpretation of what makes sense to the people concerned.[37] This approach is liable to recast in a different mould the study of standard methods in social sciences.

Our view of the State differs from both institutionalist theories and from those approaches based on 'sociogenesis' or individual 'psychogenesis', such as that advocated by Norbert Elias.[38] Of course it is quite legitimate to study the links between the evolution of institutions and that of individual citizens, as well as the extent to which 'civilised' society requires social control and personal self-control. However, we must eschew the assumption that what has happened in the West is a potentially universal dynamic process. To illustrate our viewpoint we refer to Elias' suggestion that there is a 'world of difference' between an inherently dark and dangerous medieval path and the well-ordered street of a modern city. This is true as far as it goes, but there is also a 'world of difference' between Sweden, where jay-walking never occurs; France, where pedestrians battle with drivers who seldom give way; and the utter chaos of a Lagos, where pedestrians and car drivers refuse to give way—thus provoking gigantic traffic jams.

Local notions of civic duty, State responsibilities in respect of public services or the expectations people have of its role in terms of social regulation, vary considerably according to environment. We will discuss below the case of a country where the State embodies social harmony and welfare. However, we start with the example of a

[37] See C. Geertz, 1983, 'From the Native's Point of View: on the nature of anthropological understanding' in C. Geertz, *Local Knowledge*.
[38] Elias, N., 1982 (1939), *The Civilizing Process*, vol. II.

country where the State is ostensibly very strong but where there is pride in breaking its rules—except, that is, when it is beneficial to follow them. We conclude with a discussion of a country where the notion of 'State' does not make sense and where people turn towards kinship groups or clientelistic networks in order to access officialdom or to seek protection. In such circumstances, is it still legitimate to refer to this political system as a State?

France or the ambiguous State

It has been argued that the ideal type of the State was the French model.[39] This is because it is the country where the processes of institutionalisation and differentiation have been the most thorough— due in the main to the fact that the penetration by the centre into the periphery was difficult and that resistance from civil society prompted the development of a formidable bureaucracy. Without a doubt this administrative machinery was strengthened over the centuries, most notably during the absolutist period (when royal officers already enjoyed real professional careers), during the 1789 Revolution (which asserted control over a newly administratively parcelled nation) and during the first Empire (when the prefectoral corps was set up). Fur- thermore the State reinforced its grip in other ways: through its obsessive insistence on secularity, the attempt to remove all interme- diaries between citizens and State, central monopoly over education, strong interventionism in the economy, the establishment of the famous *Ecole Nationale d'Administration* (ENA), the ethos of public service, and the exploitation of the ideology of the 'common inter- est'. This is indeed a *prima facie* case of extreme State development.

Yet if one re-examines the question of the autonomy of the State, not from an ideal or theoretical viewpoint, but by focusing attention on political and administrative actors over the last few centuries, then a different picture emerges. Here the scholarly work of historians and those political scientists specialising on the élite reveals a State that is far from the reified homogenous entity supposedly issued from the Colbertist, Jacobin and Napoleonic traditions. This also makes it easier to move away from intellectualised visions, rooted in the history of political thought, which either seek to praise or condemn the State as it developed in France.

[39] B. Badie and P. Birnbaum, 1979, *Sociologie de l'Etat*, p. 191.

Looking more closely at the absolutist period, usually seen as crucial in the formation of the State, it is not difficult to identify a number of ambiguities or paradoxes. It is true that the royal administration managed to diversify and to gain firmer control over a very divided society. At the same time a number of factors would suggest that it was at best a proto-State: offices were purchased, hereditary positions were expensively maintained (this was one of the Crown's main sources of revenues) and personal allegiances to those in power prevailed. There remained a deep and persistent fascination on the part of this *noblesse de robe* for the old aristocratic model.[40] Finally particularistic and patrimonial relations still flourished. Moreover insofar as the institutional order was embodied in the very person of the King,[41] there was a contradiction between the requirements of an emerging modern and complex bureaucracy and the ability of the monarch to exercise meaningful administrative supervision.[42]

Beyond Versailles the country remained a disunited conglomeration of social, economic and political entities—old provinces, generalities, *baillages, Sénéchaussées,* military districts, academies and dioceses—which made for an administrative, judicial and fiscal labyrinth that conspired against the establishment of an efficient State system.[43] Britain, on the other hand, though it is often seen as a far less 'advanced' State at that time, already enjoyed a more ordered juridical order. As de Tocqueville noted, there were strong continuities between the *Ancien Régime* and the Revolution. The Empire *préfets* followed in the footsteps of the royal *intendants* in surrounding themselves with patrimonial collaborators who had deep local roots.[44]

[40] On this issue, work on élite are particularly enlightening. See, for instance, G. Chaussinand-Nogaret (ed.), 1991, *Histoire des élites en France du XVIe au XXe siècle.*

[41] Louis XV reminded parliament that 'sovereign power is rooted in my very person'.

[42] For a discussion of this contradiction, see Y. Fauchois, 1997, 'L'absolutisme: un colosse aux pieds d'argile' in *L'histoire grande ouverte. Hommages à Emmanuel Le Roy-Ladurie.*

[43] See J. Godechot, 1968, *Les institutions de la France sous la Révolution et l'Empire.* Looking at some key indicators—the low percentage of officials in relation to the size of the population, the continuation of private practices of tax collection and military recruitment—one could easily argue that the State was relatively poorly developed.

[44] See, among others, R. Mandrou, 1987, *La France aux XVIIe et XVIIIe siècles.*

However, territorial unity in France was only achieved, and not without resistance, after the Revolution, underpinned by a strong nationalist ideology, simplified the country's administrative grid.[45]

It might indeed be thought that the priority placed on centralisation, further strengthened by the Napoleonian bureaucracy, had finally brought about a strong State. Yet looking at the civil service in the first half of the nineteenth century it is clear that only a small élite was actually trained and personal relations continued to predominate. The private and public spheres readily mixed and promotion depended on favour. In addition the numerous regime changes that took place during that period resulted in regular purges, notably of the *préfets*, who habitually behaved like local potentates, readily mixing political and administrative responsibilities.[46] Although the definitive establishment of the Republic did strengthen meritocratic principles, there were still variations in the extent to which a supposedly autonomous bureaucracy was able to maintain its independence in the face of social conflicts and political discord.[47]

From our point of view the State only makes sense in its relation with, or rather in the nature of its differentiation *from*, society. In the case of France even those scholars who have stressed the logic of differentiation have also had to take into account a process of 'de–differentiation'—given the importance of corporatism, the bureaucracy's intimate links with the private sector and the politicisation of the higher echelons of the civil service.[48] We know that in today's Fifth Republic the appointment of top civil servants to key positions requires a double 'sponsorship': a political one, bestowed by the President, the Prime Minister or a member of the government and a corporate one by way of the approval of the administrative 'corps' to which the individuals belong.[49] It is also common to reward political loyalty, as Mitterrand was particularly wont to do, with appointment to prestigious public office. Examples of similar practices abound:

---

[45] See M.-V. Ozouf-Marignier, 1989, *La formation des départements*. For a more general discussion, see J. Le Goff (ed.), 1989, *Histoire de la France* (2nd edn, 2000).

[46] See P. Rosanvallon, 1990, *L'Etat en France de 1789 à nos jours*.

[47] See P. Birnbaum, 1977, *Les sommets de l'Etat*.

[48] P. Birnbaum, 1985, 'L'action de l'Etat: différenciation et dédifférenciation' in M. Grawitz and J. Leca (eds), *Traité de science politique*, vol. III.

[49] E. Suleiman, 1976, *Les hauts fonctionnaires et la République*.

witness here the efforts made by prominent political actors to provide benefits to certain groups within their constituencies.[50]

From a comparative viewpoint it is well to see the French case for
what it is really. Indeed, the above remarks are intended to balance the
views of those who hold an excessively idealised notion of the
French State tradition.[51] However, we do not subscribe to the opposite stance, which considers that there is little specific about the
case of France. Within Africanist circles, for example, there is sometimes a tendency to argue that in terms of nepotism or corruption
there are only differences of degree, and not of kind, between France
and Sub-Saharan countries. Such sweeping relativism undermines
comparative analysis. There is in France an impersonal and independent civil service that is not to be found south of the Mediterranean. As we showed in *Africa Works*, both cultural context and
political behaviour are eminently different south of the Sahara.
Hence it is important to pay proper (scientific rather than normative)
attention to the political implications of such differences.[52] Otherwise comparative analysis becomes moot.

Such considerations notwithstanding, the French people harbour
a profoundly ambivalent attitude towards these central institutions.
The French State is undoubtedly both strong and ubiquitous, but a
cultural approach reveals clearly that it also elicits keen reservations
within society. A closer examination makes plain the myriad ways in
which individuals seek to evade its reach. What is significant here is
that such practices are not only the preserve of the 'populace' but also
concern the élite. Many politicians and businessmen take liberties
with the official 'rules of the game', as though they believed they had
impunity.[53] More generally, there is in society a general disdain for
officialdom and regulations. Drivers readily flash their lights to warn
their peers that police are on the road. Faced with draconian bookkeeping regulations in the public sector, numerous offices resort to

---

[50] A good example is the creation of the so-called 'fiscal exceptions'. Edgar Faure
was thus able to give special help to the pipe-makers of Saint-Claude and
spectacle-makers of Morez, both in his own Department of Jura.

[51] See here M. Crozier, 1963, *Le phénomène bureaucratique*.

[52] P. Chabal and J.-P. Daloz, 1999, *Africa Works*, Chapter 7 on corruption.

[53] See P. Lascoumes, 1997, *Élites irrégulières*. This is a sensitive issue, which may lead
to the devaluing of politics and the rise of populist extremist movements.

the setting up of 'unofficial' accounts as the only means of operating with a minimum of financial flexibility.

It is useful here to speak of 'double language'. Citizens and politicians alike eagerly call on the State when they need it, or when they can see its usefulness. Otherwise they just as readily denounce its inequities and inefficiencies. The perennial discussion about decentralisation illustrates clearly such 'schizophrenia', since it involves at the same time making greater demands on the State and seeking emancipation from it. A cultural standpoint on such phenomena, based on 'thick description', is particularly useful here as it makes it possible to refine comparative analysis. There is in France undoubtedly less respect for the State than in Sweden, though it is a far cry from the Nigerian situation we discuss below. The recent judicial cases involving the creation of fictitious jobs (amounting to illegal financial subsidies to the Gaullist party) within the office of the Paris mayor provide an interesting case study of French ambiguities. So does the long-lasting collusion between political parties and construction businesses. Although the most recent instances have implicated the very top of the French political establishment (including allegations against President Chirac), many dismiss the trials on the grounds that these are well-understood 'common practices'. Others have denounced the 'politicisation' of the magistrates. Whatever the case recent events have resulted in the indictment and the successful prosecution of a number of politicians, including Juppé, a former Prime Minister.

French ambiguities in respect of the State are particularly obvious when it comes to the implementation of public policies. As Lascoumes writes:

We live by the rule of law but the empirical analysis of numerous local and national activities makes plain the extent to which legality is the object of negotiation. Alongside the abstract, vertical, legality, to which lip service is paid, there is at all levels an horizontal legality, which derives from the actors' negotiated adjustments made in order to reconcile their interests with the rules.[54]

Let us illustrate this observation with reference to legislation about the environment. The implementation of European Union regu-

---

[54] Ibid., p. 16. See also P. Lascoumes, 1990, 'Normes juridiques et mise en œuvre des politiques publiques', *L'Année Sociologique*, 40.

lations on ecology is perennially delayed, or derailed, not just because it is against the interests of powerful agricultural lobbies but also because the administration is complicit in failing to take the necessary measures. For instance, farmers were largely able to ignore the 1991 European directive on nitrate levels simply because they exploited the loopholes made possible by the legislation's local caveats. French farmers have thus become masters at registering their support for anti-pollution regulations while finding ways to evade them at the local level. In this they benefit from the fact that the administration appears to be more concerned with general political and economic issues than with the impact agriculture has on the environment. In the end, therefore, it is the locality that sanctions the law and not European legislation.[55]

The same goes for hunting, where French 'traditions' effectively block European regulations on the protection of certain species and the safeguard of exceptional habitats. Government is torn between the political strength of the *Chasse, Pêche, Nature et Traditions* party, which is extremely powerful in some regions, and the need to conform to EU legislation. Local authorities are often complicit in the failure to implement the regulations but the State calculates that such laxity is politically beneficial—even if under pressure from environmental groups, it is frequently indicted by the courts for non-compliance with European legislation.[56]

In general France's relations with the EU are fraught with such cultural ambiguities. On the one hand, Paris seeks to use the Union to assert its European importance and project a strong international image—frequently at the cost of appearing arrogant to its partners.[57] On the other, French governments give themselves license to implement European legislation according to their own narrow political interests—even if they were fully behind the decisions made in Brussels. The point here is not that such tensions do not exist elsewhere

[55] See D. Busca and D. Salles, 2002, 'Agri-environnement: les territoires font la loi', *Environnement et société*, 26.

[56] See D. Darbon, 1997, *La crise de la chasse en France.*

[57] See, for instance, O. Costa, A. Couvidat and J.-P. Daloz, 2003, 'The French Presidency in 2000: an arrogant leader?' in O. Elgström (ed.), *European Council Presidencies: a comparative perspective*; and O. Costa and J.-P. Daloz, 2005, 'How French Policy Makers see Themselves' in H. Drake (ed.), *French Relations with the European Union.*

in Europe, but simply that in the French case they reveal how deeply ambiguous the relations between State and society are.[58]

Sweden or the State of consensus

In Sweden the situation is different: however eurosceptic government is and whatever objections it may have to Brussels legislation, it nevertheless is impelled to follow the letter of the law.

Such extreme submission to the legal framework of institutions is balanced in the country by very high levels of expectations regarding social protection and welfare provisions for the whole of the population. The State, therefore, is highly significant both because it is the guarantor of individual equality before the law and because it is seen to embody key (welfare) virtues, which entail onerous social, economic and political responsibilities. It is ever present in people's minds. It symbolises collective accountability, from the lowliest citizen to the Prime Minister.

From the viewpoint of a cultural analysis it is of course important to understand the historical factors that have brought about this somewhat unusual situation. The medieval period (understood here as post-Viking) exhibited very few State characteristics, other than limited attempts at legal codification. The kings were weak, with little executive power, since the bulk of their efforts were devoted to establishing and maintaining political alliances. They were compelled regularly to travel in order to assert their authority over their vassals, over their temporary allies and over those members of their family whose loyalty was feeble. The assemblies (*things*), which were held with some regularity, were at once political, legal, religious, social and economic.

However, from the sixteenth century there began a distinct, if halting, dynamic of State construction. Scholars speak here of *maktstaten, militärstaten* and *skattestaten*, referring respectively to the State functions linked to political power, army and taxation.[59] The Swedish

---

[58] These relations are also the product of the ambiguous stance of French citizens in relation to authority—at once feared and distrusted but equally to be evaded, or cheated, if at all possible.

[59] For a synthetic treatment, see here L. Jespersen, 2000, 'The Constitutional and Administrative Situation' in L. Jespersen (ed.), *A Revolution from Above? The Power State of 16th and 17th Century Scandinavia.*

State brought the whole of its territories under unified and legal control much earlier than the French. This came as a result not of the imposition of central control over the periphery but of socio-political processes that ensured the political participation of representatives from all areas. It entailed not just representation from all the realm's regions[60] but also from the main estates: aristocracy, bourgeoisie, clergy and free peasants. Historical sociologists of this period have stressed the importance of the absence of serfdom and of the remarkable presence of peasant delegates in Parliament, which acquired in this way undisputed representative legitimacy and promoted standardisation. Despite the huge distances involved and the difficulties in communication due to terrain and climate, Stockholm's relatively central position ensured the fairly rapid distribution of official documents. In this respect Sweden did not experience the difficulties faced by the Danish-Norwegian State where it sometimes took months for official correspondence to reach the northern regions.

The Swedish State only experienced limited absolutist periods: 1680–1718, which followed the 'long century' of conquest and regional domination; and 1772–1809, which however was marked by the assassination of Gustav III and the abdication of his son Gustav IV Adolph. Attempts to establish an absolute monarchy were swiftly stifled. By and large Parliament exercised control and constrained royal power, as is best illustrated by the famous 'Age of Liberty' that characterised most of the eighteenth century. As a consequence the State did not seek domination over society but aimed instead at achieving a general consensus, which was guaranteed by its representative sovereignty. Over the centuries there emerged a privileged relation between the citizens and the central institutions of power, in which all parts of society participated. If the nobility had influence it was less because it owned the land than because it gave service to the State, whether in the army or administration. The bourgeoisie, who were dominant in cities and who had little autonomy, also had a vested interest in the modernisation of the State.[61]

Of course it is essential not to reify the Swedish State and to scrutinise carefully the interests of political rulers. Those historians who

[60] Including that of Finland or those provinces conquered from Denmark.
[61] See H. Gustafsson, 1994, *Political Interaction in the Old Regime.*

have studied the question of who benefited most from the control of power in Sweden have concluded that no single class or group managed either to capture or instrumentalise the modern State. Often the King supported the interests of the peasantry against those of the aristocracy, whose indispensable services he still managed to retain by means of other rewards. Most of the time the monarch was no more than *primus inter pares* within a Council accountable to Parliament and his room for manoeuvre was reduced. For its part the nobility was often divided and thus sought support from other quarters in order to prevail over rival factions.

From a comparative standpoint the Swedish State was one of the earliest to achieve the establishment of monopoly control. As regards coercion, Sweden pioneered the setting up of a national army within Europe. Even if it had to have recourse to mercenaries, the bulk of its troops were composed of peasant conscripts, who signed up for 'military service' in exchange for land allocation. This was crucial for a country long committed to expansion abroad, but it was also critical in bringing about the integration of its diverse populations and in fostering a sense of national unity. As concerns taxation, payment was made to State appointed tax collectors and not to the local gentry. This was decisive in terms of the development of non-parochial social relations, since it made possible direct links between the population and State institutions, thus avoiding intermediaries.[62] In exchange the State was expected to work towards infrastructural and economic development. Because the country was heavily dependent on the export of iron ore the authorities set up an important communication network right from the eighteenth century.

The transition from a particularistic to a bureaucratic system did not occur without difficulties. On the face of it the process of administrative rationalisation was clear-cut. Right from the seventeenth century efforts were made to bring about specialisation and to allocate well-demarcated responsibilities to full-time officials. Procedures were institutionalised: for instance, public accounting was based on clear budgetary rules, required professional bookkeeping and involved auditing. Similarly the rights and responsibilities of public officials were codified precisely: for example, in order to ensure con-

---

[62] This tendency has lasted into the contemporary period, which explains why, for instance, the Social-Democrats have been opposed to cooperatives.

tinuity of service over the given area over which they had responsibility, functionaries required permission if they wanted to take leave.

Nevertheless, when it came to recruitment there continued to
prevail a venal system, which was not really compatible with a meritocratic rationale. Hence members of Swedish high society could
acquire official position by means of payment—whereas in the more
absolutist Danish-Norwegian dispensation the emphasis fell more
squarely on juridical competence, work effectiveness and career
employment.[63] In Sweden the income generated from the sale of
offices was the preserve of the sellers, who could use this as an
advance for the purchase of higher office or to subsidise their retirement. Such a system did not neglect competence since in most
cases recruitment still necessitated a university degree. Efforts were
made to provide appropriate education—for example at the University of Uppsala, where foreign teachers were employed to train the
country's future diplomats. Consequently the élite were keen to send
their children to institutions of higher education—even if they were
often too young to benefit from the teaching. However, exams were a
mere formality. In sum, at the central level and in cities civil servants
were educated, but they owed their position to their social and
financial standing.

Students of Swedish history now agree that the consolidation of a
modern, Weberian-type bureaucracy did not occur until the mid-
nineteenth century. Yet it is important to stress that the tradition of
bureaucratic transparency and of public access to administrative documents goes back to the 1760s. In this respect Sweden was far ahead
of its Scandinavian neighbours, which only adopted such open procedures after the Second World War. The same applies to the well-
known *Ombudsman*, whose role it was to protect citizens against
administrative abuse. Although this position was only formalised
constitutionally in 1809, it was already effective from the beginning
of the eighteenth century.

In sum, and from the point of view of historical sociology, it is easy
to identify the origins of today's strong, unitary, highly bureaucratised
but consensual State in the country's *longue durée*—even if the process
of differentiation, notably between high public office and the political realm is much more recent.

[63] See T. Knudsen, 1991, 'State Building in Scandinavia: Denmark in a Nordic
context' in T. Knudsen (ed.), *Welfare Administration in Denmark*.

However, our aim is not just to highlight the specific attributes of the Swedish State but to offer a cultural analysis of its place in contemporary society. In this Scandinavian country the State has virtually acquired a 'religious' aura. Every citizen is not just aware of the laws but conforms to them as though they issued from a 'sacred' text. Everyone is vigilant. Transgression brings forth vigorous admonition. In this respect the role played by Lutheran pastors in the formation of the State, especially at the local level, was very important. If the State confiscated the wealth of the old Church and annexed Protestantism, it also absorbed the spirit of the Reformation. Unlike France there is in Sweden no opposition between State and Church: the former took over the latter, but it retained its moral fibre.[64] Despite the current decline in religious activities Lutheran ethical injunctions to obey the law, which is embodied in the secular State, clearly still carry much conviction.

The Swedish State guarantees the respect of the principles of equality, integration and inclusion within the framework of participatory democracy. Depending on one's viewpoint, its ubiquitous importance in the citizens' everyday life can be seen as either reassuring or oppressive. Whatever the case it is without doubt a State that makes perfect sense to the Swedes, who have come to internalise both its reach and its wide-ranging responsibilities.

However, the picture is more complex, for Sweden also exhibits a very high degree of individualism, which on the face of it seems at odds with the ubiquitous presence of the State. It is indeed difficult for outside observers to reconcile the Swedes' apparent desire to conform and their highly prized individual autonomy.[65] A cultural approach is useful here for it makes it possible to understand that the State is the one institution that ensures a balance between the primacy of social cohesion and the respect of individual independence.[66] Relations between State and citizens are direct, unmediated.

---

[64] The Swedish Lutheran Church was the State religion until recently.

[65] See Å. Daun, 1991, 'Individualism and Collectivity among Swedes', *Ethnos*, 3–4. Of course one needs to take into account the actual cultural significance of individualism, which often points to a strong degree of self-consciousness or singularity, but which here refers primarily to the desire for autonomy.

[66] See here L. Trägårdh, 1997, 'Statist Individualism: on the culturality of the Nordic welfare State' in Ø. Sørensen and B. Stråth (eds), *The Cultural Construction of Norden*.

The State has responsibility for areas, which in other countries would be the preserve of the family, the local community, the Church, charitable organisations or private insurance. In this respect it is not dissimilar to the French case, but there is a fundamental difference: in Sweden the State is not concerned to 'tame' society; conversely, civil society is not geared to resisting the reach of an all too invasive State. In the Scandinavian country it is in fact the State that guarantees the existence, and facilitates the operation, of a strong democratic (civil) society.

A number of analysts have looked closely at more recent social (notably, feminist and environmental) movements, arguing that they show the decline of traditional corporatism and mark the rise of a more vigorous civil society—the origins of which would go back to the early nineteenth century.[67] We would not want in any way to minimise the importance of religious lobbying, anti-alcohol leagues and numerous other associations that have contributed greatly to the amelioration of living and working conditions. Yet such activities were not similar to those that obtained in more liberal and bourgeois countries, where the State had signally failed to address such social issues. These were egalitarian organisations, which readily found a place within the State.

The explanation for this lies in the country's socio-historical trajectory, which experienced little class conflict. Because the élite were not economically secure they readily sought employment within public service. Of course a number of scholars have pointed out that such an edifying vision of Swedish society could itself be an ideological smokescreen, obscuring greater social divisions. They have questioned the myth of the 'independent peasant', for instance. Nevertheless, such interpretations are as extreme as the ones they ostensibly aim to debunk. There is indeed no gainsaying that the absence of serfdom, the quite exceptional degree of peasant political representation and the alliance between the Crown and the less privileged social classes had a fundamental impact on the historical evolution of the State and must be at the core of any socio-political analysis.[68]

[67] See M. Micheletti, 1995, *Civil Society and State Relations in Sweden*.
[68] See Ø. Sørensen and B. Stråth (eds), 1997, *The Cultural Construction of Norden* together with a review of that book: P. Kettunen, 1999, 'A Return to the Figure of the Free Nordic Peasant', *Acta Sociologica*, 42, pp. 259–69.

From a comparative outlook this points to the singularity of the Swedish model, which a number of political scientists have argued exposes the limits of some theories of historical sociology.[69] The so-called Swedish 'model' can be understood not just as an ideological choice but also in cultural terms. Thus the Social Democrats, who developed the welfare State to its ultimate logical conclusion, did so within a set of cultural logics that transcended their own ambitions and constrained their choices.[70] This is a key conclusion, which lies at the heart of our approach, and which requires an interpretation of 'culture' going beyond the view that it is merely used instrumentally as 'ideology'. Our hypothesis, therefore, is that the élite operated within a cultural framework that set clear limits to their action. We will return to this very question in the next chapter, where we discuss political representation.

If the Swedes did not invent the welfare State, it is obvious that it was they who developed it furthest. For better or for worse Sweden is a country that has combined the highest rate of taxation with the most comprehensive social provisions. Specialists constantly debate the issue of which model of the welfare State arose first, which influenced the others most and what differences can be found within Europe or within Scandinavia.[71] Such discussion can often become ideological, or normative.[72] When asked about this issue the Social Democratic leaders—particularly those familiar with the so-called Golden Age when they ruled virtually unimpeded—stress the efforts

[69] They argue that the Scandinavian experience is not easily explained by structural analysis such as that proposed in B. Moore, 1966, *Social Origins of Dictatorship and Democracy*, since there was neither bourgeois revolution nor disintegration of a small-holding peasantry. See Ø. Østerud, 1977, 'Configurations of Scandinavian Absolutism' in P. Torsvik, *Mobilization, Center-Periphery Structures and Nation Building*. Similarly critiques have shown that Stein Rokkan's macro-interpretative analysis, combining cultural (North/South European cleavages) and economic (East/West distinctions) factors, paid too little attention to the national specificities of Scandinavian countries, particularly Sweden.

[70] See M. Childs, 1936, *Sweden: the middle way* and 1980, *Sweden: the middle way on trial*.

[71] See, among many, P. Flora and J. Heidenheimer, 1981, *The Development of Welfare States in Europe and America*; G. Esping-Andersen, 1990, *The Three Worlds of Welfare Capitalism*; and P. Baldwin, 1990, *The Politics of Class Solidarity*.

[72] For a panorama of the country from that angle, see L. Lewin, 1988, *Ideology and Strategy*.

made by the party and its affiliated organisations (trade unions, youth movements) to transform society. Theirs is a highly partisan political vision, which can sometimes amount to proselytism.[73]

Given the somewhat biased, but nevertheless ambivalent, views propagated by the party—highlighting a high degree of egalitarianism and redistribution but within a capitalist economy—the discussion of the Swedish experience has become highly politicised, often superficial and Manichean.[74] Piqued by the Social Democrats' tone of moral superiority, conservatives readily cast the 'model' in question as a totalitarian nightmare, a system that extinguished all individual and social initiative.[75] Radical Marxists see it as proof that capitalism could not be reformed. Such are still sometimes the views of those who are primarily concerned with normative issues, and in particular how far the Swedish 'model' either failed to live up to its propaganda or has in fact been changing under the pressures of globalisation, the European Union and the impact of high immigration.

Another interpretation is that the nature of the peculiarly generous Swedish welfare State has its roots in the country's historical culture. Some historians point to those who studied, and were inspired by, Bismarck's social legislation in the 1880s. Others refer to more local precedents (the laws protecting the poor, the role of guilds etc.) going back to the end of the Middle Ages, or at least the early nineteenth century. Similarly it is argued that there are deeply entrenched cultural reasons for the nature of the highly rationalist corporate system that emerged.[76] If the Swedish model was consolidated at the end of the Second World War, many contend that it had its roots in an earlier period of capitalist development, when a paternalist bourgeoisie was keen to cooperate with a rather reformist working class in order to maintain social peace. In sum, the Swedish consensus on the need to avoid conflict and to promote general well-being is, in this reading, the outcome of an agreement between 'capital' and 'labour' to share

[73] For a discussion of what this implies, see Chapter 1.

[74] This harks to a debate centred on whether street-sweepers should be paid less than managers and whether five years' professional experience should be equivalent to a university degree. See here L. Svensson, 1987, *Higher Education and the State in Swedish History.*

[75] See R. Huntford, 1971, *The New Totalitarians.*

[76] See T. Anton, 1969, 'Policy Making and Political Culture in Sweden', *Scandinavian Political Studies*, 4 and T. Anton, 1980, *Administered Élite.*

the benefits of economic growth under the aegis of a strong, benevolent, State guaranteeing equal social and civic rights, ensuring the
operation of extensive public services and working to make certain
that there did not emerge within society excessive income differentials.

Presented in this way these two lines of reasoning may well appear
extreme and thus unsatisfactory. The first is an intellectualist view,
which reduces politics to the question of party programmes. The
second runs the risk of offering a 'culturalist' justification for the
system—though of the two the second provides the more convincing historical evidence, as many analysts have shown.[77]

Our view derives from a more subtle interpretation of what lies
between the two, even if it leans somewhat in the direction of the
second. We consider the development of the Swedish State within
the *longue durée* and attribute the success of the Social Democrats primarily by reference to the fact that their ideology, their actions and
their construction of Swedish *identity* were in harmony with the
country's cultural milieu. In other words, they did not just evolve
policies that were popular but which also managed to embody
society's cultural concerns. The pursuit of social justice conferred on
those politicians a high degree of legitimacy and contributed to
strengthen further a notion of the welfare State that was in consonance with the population's expectations. Hence politicians both
used and were dependent upon society's cultural foundations.[78] If this
is the case then the more general comparative question is whether
such a process is universal or whether it is itself dependent on the
local world of meanings.

This is central to our argument. We do not subscribe to the view
that culture is a totally independent variable, which politics does not
affect. Nor, for that matter, do we adhere to the view that political
action can transform society wholesale, thus reducing the cultural
dimensions to mere alternative ideologies. Building on what we have
explained so far about the relationship between culture and politics,
we would want to advocate an approach that considers the cultural
framework within which politicians operate. As we showed in our
last book on Africa, political élite can manipulate cultural symbols
but they do so within a cultural environment, which they cannot

---

[77] See S. Graubard (ed.), 1986, *Norden*.
[78] See here our methodological discussion about political order in Chapter 5.

fully master and which they must respect. We thus reject both the theory that the élite merely manipulate cultural factors, behaving as though they were impervious to local codes, and the structuralist approach that sees them merely as puppets of infra-structural determinism, whatever that may be.

From the viewpoint of what the citizens expect in respect of their duties and official responsibilities, it is clear that the Swedish State is highly institutionalised. In this regard it is interesting to note that the Swedes are ambiguous about other models, even one as close as that of Denmark (let alone those further south): they envy their greater laxity, but fear possible anarchy[79].

Nigeria or the State that does not make sense

Nigeria for its part stands near the opposite end of the spectrum from Sweden, since politics in that country is primarily driven by factors of identity and exchange, which have made impossible the institutionalisation of administrative and governmental structures. In a system that is primarily plural and particularistic the State is not seen as a neutral entity charged with the protection and well being of the population. Without privileged access to individuals who are in a position to help, the ordinary member of the public can expect little from 'the State'. As a result the nature and level of trust in respect of federal states and local government are conditioned by the type of links individuals have with office holders. This explains why those who have felt excluded from the political system have sought the creation of their 'own' provincial state.[80] The extension of the federal system and the increase in the number of regional states has afforded relative autonomy to a large number of ethnic and local groupings. The quest is endless but there are limits to how many more sub-divisions can be created, since these states are both expensive and divisive.

[79] There is a strange echo in the perceptions of the Swedes who travelled to Rome in earlier centuries and those who do so today, which combines fascination and unease. The very same words are used: there is attraction for an apparently freer and more bohemian lifestyle but disquiet about looseness, disorganisation, chaos, corruption etc.

[80] As is often the case with reference to Nigeria, or even Africa as a whole, the most enlightening evidence frequently comes from literature. See here T. Aluko, 1986, *A State of our Own*.

Clientelism and factionalism, which show no sign of abating, are not congenial to the putative Westernisation of the political system. Most Nigerians today are, as they always were, obsessed with securing protection from a patron—not from the State. Communitarian solidarity and membership of a Big Man's network[81] are the only effective forms of social 'security' in what is otherwise an implacably harsh environment. People seek out the 'winners', who are likely to reward the support they receive from their followers. In this respect, as will be shown in the following chapter, the conspicuous display of wealth is a political asset, since it implies that the Big Man is unlikely to fail to reward his constituents. The élite, for their part, exploit such personal and informal relations. Nevertheless, loyalty is evanescent and competition between the politically privileged compels them to deliver resources to their clients in order to sustain their prominence.

An analysis based on the interpretation of meaning shows that in such a set up the main considerations turn around trust/distrust and about good/bad leaders. In the absence of an institutional framework that works, or makes sense, political relations are defined by primordial solidarity or clientelistic groupings. The complicated overlap between considerations of formal and informal politics makes any investigation fiendishly complex. But, as we have argued before, it is crucial to go beyond the façade of constitutional politics to uncover the subterranean logics of the exercise of power in this the 'giant of Africa'.

Unfortunately the bulk of academic writing on Nigeria rarely ventures beyond the narrow confines of the formal State. Political scientists and development 'experts', as well as local intellectuals, all continue to rely on a deductive approach, often without the historical perspective, which results in an analysis of the State that is framed by use of qualifiers, such as 'soft', 'hybrid', 'developing', 'neopatrimonial' etc. We have already explained that these mixed categories are not helpful since they suffer a double handicap: rooting in universalising models and at the same time suggesting reasons why

---

[81] We use the term of 'Big Man' because it is the one most commonly employed in Nigeria to refer to the 'protector boss'. But it is also a reference to Sahlins' anthropological model (discussed in the next chapter), which is applicable to Sub-Saharan Africa. See here J.-F. Médard, 1992, 'Le "Big Man" en Afrique—esquisse d'analyse du politicien entrepreneur', *L'Année sociologique*, 42.

Africa might be an exception. Such an approach thus manages both to give the illusion that it is merely a question of 'development' and to be ethnocentric. More worrying, it makes it difficult not just to explain African politics but even to describe concretely what is happening on the ground. Thus academic conformism, political correctness and conceptual stretching conspire to prevent understanding or insight.

The use of inappropriate comparative tools, simply because they apply in other settings, is not conducive to making sense of what is taking place in Nigeria. At best such approaches conclude that the African country is 'behind', that its development is hindered by a number of external factors linked with the impact of colonial rule, the constraints of the world market or globalisation. Concretely this means that the political analysis of the State is most often confined to the study of domination, violence or accumulation. There is too little attention paid to local political dynamics.

Our starting point is different. We seek to understand politics in Nigeria from the long historical perspective and by means of an inductive, interpretative, framework—and not in terms of how it may differ from that of the so-called developed world. Here, as anywhere else, what matters is the analysis of the political realm in its relation to the other spheres of society. Seen from this angle there are significant continuities going back earlier than the colonial period—the impact of which appears in this respect to have been rather more limited than is commonly assumed. The postcolonial era is thus better understood as one during which 'modern' politics re-appropriated its local, African heritage on the basis of long-established social and cultural codes, rather than as a phase of the continued Westernisation of colonial institutions. This does not in any way mean that there has been no political evolution since independence but merely that this evolution has been largely determined by the adaptation of what we might call a local political 'matrix' to the modern world.[82]

There is no space here to develop a political and cultural comparison between the present day country of Nigeria and the pre-colonial territory it now occupies.[83] A careful study of the historical

---

[82] See Chapter 4.
[83] Please refer here to J.-P. Daloz, 2002, *Élites et représentations politiques.*

and anthropological literature and several years of field research confirm a strong impression of heterogeneity. This is clear in relation to the question of social stratification: the argument that the pre-colonial period evidenced a 'common Nigerian heritage' is not convincing.[84] This type of approach usually goes hand in hand with the claim that ethnic groups were 'created' by the colonial rulers—an outcome that was made easier by the work of European anthropologists, who had classified Africans in this way.[85] This is a very debatable interpretation, based as it is on the assumption that the precolonial area that is today Nigeria was harmoniously homogenous, and that it was the British who exploited and fostered whatever divisions may have existed between the groups who chanced to live there.[86] Those who have studied the history and the evolution of such groups know that there were significant cultural differences between them and that these differences have regularly become politically salient since precolonial time, even if tactical alliances have prevailed during some periods.

Nevertheless, there are a number of similarities in the political systems of Nigeria's different ethnic or regional groups. For instance, whether we consider the Bornu model, Hausaland before and after the *Jihad*, 'classical' or military-type Yoruba organisations, the more egalitarian Ibo communities or many other cases, there emerge numerous common elements, which are crucial to our interpretation. Above all there was little of the kind of political differentiation, the type of institutionalisation, and the bureaucratisation that may have developed elsewhere in the world. Of course there were in

---

[84] See here E. Isichei, 1983, *A History of Nigeria*, which contrasts strongly with the more classical (more British) approach found in M. Crowder, 1962, *The Story of Nigeria*. On the question of the relations between different groups before colonial rule, see, among others, A. Afigbo, 1987, *The Igbo and their Neighbours*, Introduction.

[85] C. K. Meek, 1971 [1925], *The Northern Tribes of Nigeria*, 2 vols; S. F. Nadel, 1942, *A Black Byzantium* (about the Nupe); L. Bohannan and P. Bohannan, 1953 (2nd edn, 1969), *The Tiv of Central Nigeria*; P. C. Lloyd, 1954, 'The Traditional Political Systems of the Yoruba', *South-Western Journal of Anthropology*, IV/10; R. E. Bradbury and P. C. Lloyd, 1957, *The Benin Kingdom and Edo-Speaking People, plus the Itsekiri*.

[86] It can in fact be argued that it is postcolonial politicians who exacerbated ethnic divisions, torn as they were between their desire to transcend such splits and their inability to mobilise support other than by such means.

Nigeria strong centres of power, which controlled relatively large territories. Yet such political systems never remotely evolved in the
direction of a State differentiated from society, such as those outlined
in the case of France or Sweden. We are aware that many African and
Africanist scholars reject this view on the grounds that precolonial
'States' in Africa were powerful and well organised. However, as explained in the first part of the chapter, such systems turned on a
notion of legitimacy which was primarily underpinned by exchan-
ges of personal loyalty, ascriptive solidarity and particularistic reciprocity between patrons and clients. Nor did the distinction between
the public and private spheres make any sense.

Colonial rule had only limited success in changing those political
and administrative mechanisms and in establishing a Western political order. True the British did divide the territory by means of
arbitrary cleavages, which upset previous arrangements. Yet it would
be an exaggeration to suggest that colonial rule brought about systematic and radical political change in this respect, and this for two
reasons. Either the colonial government relied on a system of indirect
rule that depended on existing political dispensations, which such
dependence contributed to legitimise. Or the imposition of new
(Western) forms of political government was undermined by the
ways in which they were appropriated and 'Africanised' by those
who were put in charge. The British were less concerned to bring
about the 'modernisation' of politics than in the more pragmatic
need to 'exploit' the colony at the lowest possible cost. In the end,
therefore, both budgetary constraints and the necessity to maintain
legitimacy led the colonial government to rule in a fairly 'informal'
manner.

In point of fact only the first two generations of Africans educated
in mission schools were exposed to the European social and political
'ideals' that lay at the heart of the modern State.[87] This small minority
soon found itself torn between its commitment to the European
'model' and its allegiance to the rest of the population, who resisted
their influence. The British relied heavily on these Nigerians, who
worked in the colonial administration under the stewardship of a
handful of white civil servants.[88] However, a turning point occurred

---

[87] See, for example, E. Ayandele, 1966, *The Missionary Impact on Modern Nigeria
1842–1914.*
[88] See G. Olunsaya, 1975, *The Evolution of the Nigerian Civil Service 1861–1960.*

in 1890 when it was decided formally to colonise the interior. European officials now replaced the local black élite. Frustrated by their sudden downfall and unhappy at a new form of racial discrimination, these educated Africans protested in vain. Barred from the civil service, they now turned towards the professions. This newly sharpened divide between white and black élite led them and (in greater numbers) their descendents towards a nationalist position. Indeed it is they who created and led the movement for independence.

A careful study of the political evolution that took place in the decade preceding and following independence shows that the formal transformation of the political system had limited impact on the ways in which power was exercised. From the administrative point of view the agents working for the traditional authorities (maintaining order, collecting tax, or enforcing the law) remained at the mercy of their employers, who could sack them at will. There was no code regulating the employment of these civil 'servants', or granting them professional independence. Similarly, Native Authorities had complete license when it came to the remuneration of their auxiliaries. Those who had the right contacts were well paid. Others, who might have worked much more, were left to find revenues where they could—not infrequently abusing the local population they were meant to serve.

The attempts made to modernise the administration, increase specialisation and promote meritocracy were at best feeble.[89] In the North, for instance, the authorities were mainly concerned to replace southern bureaucrats with northern ones, since it was understood that the whites would leave at independence. This politics of *Northernisation* was successful in that it drove the southerners away, but this was at the expense of professional competence, since the latter were usually better qualified. Those who replaced them came from the main aristocratic families (including their palace servants of slave origin), regardless of their qualifications. It was the Emirs who appointed all, including the heads of technical departments, on the basis of political loyalty and not competence or motivation.[90]

---

[89] See here I. Nicolson, 1969, *The Administration of Nigeria 1900–1960* and A. Kirk-Greene, 1965, 'Bureaucratic Cadres in a Traditional Milieu' in J. Coleman, *Education and Political Development*.

[90] See C. Whitaker, 1970, *The Politics of Tradition*, p. 181. In the southeast and southwest of the country it was the elected officials, rather than the traditional

The same continues to apply today: the loyalty of administrative staff is not to the institution they serve. There is in this respect no lasting internalisation of 'impersonal' norms. In this area, as in most others, relations remain particularistic and negotiable. Civil servants do not see themselves as professional officials within an administrative machine and do not consider those they are meant to 'serve' as an undifferentiated ensemble of people. From this viewpoint, therefore, the State is merely a façade, the formal regulations of which are used when necessary and discarded when expedient. Only those Nigerians who have lived abroad, for instance in the UK, object to these practices and bemoan the lack of reaction on the part of those fellow Nigerians who have known nothing else.

Clientelistic networks or systems of 'co-ethnic friendship' prevent the advent of any functioning formal bureaucratic organisation. The more resources bureaucrats control the more they operate as though they were in charge of a 'business'. All civil servants, even the lowliest, find ways of negotiating the powers bestowed upon them by their office. It is often the touts, loitering around official buildings, who act as intermediaries to the office-holder, explaining that access to the service in question will have to be negotiated, in the first instance with them.[91] Most Nigerians, who know full well that there is no other way, are forced to play this game—which serves both the intermediary and the bureaucrat.[92]

There thus prevails an attitude of fatalism and an inability to conceive that the situation could be any other than it is. The common response is not to criticise such practices but to find (and to pay for) the contact within that will deliver the service. The perceptions of the bureaucrats themselves are conditioned by particularistic or extra-professional lines rather than the more impersonal ones that ought in principle to characterise a bureaucracy. Like everyone else they give preference to their ethnic group. In a country where particularistic clientelism prevails and where survival strategies require the

---

authorities, who controlled the appointment of civil servants; the result, however, was the same.

[91] As can be testified by anyone who has lived in Nigeria.

[92] The intermediary explains the situation thus: 'since you do not know anyone inside, and since I do, I offer my services to you, knowing that you will show appreciation.'

acceptance of unequal reciprocity, such an administrative 'system' is reproduced through the generations. Consequently the logic of a bureaucracy operating according to 'impersonal' norms, regulations and procedures has failed to take root. The State ideals that the colonial rulers sought (very late in the day and with little vigour) to impart to their successors did not survive long after independence. If this heterodox analysis is correct, then it becomes possible to make sense of a number of aspects of prevailing logics of representation and behaviour.

Our approach, therefore, aims to account for what happens, concretely, on the ground, above and beyond theoretical or ideological debates about the State, which often lack historical depth. For analytical reasons we have developed an argument that sought to explain how Nigerian practices differed substantively from those of the other two cases. We tried in this way to show why it is problematic to refer to the Nigerian 'State'. However necessary this was for the purpose of explaining what we mean by such a stark formulation, we would argue that the method we employed was still too deductive.[93] Ideally we would like to do away entirely with the need to explain why the modern concept of the State fails to apply to this country and devote our full attention to the empirical analysis, the 'thick description', of the nature and workings of social and political relations at the local level.[94] For us, then, a 'scientific' approach would ultimately demand that we keep our distance from a 'general' concept of the State, which in any event some argue only makes sense in the West.[95] We would hold that it is not necessary to place it at the heart of research on politics. And when it seems to make sense in a particular environment it should be analysed in terms of its local relevance and historical trajectory.

---

[93] In *Africa Works* also we were compelled to develop an analysis centred around standard political concepts (State, civil society, identity, dependence, development), which led to relatively iconoclastic conclusions in terms of the 'meaninglessness', 'non-emancipation', 'illusion', 'insignificance' of what are considered to be 'standard' political questions.

[94] Equally, we would prefer to compare the ways in which rulers exercise power without necessarily to engage in a comparative study of the State.

[95] See B. Badie and G. Hermet, 1990, *Politique comparée*.

10

THE GUISES OF POLITICAL REPRESENTATION

The following discussion of political representation will show even more clearly the heuristic advantages of a cultural approach—an approach that is based on the interpretation of local meanings. We are not concerned here, as we were in the previous chapter, with the question of assessing whether political institutions match a putative model, but rather with a political process that is to be found in most polities, albeit in an infinite variety of guises.

Although representation is at the heart of the exercise of power, and is much debated, there is little new in the way it has been studied in the recent past. The arguments seem to reflect either a legal or philosophical standpoint or, perhaps more readily, a tendency to equate representation with the disjunction between rulers and ruled. As such it is a topic that has generated much ideological controversy. Some see representation as a technical question concerned with the democratic mechanisms by which the people express political will. Others take a more radical view and consider it to be the political simulacrum that enables the élite to dominate society.

We would like to cast a fresh look at this important subject. As should be clear from previous chapters, we shall approach this question not from a narrow, abstract, legal or constitutional standpoint but much more from a comparative angle that pays full attention to local meanings. We will aim to link the standard political question about the representation of interests with the cultural contexts within which it takes place concretely.[1] We intend to give equal consideration to the various aspects of representation, from the straightforward mechanism of political delegation to the theatricalities of the

[1] On the standard approach, see A. Birch, 1971, *Representation*.

display of power. Some analysts are sceptical about such a multi-faceted approach and warn against its presumed pitfalls.[2] Others, like Bourdieu, advocate instead a reading of representation as 'alchemy', where its various aspects would all be fused.[3] Yet there have been few empirical studies to follow his injunction.[4]

Despite the reservations mentioned above we believe that a method based on the careful study of polysemy can yield rich dividends and open up a vast area of comparative research well worth exploring. This chapter, like the previous one, will begin with a number of general observations about the concept and about our approach. A detailed discussion on the cases of Nigeria, Sweden and France will then follow.

AN INTERPRETATIVE APPROACH TO REPRESENTATION

The study of political representation has often been highly theoretical. A number of writers have worked on the technical and normative aspects of questions such as the difference between national and popular sovereignty or on the autonomy of the elected officials vis-à-vis those they represent. However, research on the very person of the representative—his or her image, appearance or attitudes—makes it possible to come to more concrete conclusions. The issue is complex, for at the heart of the notion of representation lies an inherent tension between the need for the representative to show distinction *and* to demonstrate affinity, similarity and proximity. We shall first explain why we find existing approaches limiting. We shall then develop our argument in respect of these two key dimensions of representation.

[2] See several of the chapters in F. d'Arcy (ed.), 1985, *La représentation*. This unease in the face of ambiguity is not new: see in this respect H. Pitkin, 1967, *The Concept of Representation*.

[3] See, among others, P. Bourdieu, 1980, *Questions de sociologie*, p. 149 and P. Bourdieu, 1982, *Ce que parler veut dire*, p. 101.

[4] In point of fact, what Bourdieu is most interested in is 'le coup de force symbolique de la représentation'—by which is meant the process whereby self-proclaimed representatives can 'generate' the collective grouping, which they aim to represent. See, for example, P. Bourdieu, 1984, 'La délégation et le fétichisme politique', *Actes de la Recherche en Sciences Sociales*, 52–3 (June). This Bourdieusian journal also produced a double number (36–7, 1981) dedicated to the question of political representation.

A few considerations on the study of political representation

The classical approach to the question of political representation is in our view confined to fairly dogmatic visions of society and voluntarist conceptions of politics. For instance, the debate between those who are concerned to represent the unity of a 'people' and those who privilege the representation of a society's diverse components is a good illustration of the ideological and normative considerations that affect analysis.

In societies such as the French Ancien Régime, which were composed of different estates, representation was not a problem. There was a fit, as it were, between social groupings and political categories. Political representation was rooted in an existing social order of which it was merely the outcome. The situation is infinitely more complicated within an environment in which politics is more differentiated and where society is organised on an individualist and contractual basis. In such cases it has become necessary to invent new categories and to develop new procedures in order to allow the representation of citizenship. This has led to sharply divergent views about the nature of the political system.[5]

The French case is instructive in this respect. Those who wanted to do away with the old social order, and who were suspicious of local parochial interests, conceived representation as the embodiment of the 'general will' and as an instrument of national unification. Two other groups later contested this vision. The liberals wanted to favour the expression of different social interests within a Parliament that would allow for negotiation and compromise. The radicals distrusted the imagery of unity that obscured class divisions and saw representation as the mirror that reflected divergent socio-economic interests.

This debate, which started in the eighteenth century, has never abated. Today, for example, it turns on the sensitive issue of parity between men and women or the representation of 'cultural' minorities. Those who give preference to a 'photographic' notion of representation that reflects a society's different groupings argue that a homogenous vision privileges the dominant strata. Their opponents ask, not without reason, how far such representation needs to go if it is to give voice to all types of identity or particularism. Who will be

[5] See J. Roels, 1969, *Le concept de représentation politique au dix-huitième siècle français.*

entrusted to adjudicate about the legitimacy of representation? As is obvious, therefore, this kind of debate is normative rather than analytical.

Concerning the feminist argument, for example, it is not clear whether the claim for parity is based on the fact that women make up roughly half the electorate or whether it derives from the argument that there are irreconcilable gender differences in the approach to politics. When it comes to ethnic, religious and other minorities, there is obviously a danger that the exaltation of multiculturalism will result in representative atomisation.[6] Furthermore such considerations have immediate practical consequences. Is it possible to conjure techniques of proportional representation that can mirror social diversity accurately? Is there not a serious risk that such political dispensations could lead to constant political instability, resulting in weak governing coalitions unable to agree on policy?

It would not be difficult to furnish other examples of approaches to the question of political representation of dubious analytical neutrality. Let us take, for instance, the issue of the nature of the representative mandate. At one end of the spectrum stand the sceptics who, since Rousseau, have remained hostile to the very notion of representation. Next are those who favour highly restrictive mandates, maintaining that true representation occurs only when the representative acts on explicit instruction. Different still are the advocates of a realist conception of representative democracy, who accept that the representative cannot automatically be bound by the opinions of the electorate. Finally there is a research agenda that stresses the defence of the interests of political classes, above and beyond ideological cleavages.

We might have expected that political sociology would make possible a less partisan method. But such is not the case. Numerous studies of representation, which are based on the survey of objective factors, often display a normative bias—seeking for instance to demonstrate that there is an overload of 'élite' within elected bodies. Equally, ideological considerations clearly impinge on the current debate on the crisis of representation within Europe. Arguments range from the fact that some societies are too politically volatile to the complaint that present day political marketing obscures any real debate

---

[6] We discuss the analytical pitfalls of such a position in Chapter 3.

about fundamental political issues. The proponents of rational choice theory, for their part, reduce representation to political calculus: electoral success is to be understood in terms of cost/benefit analysis. In sum, even empirical research on political representation remains mired in ideological, normative or instrumentalist considerations.

The cultural framework of representation

Our approach, both cultural and comparative, is very different. Admittedly we recognise that there is an inescapable tension between the pressures of social heterogeneity (although social cleavages vary greatly across the world) and the need for a system of representation that facilitates political cohesion. Yet this should not be cause for universalistic interpretations. If we study concretely the nature of the relationship between the representative and the represented it becomes obvious that the standard interpretations discussed above are less than enlightening.

Witness, for example, the case of plural societies where political relations are determined primarily by clientelistic links between patrons and their supporters. In such settings political accountability takes on a very different complexion from that which prevails in political systems where party allegiance and ideological commitments are key. In the first case representation is particularistic and legitimacy is tied to patrimonial redistribution. In the second, relations of representation are markedly more impersonal. As explained in Part III, we want to study these cases inductively, based on a semiotic interpretation of the evidence.

It is true that politics can be, and probably is, about both a question of general political programmes and the common good *as well as* of instrumental loyalties and particularistic benefits. Proponents of development theories have put forward a model of the evolution from local clientelistic logics to the more universal party political system that characterises the West.[7] Nevertheless, empirical research reveals variations that are not easily encompassed within a single theory. It is not really possible to understand fully the complexities of political representation without taking into account the cultural dimensions of the relationship between representatives and repre-

---

[7] See, for example, S. Huntington, 1968, *Political Order in Changing Societies.*

sented. Put differently, our argument is that the nature of that link is itself dependent on the (explicit and implicit) notion that both sides have of the very meaning of representation. It is also the outcome of the way representatives portray the represented as a group *as well as* of their own, conscious or unconscious, presentation of their role.

The analysis of the cultural dimensions of representation goes beyond the mere recording of political opinions and viewpoints. It must extend to the study of what lies behind such attitudes—that is, the thought patterns and forms of reasoning linked to the environment that conditions the behaviour of both represented and representatives. In this respect it is necessary to make sense of the ways both the élite and the general public are influenced by the cultural milieu they share. The social imaginary and the diverse forms of collective representation condition the texture of political delegation. Hence, there are in each instance more or less plausible, more or less successful, practices of representation.

Our approach thus consists in testing the extent to which people feel that they are properly represented and the degree to which representatives are concerned to reflect the opinion of those on whose behalf they speak. In some circumstances there are severe constraints on representatives, who are expected to reproduce strictly the ideals and socio-cultural interests of the community for which they stand. Only at this price are they empowered to act on their behalf. We are faced here with the sensitive issue of political identity and identification, as discussed in Chapter 4—that is, instances where the population only accept as 'representatives' those who belong to their own (for example, ethnic or religious) community. However, as we shall see below in the case of Nigeria, the widening of political competition often makes such simple practices of delegation impossible and forces politicians to align themselves with other groups in order both to increase representation at the national level and maximise the delivery of resources to their supporters in a context of fierce factional antagonisms.

Conversely there are cases where it is the very claim of being a representative that creates, shapes and defines the nature of the grouping for which one purports to act. In this instance the political discourse becomes 'performative',[8] aiming to give body and public presence to

---

[8] In linguistics, the 'peformative' denotes discourses that contain within themselves

a regional identity or to other 'virtual' social groups. It becomes a matter of imposing a new vision and a new division of the social or territorial world, of redefining the contours of the arena within which struggles to sustain, or deny, particular forms of identity take place.[9] For example, in France the representation of 'cadres' (managers) was made possible by the demands of those who claimed to speak on their behalf and thereby established the legitimacy of a category that was not encompassed within the traditional vision of labour division between workers and employers.[10]

Clearly our aim is not to reduce the question of interpretation to a few 'ideal types' and even less to narrow it down to a number of structural variables claiming to explain different practices. It is, rather, to attempt to use 'thick description' in order to tease out the evidence with which to throw some light on the local logics underpinning distinct modes of representation. However, before we do so we would like to discuss the two key aspects of representation: the principle of distinction and the demands of similarity. These are not the only relevant questions, clearly, but they are fundamental. The way we tackle them will help to explain the specificities of our approach.

Representatives need to remain proximate enough to those for whom they speak. At the same time they must maintain suitable distance, so that they can demonstrate the value of their role as spokesperson. In other words, it is often important for these political actors not to appear cut off from those they represent—that is, in some sense to embody their identities and interests. Yet they cannot merely act as a 'mirror' since those for whom they stand frequently aspire to elevate themselves, in part at least by way of the individual they have chosen as representative.

So it may well be the case that the most profitable strategy in this respect is to combine proximity with distinction. In some societies, as we shall see later, there is little space for manoeuvre: for instance, a

the act to which they refer—in other words bringing to life what they claim to formulate.

[9] See P. Bourdieu, 2001, 'L'identité et la représentation' in P. Bourdieu, *Langage et pouvoir symbolique* (previously published, in 1984, as 'Le pouvoir de la représentation').

[10] L. Boltanksi, 1982, *Les cadres*. Other examples will be found in P. Bourdieu, 'La délégation et le fétichisme politique'. We do not reject this type of analysis but would express some disquiet at its universalising ambition and its one-dimensional interpretation in terms of 'usurpation'.

display of ostentation may be either indispensable or completely unacceptable. The nature and consequence of this tension between similarity and difference are both complex and extremely significant. Our point here is that they can only be properly analysed in terms of the interpretation of the local cultural context.

We shall discuss below the 'theatrical' dimensions of representation. Suffice it to point out here that there is in the social sciences too little attention paid to the symbolic aspects of élite superiority. Most analysts limit their research to universalist reflections on the questions of inequality and political consciousness. Yet it is comparatively more rewarding to study the extent to which different peoples tolerate symbolic distance between representatives and represented. Understanding how and why it matters entails looking beyond the so-called 'objective' social factors extant and entering the world of mentalities. In many settings the political élite need not apologise for its eminence, which is easily accepted and merely generates deference or indifference, admiration or envy. For their part the behaviour of the élite ranges from ostentatious display to ostensible generosity, with a view to meet the expectations of their supporters by way of largesse.[11]

Historically one of the most interesting research areas is that which studies the impact that the advent of democracy and universal suffrage have had on the image of the representative. We know that the increase in purchasing power brought about by economic development created the modern 'consumer', who acquired the right to be treated with respect by businesses competing for custom. We know too that the narrowing of the gap between social classes (in Western Europe and North America) has led to less unequal living conditions. Could it also be the case that the acquisition of the full rights of citizenship, including the vote that confers upon ordinary people control over the fate of government,[12] reduces the 'prestige' of political actors?[13] Perhaps. However, we shall show why it cannot simply be assumed that deference towards politicians is lessened by the obligation they have of treating every citizen equally.[14] There are

---

[11] See P. Veyne, 1976, *Le pain et le cirque.*
[12] Although this issue is complex, since it hinges partly on questions of socialisation and of the understanding of political relations.
[13] See W. Goode, 1978, *The Celebration of Heroes.*
[14] See E. Shils, 1969, 'Reflections on Deference' in A. Rogow, (ed.), *Politics, Personality and Social Science in the Twentieth-Century.*

huge cultural variations in this regard even among ostensibly similar democratic countries.

Political representation as theatre

It is because of this that we favour the comparative analysis of the theatrical aspects of representation. They provide crucial evidence of the ways political actors use various cultural registers in order to seek to impress putative constituents or to symbolise unity. Although most studies of political élite tend to concentrate on key socio-economic questions—such as accumulation, reproduction, circulation—this section focuses attention on the more elusive, but no less significant, dramatic aspects of politics. Indeed, acting is an integral part of the political behaviour of representatives, whether it is to demonstrate distinction or, conversely, modesty. Understanding how it works clearly requires an interpretative approach. An important area for research is how the display of the outward (or internalised) signs of distinction and power contribute to the legitimacy of political actors. This, in addition to the relationship between cultural attributes and the efficacy of the defence of the interests of a constituency, complements the analysis of political representation.

Before proceeding we want to discuss first the relevance, but also the limits, of historical, anthropological and sociological research in this respect. We shall then develop our own, more political approach to the comparative investigation of political representation.

As already explained, the strength of cultural anthropology is to pay suitable attention to the immense diversity and 'plasticity' of societies across the globe. One conventional approach to the symbolic and theatrical dimensions of power in the social sciences is to stress the links between eminence, deference and respectability. Balandier,[15] in a book dedicated to 'princes of all colours', offers a reading of politics as theatre, which is akin to C. Wright Mills' arguments about 'master symbols'[16] and Edelman's discussion of the political uses of the symbolic.[17] Above and beyond these studies, which lay emphasis on political manipulation,[18] the merit of cultural anthro-

---

[15] G. Balandier, 1980, *Le pouvoir sur scènes.*
[16] C. Wright Mills, 1961, *The Sociological Imagination.*
[17] M. Edelman, 1964, *The Symbolic Uses of Politics.*
[18] As does the work of Victor Turner (1967, *Schism and Continuity in an African*

pology is to offer approaches that demonstrate the complex relevance of the symbolic. One must refer here to Firth, who discussed with great subtlety how different 'spectators' make different sense of rituals,[19] but above all to the magisterial *Negara*, by Clifford Geertz, in which the author shows how 'thick description' enables the analyst to transcend simplistic interpretations of political representation.[20]

Among others it is well to mention here those studies that concentrate on systems based on prestige goods and gift giving.[21] Such political arrangements lead to the exaltation of those who own such goods and foster a common feeling of identification—a factor that is obviously relevant to the understanding of representation in these societies. It also raises very interesting questions about the relationships between objects and the owners of objects within societies that do not (yet) subscribe to a logic of object reification. Additionally the reading of such monographic studies renders even more palpable the distinct cultural perceptions to be found in differing environments.

As concerns gift giving, Mauss' writings[22] are well known; they are impressive from a theoretical viewpoint but perhaps overly universalising.[23] They are useful to political analysis because they point to the collective aspect of gift exchange. For instance, in the Amerindian potlatch there was reciprocal obligation between clans and not between individuals. It is the group as a whole, embodied in the person of the chief, which had to give, and receive, with 'dignity', or indulge in ostentatious 'consumption'. Here too, therefore, anthropology discusses representation in its manifold manifestations, including the theatrical. As Sahlins showed in his comparative work, such displays of prestige acquire immense importance in societies without clear political hierarchies and where relations are highly

---

Society) or of Abner Cohen, who is interested in the instrumental aspect of the symbolic (1981, *The Politics of Élite Culture*).

[19] R. Firth, 1973, *Symbols*.

[20] C. Geertz, 1980, *Negara*.

[21] See M. Godelier, 1973, *Horizons, trajets marxistes en anthropologie*, vol. II, and M. Godelier, 1996, *L'énigme du don*.

[22] See M. Mauss, 1950 (1924), 'Essai sur le don' in M. Mauss, *Sociologie et anthropologie*.

[23] Instead of assuming like Mauss that gift giving is at the heart of all 'primitive societies', it is important to study its historical and very culturally specific discussions. See P. Veyne, 1976, *Le pain et le cirque*.

personalised.[24] His work thus links with our earlier discussion of identity as well as with the complex nature of the relationships between individual and collective political actors, which can only be fully appreciated within the local context. It shows how contextually bound the notion of political representation is.

These all too brief examples show why anthropology is salutary to political science: it makes it glaringly obvious that the Western developmental path—and by implication our concepts of representation as well as our analytical frameworks—is relatively singular. Some anthropologists argue that when it comes to questions of distinction and prestige there is a wide variety of different situations that are quite distinct from our own. On the other hand, anthropology is much less convincing when it seeks to develop a 'fundamental science' of mankind by means of the identification of the 'constant' attributes shared by all and transcending local variations.

The (direct or indirect) contribution of historians to the question of representation is immense and we cannot here pretend to engage their work seriously and meaningfully in the few paragraphs that follow. History at its best reveals the broad dynamics of social and political change (without falling into the trap of evolutionary theory). Given our approach it stands to reason that we find most to admire in what is called in France 'histoire des mentalités' and what has been published in the English-speaking world under the guise of 'New Cultural History'.[25] This scholarly corpus is particularly sensitive to the risks of anachronism and of 'false historical continuities' when it comes to the study of forms of representation, which are rendered obsolete in later periods. The pace at which 'mentalités', or culture, evolve is rarely the same as that of political, economic or ideational history.[26]

One of the merits of this historiography is that it does not just work diachronically, with a view to explaining historical transformations, but also synchronically, as it studies in depth the singularities

[24] See, for example, M. Sahlins, 1963, 'Poor Man, Rich Man, Big Man, Chief: political types in Melanesia and Polynesia', *Comparative Studies in Society and History*, 2/3 (April) and M. Sahlins, 1972, *Stone Age Economics*.

[25] See, among others, L. Hunt (ed.), 1989, *The New Cultural History*; P. Burke, 1997, *Varieties of Cultural History*; and P. Burke, 2004, *What is Cultural History?*

[26] We refer here to what is discussed in Chapter 6 above about the cultural 'tectonic' dynamics of change.

of earlier environments. Here historians (like anthropologists) account for modes of thought, behaviour and motivation, as well as of political calculus, which are completely at odds with contemporary ones. Therefore, it is easy to understand why Geertz's method has had such commanding influence over so many historians.[27] There are of course important differences between the two disciplines—the most critical of which is that anthropologists are able to root their analysis in direct observation. Nevertheless, Geertz's definition of culture (notably its 'public' texture), his emphasis on the fact that it can be understood in terms of the study of 'texts', 'staging' and symbolic systems, are all congenial to historians. The point here is not to exalt an empathetic approach to the peoples concerned. Nor is it to suggest that such a method enables the analyst to uncover 'unconscious' structures of agency. It is merely—but that is already a great deal—to call for the analysis of the words, images and institutions by which people perceive and represent themselves.[28]

As comparativists we are of course interested in the monographs available about those places and periods in which the theatre of political representation was most exuberant: the Antiquity's Epiphanic monarchs; the extravagant Roman Empire; the pomp of Italian Renaissance; the pageantry of the court of Burgundy, of England at the end of the Elizabethan period, of the Stuarts, and particularly, Versailles; the world of the sultans, maharajas, emperors *et al*. Conversely we learn a great deal from the periods of reaction against ostentation: for instance, the 1789 Revolution and the political behaviour that marked the beginnings of the first French Republic.[29] At the same time more ambiguous environments are also instructive for a comparative analysis of representation in this perspective.[30]

Equally there is much to learn from more synthetic books, which examine how ruptures occur in the *longue durée*, or those that study the transmission of models from one society or one period to another.

---

[27] See here W. Sewell, 1977, 'Geertz, Cultural Systems and History: from synchrony to transformation', *Representations*, 59 (summer).

[28] C. Geertz, 1983, 'From the Native Point of View' in C. Geertz, *Local Knowledge*.

[29] See L. Hunt, 1984, *Politics, Culture and Class in the French Republic*.

[30] We refer here, for example, to the Reformation countries. See Schama's reflections on the 'embarrassment of riches' in the seventeenth-century Netherlands—which is also a fine illustration of the insights of cultural analysis. S. Schama, 1987, *The Embarrassment of Riches*.

For example, it is enlightening to analyse the changes in the 'visibility' of power holders over time. For a long time 'contact' with rulers only applied to the limited number of people who could be in their physical proximity. Within proto-States political aristocrats had to make a show of their existence all over their territory, and even more so in newly conquered lands. The sovereign's entrance into the cities was thus an occasion for all, and not just the notables, to witness his existence—even if the local élite also attended other events, such as banquets or tournaments. With the rise of absolutism, courtly society and centralisation rulers became more remote and they restricted the occasions on which the crowds would see them. This trend continued over the period that followed. With the development of contemporary mass media, however, there is a virtual form of ubiquitous presence: we can see, but not engage with, our rulers. The continuous flow of information—first in print, then on radio and finally on screen—generates a feeling of 'instrumentalisable' intimacy.[31]

We could also mention here many studies about the relevance of the relationship between public and private spheres to the modalities of political representation. Clearly such a distinction is not equally pertinent to all cases: for instance, it does not make sense in so-called 'pre-modern' or even totalitarian societies.[32] Of interest to us is the putative connection between personal ostentation and political prominence. Present day decorum in Western democratic countries (whether republican or not) holds that those earlier displays of pageantry are only legitimate insofar as they are the preserve of the State and not of a political class seeking to appropriate them. When contemporary political élite are but temporary office holders, the ostentation displayed in, say, the banquets they organise in their capital's palaces is perceived as a reflection of the country's standing, which it is sometimes necessary to project, and not of that of its politicians. Nevertheless, there are still significant differences between countries, as will be shown later in regard of France and Sweden. Finally it is useful to compare attitudes towards the private lives of politicians,

---

[31] The literature on this subject is too large to be cited here.

[32] See here the series of volumes on the history of private life published by the French publisher Le Seuil under the editorship of Ph. Ariès and G. Duby.

and in particular the tension between the protection of privacy and freedom of information. Here too there are wide differences between periods or nations.[33]

Let us now complete our discussion of the literature on the theatrical aspects of representation with a brief look at sociology, undoubtedly one of the disciplines that have most influenced political science. The founders of sociology were primarily concerned with social change in nineteenth- and twentieth-century Western societies. However, a few (like Weber or Elias) sought to essay a theory of historical dynamics and, for this reason, set out to analyse the social aspects of 'pre-modern' or extra-European communities.

For our part, we have a mixed appreciation of sociologists' efforts at theory building. Obviously political scientists who study representation make constant use of a range of useful, even indispensable, concepts such as stratification, status, class, prestige etc. At the same time we have reservations about those sociologists who hold a monolithic view of the social order and claim to draw conclusions by means of a study of sociological 'laws'. Many of them are analytically stimulating but, from our viewpoint, fall into the trap of making generalisations they hold to be universally valid.

This is quite clearly the case for sociological research on the symbolic factors of domination. Anyone interested in élite social distinction is familiar with the body of studies on consideration, eminence, imitation, trickle down effects, conspicuous consumption etc. We would in this respect need to assess, from a cultural viewpoint, the work of Weber, Veblen, Tarde, Simmel and Bourdieu as well as that of Sombart, Elias, Parsons, Merton, Goffman, E. P. Thomson, Duncan and Baudrillard. However, the main problem with the sociologists cited above is that, on the basis of the analysis of one case study, they generalise to other settings and other periods.

Elias criticised Veblen for failing to understand the behavioural logics and the mentalities of environments different from the

---

[33] Our purpose here is not simply to offer multiple illustrations of topics that are relevant to the analysis of political representation but to stress how historical research also contributes to widen our horizons and our reference points. In this way it enriches our comparative reflection and makes it possible to approach the question other than by way of the theoretically abstract viewpoints discussed above.

American bourgeois society he knew best.[34] Yet Elias too can be taken to task for his debatable links between courtly society and the potlatch. Simmel offered an enlightening method for the study of Berlin's bourgeoisie in the early twentieth century, but the extension of this model to other cases is less convincing. Bourdieu wrote rich chapters on French society in the 1970s, but here too his extrapolation to other terrains is debatable. Within societies organised in vertical (clientelistic, factional, identity or religious) relations, as opposed to class structures, his model of 'symbolic struggles' does not really apply—as will be shown in the case of Nigeria.[35]

Thus we need to proceed cautiously. We acknowledge our debt to these scholars but are mindful of the limits of their models when it comes to a comparative interpretation of meaning. Indeed, their work derived from different theoretical approaches. Other than Veblen they all considered the question of élite symbolic superiority within the ambit of a general sociological model. Although as a result their writings are theoretically coherent, they are not as useful as they might have been for the comparative analysis of élite distinction. As already argued, and again to be explained in the Conclusion, an approach in terms of relevant theoretical eclecticism does provide a way of overcoming this contradiction between the theoretical and empirical.

Let us now come to our own discipline. Clearly the question of the legitimacy of political power cannot simply be reduced to that of 'social' legitimacy. For this reason the study of the possible eminence and ostentation of the political élite is not exactly the same as that of the social élite. Indeed, one of the key differences here is that modern democracies are constructed around a precise notion of representation and that professional politicians are politically dependent on the population they represent.

Again we are confronted with the question of the very definition of the political realm, the degree of differentiation between the political and social spheres and the extent of the institutionalisation of specialised political roles. Ethnology provides evidence that the distinction between the political and social does not always make sense: a number of societies do not have separate mechanisms of political

---

[34] N. Elias, 1974, *La société de cour*, pp. 48–9.
[35] See our brief discussion of Bourdieu in Chapter 2.

control. Historians of Europe have provided us with numerous examples of aristocracies claiming an innate right to rule, as though their authority derived from a timeless political 'vocation'. Even in nineteenth-century France, the legitimacy of ministers like Thiers or Guizot did not rest on the fact that they held any official post. It was only at the end of the century, with the advent of professional politicians earning their living in politics that the distinction truly began to matter.[36] From a comparative standpoint it is interesting to contrast this with the situation of political actors in non-Western settings, where politics is not distinct from other social spheres and where, therefore, politicians straddle different (political, economic, social, NGO) spheres.

True it is often argued that today's politicians more often that not belong to the upper classes (insofar as it is possible objectively and subjectively to identify such classes). Thus many political sociologists readily see social and political domination as homologous. But this is far from being the rule. Witness how common it is for junior officers to seize power by means of a coup. Furthermore the contention that there is 'objective' collusion between political and socio-economic élite is often ideologically driven, with a view to denouncing the hegemony of the ruling classes. And yet the comparative study of élite reveals a real diversity of cases, to such an extent that it is often debatable whether there ever is a ruling *class* as such.[37]

The same applies to the tension between distinction and similarity. Within a competitive political context it is crucial for would-be representatives to stand out.[38] Whether they aim to distinguish themselves from the other candidates seeking endorsement by a political group or, at a later stage, from other parties' representatives, politicians want to appear 'different'. This is especially important during the run up to elections, when candidates attempt to exhibit the qualities that would make them suitable MPs and prove that they would defend the interests of their constituents. In some settings this might extend to the deployment of extra-ordinary imagery, even suggesting hero-like qualities, or at least the claim to be able to use political power for the direct benefit of the constituents.

[36] M. Weber, 1919 (1959), *Le savant et la politique.*
[37] See M. Dogan, (ed.), 2003, *Élite Configuration at the Apex of Power.*
[38] B. Manin, 1996, *Principes du gouvernement représentatif,* 2nd edn, pp. 179–84.

A representative's assertion of singularity could arise from competence, social origins or from outward signs of eminence. There were periods in history (as in the case of the Ancien Régime in France) when all three dimensions were combined in what appeared to be 'natural' superiority. There was immediate acceptance of the representative's claims, for instance, to be more qualified, to issue from the right social background, to be wealthy, to have significant political weight, to have access to the monarch or to protect regional interests. In contemporary democracies this is no longer the case: the basis of the legitimacy of candidate representatives cannot simply be taken for granted.

Today competence is a valuable resource because it confers rational prominence; it confirms merit and efficacy. However, this may not be the case with the marks of 'distinction' derived from upper class origins—which is now rarely a political advantage. Here the context of political competition is all-important. At times social origin is less important than local roots: what matters is to live in one's region of birth. On the other hand, social origin might be critical in an area with strong class rivalry and deep partisan cleavages. Of course there are also cases where these two requirements are combined. In an environment where a particular socio-economic activity prevails the representative will be expected to belong: for instance, to be a farmer in a rural community. Quite often representation will demand of the person concerned that (s)he embody the qualities most prized locally in terms of identity, wealth, notoriety, profession etc. In the former Soviet Union it was important to claim working class origins and many politicians 'invented' such ascendancy in order to gain legitimacy. Thus the representative's political authority derives in part from criteria of social authenticity that can vary greatly from one society to the next.

The relevance of outward signs of superiority is a more symbolic dimension of representation. In some settings it may sometimes result in ostentatious display whilst in others representation of the less advantaged strata may require adherence to demonstrable modesty. For example, going against a strong republican and liberal tradition of representation based on personal merit, some French working class organisations proposed in 1860–70 to send to parliament the humblest of their numbers so that they would better resist the temptation to 'betray' their constituency. The handicaps due to their origins (especially not being able to express themselves properly) were adjudged to be secondary to the fact they would bear witness to the condition of their peers. In this view the representative's role was to appear as a living symbol of his collective identity. In 1889 one such deputy created a scandal when he appeared dressed in his working clothes—a gesture intended to remind him, and everyone else, of his social origins and obligations.[39] This shows how the three aspects of representation discussed above—mental representations, embodiment and presentation of self—are combined. Actual professional homology acted as a badge of legitimation. Conversely there was great suspicion of those issued from higher classes (lawyers, journalists, doctors) who claimed to represent the proletariat.

This raises the issue of the relative independence of the political realm and of the emergence of 'professional representatives', which is virtually the norm today. Such politicians are often compelled to manufacture a contrived, when not downright artificial, relation with their putative constituency: buying a house locally, attending local events and, during campaigns, walking the crowds, shaking hands and smiling to the cameras. The effects they seek to achieve dictate their behaviour on the stump. There are strong elements of 'staging', as analysed by Goffmann, which are dictated by the need to compose their image in public—hence the differences between the 'front' and 'back' regions of the campaigning displays as well as the 'theatrical' variations before different audiences.[40] Important as these considerations are—and they do merit in-depth study—we do not subscribe to the (presently fashionable) view that contemporary political representation is merely a question of communication, or PR. The question is far more complex, especially when it comes to comparative analysis.

The merit of our approach is to make clear the cultural constraints that affect representation in different settings and to stress the need to understand the import of mental perceptions and local meanings to political practices. The legitimacy of the representative is thus intimately tied to the ability to meet specific expectations whilst displaying those personal, social and cultural qualities that make most

[39] P. Rosanvallon, 1998, *Le peuple introuvable.*
[40] E. Goffmann, 1959, *The Presentation of the Self in Everyday Life.*

sense to the people concerned. To represent is in this way to embody the grouping on whose behalf one claims to speak.

OSTENTATION, MODESTY AND LEGITIMACY: REPRESENTATION IN CONTEXT

Our comparative research suggests that it is crucial to examine the three dimensions of political representation: cultural representation, the representation of interests and the theatre of representation. These mix differently across the world. The second part of this chapter will present a comparative analysis of three distinct societies—Nigeria, Sweden and France—that applies the method outlined in Part III.[41] The research in progress focuses on five areas: the display of prestigious goods (clothes, dwelling, vehicle, cuisine etc.), refined manners, pomp entourage and (when appropriate) physical appearance. The aim is obviously not to generate statistical data but, based on interviews and observation *in situ*, to explain how political representation occurs and why.

We return to the three case studies discussed in the previous chapter. Here too a study of ostentation will show that Nigeria and Sweden are at the opposite ends of the spectrum, while France is mired in ambiguity. Our aim in the remainder of this chapter is to engage in 'thick description' and not in the least to limit enquiry to a particular category of representatives (for which, in any event, it would be difficult to find satisfactory 'equivalents' in each country). What we want to do is to cast light on the cultural dimensions of representation, so as to evolve a comparison by means of contrast.

As we shall see, in Sweden the legitimacy of representation demands the lowest personal profile and the avoidance of ostentation. In Nigeria representative legitimacy is rooted in the display of external signs of power, of which conspicuous flamboyance is key since it is the material proof of the ability to nourish clientelistic networks. So long as clients are placated the show of wealth is a political virtue, casting as it does a flattering image on the community being 'represented'. France is troubled by its double heritage—Versailles and the

---

[41] For a detailed discussion of the methodology, see J.-P. Daloz, 2003, 'Ostentation in Comparative Perspective: culture and élite legitimation', *Comparative Social Research*, 21, pp. 29–62.

Revolution—that requires a contradictory approach to representation. In effect representatives must play on two distinct, and not easily compatible, registers by simultaneously proving and transcending proximity.

Compulsory ostentation: the pageantry of representation in Nigeria

The previous chapter highlighted the particularistic and vertical nature of political relations in Nigeria. This is equally relevant to political representation. Given the importance of infra-national identities, of the ways in which political leaders seek to advance the interests of their community or factions and of the manner in which clients associate with their patrons' *desiderata*, there is virtually no scope for horizontal representation. Politics link leaders and followers within a well-understood relation of unequal reciprocity that is rooted in patrimonialism.

Yet, for analytical or ideological reasons, the bulk of the political studies continue to focus on the political consequences of the supposed gap between élite and populace.[42] Such essays are prone to rely on debatable dichotomies, which seem rather artificial and not to reflect the realities of political behaviour in this country. Moreover they largely fail to account for the intricacies of political representation in Nigeria. They obscure rather than illuminate actual practices.

An inductive approach, on the other hand, starts from empirical observation, regardless of whether what is being observed conforms or not to theories of representation. We have already explained how in Nigeria (as elsewhere in Africa) relations between leaders and followers are conditioned by the politics of reciprocity. Within such an environment even the lowliest members of the grouping feel closer to their Big Man than to those who may share the same socio-economic conditions at the other end of the country. Since the State, as we have seen, is so poorly differentiated, people always seek protection from patrons whose reputation derives from their ability to safeguard particularistic interests. Faced with such evidence those analysts who favour a class analysis are prone to suggest that this

---

[42] For a discussion of this literature, see J.-P. Daloz, 1992, *Société et politique au Nigéria*.

behaviour is the result of 'false consciousness' among the poorer people. Yet the indication is that all, from top to bottom, share such a notion of representation. Far from being a mere ideological smoke-screen, this deeply engrained patrimonial vertical relationship is part of a common cultural heritage.

In Nigeria it is not sufficient to accumulate and display one's wealth in order to acquire political authority; one needs to give evidence of appropriate munificence. It is the generous patron who will gain prestige and assert dominance. However, the price to pay is that Big Men are under constant pressure from their constituents to deliver more and more. Such competition forces them into a frantic search for the resources that will make it possible for them to convert wealth into political support and prominence. This 'bigmanic' quest for the means to secure ascendancy over rivals translates into an obsession to acquire and display tokens of prosperity, which convey the promise of generosity. In this sense political representation rests on the dramatisation of power, at the heart of which lies ostentation or 'showing off'.

The unstable pecking order between traditional chiefs, wealthy politicians, businessmen, high ranking military officers, religious leaders and others claiming to represent a particular community,[43] leads to rivalry, confusion and instability. Big Men are often pre-occupied with their outward appearance and try, therefore, to deploy every conceivable sign of distinction. Although this concern with magnificence sometimes harks back to ancient 'traditions', it has been strongly accentuated by contemporary political rivalry. Pro-jecting an image of substance is imperative for politicians, if they are to convince their potential followers of their authority. To that end they have recourse to a wide variety of strategies intended to demon-strate eminence. They seek to acquire prestige goods as a means of self-promotion. This results in the conspicuous exhibition of wealth: cars; houses often located in the community of origin, even it is a miserable village or an overcrowded suburb; clothing and glamorous (particularly female) company, whose display is critical to the asser-tion of social status.[44]

---

[43] See J.-P. Daloz, 2002, 'Big Men in Sub-Saharan Africa: how élites accumulate positions and resources', *Comparative Sociology*, 2/1, pp. 271–85.
[44] See J.-P. Daloz, 2002, *Élites et représentations politiques*, Chapter 5.

Ostentation always proceeds from a sharp contrast with regard to the common lot.[45] Faced with what appears to be widespread excesses in this respect, outside observers of Africa and foreigners who live there profess indignation. To them it is offensive that there should be such a surfeit of prestige spending when a large proportion of the population lives in utter desolation. However, what is bound to strike the researcher who studies these questions in some depth is the *relative* absence of popular resentment against such practices, at least within the politician's constituency.[46] This shows clearly that an appreciation of the legitimacy of élite ostentation requires an understanding of the socio-cultural context within which Big Men seek to obtain, and maintain, support from their 'constituents'.

Therefore, the dramatisation of affluence meets the needs of both the actor (patron) and the public (clients). From a Western point of view, it may be difficult to accept that in a country as poor as Nigeria such considerable resources should be devoted to the purchase and display of prestige goods, to the holding of lavish feasts, and to the distribution of money far and wide. Nevertheless, we have to go beyond immediate and instinctive recoil in order to make sense of patterns of behaviour that have significant influence on the exercise of power, and more particularly on the reality of political representation.

This approach enables us to understand that the 'staging' of ostentation, or more simply the demonstration of success, fulfils clear needs both for the political actors concerned and for the 'spectators'. Here we must accept that such practices are not stigmatised in the way they often are in the West. On the contrary, it is expected of political leaders that they should publicly manifest their dominance, and assert distinction, through the attributes of material success and opulence. Conspicuous consumption is acceptable so long as the Big Men

---

[45] The word derives from the Latin *ostentatio*, which comes from the verb *ostentare*, meaning to view with insistence. For the Romans, *ostentatio* referred to the composition of a favourable outside persona.

[46] We would stress here that we are referring to cases of 'normal' ostentation and not to those more familiar (at least in the West) instances of blatant enrichment by politicians (like the late Abacha) whose concerns are to spirit as much as possible out of, rather than to redistribute within, the country. This may appear an arbitrary difference to the outside observer but Africans themselves are perfectly capable of making the distinction between the rich Big Men who are 'representative' because they redistribute and those who are not.

continue to 'reward' their supporters generously. If redistribution meets the expectations of the followers, there is (virtually) no limit to the level of luxury that may be publicly exhibited. The most destitute clients are likely to show pride in the construction of the patron's mansion, or in the car in which he travels, as though they partook directly of the affluence on show.[47] As though their community, and neighbourhood, were honoured in this way. Luxury confers upon ordinary people a certain aura, which we would identify as 'vertical symbolic redistribution'.

Typically, and this is a key argument for us, clients expect of their patrons that they uphold their rank—that is, show off their wealth. The inability to do so would come as a grave disappointment since it would denote the community's lack of substance. Any deficiency in this respect would not only be seized upon by political competitors, but would also appear suspicious to the community, the image of which would be tarnished, since the politician is taken to be its representative embodiment. Therefore, would-be representatives are pre-occupied about any possible lacunae in distinction. For example, those who have little education will attempt to obtain an *honoris causa* degree. More generally Big Men are extremely suspicious of any move that could deprive them of their badges of distinction.[48]

Because social prominence and ranking are eminently insecure and subject to dispute, representatives are keen to buttress their claims through the display of eye-catching prosperity. In a context where there is no clear hierarchy of power among many of these politicians it is imperative to assert prominence vicariously.[49] Seeing that Nigeria is large and heavily populated by African standards, its élite is

---

[47] See here, among others, the novel by N. Nwankwo, 1975, *My Mercedes is Bigger than Yours.*

[48] In the course of our research we verified on many occasions how local government officials were punctilious in having meeting minutes corrected so as to include all their titles: the longer the list, the better. We have seen countless cards that include such designations as Honourable Chief, Commissioner, Doctor, Alhaji etc. See here humorous passages in C. Achebe, 1966, *A Man of the People,* and T. Aluko, 1986, *A State of our Own.*

[49] In Nigeria, unlike Western Europe, conspicuous ostentation does not require originality. On the contrary, politicians seek above all to display the 'standard' attributes of power, which results in 'smaller' Big Men imitating more powerful ones.

uncommonly numerous and dispersed. In such a situation political standing is not self-evident and must be symbolically demonstrated at all times by means of magnificence and munificence. Obviously Big Men need to be resourceful in order to maintain a balance between display and distribution if they are to court, gain and maintain political legitimacy. Thus their behaviour conforms less to that discussed in sociological or anthropological accounts of the dramatisation of power aimed at marking distinction from lower classes than to the harder edge needed to survive intra-élite competition in a context of inter-communitarian or inter-factional politics.

Within such a society ostentation is in fact a mandatory attribute of power. In Nigeria, therefore, the need to balance distinction and similarity, which lies at the heart of representation, is resolved in a singular fashion: that is, the vicarious proxy 'enjoyment' by the represented of the representatives' prestige goods. Paradoxically, at least from a Western point of view, such a process calls for the exacerbation of the gap in affluence between the two. This state of affairs may seem peculiar to outside observers. How is it possible that people should be content with such a blatantly unequal set up? Our concern is not to judge the merit of this type of arrangement. It is to explain how a cultural approach—as opposed to analytical frameworks derived from the experience of other polities—helps to explain why such a mechanism lies at the heart of the symbolic representation of power in Nigeria.

Ostentation forsaken: the diffidence of representation in Sweden

For the comparative analyst interested in the political élite the situation in Scandinavia is at the opposite end of the spectrum. There politicians cultivate an image of modesty, which is rarely found in the rest of the world. The effects of *Jante lagen* (meaning the informal rule that discourages feelings of superiority) can be felt amongst all members of the élite,[50] but they are even more powerful when it comes to politicians who cannot be seen to ignore its application.[51]

---

[50] Admittedly this rule appears less effective in respect of today's *nouveaux riches* but even here it is well to point out that few will ignore it. Displays of ostentation are usually possible outside their native country, for example when they are on holiday in the Mediterranean or the Swiss Alps.

[51] See J.-P. Daloz and K. Barrling-Hermansson, 2004, 'Représentation politique et modestie ostensible en Europe du Nord', *Nordiques*, 4 (April).

There are indeed few countries in the world where ministers cycle to work, use public transport, queue in the cafeteria, swim in the municipal pool on Sunday mornings and allow their private telephone number to appear in the phone book.[52] More recently concerns about security, rather than the desire for distinction, has forced politicians to accept greater separation from the public.[53] This attitude is all the more remarkable for being common to political parties of both left and right.

Although merit is highly prized in Sweden, it is crucial that praise should come from others and never from self-publicity. Swedish politicians are expected to downplay their achievements and if need be to explain them in terms of the support they have received from others or attribute them to chance. Even timidity is seen as virtue so long as it evokes modesty.[54] As a result political representatives are often loath to stand out. It is sometimes necessary to prod or cajole them before they agree to appear on official photographs.

Eloquence is possibly the one political attribute that escapes such rigorous censorship, since the capacity of a politician to be articulate is much admired. Nevertheless, the Swedes remember well the 1976 debate between Olof Palme, the brilliant intellectual, and Thorbjörn Fälldin, the Centre (ex-Agrarian) party, whose electoral posters showed him on a tractor in front of his farm. The former, who was clever and extremely self-assured, clearly prevailed in the debate over his tongue-tied and hesitant opponent. Yet Palme went on to lose the elections partly because, according to opinion surveys, voters had found him too arrogant, too assertive and therefore insufficiently 'Swedish'.[55]

---

[52] Examples abound: Tage Erlander (who dominated Swedish politics from 1946 to 1969) cycled to work and Olof Palme, the former Prime Minister, used the bus. Bengt Göransson, a former minister of culture, recalls how he used to debate with the public in the Metro.

[53] The assassination of Olof Palme was traumatic in this respect and forced a change. Nevertheless, Birgitta Dahl, the former leader of Parliament used to go from her modest flat in Uppsala to parliament by train until she was forced to use an official car. More recently, Anna Lindh, the foreign minister, was stabbed to death when she was shopping, without protection, in one of Stockholm's main department stores.

[54] See Å. Daun, 1999 (1989), *Swedish Mentality.*

[55] For a comparative discussion of political communication in Scandinavia today, see K. Gomard and A. Krogstad (eds), 2001, *Instead of the Ideal Debate.*

However, this need to appear 'ordinary' is not incompatible with strong leadership—as is clear in the cases of Carl Bildt in the early 1990s or later with Göran Persson. Nor does it necessarily carry over into attire codes. Most politicians dress formally, but perhaps more out of respect for their profession than as a sign of distinction. It is interesting to remember here that when the Greens first entered parliament they debated whether the men should wear suits and the women skirts. They were torn between the wish to express their different politics sartorially and the realisation that they might have to sacrifice their ideals in order to be taken seriously. Yet compared to most other similar countries Swedish politicians remain highly informal. They are easily accessible and are very relaxed about debating opinions contrary to their own. Perhaps this is at the price of strong self-control and a lack of spontaneity—an area where they do seem to be more formal. In any event a cultural approach makes it possible to tease out the political significance of these subtle dynamics.

It might have been expected that the politicians' modesty would be compensated by the royal family's pomp. However, even here there is a vast dissimilarity from, for instance, the British sovereign's demeanour. True the King of Sweden has been seen to drive a Ferrari. True also, television cameras must abstain from showing him eating during the Nobel Prize ceremony. Nevertheless, he lives a much more unassuming life than many other European royals. Apart from Gustav III, at the end of the eighteenth century, the Swedish monarchs have remained fairly close to their people. The question is whether this behaviour is due to the constraints of the cultural environment from the early days of the modern period or whether this is merely part of the royal 'theatre'.[56] Whatever the cause the contrast with other royal families is significant.

Contemporary politicians in Sweden enjoy few privileges and they remain under the constant scrutiny of a very vigilant press and media. Furthermore the existing legislation on transparency makes it possible for any citizen to have access to all manner of information, such as their official expenditures. It is thus preferable for them not to take advantage of their official position or to indulge in private gain.

---

[56] P. Burke, 1997, 'State-Making, King-Making and Image-Making from Renaissance to Baroque: Scandinavia in a European context', *Scandinavian Journal of History*, 22.

One of the ways in which it is possible to gauge public perceptions in this respect is to study closely what is taken to be socially most reprehensible, both at home and abroad. For us then the comparative analysis of what constitutes a 'political' scandal is always revealing. In some countries sexual misdemeanours are utterly unacceptable. In others it is financial impropriety that is most culpable. The key issue here, quite clearly, is how the cultural environment defines the limits of the public and private spheres.

In this respect what does Swedish public opinion most censure? Because of the influence of the Lutheran Church on society there is little scope for dissociating personal behaviour from political role.[57] The probity expected of someone discharging official functions needs, as it were, to be confirmed by impeccable moral credentials. What happened to Mona Sahlin when she was a minister is here emblematic. Whilst on holiday she used her official credit card to buy nappies and a few bars of chocolate. Although the amount was insignificant and was promptly reimbursed, suspicion was immediately cast upon her integrity—a slur that her Social Democratic rivals were not slow to exploit. The problem was not dishonesty, abuse of public funds or of public position (which is wholly unacceptable in Sweden), rather it was the fact that she gave the appearance of someone unable to manage her affairs satisfactorily. Perhaps such close scrutiny of her private life was due to the fact that at the time she was expected to succeed the Primer Minister. This, as well as a few other minor incidents, effectively ruled her out.

On the other hand, Swedish newspapers have usually exercised considerable discretion regarding the intimate details of politicians' lives. Revelations are usually only made posthumously. Admittedly this is now beginning to change, adding further pressure of scrutiny on those who choose to serve as representatives. Locally this is seen as the 'Americanisation' of politics, that is, the increasing obsession with the personality of political actors and with public relations. Nevertheless, there is continued unease in Sweden with the dramatisation of politics. Public figures must behave responsibly and avoid giving

---

[57] For a comparative study of the influence of Protestantism, see D.-L. Seiler, 'L'usage politique de la vie privée des hommes publics en démocratie' in P. Baudry, C. Sorbets and A. Vitalis (eds), 2002, *La vie privée à l'heure des médias*, pp. 146–65.

themselves in spectacle. The theatre of representation is only allowed if it is meant to convey the legitimate 'rituals' of a particular office. Older politicians reject the present trend whereby politicians and media conspire to stage public political 'performances', notably on television.[58] In any event there is in Sweden permanent hostility to the outward display of power or wealth. The case of Mona Sahlin cannot simply be dismissed as an instance of partisan infighting. It is a reflection of a cultural environment in which there is very strong social control, bordering at times on an obsession to denounce wrongdoing.[59]

This may well explain why there is in the country such scepticism about the European Union. The Swedes are suspicious of an institution that is not transparent and that keeps excessive distance from European citizens. When Sweden held the EU Presidency in 2001 it attempted to fashion a different image. This failed, in part because of concerns about the security of politicians. Swedish officials consider southern European politicians (including Mitterrand and Chirac) as 'anti-models' in this respect. For example, Jack Lang's behaviour at a European summit of ministers of culture held in Granada was seen as being particularly shocking. The French minister arrived late, made a very 'theatrical' entrance surrounded by his entourage and journalists, hurried through his speech and left immediately afterwards. The Swedish delegation, which had participated actively in the meeting, disapproved of this 'media show' and resented such unacceptably patronising behaviour.[60]

Swedish party activists are also amazed by the excessive deference afforded party leaders in southern Europe. And they are positively appalled by the behaviour of Third World politicians, diplomats and officials. As far as they see it the poorer a country the more ostentatious the behaviour of its representatives.[61] From a comparative point of view, and especially in view of what we have indicated in the section on Nigeria, such behaviour is far from unusual: it is in fact utterly

---

[58] Here the rise of populist politicians like Ian Wachtmeister and Bert Karlsson, who readily mock the style of establishment politicians, has contributed to a less traditional image of politics.

[59] As was already made clear in the previous chapter in respect of the nature of the cleavage between State and society.

[60] Source: personal interviews in Sweden, May 2001.

[61] Ibid.

'rational'. However, the study of the Swedish reaction helps us make better sense of the meanings of political representation in that country. A cross-cultural analysis of that kind is thus most enlightening.

There are a number of excellent studies in the political sociology of Scandinavian parliaments, which examine in detail such factors as social or geographical origins, women participation and the like.[62] Yet our emphasis on 'thick description' type research makes it possible to provide a complementary approach, which does confirm the importance of modesty for politicians. A recent survey of fifty-three MPs, with added participant observation, proves that they positively want to project an image of 'banality and 'ordinariness'—in other words, to appear to be 'like every other Swede'.[63] The study was based on the MPs' self-portrait: it asked them to choose the image they would like to give of themselves. Obviously their replies may have fitted their own PR strategy but they are nevertheless useful in that they allow assessment of the criteria they adjudged to be most relevant in this respect.

The majority of respondents wanted to be depicted in some ordinary everyday activity: house cleaning, gardening, looking after the children, taking a walk etc. Without going into undue detail, a few conclusions will illustrate our point. A number of MPs did not even register the question, as though the portrayal of their person was irrelevant. Others were embarrassed, explaining they had never envisaged such portrayal. Yet others explained that party, not person, mattered. Asked about clothes, most favoured casual wear, thus ruling out any exclusive elegance. Also instructive were the responses of those who changed their minds: one realised that a picture in an expensive restaurant would be inappropriate and proposed instead to be photographed hunting in the woods; another revised her earlier idea of a golf course and suggested a summer family photograph in the garden. Finally one the most revealing conclusions from the survey is that the responses did not differ according to party affiliation.[64]

---

[62] See, among others, P. Esaiasson and S. Holmberg, 1996, *Representation from Above*; and P. Esaiasson and K. Heidar (eds), 2000, *Beyond Westminster and Congress.*

[63] This paragraph summarises some of the conclusion of Katarina Barrling-Hermansson's survey. See J.-P. Daloz and K. Barrling-Hermansson, 'Représentation politique et modestie ostensible en Europe du Nord', *Nordiques*, 4 (April), and K. Barrling-Hermansson, 2004, *Partikulturer.*

[64] Even if there are clearly different party 'sub-cultures' when it comes to other issues.

Returning now to an issue mentioned above in respect of the behaviour of Nigerian politicians—that is, the display of female company—the situation in Sweden is again wholly different. In Nigeria the conspicuous affirmation of predatory sexuality enhances the political profile of politicians, who frequently seek to assert their authority by seducing their opponents' female companions.[65] If in the African country such demonstration of 'virility' is more often than not a political asset for the legitimation of power, the reverse is true in Sweden.[66]

The case of Gudrun Schyman, who was until recently the leader of the Left (ex-Communist) Party, is instructive in this regard. Schyman has been much in the news because of her alcoholism. Although ostensibly a feminist, she has spoken publicly of her private life, saying that she was not just a politician but also a human being—'mother, 'lover' etc. Her confessions about a singularly messy love life seem to have done her standing no harm, particularly among the party members. During one of the last election's debates, when party leaders were asked to summarise their programme, she began by saying: 'I am Gudrun Schyman; I am an alcoholic...' and went on to speak of her chaotic personal life. In other words, she sought support by stressing her private weaknesses, which are obviously widely shared in society. Although this may well be an extreme occurrence, it serves to illustrate the point that in Sweden representative legitimacy derives largely from a demonstration of a type of ordinariness that is appealing to the voters concerned.

How can one best explain such disdain for ostentation in political life? Some scholars stress a mentality[67] fashioned out of the perennial need for solidarity within a harsh Scandinavian environment in which low population density and a widely dispersed habitat favoured self-control, equality and the avoidance of conflict.[68] This is far from being the same as egalitarianism since, as we saw, the Nordic societies privilege individuality, even if they stress the importance of

---

[65] For a discussion of the risks involved in such 'games', see D. Bourmaud, 1995, 'Le pouvoir au risque du sexe', *Politique africaine*, 59.

[66] J.-P. Daloz, 2002, 'L'étalage de la vie sexuelle en tant que facteur de légitimation politique' in P. Baudry, C. Sorbets and A. Vitalis (eds), *La vie privée à l'heure des médias*.

[67] See, for example, Å. Daun, 1999 [1989], *Swedish Mentality*.

[68] See S. Graubard (ed.), 1986, *Norden*.

the collective. It is different both from the American notion of equality of opportunities and from the French emphasis on civic equality. It is, rather, a matter of similitude—the importance of avoiding distinction from one's peers—which is perhaps best conveyed by the Swedish word *lagom*, meaning behaving 'as one should', with moderation. Similarly the adjective *duktig* is commonly used to refer positively to competence, cleverness and efficacy—attributes that result from work and not from ascriptive or social factors.

For their part, historians trace some of the country's cultural roots to the lack of class divisions during the Viking period, the virtual absence of feudalism and the weakness of the aristocracy. Yet, as shown in the last chapter, there has recently emerged a view that such factors have been exaggerated. Historical and archaeological research has not provided much information about the early period, particularly about Viking communities. Even the specialists of the Middle Ages (which in Scandinavia is defined as post-eleventh century) readily admit to lack of information.[69] What is undoubtedly relevant to an explanation of the rejection of excessive social distinction is the influence of Lutheranism, with its moral code of austerity.

Social Democratic politicians, especially those from the older generations, argue that the origins of such attitudes are not to be found in ancient history. They believe that the primacy of anti-ostentatious behaviour stems from the efforts of their predecessors who, at the end of the nineteenth century, were responsible for the creation of influential popular movements. Since the members of these movements often came from humble backgrounds themselves and had been socialised in the trade union tradition, they brought to the fore a concern for modesty and proximity. It is this heritage that made them immune to ministerial pomp when in office and, it is argued, their attitude would then have filtered through to the whole body politic. This thesis is reminiscent of the view that what has prevented the Swedish middle and upper classes from displaying wealth and distinction is the hegemonic influence of Social Democratic ideology.[70]

We cannot here enter into the debate about the nature of the relationship between social democracy and capitalism in Scandinavia, which has spawned a huge literature, or revisit the discussions about

[69] See B. Sawyer and P. Sawyer, 1993, *Medieval Scandinavia*.
[70] See J. Pontusson, 1988, *Swedish Social Democracy and British Labour*.

the welfare State adumbrated in Chapter 9. Suffice it to say that one incontrovertible consequence of this political orientation is the considerably reduction of socio-economic inequalities through the control of salaries and tight fiscal discipline. The Social Democratic party emphasises the import of their reforms following a nineteenth century characterised by the exploitation of rural workers, the need for emigration and a frightening level of alcoholism. On the other hand, their liberal adversaries point to the smooth process of industrialisation, the swift development of consultative bodies and the impact of the provisions of early social protection (from the 1890s) under the benign oversight of the bourgeoisie. To them, therefore, Social Democratic governments consolidated but did not initiate these momentous changes.[71]

Whatever the origins of such behaviour, there is no gainsaying the importance of humility for the political élite. This appears clearly in, for instance, the patterns of party recruitment and socialisation. Although some politicians are still coming to the Social Democratic party by way of popular organisations (like trade unions), most members of the youth section of the party now have a university education. This is an important change. Yet they must still serve their 'apprenticeship' within the lower rungs of the party and uphold the required image of earnest modesty. In such an environment, therefore, power appears to lie more with the party structures than with the individuals who run them. In other words, legitimacy derives from a strong commitment to such supra-personal bodies and it is imperative both to keep a low profile and to be seen to work as a team player.[72]

Returning to our interpretative framework, we would argue for an explanation that goes beyond these two—respectively culturalist and ideological—approaches. Indeed, we would suggest that the two are not mutually exclusive. There is little doubt that the Social Democrats were responsible for the emergence of the type of political legitimation that still prevails today across the political spectrum. At the same time their success was due in no small measure to the fact that the model they helped fashion was in harmony with the pre-

---

[71] See, for instance, H. Dahl, 1986, 'Those Equal Folks' in S. Graubard (ed.), *Norden*.
[72] Such is less clearly the case within the liberal and conservative parties, where individual brilliance is now more likely to secure (faster) promotion than in the past.

vailing socio-cultural norms. In other words, they succeeded in evolving a specific attitude to political representation precisely because that brand of political behaviour fitted the environment within which modern politics developed.

Therefore, our approach rests on a conception of the cultural system as simultaneously a framework that shapes, and is in turn shaped by, existing (cultural) realities.[73] This makes it possible to offer an analysis of politics that goes beyond the two dominant schools of thought: the one assuming that it is merely a reflection of socio-economic trends and the other reducing it to the outcome of voluntarism. From our viewpoint the cultural matrix is at once a constraint and a source of creativity, which can in turn contribute to alter the very foundations from which it issues.

In a country like Sweden, where the State is so prominent, the legitimacy of political representation derives above all from the proof that politicians are at the service of the 'people'. American style self-promotion ('I am a winner'; 'See how successful I was in my professional career', 'I am your best choice') would be counter-productive in the Swedish context. It is instead the evidence of one's ordinariness, one's honesty and one's humble devotion to the public, which will carry conviction and strengthen the claim to act as 'representative'.

The Republic's monarchs: the ambiguities of representation in France

In contrast to the two previous cases—one where eminence and the other where similitude best served political representation—there are cultural milieus where the situation is ambivalent, where the behaviour of political actors is more ambiguous. The French case is in this respect quite fascinating since it exhibits the most violent swing from the one to the other. During the absolutist period centralisation of power went hand in hand with an excess of flamboyance and pageantry that was intended to seal the sovereign's supremacy. Clearly Louis XIV's court in Versailles was by far the most ostentatious in Europe. On the other hand, the 1789 Revolution brought about an extreme reaction against such courtly pomp. Since then French

[73] See C. Geertz, 1973, 'Religion as a Cultural System' in C. Geertz, *The Interpretation of Cultures*.

political élite have swayed from one tradition to the other. Respect for authority is believed to require the display of grandeur. Indeed, commentators have pointed to the royal tendencies of the Fifth Republic presidents. At the same time the legacy of the Revolution impels political actors to seek proximity with their constituents.

There is in France a long tradition of essays on the exercise of power, which reflect quite accurately the tension between these two political tendencies: the fascination for the Elysée's sumptuous decorum as well as the disdain for a spectacle that is far too reminiscent of the pre-democratic *Ancien Régime*. This is well illustrated by the back cover of a book on the French '*nomenklatura*', which reflects these two registers. The reader is meant to be drawn in by the revelations about the secret prerogatives of the top political echelons—of which (s)he has scant knowledge—and at the same time encouraged to denounce such exorbitant privileges.[74]

As explained before, there is no reason to suppose that a society's cultural matrix is necessarily monolithic. The specificities of certain cultures can just as well come from the constant stress between two contradictory imperatives, as is plainly the case in France. Here political analysts must take into account the consequences of these two antagonistic modes of political legitimation. Both make sense, to the élite as well as the general public; to the represented as well as to the representatives. A cultural approach allows us to take both into account, avoiding the trap of dismissing the desire for proximity as mere rhetoric and the exhibition of the prestige of power as an archaic leftover. Indeed, the question of political representation in France is more complex than a simple public relations exercise.

Here, as in the other two cases, it is useful to start with a brief account of the complexities of the country's historical trajectory. Historians of seventeenth-century Europe believe that Ancien Régime France, obsessed as it was with the defence of privileges and with hierarchies of social differentiation, exhibited the most extreme socio-economic gap between the top and bottom of society.[75] Life at

---

[74] See A. Wickham and S. Coignard, 1986, *La Nomenklatura française*. There is in this book a deliberate parallel with a well-know essay on the Soviet Union: M. Voslensky, 1980, *La Nomenklatura. Les privilégiés en URSS*. The implication here is that the privilege enjoyed by the political élite in France is as offensive as that of the former Soviet Union.

[75] See O. Hufton, 2000, *Europe*.

the court of Versailles entailed a lavishly luxurious existence; the use of rarefied 'pure French'; the strictest control over demeanour during audiences, dinners and balls; and the most stringent observation of daily rituals. Within such a context theatrical ostentation both derived from, and consolidated, courtly hierarchies. The refinement of some led to the exclusion of others, within the élite and beyond. The courtier was at once a contributor to, and a spectator of, kingly pomp, which aimed to exalt the figure of the monarch—at once God's representative on earth and supreme temporal authority.

The eighteenth century witnessed a decline in courtly etiquette. The protagonists became more lax as the theatre of power began to lose its lustre and relevance. Nevertheless, there still prevailed a notion of eminence that was intimately linked with the outward expression of the symbols of authority. Even today it is a cultural attribute of the exercise of power in France.

The 1789 Revolution was a radical rejection of the *Ancien Régime* and it brought about a strong reaction against the court's wastefulness, which had led to such large rises in taxation. Even before it was well understood that the aristocracy's extravagance was paralleled by the ordinary people's misery, the pageantry had ceased to provoke wonderment, or respect, but evoked a type of parasitic oppression that was taking the country to ruin. Those obscure servants, without whom the nobility could not have displayed its brilliance, began to express their dissatisfaction. The court's excesses now appeared more and more mindless.[76]

Consequently the Revolution set out to wipe out the previous regime's symbolic splendour and to obliterate all social distinctions that were not justified by utilitarian principles. The only permissible honour was that which signalled function, not title.[77] From 1792 elegance and style became suspicious, taken to indicate a form of social selfishness that was no longer acceptable. The use of simple, even worn out, clothing was now a token of patriotism. This attitude grew to be even more acute with the advent of the *sans-culottes*.[78]

---

[76] Marie Antoinette's wardrobe (she ordered about 150 new dresses every year and refused to reduce her expenses even at the height of the financial crisis) was so extravagant that it became the symbol of such excesses. See A. Ribeiro, 2002, *Dress in Eighteenth-Century Europe*.

[77] Concerning dress codes, see R. Wrigley, 2002, *The Politics of Appearances*.

[78] The paradox, from our point of view, is that Robespierre, its leader, always dressed

Indeed, it was not until the Thermidorian reaction that austerity came to an end and that the bourgeoisie allowed itself the pleasure of displaying the riches they enjoyed.

Politically the nineteenth century and the first half of the twentieth century were ambiguous, with a succession of conservative, at times reactionary regimes, followed by revolutionary episodes. There was clearly a strong ambivalence in conceptions of representation between Napoleonian pageantry and the republican *fêtes*, which celebrated the virtues of social equality. It is worth remembering that the First Empire indulged in paroxysms of ostentation: the Emperor wanted to legitimise the new dynasty by exhibiting a degree of magnificence that would provoke deference.[79] This was crucial not just in respect of his subjects but also *vis-à-vis* the long-established European royal families.

Work on the theatre of power and the dramatisation of politics usually concentrates attention on the relationship between the leaders and the led, the dominant and dominated classes. Some analysts (like American functionalist political scientists) stress the positive aspects of such symbolic factors, which facilitate integration. Others (such as those who favour a class analysis) see them in terms of manipulation. However, both seem to neglect the fact that, historically, ostentation was primarily intended to mark differentiation *within* the élite, rather than from the (generally much more distant) populace. This is a rich area for research, where one might, for instance, look at competition within a single organisation or faction, domestically or in an international context, as well as contrasts between élite in different sectors.

The period of restoration that followed the First Empire sought to bring back Versailles' elegance and refinement. However, there was an evolution away from the enclosed aristocratic courtly pageantry towards a more open type of social intercourse within a far broader circle of élite.[80] This trend was further accentuated under the July Monarchy: Louis-Philippe's style emulated that of the bourgeoisie,

---

well (wearing silk) and took great care of his appearance (even powdering his hair).

[79] See, among others, Ph. Mansel, 1987, *The Eagle in Splendour*.

[80] Which Balzac dubbed *vie élégante*. See A. Martin-Fugier, 1990, *La vie élégante ou la formation du Tout-Paris*.

who had brought him to power. If this 'familiar' fashion served him well with the bulk of public opinion, it entailed the risk of raising the question of the legitimacy of a type of royalty that was no longer distinguished by etiquette and decorum. For his part Louis-Napoléon (Napoleon III) went the other way. Although his ostentatious tendencies were checked by parliament under the Second Republic, they were allowed free expression under the Second Empire, resulting in much pageantry at the Tuileries court, royal balls in Saint-Cloud and parades in Biarritz.

From the point of view of political representation the transition to the Third Republic is fascinatingly rich in ambiguity. The Republicans combined a high degree of respect for the people they meant to represent with an elevated conception of their official functions. This caused them, for example, not to erect new buildings in order to symbolise their regime, but instead to occupy existing palaces (Bourbon) and private *hôtels* associated with the monarchy (Matignon, Lassay) or with an élitist connotation (Elysée). The remnants of older opulence were now meant to be converted into public or official luxury—luxury sanctioned by the new social and political morality of the national 'common weal'. Similarly, republican protocol replaced etiquette, demonstrating thereby the 'de-patrimonialisation' of a State that had now acquired its independence from the personal standing of those who worked in it.[81] Nevertheless, public authority continued to rest on 'traditional' signs of eminence. The notion of Head of State, applied both to the *Ancien Régime* monarchs and to contemporary Presidents of the Republic, is an indication of this lasting ambiguity.[82]

Looking more closely at the Presidents from that period, there are clear contrasts. Jules Grévy (1879–87) behaved with modesty and led a very parsimonious life at the Elysée. The press mocked his ubiquitous black suit and the fact that his daughter, also poorly dressed, remained unmarried. On the other hand, he behaved with immense ostentation in his Jura native region—going as far as having his own private railroad line and a station in his hometown of Mont-sous-Vaudrey that was more luxurious than that of James Rothschild, who

---

[81] See Y. Déloye, C. Haroche and O. Ihl (eds), 1996, *Le protocole ou la mise en forme de l'ordre politique.*
[82] See M. Morabito, 1996, *Le Chef de l'Etat en France.*

was then the owner of the *Chemins de Fer du Nord*.[83] His successor, Sadi Carnot, also cultivated an austere demeanour, but he liked to hold parties in the Republic's châteaux.

Other Presidents behaved more ostentatiously or, conversely, with excessive sobriety, reflecting in this way the country's deep ambivalence with regard to the vicarious aspects of representation. There could hardly have been a greater contrast between Félix Faure's (1895–9) *folies des grandeurs* and Paul Doumer's (1931–2) immense puritanism. The former liked to sail down the Seine in his yacht, ride horses in the mornings in the Bois de Boulogne, go hunting in Austria and put on sumptuous feasts. He died in the arms of his mistress at the Elysée.[84] Doumer, however, maintained an image of utter austerity. He worked from five in the morning until midnight every day, never took any holiday and went as far as to open the shutters of his official residence himself so as not to disturb his guards.[85] These may well have been extreme cases but they are no less revealing. If, by then, dynastic logics had largely been replaced by social recognition based on political activities or merit, those at the top of the French State continued to be partial to external symbols of prestige.

The advent of the Fifth Republic, and with it the institutionalisation of a Presidential political system, led to even greater ambiguity. De Gaulle's stature, his personality, his obsession with the country's grandeur, and his ready recourse to the plebiscite lent his presidency an aura that some linked back to the Second Empire. Privately he showed haughty contempt for wealth and luxury; he maintained a stern military deportment. Yet in public he controlled tightly all aspects of state ceremonial and dictated the rules of protocol. A master of the theatre of politics (he was without rival on television), his political demeanour was in keeping with the very elevated notion he had of the position of Head of State. Valéry Giscard d'Estaing, one of his successors, tried hard to demystify his position but never managed to shake off his élitist image. He would go to the Elysée on foot, avoid displaying his *Grand collier de la Légion d'Honneur*, play the

[83] See P. Jeambrun, 1991, *Jules Grévy ou la République debout.*
[84] Some commentators attributed this ostentatious behaviour to the need to give an image of the French Republic commensurate with that exhibited by European royal families. See T. Billard, 1995, *Félix Faure.*
[85] See P. Miquel, 2001, *Les rois de l'Elysée.*

accordion, dine with 'ordinary' citizens, share his breakfast with dustmen and hold informal fireside 'talks' in the presence of his wife. Yet he was remorselessly lampooned as Louis XV in the satirical press and his attempts were seen as either instrumental or simply condescending. His successor François Mitterrand, who claimed to usher in a socialist renewal, was also caricatured as a monarch, surrounded by PR courtiers. Although he sought to give an air of avuncular familiarity, he never neglected the display of presidential pomp when he travelled in the country.

The same is true today of Jacques Chirac, who readily mixes a relatively relaxed style with a more solemn exhibition of republican magnificence. Lionel Jospin, the former Prime Minister, was often (according to some observers) seen to be more in tune with French society, which expected a degree of humility from its politicians. Although there is no simple explanation as to why he received fewer votes than Jean-Marie Le Pen in the (first round of the) last presidential elections—the chief causes seem to have been a dispersion of left votes, the absence of a clear socialist programme and an under-estimation of the 'insecurity' factor—it is also true that Jospin undoubtedly appeared to lack the 'majesty' the French expect of their president.

This ambivalence in political representation between the need for eminence and the importance of proximity remains significant at all levels—from President to mayor. It is particularly visible in the behaviour of parliamentary deputies, who must combine the image of power bestowed upon them by their meetings in Paris with national politicians *with* careful attention to the more prosaic political demands at constituency level.[86] France is thus a country of contradictions, where local politicians may indulge in megalomaniac architectural folly, which is supposed to heighten the grandeur of their region, whilst at the same time paying scrupulous attention to the vagaries of regional democracy. The point we wish to stress is that, incongruous as these two aspects of representation may appear to the outside observer, both make perfect sense within France.

It would have been possible to offer other illustrations of our approach to political representation. As in the previous chapter, the three case

---

[86] M. Abélès, 2000, *Un ethnologue à l'Assemblée*, pp. 240 ff.

studies were only meant to give examples of how our method can profitably be applied to comparative analysis. A systematic study of either the State or of political representation would obviously demand a book-length treatment. Our aim in Part IV was to show that a cultural framework makes it possible to combine in-depth understanding of individual cases with enlightening comparison. We develop this last point more thoroughly below, in the book's Conclusion.

CONCLUSION

IN DEFENCE OF ECLECTICISM

If it is true that paradigms act as meta-theoretical frameworks for research, then it might be argued that in comparative politics there are two camps: the universalist and the relativist. However, a more systematic examination of the main schools of thought would reveal that there are a large number of distinct viewpoints. For example, both structuralist and rational choice theories are universalist. Similarly, and as we have pointed out repeatedly, there is a wide variety of cultural approaches.

In the social sciences there has always been an ambition to emulate the physical sciences in the search for the most 'advanced' theoretical synthesis. The latest trend in comparative politics is to favour ecumenism and certain scholars envisage the possibility of marrying rationalist, cultural and structuralist approaches.[1] We shall explain below why we think this trend is unpromising. Our view is that there is little possibility of analytical dialogue, or convergence, between the holders of different paradigms, since they work within what are effectively incompatible frameworks of investigation.

Our argument is that the interpretativist standpoint we advocate leads to theoretical eclecticism. If, as we believe, theory in the social sciences consists of a series of propositions to be confronted with the evidence of field data, then our approach makes it possible to overcome the limitations of universalist models of interpretation. Our contention is not that such models should be rejected on ideological or partisan grounds, but simply that we should be aware of their con-

---

[1] See M. Lichbach and A. Zuckerman (eds.), 1997, *Comparative Politics*; J. Blondel, 1994, 'Plaidoyer pour une conception œucuménique de la politique comparée', *Revue Internationale de Politique Comparée*, 1, 1 (April); and N. Smelser, 2003, 'On Comparative Analysis: interdisciplinarity and internationalisation in sociology', *International Sociology*, 18, 4 (December).

siderable heuristic limits. We are critical of those paradigms that assume that a single analytical grid enables the analyst to explain all and every observable event. We consider that such a grid[2] is instead likely to imprison empirical reality within an *a priori* set of conclusions.

A cultural approach, on the other hand, is a paradigm open to all manner of theories, so long as they enable us to make better sense of empirical reality. For us, therefore, the test of theoretical relevance is entirely practical.

THE ILLUSIONS OF PARADIGMATIC ECUMENISM

We would like at this juncture to reflect on our own paradigm, open up a discussion of how it differs from others and, most important, why it is incompatible with those that advocate exclusivist conceptual or theoretical methods. Indeed, ours is a non-dogmatic approach. It might be worth pointing out here that such an explicit dialogue about analytical frameworks is uncommon in our discipline—which all too often proceeds on the basis of theoretical excommunication. However, we believe that it is not just useful but also necessary to conclude a volume such as this with a frank debate about theory and method.

Epistemology—the 'science of science', which contemplates the modalities of the production of knowledge—helps to reveal the long-established hegemonic tendencies of the paradigmatic quest in the Western world, from the Renaissance to the mid-twentieth century. Without a doubt some of these periods were characterised primarily by the dominance of one particular paradigm of the physical or social world. As in the arts, there was often a sense that it was possible to achieve paradigmatic 'improvement': the later building on but transcending the earlier ones.[3]

In the last few decades it has become banal to highlight the crisis of grand social theorising. In point of fact there is now a tendency to reject once dominant paradigms, such as functionalism or Marxism.[4]

---

[2] The grid, or *grille*, is understood here as arising from the metaphor of the prison cell, as used by R.-P. Droit as quoted in F. Dosse, 1992, *Histoire du structuralisme*, p. 349.

[3] See Kuhn, 1962, *Structure of Scientific Revolution*.

[4] It would, however, be both unrealistic and short sighted to underestimate the extent to which they may be 're-cycled'.

We seem to have moved beyond the stage of ideological theoretical competition that reduced debate to starkly simple dichotomies. Western post-modernity rhymes with the flowering of myriad divergent outlooks. We no longer conceive of the social sciences in terms of the accumulation of 'definitive' knowledge. Each school of thought has become increasingly self-referential, confining attention to 'its' authors and publications. We have outlived the moment of paradigmatic 'triumph', when one viewpoint claimed supremacy and we now inhabit a world of multiple scientific 'networks'.

In some ways this is a more congenial universe. There is presently a greater diversity of approach. Social scientists can choose the one they prefer and disregard competing paradigms. Nevertheless, there are a number of scholars who are uncomfortable with this state of affairs and would prefer a more synthetic method. Thus in our field we find political scientists who advocate the merging of neo-institutionalist methods with those focusing on actors; and others who favour combining an emphasis on social configurations with the study of interest or cultural cleavages. There is in this regard an assumption that, following the epoch of paradigmatic opposition, political science would be more likely to 'progress' by means of a synthesis of distinct methodologies.

We are clearly sympathetic to this impetus towards a less dogmatically constrained, or school-bound, approach to our discipline. It is obviously desirable to make explicit the shortcomings of all would-be grand theory. Without doubt it makes sense to go beyond the perennial dichotomy between agency and structure, which so many social scientists (from Bourdieu to Giddens) have sought to overcome. It is clearly sensible, for instance, to consider that Louis XIV was both the *architect* and the *product* of the Versailles political system. We no longer need to pretend, as was current in the mid-twentieth century, that institutions merely 'reflect' social reality or, alternatively, that they contribute to 'creating' it.

However, attractive as such synthetic approaches may appear to be, they often conceal serious methodological incompatibilities. Paradigmatic ecumenism can easily lead to analytical incoherence. As adherents of a cultural interpretation, we are particularly mindful of the gap between our perspective and that of those who support a universalist approach in the social, and particularly political, sciences.

The interpretativist approach we advocate differs crucially from other meta-theoretical frameworks in that it does not rely on a single universal explanatory scheme, such as rational choice or structuralism, for example. In particular it eschews the claim that a single key can open all doors,[5] or that a theory of politics can be derived from a single, cardinal principle. In fact the opposite is the case, as we have argued throughout the book. A cultural methodology rests on an inductive approach, which starts from an examination of empirically observed reality and then proceeds to select (or if need be devise) the most appropriate analytical instruments. Contrary to a common (and fashionable) criticism, such an approach has no need to reject *a priori* any theory—whether, say, rational choice, historical materialism or institutionalist. However, what it does discard is any dogmatic and abstract theoretical pre-condition, no matter how canonical. In other words, our approach is in this respect entirely non-aligned.

A perspectivist approach, nonetheless, is not a deconstructionist approach—as propounded, for instance, by Derrida or Foucault. As explained in Parts I and III, a cultural method is indeed scientific—in the sense in which we have defined it above. However, our notion of science is distinct from that entailed either by grand theory or by a postmodernist point of view. It aims above all at offering a synoptic vision of cultural differences.

Structuralists charge those they classify as 'culturalist' with an overly impressionistic, anecdotic, viewpoint. The latter, for their part, consider that a structuralist approach is prone to fitting reality into pre-conceived moulds. Let us illustrate this debate with two fairly common but nevertheless enlightening examples. The first raises the issue of the construction of *a priori* categories. For instance, structuralists who study social stratification make assumptions about general models whereas those who are sensitive to cultural issues focus instead on local perceptions of success, distinction or prestige. The second addresses the question of explanation. For example, structuralists argue that the reason why believers, when they enter a sacred

---

[5] Here again we cannot resist quoting Geertz: 'Though those with what they take to be one big idea are still among us, calls for a "general theory" of just about anything social sound increasingly hollow, and claims to have one megalomaniac.' C. Geertz, 1993, *Local Knowledge*, p. 4.

site, either cover or uncover their heads, is because these two types of behaviour both convey respect. A more culturally attuned method would avoid making assumptions in this respect and would instead study these two different types of behaviour within the overall societal context *before* proposing a single explanation of such religious public deportment.

Structuralists are concerned to identify fundamental objective causalities. Hence they are interested principally in establishing correlations based on a distinction between independent and dependent variables. For this reason they reject as 'essentialist' the argument that social cleavages are not easily reducible to structure. The proponents of a cultural perspective, on the other hand, are wary of such correlations, which they consider to be largely tautological. As we have shown already, they reject the argument that culture is merely derived from other, more consequential, processes. To conclude, then, structuralist and cultural approaches are quite clearly epistemologically, and hence methodologically, incompatible.

Moving on to another important analytical framework, it is equally obvious that there is no common methodological ground between cultural approaches and the rational choice perspective. The one seeks to identify universal 'laws' on the maximisation of power based on the assumption that all political actors are bent on achieving broadly similar objectives, by means of relatively similar strategies, regardless of historical and socio-cultural context. The other argues that, according to empirical observation, motivation and interest are culturally bound. As we have mentioned on several occasions, we do not deny that a study of interest or rationality is relevant to comparative analysis. We hold only that making comparative sense of political action involves an appreciation of these factors within their own environment. Here too, therefore, there is a fundamental opposition between the two approaches.

In sum, a cultural approach is complex, contingent, mindful of the past, sensitive to the multiple dimensions of the contemporary period and open to many possible futures. That is why it is at odds with those paradigms that seek to minimise difference, to transcend cultural resistance, in order neatly to fit the Other, the Exotic, into universalist and usually ethnocentric moulds.

THE PERENNIAL DILEMMA OF ETHNOCENTRISM OR
THE PROBLEM OF REFERENCE

Western thought tends to proceed by means of the absorption of difference. The realisation that there are other cultural codes leads us not to reconsider our own as one only among many, but to integrate them all into what we claim to be the 'unity' of mankind. The paradox is that this universalist approach reinforces a very ideological or voluntarist tendency towards ethnocentrism or 'sociocentrism', insofar as we project our own conceptual categories onto the rest of the world. For example, we continue to view people across the globe principally as 'individuals' and, from the political viewpoint, as 'citizens', even when it is clear that in what we might call 'holistic' societies these notions do not make sense.[6]

On the face of it the problem of ethnocentrism in comparative politics is without solution. Indeed, on what basis does one compare? Compare what with what? According to what criteria? It seems difficult, if not impossible, to avoid doing so from a specific reference point. Given its present level of economic, social, political and scientific 'development', is the West not automatically going to be seen as the 'gold standard'? Is there not a danger, therefore, that all comparative analysis is vitiated right from the outset? Whether one views the non-Western world as 'backward' or whether, on the contrary, one sees it as that repository of the 'wisdom' the West has lost, one seems not to be able to resolve the conundrum of the reference point.

Let us illustrate this dilemma with the issue of corruption. As we suggested in *Africa Works*, such a negatively connoted notion only adds up in respect of societies where pre-existing norms are clearly delineated and widely respected. But there is a problem in comparative analysis: how best to explain behaviour that fails to conform to Western-derived legislation? Here it is best to avoid an argument based on a bureaucratic ideal with universal pretensions. If, for example, it is the case that African States do not function in terms of their official legal obligations, but according to instrumental and culturally based informal relations, then comparison will have to take such facts into account. Where there is no respect for the institutional environment, which in any event does not work, then the Western

---

[6] See R. Dumont, 1985, *Essais sur l'individualisme.*

notion of corruption makes little sense. This does not mean that there is no way of conceptualising corruption, but simply that in order to identify what it is, it becomes necessary to explain what is understood as such on that continent.[7]

More generally, the dominance of a social science lexicon drawn from the experience of Europe and North America, which is supposed to apply to the whole world, is problematic—particularly for those who hold that there is no universal definition of 'the politic'. In this regard there is some merit to the postmodernist argument that this conceptual dominance amounts to a 'second colonisation'. But that critique is all too easily transmuted into a systematic denunciation of Western 'culture' and a systematic devotion to non-Western 'beliefs'. It might be noted here that the curiosity towards and the fascination for foreign cultures—which lie at the root of anthropology—are themselves very Western phenomena, and not necessarily shared by all societies.

As discussed above, a scientific approach in comparative politics involves an effort to factor the relevance of our own intellectual cultural socialisation into the analysis. This is not easy. Culture acts as a powerful filter in the perception of the outside world. Therefore, we realise that to seek 'objectivity' in this way is arduous, but we do not believe that it is impossible to maintain the required self-critical stance. At the very least comparativists must attempt to understand their own preconceptions, assumptions and biases. They also need to abstain from *a priori* judgemental, normative or proselytising attitudes.

From a more academic viewpoint it seems to us important to avoid making a fetish out of theory or concept. Indeed, one the defects of our discipline (particularly within positivist circles) is the excessive attention devoted to this methodological preoccupation, as though it perennially had to justify its 'scientific' credentials. Such a stance is usually at the expense of a more pertinent discussion of the conceptual complexities and research difficulties of the comparative research being undertaken. On the other hand, for analysts who approach comparative questions in a more discursive essay form, the problem lies with the use of metaphor. In political science it is common to invoke military, sporting or theatrical images. But here too the ethnocentric risk is high since such writers are likely to use

---

[7] See P. Chabal and J.-P. Daloz, 1999, *Africa Works*, Chapter 7.

metaphors that make sense within their own environment, rather than within those being studied.

Let us look more closely at the example of theatre. Above and beyond its contested use as a general model in the social sciences,[8] the theatrical metaphor has been used analytically in three different ways. There is first the question of the (functional) demands of any political role. What is stressed here is the 'dramatic' persona to which social or political actors must conform: a publicly salient position entails a certain type of demeanour, with limited leeway. The second concerns the study of the theatrical techniques, which enable political actors to achieve the desired effects. Finally there is a body of work on the processes of public identification with public actors.

However, the question is to which type of theatre such a metaphor refers. Even within the so-called Western world there has been a continuous evolution in what we identify as drama—from the early days of Greek comedy and tragedy to the medieval type of public liturgy (is the Catholic mass not theatre?), the *charivari*, the more modern forms of courtly entertainment, to popular or avant-garde theatre. Further complications arise when we take into consideration non-Western examples, such as the multiform rituals of so-called 'primitive' societies or, for example, the highly stylised forms of Japanese drama. Of course structuralists argue that underneath the differences in expression it is possible to identify 'fundamental' structures. But which are those: the meaning of the role, the relationship between actor and spectator, the repertoire or the theatrical traditions? Clearly it is not that simple. There is in fact no way of bypassing a cultural analysis of theatrical conventions or social codes. The danger here is that of extrapolation: generalising from a particular case, or a given metaphor, to a theory or a methodology that is then erected as a model.

Of course all social scientists need to start from somewhere. It would be instructive in this respect to study the intellectual origins or the field experiences that have most influenced our scholarly work—as it would be to assess the impact of the fortune of early publications on the rest of our professional career. There is clearly a tendency to rely on the analytical framework or on the material from monographic publications, which have given social scientists prominence.

[8] See F. Mount, 1972, *The Theatre of Politics* and, as a critique, E. Burns, 1972, *Theatricality* or R. Wilshire, 1982, *Role Playing and Identity.*

Witness here de Tocqueville's acknowledgment that his study of the United States was intended to uncover the 'tendencies, characteristics and prejudices' of democracy.[9] Or the belief that Banfield[10] was principally trying to derive 'universal applications' from the case study of southern Italy.[11]

The chief merit of an approach in terms of 'thick descriptions' is precisely that it avoids the temptation to generalise on the basis of apparently objective, but in fact superficial, observations. The in-depth study of local meaning does not necessarily result in mere subjectivity. In point of fact the interpretativist method rejects the dichotomy between objectivity and subjectivity.[12] It claims instead, and quite rightly, to advance knowledge further than the 'thin descriptions' of behaviouralism or the vast statistical surveys it has spawned.

For our part we do not seek to unearth 'general tendencies', or 'significant regularities'. We merely attempt to shed some light on the logics of local actions and processes. It is well to remember here that a large number of so-called fundamental dichotomies at the heart of Western thought (body/mind, theory/practice etc.)—which are self-evident in that part of the world—do not make much sense in other settings. In comparative politics, then, the study of behaviour or opinion is unlikely to be informative unless it takes into account the local modalities of political expression. The formulation of survey questions is almost always liable to over-determine the responses. It is sometimes argued that globalisation has contributed to dissipate such misapprehensions. But, as discussed in Chapter 6, it is very far from clear that the worldwide spread of capital, information and technology has brought about a globalisation of meaning.

ON THE MERIT OF CONCEPTUAL
AND THEORETICAL ECLECTICISM

The quandary of the reference point is particularly acute when it comes to conceptualisation. As many scholars have stressed, to reduce

[9] A. de Tocqueville, 1968 [1835], *De la démocratie en Amérique*, pp. 37–8.
[10] E. Banfield, 1958, *The Moral Basis of a Backward Society.*
[11] See L. Harrison, 2000, 'Introduction' in L. Harrison and S. Huntington (eds), *Culture Matters*, p. xxi.
[12] C. Geertz, 1973, *The Interpretation of Cultures.*

the range of the notions we use only to those that arise from a case study is to fall into the trap of 'localism'. It leads to a lack of distance from the societies under examination and the artificial elaboration of *ad hoc* terminology. If each new terrain generates new concepts, it is argued, comparison is by definition impossible. This is certainly correct.

However, the opposite hazard is the recourse to a given (universal) conceptual apparatus, regardless of the specificities of the research terrain. It is of course true that the more abstract concepts are, the more likely they are to be applicable to a wide range of distinct cases. But the price to pay might well be the use of a *passe partout* and doctrinaire taxonomic jargon that merely obscures local realities.[13] Here it is obvious that the social sciences are often constrained by the philosophical tradition within which they have evolved and which they claim to have transcended. As suggested in Chapter 6, however, they have not really broken with its vision in terms of dichotomies.

Each side charges the other with 'nominalism'. Structuralist political scientists[14] argue that it is necessary to avoid being blinded by the complexities of local, autochthonous notions; that it is imperative to seek out general, functionally equivalent categories of analysis (as discussed in Chapter 2). Those who advocate a cultural approach contend that such universalist methods run the risk of misreading the situation: apparently similar functional actions may serve instrumentally different purposes. What matters politically is thus not to be found in the study of structural variables.[15]

If we assume that every society has been, is, and will for ever be confronted with broadly the same type of political problems; and additionally that there are only a limited number of ways of dealing with them, then we will be tempted to consider local factors as secondary, or analytically negligible. If, on the other hand, we take seriously the importance of cultural discordances—understood here geologically or tectonically—then we will have to pay special attention to the local meanings of political actions and processes, so as to

---

[13] For this reason it is wise to advise research students going into the field of the need to maintain a balanced approach between the need to focus on a tightly defined topic and the need to keep an open mind.

[14] See here M. Thompson, R. Ellis and A. Wildavski, 1990, *Cultural Theory.*

[15] As we have shown in respect of Africa in *Africa Works.*

construct political comparison accordingly. In any event analysts need to operate at a certain level of generalisation—one at which concepts are operational—without falling prey to excessive universalism. One possible approach is to make a distinction between concepts that are trans-cultural (such as the notion of norm) and those that are mono-cultural (such as the notion of the State).[16] Yet this is not simple. How do we use ideologically connoted notions like, positively, democracy or, negatively, despotism and imperialism?

Political theorists readily point out that the genealogy of these concepts matters little, since they evolve over time to transcend their origins and they cross national boundaries. All societies eventually make use of them. Our approach to this conceptual and theoretical conundrum is different. We are not primarily concerned with the debate about the historical and cultural origins of concepts or with the issue of whether social sciences can be 'meta-cultural'. We advocate instead a well-considered scientific eclecticism. As we see it an interpretative approach avoids a rigid theoretical standpoint, setting one theory against another. Instead, it uses that which makes it possible most plausibly to account for actual observable processes or events. We do not believe there is a need to make a choice of analytical framework and to apply its concepts, methods and instruments systematically, regardless of conditions on the ground. Our view is that a cultural approach needs to respond to the complexity and plurality of the cases under study and have appropriate recourse to the (existing or new) theoretical and conceptual perspectives that can best explain how to compare what happens concretely in different settings.

From our standpoint, therefore, there is no such thing as a 'good' or 'bad' concept, but only concepts that are applicable, or not, to the case studies. Of course we are well aware that concepts are not neutral, that they derive from specific intellectual, scientific or theoretical traditions. It is thus not possible simply to juxtapose or mix notions without any reference to their genesis, and even less to deploy those that are clearly incompatible. However, within reasonable analytical limits it is well not to be constrained by ideological considerations. Where it makes sense there is no reason not to be conceptually eclectic. It is not just a matter of combining apparently diverse notions, but

[16] See B. Badie and G. Hermet, 1990, *Politique comparée*, pp. 26 ff.

much more to discuss how their use can help illuminate social or political processes—regardless of whether these originate in ostensibly distinct theoretical traditions. It is the tendency to erect one interpretation as all explanatory that leads to analytical dead-ends.

Let us illustrate our argument with a few examples. In (political) sociology it is customary to oppose Marxist and Weberian approaches. As regards social stratification, for instance, Weber argued that power and influence were not merely determined by economic wealth. He introduced the notion of status, which in pre-capitalist societies derived from distinct, long-established systems of prestige and styles of life.[17] Seen from the outside these may appear to us arbitrary, but for Weber it was crucial to assess their importance. Following this train of thought it is possible to suggest that there were social classes before the development of market capitalism but that they had had only minor effects on stratification. The proponents of a Marxist analysis, on the other hand, stress the primacy of economic factors, the causal importance of class and the superficial relevance of status—which they see as nothing more than ideological mystification. Unlike Weber they deny the significance of the transition from status-based to class-based societies since for them class factors, however invisible, always were (and are) determinant.[18]

From a theoretical point of view Weber argued that social prestige enjoys relative autonomy from what the Marxists call material forces. Indeed, sociologists have shown clearly that in modern societies there is both an increasing division of labour and a diversification in the criteria of prestige. Positions of superiority are not as cumulative as they were in the past, even if socio-economic standing remains the dominant criterion. Social superiority, in other words, has become more multiplex. Comparative analysis thus demonstrates the limits of the purely economic interpretation of social stratification.[19]

---

[17] M. Weber, 1978, *Economy and Society* (edited by G. Roth and C. Wittich), pp. 1239 ff.

[18] Bukharin, for example, argued that the tripartite social division extant was merely hiding the more significant social classes. See N. Bukharin, 1921, *Historical Materialism*.

[19] See for instance F. Anthias, 2001, 'The Material and Symbolic in Theorizing Social Stratification: issues of gender, ethnicity and class', *British Journal of Sociology*, 52 (September) and M. Pinches (ed.), 1999, *Culture and Privilege in Capitalist Asia*.

A third analytical tradition adds further theoretical complexity. Scholars interested in social élite have focused attention on the processes of stratification and domination related both to the rise of 'managers' in Western Europe and the United States *and* to the preponderance of a political-cum-administrative 'nomenklatura' in the former Soviet Union. The power wielded by these two categories of élite did not derive either from traditional status or from the control of capital. It issued from other cognitive resources or institutional assets, which commanded authority.[20] The chief executive is distinct from the capitalist investor. Unlike the bourgeois who owned wealth and therefore ruled, the communist apparatchik ruled and therefore acquired riches. Of course there are vast differences between the American manager, the Russian planner and the French ENA-trained civil servant. Yet all three evince a form of superiority that is neither strictly economic nor simply rooted in 'tradition'.

In many ways theories such as the ones we have just discussed are taken by their adherents to be mutually exclusive. Many Marxists and Weberians simply refuse to contemplate the causal relevance of the other side's argument. For their part, Pareto and Mosca, the founders of the sociology of élite, sought to differentiate themselves radically from the Marxist class perspective. Pareto, who had stern scientific ambitions, relegated Marx's theory to nothing more than propaganda for the masses. Marxists in turn denounced the sociology of élite as bourgeois ideology. Still today some consider élite networks as a threat to democracy whereas others see them as the guarantor of pluralism.[21]

Leaving aside normative disagreements, it is clear that all three of these theories provide analytical insight. We see every reason, for example, to study political standing in terms of class cleavages, which are clearly critical in post eighteenth-century Western societies. On the other hand, to employ a class analysis for all societies, at all times, seems to us heuristically dogmatic. Such an approach makes little sense in settings where conflicts are based on factional or intercommunal rivalries. As we noted in respect of Africa, clientelistic networks are undeniably based on inequality. Yet the demands for

[20] See, among very many, J. Burnham, 1941, *The Managerial Revolution*.
[21] For a general discussion of these issues, see E. Etzioni-Halevy, 1993, *The Élite Connection*.

reciprocity impinge on the élite in ways that constrain them significantly. Here competition between vertical networks is more significant than class conflicts. To deny such evidence on the grounds of 'false consciousness' is merely to obscure understanding of what is happening in that part of the world.

Turning now to another contentious issue, the theory that North-South relations are conditioned by a form of imperialism, which binds capitalists from the core countries to the exploiting élite from the periphery, is excessively reductive. The behaviour of multinationals is by no means the same in all Third World countries. Equally, southern politicians exhibit very diverse attitudes: in Thailand, nationalist politicians are inclined to favour redistribution along the lines of the Buddhist ethos; in much of Africa, they are liable to act as particularistic Big Men. Equally, a slavish adherence to Weberian ideal-types—however useful these are conceptually—is likely to be analytically self-defeating. We have already shown why we think that hybrid categories, like neo-patrimonialism, may not be appropriate to the study of certain non-Western settings.

In sum, using the same conceptual vocabulary for widely divergent political realities amounts to the forcing of evidence into a limited number of models of historical development. It reduces comparative analysis to the identification of simplistic dichotomies or the contrast between a limited number of 'evolutionary' models. To us such approaches are thus 'pre-scientific' in that they merely engage in value judgements without taking into account the evidence on the ground. They exhibit the worst features of an intellectually normative approach—that is, a method that fails to allow for the largely ethnocentric character of the analytical categories used.

An eclectic approach, such as we propose, does not consist in juxtaposing more or less compatible theories.[22] It entails instead an awareness of the limited validity of certain concepts, certain forms of reasoning and certain theories for the understanding of given situations. Thinking inductively means here having recourse to those instruments that have relevance to the explanation of empirical realities on the ground. We employ those concepts and theories that help us to make sense of what we observe, free from ideological or

---

[22] On this point, and in relation to the discussion of social stratification, see John Scott, 1996, *Stratification and Power*.

intellectual pre-conceptions. Where a given approach brings no heuristic added value, it is of no analytical consequence. Indeed, it may sometimes be necessary to fashion different conceptual or theoretical tools.

Such eclecticism also concerns methodology. As shown in Part III, we advocate flexibility in this respect. We do not see the point of asserting *a priori* the superiority of some research techniques over others. For instance, any comparative analysis of the sociology of local power needs in our view to be pragmatic. This field has largely been the preserve of American social scientists and their methods have evolved over time: the new ones challenging the existing ones.[23] There is thus a wide variety of different approaches: those issued from the study of 'position', stipulating that an actor's power is directly related to his/her official position; those linked to 'reputation',[24] which state that reputation derived from power is a good indicator of actual power; those which hold that power is related to 'decision-making'[25] or, alternatively, to be understood in terms of the institutional and ideological causes of 'non-decision making'.[26]

Admittedly these different methods rest on dissimilar social theories and most of these scholars feel the need to challenge the premises on which earlier approaches have been constructed.[27] The 'positional' approach has been criticised as overly simplistic: confusing potential and real power. Dahl attacked the reputation standpoint, which he considered as being too subjective. He favoured a 'decisional' method in his work on the city of New Haven[28]—a study that was assailed by the founders of the 'non-decisional' approach. A more balanced view might suggest that both have their limits. The former probably neglects the hidden aspects of power, such as, how decisions that go against certain interest groups are blocked. The latter may tend to focus excessively on the (ideological or other) manipulations

---

[23] For a survey of this literature see, among others, H. Elcock, 1976, *Political Behaviour.*

[24] Of which the pioneer was F. Hunter, 1953, *Community Power Structure.*

[25] See R. Dahl, 1961, *Who Governs?*, and R. Presthus, 1964, *Men at the Top.*

[26] See P. Bachrach and M. Baratz, 1963, 'Decisions and Non-Decisions: an analytical framework', *American Political Science Review,* 57 (September).

[27] See P. Birnbaum, 1973, 'Le pouvoir local, de la décision au système', *Revue française de sociologie,* xiv, 3 (July).

[28] R. Dahl, 1964, *Who governs?*

that lead to non-decision making whilst neglecting the structural aspects of power.[29]

For us it is important not to favour an approach because it fits with a given socio-political outlook, but on the contrary to use those methods that are most appropriate to the case studies. In a country like the United States, where formal power is fragmented and frequently entails informal influences, it is natural that researchers should seek to go beyond an analysis in terms of 'position' in order to find out who really governs. In countries where local power is more visible (as in the United Kingdom) or less fragmented (as in France), there is greater interest in other questions (electoral sociology, access routes etc.)—although the study of the structures of power (for which a 'positional' line of attack is more straightforward) is by no means neglected.[30] In Africa approaches either in term of 'reputation' or of 'decision-making' are problematic. Given the overall clientelistic context, the first tells us more about the actors' perceptions than about effective power. The second is virtually impossible to achieve, since the main determinants of decision-making are informal.

In our discipline, as in much social science, there are close links between theory, methodology and concepts. It is common to relate research to a school of thought, thereby limiting it to the confines of a given analytical and conceptual framework. However, this attitude has perverse effects. First the identification and use of concepts can all too easily be driven more by the need to assert originally vis-à-vis competitors than by a reflection upon the empirical evidence. In other words, a number of conceptual debates have nothing to do with comparative work but are in fact the result of disputes between various intellectuals and their disciples. Such rivalry gives pride of place to discussion about methods and neglects to address the heuristic quality of the contending positions. Eclecticism here means judging method purely on results.

Second there is a danger of using over-general concepts. Here the defect is to suggest that a simple analytical instrument is sufficient to account for vastly different situations, thus obviating the need for more sophisticated, or different approaches. Let us take the example of the study of leadership. A number of political scientists have argued

[29] See here S. Lukes, 1974, *Power.*
[30] J. Becquart-Leclercq, 1976, *Paradoxes du pouvoir local.*

that leadership is a universal phenomenon—research on which can safely be confined to 'style' (of leadership)—or that it is a political 'model' towards which all polities tend to evolve. In the 1970s it was even claimed that an approach in terms of 'leadership' provided a new theoretical framework for political analysis *in toto.* The contention was that this notion had been 'scientifically' neglected, but that its use would render obsolete most previous approaches.[31] The result was a tendency to produce either universalist or normative work.[32]

Our approach does not denigrate the concept. It suggests instead its judicious use: theories of leadership must be judged on merit, which implies that greater definitional clarity needs to be achieved. For us the notion of leadership is useful insofar as it is analytically distinct from that of élite domination or of institutionalised rulership. Indeed, in our view, leadership implies an important degree of proximity with particular groupings within a context of particularistic exchange relations.[33] Defined in this way, the concept is clearly relevant to certain political environments and not others.

In the United States, where the study of business management techniques is highly developed, there is much emphasis on the notion of leadership. What is meant there is that some managers are able to project an aura of belief and self-confidence that conveys conviction and helps to mobilise others. This definition of the concept stresses the competitive nature of the business world, the rivalry between putative managers, the leaders' individual qualities, the rationality of those who choose to follow them and, finally, the need to achieve concrete results. In other words, this approach rests on a number of assumptions: for example, equality of opportunities for all would-be leaders, a cohesive team dedicated to performance and the success of the enterprise.

Yet, as numerous studies have shown, such are not the conditions that obtain in other societies, where cultural factors impinge on

---

[31] See G. Paige (ed.), 1972, *Political Leadership* and 1977, *The Scientific Study of Political Leadership.*

[32] Cf. for instance J. M. G. Burns, 1978, *Leadership* and J. Blondel, 1987 *Leadership.*

[33] For a systematic discussion of this question, see J.-P. Daloz, 2003, 'Reflections on the Comparative Study of Political Leadership' in H. Baldersheim and J.-P. Daloz (eds), *Political Leadership in a Global Age.*

hierarchy and authority and where leadership potential is restricted to the few. Here priority is given to clarity and continuity in power relations. In France,[34] for instance, as in Asian countries where Confucian traditions matter,[35] there is respect for one's superiors regardless of their personal qualities as managers or their capacity to maintain team harmony. Although our approach here is slightly different, since we are primarily concerned with *political* leadership, we feel affinity with those methods that eschew universal pretensions and focus on the study of the importance of local cultures, mentalities and attitudes.

To sharpen definition in this way is liable to disqualify whole sections of the literature on leadership, but it is likely to make possible much less ambiguous analysis[36] and to provide more precise conceptual instruments. The ideal would be that each instrument should be unique and, as concerns the approach we advocate, that we would be able to use all potential instruments without any *a priori* caveat.

In sum, we start from a very simple observation: people from different cultural origins find it difficult to communicate properly and to understand each other. What seems obvious to some is incomprehensible or absurd to others and even the translation of the relevant words, ideas or concepts from one language into another is rarely sufficient to eliminate misunderstanding or confusion. In the end the difficulties inherent in making sense of the 'other' are caused less by language than by cultural cleavages, differences in mentalities, distinct prejudices or logics.[37]

Because there is in the world almost infinite cultural variation it is impossible to devise comparative analysis other than by means of a cultural approach, or what we call a perspectivist paradigm. Here we use a hard (rather than soft) concept of paradigm since we are not dealing with minor comparative issues but with a way of looking at the world and a method for the scientific study of political systems across the globe. To understand others it is necessary to understand

---

[34] See G. Hofstede, 1997, *Cultures and Organizations.*

[35] See R. Westwood and A. Chan, 1992, 'Headship and Leadership' in R. Westwood (ed.), *Organizational Behaviour.*

[36] Leadership is often used as a synonym for other power relations, such as that between 'governors' and 'governed', 'rulers' and 'ruled', 'élite' and 'masses', 'elected' and 'electors', 'representatives' and 'represented' etc.

[37] P. Burke, 1997, *Varieties of Cultural History,* p. 167.

how they understand themselves. Therefore, the ambition is to seek to interpret meaning in terms of their own ways, even if these ways may appear to us opaque or bizarre.

It remains difficult to convince our peers that the fact we live in very dissimilar cultural worlds is of analytical significance. The problem is that our line of attack demands a drastic revision of the notion of 'scientific' in the social sciences. It implies that we cease to think of the attributes of mankind and of the characteristics of the body politic purely in universal terms. In other words, that we stop operating on the assumption that observable diversity is but a veil over fundamentally similar processes. Our approach rejects the illusion of paradigmatic ecumenism because, as we see it, its meta-theoretical assumptions lead inevitably to theoretical, conceptual and methodological exclusiveness based on deductive reasoning. The illusion of universality generally leads to universalism. Yet we believe it is possible to escape the ethnocentric dilemma by means of an eclectic methodology: a methodology that pays attention to the benefits as well as the limits of the various theoretical, conceptual and methodological instruments as they are applied concretely to empirical research.

BIBLIOGRAPHY

The bibliography is divided into two sections. The first lists those books and articles, which have been most useful to the authors and have most directly informed their reflection. The second is a record of the volumes they consulted in the course of their research, including all those cited in the footnotes.

I

Badie, B., 1983, *Culture et Politique*, Paris: Economica.

———— and P. Birnbaum, 1979, *Sociologie de l'Etat*, Paris: Grasset (English version, *The Sociology of the State*, University of Chicago Press, 1983).

———— and G. Hermet, 1990, *Politique comparée*, Paris: Presses Universitaires de France.

Bastide, R., 1970, 'Mémoire collective et sociologie du bricolage', *L'Année sociologique*.

Berman, B. and J. Lonsdale, 1992, *Unhappy Valley: conflict in Kenya and Africa*, 2 vols, London: James Currey.

Burke, P., 1992, *History and Social Theory*, Cambridge: Polity Press.

————, 1997, *Varieties of Cultural History*, Cambridge University Press.

————, 1997, 'State-Making, King-Making and Image-Making from Renaissance to Baroque: Scandinavia in a European context', *Scandinavian Journal of History*, 22.

————, 2004, *What is Cultural History?*, Cambridge: Polity Press.

Chabal, P., 1994, *Power in Africa: an essay in political interpretation*, Basingstoke: Macmillan.

————, 1998, 'A Few Reflections on Democracy in Africa', *International Affairs*, 74 (2).

————, 2002, 'The Quest for Good Government and Development in Africa: is NEPAD the answer?', *International Affairs*, 78 (3).

———— and J.-P. Daloz, 1999, *Africa Works: disorder as political instrument*, Oxford: James Currey; Bloomington: Indiana University Press.

Daloz, J.-P., 1997, '"Can we eat Democracy?"'—Perceptions de la "démocratisation" zambienne dans un quartier populaire de Lusaka' in J.-P. Daloz and P. Quantin (eds), *Transitions démocratiques africaines. Dynamiques et contraintes*, Paris: Karthala.

———, 2002, *Élites et représentations politiques: la culture de l'échange inégal au Nigeria*, Presses Universitaires de Bordeaux.

———, 2003, 'Ostentation in Comparative Perspective: culture and élite legitimation', *Comparative Social Research*, 21.

———, 2003, 'Reflections on the Comparative Study of Political Leadership' in H. Baldersheim and J.-P. Daloz (eds), *Political Leadership in a Global Age: the experiences of France and Norway*, Aldershot: Ashgate.

Dumont, L., 1985, *Essais sur l'individualisme. Une perspective anthropologique sur l'idéologie moderne*, Paris: Seuil (2nd edn) (English version, *Essays on Individualism: modern ideology in anthropological perspective*, University of Chicago Press, 1986).

Geertz, C., 1963, *Peddlers and Princes*, University of Chicago Press.

———, 1963, *Old Societies and New States*, New York: Free Press.

———, 1963, *Agricultural Involution: the process of ecological change in Indonesia*, Berkeley and Los Angeles: University of California Press.

———, 1965, *The Social History of an Indonesian Town*, Cambridge, MA: MIT Press.

———, 1973, *The Interpretation of Cultures: selected essays*, New York: Basic Books.

———, 1979, *Meaning and Order in Moroccan Society*, Cambridge University Press.

———, 1980, *Negara: the theatre state in nineteenth-century Bali*, Princeton University Press.

———, 1983, *Local Knowledge: further essays in interpretive anthropology*, New York: Basic Books.

———, 1984, 'Anti Anti-Relativism', *American Anthropologist*, 86.

———, 1988, *Works and Lives: the anthropologist as author*, Cambridge: Polity Press; Oxford: Blackwell.

———, 1995, *After the Fact: two countries, four decades, one anthropologist*, Cambridge, MA: Harvard University Press.

———, 2000, *Available Light: anthropological reflections of philosophical topics*, Princeton University Press.

Goldenweisser, A., 1936, 'Loose Ends of a Theory on Individual Patterns and Involution in Primitive Society' in R. Lowie (ed.), *Essays Presented to A. L. Kroeber*, Berkeley: University of California Press.

Hall, E., 1966, *The Hidden Dimension*, New York: Doubleday.

Hunt, L., 1984, *Politics, Culture and Class in the French Republic*, Berkeley: University of California Press.

——— (ed.), 1989, *The New Cultural History*, Berkeley: University of California Press.

Hydén, G., 1980, *Beyond Ujamaa in Tanzania: underdevelopment and an uncaptured peasantry*, London: Heinemann; Berkeley: University of California Press.

Lévy-Bruhl, L., 1960, (1921) *La mentalité primitive*, Paris: Presses Universitaires de France (English version, *Primitive Mentality*, London, George Allen & Unwin, 1923).

Lonsdale, J., 1992, 'The Moral Economy of Mau Mau' in J. Lonsdale and B. Berman, *Unhappy Valley: conflict in Kenya and Africa*, London: James Currey.

———, 1994, 'Moral Ethnicity and Political Tribalism' in P. Kaarsholm and J. Hultin (eds), *Inventions and Boundaries: historical and anthropological approaches to the study of ethnicity and nationalism*, papers from the Researcher Training Course held at Sandbjerg manor, 23–29 May 1993, IDS Roskilde University, Denmark.

———, 1995, 'Moral Ethnicity, Ethnic Nationalism and Political Tribalism: the case of the Kikuyu' in P. Meyns (ed.), *Staat und Gesellschaft in Afrika. Erosions und Reformprozesse*, Hamburg: Lit Verlag.

———, 2003, 'Moral and Political Argument in Kenya' in B. Berman, D. Eyoh and W. Kimlycka (eds), *Ethnicity and Democracy in Africa*, Oxford: James Currey.

———, 1996, 'Ethnicité morale et tribalisme politique', *Politique Africaine*, 61 (March).

Ross, M. H., 1993, *The Culture of Conflict: interpretations and interests in comparative perspective*, New Haven, CT: Yale University Press.

———, 1997, 'Culture and Identity in Comparative Political Analysis' in M. Lichbach and A. Zuckerman (eds), *Comparative Politics: rationality, culture and structure*, Cambridge University Press.

———, 2001, 'Psychocultural Interpretations and Drams: identity dynamics in ethnic conflicts', *Political Psychology*, 22 (1).

Sahlins, M., 1963, 'Poor Man, Rich Man, Big Man, Chief: political types in Melanesia and Polynesia', *Comparative Studies in Society and History*, 2 (3) (April).

———, 1972, *Stone Age Economics*, Chicago, IL: Aldine.

———, 1976, *Culture and Practical Reason*, University of Chicago Press.

———, 1995, *How 'Natives' Think: about Captain Cook, for example*, University of Chicago Press.

———, 2000, *Culture in Practice*, New York: Zone Books.

Sartori, G., 1970, 'Concept Misformation in Comparative Politics', *American Political Science Review*, 64 (December).

———, 1994, 'Compare Why and How: comparing, miscomparing, and the comparative method' in M. Dogan and A. Kazancigil (eds), *Comparing Nations: concepts, strategies, substance*, Oxford: Blackwell.

———, 1994, 'Bien comparer, mal comparer', *Revue Internationale de Politique Comparée*, 1 (1) (April).

Schama, S., 1987, *The Embarrassment of Riches: an interpretation of Dutch culture in the Golden Age*, London: Collins.

Shweder, R. A., 2000, 'Moral Maps, "First World" Conceits and the New Evangelists' in L. E. Harrison and S. P. Huntington (eds), *Culture Matters: how values shape the human progress*, New York: Basic Books.

Trägårdh, L., 1997, 'Statist Individualism: on the culturality of the Nordic welfare State' in Ø. Sørensen and B. Stråth (eds), *The Cultural Construction of Norden*, Oslo: Scandinavian University Press.

Veyne, P., 1976, *Le pain et le cirque. Sociologie historique d'un pluralisme politique*, Paris: Seuil (English version, *Bread and Circuses: Historical sociology and political pluralism*, London, Allen Lane, 1990).

II

Abel, T., 1970, *The Foundation of Sociological Theory*, New York: Random House.

Abélès, M., 2000, *Un ethnologue à l'Assemblée*, Paris: Odile Jacob.

——— and H.-P. Jendy (eds), 1997, *Anthropologie du politique*, Paris: Armand Colin.

Abrams, P., 1982, *Historical Sociology*, Ithaca, NY: Cornell University Press.

Abu-Lughod, L., 1997, 'The Interpretation of Culture(s) after Television', *Representations*, 59.

Abu-Rabi', I., 2004, *Contemporary Arab Thought: studies in post-1967 Arab Intellectual History*, London: Pluto Press.

Achebe, C., 1966, *A Man of the People*, London: Heinemann.

Adorno, T., 1976, *The Positivist Dispute in German Sociology*, London: Heinemann.

Afigbo, A., 1987, *The Igbo and their Neighbours*, Ibadan University Press.

Agulhon, M., 1979, *La République au village: les populations du Var, de la Révolution à la Deuxième République*, Paris: Seuil.

Aho, J., 1999, *This Thing of Darkness: a sociology of the enemy*, Seattle: University of Washington Press.

Akindés, F., 1996, *Les mirages de la démocratie en Afrique subsaharienne francophone*, Dakar: CODESRA.

Alexander, J. and S. Seidman (eds), 1991, *Culture and Society: contemporary debates*, Cambridge University Press.

Almond, G., 1990, *A Discipline Divided: schools and sects in political science*, Newbury Park, CA: Sage.

———, 1996, 'Political Science: the history of the discipline' in R. Goodin and H. Klingeman (eds), *A New Handbook of Political Science*, Oxford University Press.

——— and J. Coleman (eds), 1960, *The Politics of Developing Areas*, Princeton University Press.

Almond, G. and G. B. Powell, 1966, *Comparative Politics: a developmental approach*, Boston, MA: Little, Brown.

—— (eds), 1966, *Comparative Politics Today: a world view*, Glenview, IL: Scott, Foresman and Company, 1988 (4th edn).

Almond, G. and S. Verba, 1963, *The Civic Culture: political attitudes and democracy in five countries*, Princeton University Press.

—— (eds), 1980, *The Civic Culture Revisited*, Boston, MA: Little Brown.

Aluko, T., 1986, *A State of our Own*, London: Heinemann.

Amselle, J.-L., 1990, *Logiques métisses: anthropologie de l'identité en Afrique et ailleurs*, Paris: Payot.

——, 1996, *Vers un multiculturalisme français. L'empire de la coutume*, Paris: Aubier.

Anderson, B., 1990, *Language and Power: exploring political cultures in Indonesia*, Ithaca, NY: Cornell University Press.

——, 1991, *Imagined Communities: reflections on the origins and spread of nationalism* (revised edn) London: Verso.

Anderson, D. and V. Broch-Due (eds), 2000, *The Poor are not Us: poverty and pastoralism*, Oxford: James Currey.

Anderson, P., 1992, *A Zone of Engagement*, London: Verso.

Ansari, H., 2004, *'The Infidel Within': the history of Muslims in Britain from 1800 to the present*, London: Hurst.

Anthias, F., 2001, 'The Material and Symbolic in Theorizing Social Stratification: issues of gender, ethnicity and class', *British Journal of Sociology*, 52 (September).

Anton, T., 1969, 'Policy Making and Political Culture in Sweden', *Scandinavian Political Studies*, 4.

——, 1980, *Administered Élite: élite political culture in Sweden*, Boston, MA: Martinus Nijhoff.

Appadurai, A. (ed.), 1986, *The Social Life of Things: commodities in cultural perspective*, Cambridge University Press.

——, 1991, 'Global Ethnoscapes: notes and queries for a transnational anthropology' in R. Fox (ed.), *Recapturing Anthropology: working in the present*, Santa Fé, NM: School of American Research Press.

——, 1997, *Modernity at Large: cultural dimensions of globalization*, Minneapolis: University of Minnesota Press.

Appiah, A., 1992, *In my Father's House: Africa in the philosophy of culture*, New York: Oxford University Press.

Apter, A., 1992, *Black Critics and Kings: the hermeneutics of power in Yoruba Society*, University of Chicago Press.

Apter, D., 1972 (1955), *The Gold Coast in Transition*, Princeton University Press (2nd edn).

——, 1961, *The Political Kingdom in Uganda*, Princeton University Press.

————, 1965, *The Politics of Modernization*, New Haven, CT: Yale University Press.

————, 1973, *Political Change: collected essays*, London: Frank Cass.

Archer, M., 1995, *Realist Social Theory: the morphogenetic approach*, Cambridge University Press.

————, 1996, *Culture and Agency: the place of culture in social theory*, Cambridge University Press.

Ariès, Ph. and G. Duby (eds), *Histoire de la vie privée* (5 vols), Paris: Seuil (English version, *A History of Private Life*, Cambridge, MA: Harvard University Press, 1987–91).

Arrow, K., 1951, *Social Choice and Individual Values*, New York: Wiley.

Asad, T., 1993, *Genealogies of Religion: discipline and reasons of power in Christianity and Islam*: Baltimore, MD: Johns Hopkins University Press.

Atkinson, P., 1990, *The Ethnographic Imagination: textual constructions of reality*, London: Routledge.

Augé, M., 1979, *Symbole, fonction, histoire: les interrogations de l'anthropologie*, Paris: Hachette (English version, *The Anthropological Circle: symbol, function, history*, Cambridge University Press, 1982).

————, 1983, *Le sens des autres*, Paris: Fayard.

Avineri, S. and A. de Shalit (eds), 1992, *Communitarianism and Individualism*, Oxford University Press.

Ayandele, E., 1966, *The Missionary Impact on Modern Nigeria 1842–1914: a political and social analysis*, London: Longman.

Ayer, A., 1971, *Language, Truth and Logic*, Harmondsworth: Penguin (2nd edn).

Bachrach, P. and M. Baratz, 1963, 'Decisions and Non-Decisions: an analytical framework', *American Political Science Review*, 57 (September).

Badie, B., 1986, *Les deux Etats. Pouvoir et société en Occident et en terre d'Islam*, Paris: Fayard.

————, 1992, *L'Etat importé. L'occidentalisation de l'ordre politique*, Paris: Fayard (English version, *The imported State: the westernization of the political order*, Stanford University Press, 2000).

————, 1995, *La fin des territoires*, Paris: Fayard.

————, 1999, *Un monde sans souveraineté*, Paris: Fayard.

Bailey, F. G., 1969, *Stratagems and Spoils: a social anthropology of politics*, Oxford: Blackwell.

Baker, M. (ed.), 1987, *The Political Culture of the Old Regime*, vol. I: *The French Revolution and the creation of modern political culture*, Oxford: Pergamon Press.

Bakker, J.-W., 1988, *Enough Profundities Already! A reconstruction of Geertz's interpretive anthropology*, Utrecht: ISOR.

Balandier, G., 1967, *Anthropologie politique*, Paris: Presses Universitaires de France.

————, 1971, *Sens et puissance: les dynamiques sociales*, Paris: Presses Universitaires de France.

————, 1980, *Le pouvoir sur scènes*, Paris: Balland.

Baldwin, D. (ed.), 1993, *Neorealism and Neoliberalism: the contemporary debate*, Princeton University Press.

Baldwin, P., 1990, *The Politics of Class Solidarity: class bases of European Welfare States*, Cambridge University Press.

Balibar, E. and I. Wallerstein, 1991, *Race, Nation, Class: ambiguous identities*, London: Verso.

Balogun, M., 1983, *Public Administration in Nigeria: a developmental approach*, London: Macmillan.

Banfield, E., 1958, *The Moral Basis of a Backward Society*, New York: Free Press.

Banton, M., 1997, *Ethnic and Racial Consciousness*, London: Longman.

Barber, K. (ed.), 1997, *Readings in African Popular Culture*, Bloomington: Indiana University Press.

Barnes, S. and M. Kaase, 1979, *Political Action*, London: Sage.

Barrling-Hermansson, K., 2004, *Partikulturer. Kollektiva självbilder och normer I Sveriges riksdag*, Uppsala: Acta Universitatis Upsaliensis.

Barry, A., T. Osborne and N. Rose (eds), 1996, *Foucault and Political Reason*, London: UCL Press.

Barry, B., 1970, *Sociologists, Economists and Democracy*, Basingstoke: Macmillan.

Barth, F. (ed.), 1969, *Ethnic Groups and Boundaries*, Boston, MA: Little, Brown.

Barthes, R., 1964, *Eléments de Sémiologie*, Paris: Seuil.

Bartolini, S. and P. Mair, 1990, *Identity, Competition and Electoral Availability: the stabilization of European electorates 1885–1985*, Cambridge University Press.

Bary, de W., 1998, *Asian Values and Human Rights: a Confucian communitarian perspective*, Cambridge, MA: Harvard University Press.

Bastide, R., 1970, *Le prochain et le lointain*, Paris: Cujas.

————, 1971, *Anthropologie appliquée*, Paris: Payot.

Bates, R., 1983, *Essays on the Political Economy of Rural Africa*, Cambridge University Press.

————, 1989, *Beyond the Miracle of the Market: the political economy of agrarian development in Kenya*, Cambridge University Press.

———— et al., 1998, *Analytic Narratives*, Princeton University Press.

Baudrillard, J., 1970, *La société de consommation*, Paris: Denoël (English version, *The Consumer Society: myths and structures*, Thousand Oaks, CA: Sage, 1996).

Bauman, G., 1997, *Contesting Culture*, Cambridge University Press.

Bauman, Z., 1978, *Hermeneutics and Social Science: approaches to understanding*, London: Hutchinson.

———, 1990, *Thinking Sociologically*, Oxford: Blackwell.

———, 1999, *In Search of Politics*, Stanford University Press.

———, 2000, *Liquid Modernity*, Cambridge: Polity Press.

———, 2001, *The individualized Society*, Cambridge: Polity Press.

Bayart, J.-F., 1986, 'Civil Society in Africa' in Chabal, P. (ed.), *Political Domination in Africa*, Cambridge University Press.

———, 1989, *L'Etat en Afrique. La politique du ventre*, Paris: Fayard (English version, *The State in Africa: the politics of the belly*, London: Longman, 1993).

———, 1996, *L'illusion identitaire*, Paris: Fayard (English version, *The Illusion of Cultural Identity*, London: Hurst, 2005).

———, 2004, *Le gouvernement du monde. Une critique politique de la globalisation*, Paris: Fayard.

——— et al., 1992, *Le politique par le bas en Afrique noire. Contributions à une problématique de la démocratie*, Paris: Karthala.

Bayly, C. A., 1996, *Empire and Information*, Cambridge University Press.

———, 1998, *Origins of Nationality in South Asia: patriotism and ethical government in the making of modern India*, New Delhi: Oxford University Press.

———, 2004, *The Birth of the Modern World, 1780–1914*, Oxford: Blackwell.

Bayly, S., 1989, *Saints, Goddesses and Kings: Muslims and Christians in South Indian societies*, Cambridge University Press.

———, 1999, *Caste, Society and Politics in India: from the eighteenth century to the modern age*, Cambridge University Press.

Beasley, C., 1999, *What is Feminism? An introduction to Feminist Theory*, London: Sage.

Beattie, J., 1980, 'Representations of the Self in Traditional Africa', review article, *Africa*, 50 (3).

Beauchamp, T. and Rosenberg, A. 1981. *Hume and the Problem of Causation*. Oxford: Clarendon Press.

Becker, G., 1976, *The Economic Approach to Human Behaviour*, University of Chicago Press.

Becker, M., 1994, *The Emergence of Civil Society in the Eighteenth Century: a privileged moment in the history of England, Scotland and France*, Bloomington: Indiana University Press.

Becquart-Leclercq, J., 1976, *Paradoxes du pouvoir local*, Paris: Presses de la Fondation Nationale des Sciences Politiques (FNSP).

Beer, S. and A. Ulam (eds), 1958, *Patterns of Government: the major political systems of Europe*, New York: Random House.

Behrend, H. and U. Luig (eds), 1999, *Spirit Possession: modernity and power in Africa*, Oxford: James Currey.

Beitz, C., 1979, *Political Theory and International Relations*, Princeton University Press.

Bell, D., 1960, *The End of Ideology*, New York: Free Press.

Bellamy, R. and M. Hollis (eds), 1999, *Pluralism and Liberal Neutrality*, London: Frank Cass.

Benedict, R., 1934, *Patterns of Culture*, Boston, MA: Houghton Mifflin.

———, 1946, *The Chrysanthemum and the Sword: patterns of Japanese culture*, Boston, MA: Houghton Mifflin.

Benn, S. and G. Mortimore (eds), 1976, *Rationality and the Social Sciences*, London: Routledge and Kegan Paul.

Bennett-Jones, O. 2002. *Pakistan*. New Haven: Yale University Press.

Beran, H., 1987, *The Consent Theory of Political Obligation*, London: Croom Helm.

Berdal, M. and D. Malone, 2000, *Greed and Grievance: economic agendas in civil wars*, Boulder, CO: Lynne Rienner.

Berger, B., 1995, *An Essay on Culture: symbolic structures and social structures*, Berkeley: University of California Press.

Berger, P. and T. Luckmann, 1971, *The Social Construction of Reality: a treatise in the sociology of knowledge*, Harmondsworth: Penguin.

Berger, P. and M. Hsiao (eds), 1988, *In Search of an East Asian Model*, New Brunswick, NJ: Transaction.

Berghe, P. van den, 1981, *The Ethnic Phenomenon*, New York: Elsevier.

Berlin, I., 1979, *Russian Thinkers*, London: Hogarth Press.

———, 1980, *Concepts and Categories: philosophical essays*, Oxford University Press.

Berman, B., 1998, 'Ethnicity, Patronage, and the African State', *African Affairs*, 97 (389).

Berman, S., 1998, *The Social Democratic Moment: ideas and politics in the making of interwar Europe*, Cambridge, MA: Harvard University Press.

Bernard, R., 1994, *Research Methods in Anthropology: qualitative and quantitative approaches*, London: Sage.

Bernstein, R., 1976, *The Restructuring of Social and Political Theory*, London: Methuen.

Berstein, S. (ed.), 1999, *Les cultures politiques en France*, Paris: Seuil.

Berry, S., 1993, *No Condition is Permanent: the social dynamics of agrarian change in Sub-Saharan Africa*, Madison: University of Wisconsin Press.

Bevir, M., 1999, *The Logic of the History of Ideas*, Cambridge University Press.

Bevir, M. and R. Rhodes, (2002) 'Interpretive Theory' in *Theory and Methods in Political Science*, 2nd edn, ed. D. Marsh and G. Stoker (Basingstoke and New York: Palgrave Macmillan).

Bhabha, H., 1994, *The Location of Culture*, New York: Routledge.

Biersack, A., 1989, 'Local Knowledge and Local History: Geertz and beyond' in Hunt, L. (ed.), *The New Cultural History*, Berkeley: University of California Press.

Bierschenk, T. and J.-P. Olivier de Sardan, 1998, *Les pouvoirs au village: le Bénin rural entre democratisation et decentralisation*, Paris: Karthala.

Bill, J. and R. Hardgraves, 1973, *Comparative Politics: the quest for theory*, Columbus, OH: Charles Merrill.

Billard, T., 1995, *Félix Faure*, Paris: Julliard.

Birch, A., 1971, *Representation*, London: Macmillan.

Birnbaum, P., 1973, 'Le pouvoir local, de la décision au système', *Revue française de sociologie*, xiv (3) (July).

———, 1977, *Les sommets de l'Etat: essai sur l'élite du pouvoir en France*, Paris: Seuil. *The Heights of Power: an essay on the power élite in France*, University of Chicago Press, 1982.

———, 1985, 'L'action de l'Etat: différenciation et dédifférenciation' in M. Grawitz and J. Leca (eds), *Traité de science politique*, vol. III, Paris: Presses Universitaires de France.

——— (ed.), 1997, *Sociologie des nationalismes*, Paris: Presses Universitaires de France.

Blalock, H. (ed.), 1972, *Causal Models in the Social Sciences*, Basingstoke: Macmillan.

Blaug, M., 1980, *The Methodology of Economics*, Cambridge University Press.

Bloch, M. and J. Parry (eds), 1982, *Death and Regeneration of Life*, Cambridge University Press.

——— (eds), 1989, *Money and the Morality of Exchange*, Cambridge University Press.

Blondel, J., 1987, *Leadership: towards a general analysis*, London: Sage.

———, 1994, 'Plaidoyer pour une conception œcuménique de la politique comparée', *Revue Internationale de Politique Comparée*, 1 (1).

Blumberg, P., 1974, 'The Decline and Fall of the Status Symbol: some thoughts on status in post-industrial society', *Social Problems*, 21 (April).

Blyth, M., 2002, *Great Transformations: economic ideas and political change in the twentieth century*, Cambridge University Press.

Boas, F., 1940, *Race, Language and Culture*, New York: Macmillan.

Bohannan, L. and P. Bohannan, 1969 (1953), *The Tiv of Central Nigeria*, London: International African Institute (2nd edn).

Bohman, J., 1991, *New Philosophy of Social Science*, Cambridge, MA: MIT Press.

Boix, C., 1998, *Political Parties, Growth and Equality*, Cambridge University Press.

Boltanksi, L., 1982, *Les cadres: La formation d'un groupe social*, Paris: Minuit.

Bonnell, V. and L. Hunt (eds.), 1999. *Beyond the Cultural Turn*. Berkeley: University of California Press.

Booth, W. *et al.* (eds), 1993, *Politics and Rationality*, Cambridge University Press.

Boudon, R., 1991, *La place du désordre*. Paris: Presses Universitaires de France (English version, *Theories of Social Change: a critical appraisal*, Berkeley: University of California Press, 1986).

——, 1998, 'Limitations of Rational Choice Theory', *American Journal of Sociology*, 104 (3).

Boukharine, N., 1969 (1921), *Théorie du matérialisme historique*, Paris: Anthropos (English version, Bukharin, N., *Historical Materialism: a system of sociology*, New York: International Publishers, 1925).

Bourdieu, P., 1972, *Esquisse d'une théorie de la pratique*, Geneva: Droz (English version, *Outline of a Theory of Practice*, Cambridge University Press, 1977).

——, 1979, *La distinction: critique sociale du jugement*, Paris: Minuit (English version, *Distinction: a social critique of the judgement of taste*, Cambridge, MA: Harvard University Press, 1984).

——, 1980, *Questions de sociologie*, Paris: Minuit.

——, 1982, *Ce que parler veut dire: l'économie des échanges linguistiques* (English version, *Language and Symbolic Power*, Cambridge: Polity Press, 1994).

——, 1984, 'La delégation et le fétichisme politique', *Actes de la Recherche en Sciences Sociales*, 52–3 (June).

——, 1987, 'Espace social et pouvoir symbolique' in *Choses dites*, Paris: Minuit (English version, 'Social Space and Symbolic Power', *Sociological Theory*, 7, 1989).

——, 2001, 'L'identité et la représentation' in P. Bourdieu, *Langage et pouvoir symbolique* (previously published as 'Le pouvoir de la représentation'), Paris: Seuil.

Bourmaud, D., 1995, 'Le pouvoir au risque du sexe', *Politique africaine*, 59.

Bouzar, D., 2001, *L'Islam des banlieues*, Paris: Syros.

Bowen, J. and R. Petersen, 1999, *Critical Comparisons in Politics and Culture*, Cambridge University Press.

Boyd, R. and P. Richerson, 1985, *Culture and the Evolutionary Process*, University of Chicago Press.

Bradbury, R. E. and P. C. Lloyd, 1957, *The Benin Kingdom and Edo-Speaking People, plus the Itsekiri*, London: International African Institute.

Brass, P. (ed.), 1985, *Ethnic Groups and the State*, Totowa, NJ: Barnes and Noble.

Bratton, M., 2003, 'Briefing: Islam, democracy and public opinion in Africa', *African Affairs*, 102 (408).

—— and N. Van de Walle, 1997, *Democratic Experiments in Africa: regime transitions in comparative perspective*, Cambridge University Press.

Braudel, F., 1987, *Grammaire des civilisations*, Paris: Flammarion.

Briquet, J.-L. and F. Sawicki (eds), 1998, *Le clientélisme politique dans les sociétés contemporaines*, Paris: Presses Universitaires de France.

Brown, A. (ed.), 1984, *Political Culture and Communist Studies*, Basingstoke: Macmillan.

—— and J. Gray (eds), 1977, *Political Culture and Political Change in Communist States*, London: Macmillan.

Brown, C., 1995, *Serpents in the Sand: essays on the nonlinear nature of politics and human destiny*, Ann Arbor: University of Michigan Press.

Brubaker, R., 1996, *Nationalism Reframed: nationhood and the national question in the new Europe*, Cambridge University Press.

——, 1997, *Citoyenneté et nationalité en France et en Allemagne*, Paris: Belin.

Bruce, S., 1994, *The Edge of the Union: the Ulster nationalist political vision*, Oxford University Press.

Bryman, A., 1988, *Quantity and Quality in Social Research*, London: Routledge.

Bryson, V., 1999, *Feminist Debates*, Basingstoke: Macmillan.

Bukharin, N., 1969 (1921), *Historical Materialism: a system of sociology*, Ann Arbor: University of Michigan Press.

Bull, H., 1977, *The Anarchical Society: a study of order in world politics*, Basingstoke: Macmillan.

Bunge, M., 1996, *Finding Philosophy in Social Science*, New Haven, CT: Yale University Press.

Burke, P. (ed.), 1973, *A New Kind of History: from the writings of Febvre*, London: Routledge and Kegan Paul.

——, 1990, *The French Historical Revolution: the Annales School, 1929–89*, Cambridge: Polity Press.

Burkitt, I., 1991, *Social Selves: theories of the social formation of personality*, London: Sage.

Burnham, J., 1941, *The Managerial Revolution*, New York: John Day.

Burns, E., 1972, *Theatricality: a study of convention in the theatre and in social life*, London: Longman.

Burns, J. M. G., 1978, *Leadership*, New York: Harper and Row.

Busca, D. and D. Salles, 2002, 'Agri-environnement: les territoires font la loi', *Environnement et société*, 26.

Butler, J., 1993, *Bodies that Matter: on the discursive limits of 'sex'*, London: Routledge.

Cahen, M., 1994, *Ethnicité politique: pour une lecture réaliste de l'identité*, Paris: L'Harmattan.

Calhoun, C., 1982, *The Question of Class Struggle: social foundations of popular radicalism during the Industrial Revolution*, Oxford: Blackwell.

————, 1995, *Critical Social Theory: culture, history and the challenge of difference*, Oxford: Blackwell.

Cantori, L. and A. Ziegler Jr., 1988, *Comparative Politics in the Post-Behavioral Age*, Boulder, CO: Lynne Rienner.

Caporaso, J., 2000, 'Comparative Politics: diversity and coherence', *Comparative Political Studies*, 33.

Carré, O. (ed.), 1982, *L'Islam et l'Etat dans le monde d'aujourd'hui*, Paris: Presses Universitaires de France.

———— (ed.), 1993, *L'islam laïque ou le retour. La grande tradition*, Paris: Armand Colin.

Carrier, J., 1995, *Gifts and Commodities: exchange and Western capitalism since 1700*, London: Routledge.

————, 1995, *Occidentalism: images of the West*, Oxford: Clarendon Press.

————, 1997, *Meanings of the Market*, Oxford: Berg.

Carrithers, M., 1992, *Why Humans Have Cultures: explaining anthropology and social diversity*, Oxford University Press.

Castells, M., 1996, *The Rise of Network Society*, vol. I of *The Information Age*, Oxford: Blackwell.

Catt, H., 1996, *Voting Behaviour: a radical critique*, London: Cassell.

Cefai, D., 2000, *Cultures politiques*, Paris: Presses Universitaires de France.

Certeau, M. de, 1993 (1974), *La culture au pluriel*, Paris: Seuil (2nd edn).

Chabal, P., 1983, *Amílcar Cabral: revolutionary leadership and people's war*, Cambridge University Press.

———— (ed.), 1986, *Political Domination in Africa: reflections on the limits of power*, Cambridge University Press.

————, 2004. "La politique comparée et les études en termes d'aires culturelles" in C. Thiriot, Marty, M. Nadal, E. (eds.), 2004. *Penser la politique comparée. Un état des savoirs théoriques et méthodologiques*. Paris: Karthala.

Champney, L., 1995, *Introduction to Quantitative Political Science*, New York: HarperCollins.

Chan, S., 2002, *Liberalism, Democracy and Development*, Cambridge University Press.

Chang, H.-J., 2002, *Kicking Away the Ladder: development strategy in historical perspective*, London: Anthem Press.

Chant, S., 1997, *Women-Headed Households: diversity and dynamics in the developing world*, Basingstoke: Macmillan.

Charlesworth, J. C., 1962, *The Limits of Behavioralism in Political Science*, Philadelphia, PA: American Academy of Political and Social Science.

Chatterjee, P., 1993, *The Nation and its Fragments: colonial and postcolonial histories*, Princeton University Press.

Chaussinand-Nogaret, G. (ed.), 1991, *Histoire des élites en France du XVIe au XXe siècle*, Paris: Tallandier (2nd edn, Paris: Hachette, 1994).

Cheal, D., 1988, *The Gift Economy*, London: Routledge.

Cheater, A. (ed.), 1999, *The Anthropology of Power: empowerment, disempowerment and changing structures*, London: Routledge.

Chelhod, J., 1958, *Introduction à la sociologie de l'Islam*, Paris: Besson-Chantemerle.

Chie, N., 1970, *Japanese Society*, Berkeley: University of California Press.

Chilcote, R., 1994, *Theories of Comparative Politics: the search for a paradigm reconsidered*, Boulder, CO: Westview.

Childs, M., 1936, *Sweden: the middle way*, London: Faber and Faber.

————, 1980, *Sweden: the middle way on trial*, New Haven, CT: Yale University Press.

Chrétien, J.-P., 1993, *L'invention religieuse en Afrique: histoire et religion en Afrique noire*, Paris: Karthala.

Clapham, C., 1999, 'Sovereignty and the Third World State', *Political Studies*, 47, 522–37.

Clark, T. and V. Hoffmann-Martinot (eds), 1998, *The New Political Culture*, Boulder, CO: Westview.

Clarke, L. and L. Lange, 1979, *The Sexism of Social and Political Theory: women and reproduction from Plato to Nietzsche*, Toronto University Press.

Clifford, J., 1988, *The Predicament of Culture: twentieth-century ethnography, literature and art*, Cambridge, MA: Harvard University Press.

———— and G. Marcus (eds), 1986, *Writing Culture: the poetics and politics of ethnography*, Berkeley: University of California Press.

Cohen, A., 1969, *Customs and Politics in Urban Africa*, London: Routledge and Keegan Paul.

————, 1981, *The Politics of Élite Culture: exploration in the dramaturgy of power in a modern society*, Berkeley: University of California Press.

Cohen, D. and E. S. Odhiambo, 1992, *Burying SM: the politics of knowledge and the sociology of power in Africa*, Porstmouth, NH: Heinemann.

Cohen, J. and A. Arato, 1992, *Civil Society and Political Theory*, Cambridge, MA: MIT Press.

Coleman, J., 1963, *Nigeria: background to nationalism*, Berkeley: University of California Press.

Collier, D. and J. Mahon, 1993, 'Conceptual "Stretching" Revisited: adapting categories in comparative analysis', *American Political Science Review*, 89.

Collingwood, R., 1993, *The Idea of History*, revised edn, Oxford University Press.

Collins, R., 1986, *Weberian Sociological Theory*, Cambridge University Press.

Comaroff, J. and J. Comaroff (eds), 1993, *Modernity and its Malcontents: ritual and power in postcolonial Africa*, University of Chicago Press.

————, 1997, *Of Revelation and Revolution: the dialectics of modernity on a South African frontier*, University of Chicago Press.

———, 1997, *Ethnography and the Historical Imagination*, Boulder, CO: Westview.

——— (eds), 1999, *Civil Society and the Political Imagination in Africa: critical perspectives*, University of Chicago Press.

Connell, R., 1987, *Gender and Power: society, the person and sexual politics*, Cambridge: Polity Press.

Coombes, A., 1994, *Reinventing Africa: museums, material culture and popular imagination in late Victorian and Edwardian England*, New Haven, CT: Yale University Press.

Cook, T. and D. Campbel, 1979, *Quasi-Experimentation: design and analysis issues for field settings*, Boston, MA: Houghton Mifflin.

Cook, T. and C. Reichardt (eds), 1979, *Qualitative and Quantitative Methods in Evaluation Research*, New York: Sage.

Cooper, F. and A. L. Stoller (eds), 1997, *Tensions of Empire: colonial cultures in a bourgeois world*, Berkeley: University of California Press.

Copans, J., 1989, *Les marabouts de l'arachide: la confrérie Mouride et les paysans du Sénégal*, Paris: L'Harmattan.

———, 1990, *La longue marche de la modernité africaine: savoirs, intellectuels, démocratie*, Paris: Karthala.

Coppet, D. de, 1992, *Understanding Ritual*, London: Routledge.

Corbin, A., 1999 (1987), 'coulisses' in Perrot M. (ed.), *Histoire de la vie privée*, vol. IV, *De la Révolution à la Grande Guerre*, Paris: Seuil (2nd edn).

Coronil, F., 1996, 'Beyond Occidentalism: towards nonimperial geo-historical categories', *Cultural Anthropology*, 11 (1).

Corrin, C., 1999, *Feminist Perspectives on Politics*, London: Longman.

Costa, O., A. Couvidat and J.-P. Daloz, 2003, 'The French Presidency in 2000: an arrogant leader?' in O. Elgström (ed.), *European Council Presidencies: a comparative perspective*, London: Routledge.

Costa, O. and J.-P. Daloz, 2005, 'How French Policy Makers see Themselves' in Drake, H. (ed.), *French Relations with the European Union*, London: Routledge.

Coulon, C., 1981, *Le marabout et le prince. Islam et pouvoir au Sénégal*, Paris: Pedone.

———, 1983, *Les musulmans et le pouvoir en Afrique noire. Religion et contre-culture*, Paris: Karthala.

Cowling, M., 1963, *The Nature and Limits of Political Science*, Cambridge University Press.

Crane, D. (ed.), 1994, *The Sociology of Culture: emerging theoretical perspectives*, Oxford: Blackwell.

Cresswell, J., 1994, *Research Design: qualitative and quantitative approaches*, London: Sage.

Crew, I. and D. Denver, 1985, *Electoral Change in Western Democracies*, London: Croom Helm.

Crick, B., 1964, *The American Science of Politics*, Los Angeles: University of California Press.

Croft, S. and T. Terriff, 2000, *Critical Reflections on Security and Change*, London: Frank Cass.

Crook, R. and J. Manor, 1998, *Democracy and Decentralization in South Asia and West Africa: participation, accountability and performance*, Cambridge University Press.

Crotty, W. (ed.), 1991, *Looking to the Future: comparative politics, policy and international relations*, Evanston, IL: Northwestern University Press.

Crowder, M., 1962, *The Story of Nigeria*, London: Faber and Faber.

Crozier, M., 1963, *Le phénomène bureaucratique*, Paris: Seuil. *The Bureaucratic Phenomenon*, Univeristy of Chicago Press, 1964.

Cruise O'Brien, D., 1971, *The Mourides of Senegal*, Oxford University Press.

Cuche, D., 1998, *La notion de culture dans les sciences sociales*, Paris: La Découverte.

Curtin, P., 1984, *Cross-Cultural Trade in World History*, Cambridge University Press.

Daalder, H. (ed.), 1997, *Comparative European Politics: the story of a profession*, London: Pinter.

D'Andrade, R., 1995, *The Development of Cognitive Anthropology*, Cambridge University Press.

D'Arcy, F. (ed.), 1985, *La représentation*, Paris: Economica.

Dahl, H., 1986, 'Those Equal Folks' in Graubard, S. (ed.), *Norden: the passion for equality*, Oslo: Norwegian University Press.

Dahl, R., 1964, *Who Governs?* New Haven, CT: Yale University Press.

———, 1971, *Polyarchy: participation and opposition*, New Haven, CT: Yale University Press.

Daloz, J.-P., 1992, *Société et politique au Nigeria. Bibliographie annotée, réflexions sur l'état d'avancement des connaissances*, Bordeaux-Talence: C.E.A.N.

———, 2002, '"Big Men" in Sub-Saharan Africa: how élites accumulate positions and resources', *Comparative Sociology*, 2 (1).

———, 2002, 'L'étalage de la vie sexuelle en tant que facteur de légitimation politique' in Baudry, P. , C. Sorbets and A. Vitalis (eds), *La vie privée à l'heure des médias*, Presses Universitaires de Bordeaux.

——— and K. Barrling-Hermansson, 2004, 'Représentation politique et modestie ostensible en Europe du Nord', *Nordiques*, 4 (April).

——— and M.-H. Heo, 1997, 'La corruption en Corée du Sud et au Nigeria. Quelques pistes de recherche comparatives', *Revue Internationale de Politique Comparée*, 4 (2) (September).

Dalton, R., S. Flanagan and P. Beck, 1984, *Electoral Change in Advanced Industrial Democracies: realignment or dealignment*, Princeton University Press.

Daniel, V., 1996, *Charred Lullabies: chapters in an anthropology of violence*, Princeton University Press.

Daniels, N. (ed.), 1978, *Reading Rawls: critical studies on Rawls' 'A Theory of Justice'*, Oxford: Blackwell.

Darbon, D. (ed.), 1995, *Ethnicité et nation en Afrique du Sud. Imageries identitaires et enjeux sociaux*, Paris: Karthala.

———, 1997, *La crise de la chasse en France. La fin d'un monde*, Paris: L'Harmattan.

——— and J. de Gaudusson (eds), 1997, *La création du droit en Afrique*, Paris: Karthala.

Darnton, R., 1985, *The Great Cat Massacre and Other Episodes in French Cultural History*, New York: Basic Books.

Daun, Å., 1991, 'Individualism and Collectivity among Swedes', *Ethnos*, 3–4.

———, 1999 (1989), *Swedish Mentality*, University Park, PA: Penn State Press.

Delannoi, G. and P.-A. Taguieff (eds), 1991, *Théories du nationalisme: nation, nationalité, ethnicité*, Paris: Kimé.

Déloye, Y., 1997, *Sociologie historique du politique*, Paris: La Découverte.

———, C. Haroche and O. Ihl (eds), 1996, *Le protocole ou la mise en forme de l'ordre politique*, Paris: L'Harmattan.

Denzin, N., 1997, *Intepretative Ethnography: ethnographic practices for the twenty-first century*, London: Sage.

Derrida, J., 1976, *Of Grammatology*, Baltimore, MD: Johns Hopkins University Press.

Detienne, M., 2000, *Comparer l'incomparable*, Paris: Seuil.

Deutsch, J-G., P. Probst and H. Schmidt (eds), 2002, *African Modernities*, Oxford: James Currey.

Deutsch, K., 1963, *The Nerves of Government: models of communication and control*, New York: Free Press.

Devine, F. and S. Heath, 1999, *Sociological Research Methods in Context*, Basingstoke: Macmillan.

Devish, R., 1993, *Weaving the Threads: the Khital gynecological healing cult among the Yaka*, University of Chicago Press.

Dews, P., 1986, *Logics of Disintegration*, London: Verso.

Diamond, L. and F. Plattner (eds), 1999, *Democratization in Africa*, Baltimore, MD: Johns Hopkins University Press.

Diaw, A., 1994, *Démocratisation et logiques identitaires en acte. L'invention de la politique en Afrique*, Dakar: CODESRA.

Dieterlen, G. (ed.), 1973, *La notion de personne en Afrique noire*, Paris: Editions du CNRS.

Dion, D., 1998, 'Evidence and Inference in the Comparative Case Study', *Comparative Politics*, 30.

Dirks, N., G. Eley and S. Ortner (eds), 1994, *Culture, Power, History: a reader in contemporary social theory*, Princeton University Press.

Dodge, T., 2003, *Inventing Iraq: the failure of nation building and a history denied*, New York: Columbia University Press.

———— and S. Simon (eds), 2003, *Iraq at the Crossroads: state and society in the shadow of regime change*, London and Oxford: International Institute for Strategic Studies and Oxford University.

Dogan, M., 1994, 'L'analyse quantitative en science politique', *Revue Internationale de Politique Comparée*, 1/1 (April)

———— (ed.), 2003, *Élite Configuration at the Apex of Power*, Leiden: E. J. Brill.

———— and D. Pelassy, 1981, *Sociologie politique comparative*, Paris: Economica (English version, *How to Compare Nations: strategies in Comparative Politics*, Chatham, NJ: Chatham House, 1984).

———— and A. Kazancigil (eds), 1994, *Comparing Nations: concepts, strategies, substance*, Oxford: Blackwell.

Donham, D., 1990, *History, Power, Ideology: central issues in Marxism and anthropology*, Cambridge University Press.

Dörner, A., 1999, 'Politische Kulturforschung und Cultural Studies' in O. Haberl and T. Korenke (eds), *Politische Deutungskulturen*, Baden-Baden: Nomos.

———— and L. Vogts (eds), 2002, *Wahl-Kämpfe: Betrachtungen über ein demokratishes Ritual*, Frankfurt: Suhrkamp.

Dorronsoro, G., 2004, *Revolution Unending: Afghanistan, 1979 to the present*, London: Hurst.

Dosse F., 1992, *Histoire du structuralisme* (2 vols), Paris: La Découverte.

Douglas, M., 1973, *Natural Symbols*, Harmonsdworth: Penguin.

————, 1986, *How Institutions Think*, Syracuse University Press.

———— and A. Wildavsky, 1982, *Risk and Culture: an essay on the selection of technological and environmental dangers*, Berkeley: University of California Press.

Dowding, K. and D. King (eds), 1995, *Preferences, Institutions and Rational Choice*, Oxford University Press.

Downs, A. 1957. *An Economic Theory of Democracy*. New York: Harper Row.

Dozon, J.-P., 1995, *La cause des prophètes: politique et religion en Afrique contemporaine* (followed by M. Augé, *La leçon des prophètes*), Paris: Seuil.

Dreyfus, H. and P. Rabinow (eds), 1982, *Michel Foucault: beyond structuralism and hermeneutics*, London: Harvester Wheatsheaf.

Dryzek, J., 1990, *Discursive Democracy: politics, policy and political science*, Cambridge University Press.

Duby, G., 1973, *Le dimanche de Bouvines*, Paris: Gallimard (English version, *The Legend of Bouvines*, Cambridge: Poliy Press, 1990).

Duffield, M., 2001, *Global Governance and the New Wars: the merging of development and security*, London: Zed Press.

Dumont, L., 1967, *Homo hierarchicus. Essai sur le système des castes*, Paris: Gallimard (English version, *Homo Hierarchicus: an essay on the caste system*, London: Weidenfeld and Nicholson, 1970).

Dunleavy, P., 1991, *Democracy, Bureaucracy and Public Choice: economic explanations in political science*, Hemel Hampstead: Harvester Wheatsheaf.

During, S. (ed.), 2000, *The Cultural Studies Reader*, London: Routledge (2nd expanded edn).

Durkheim, E., 1983 (1894), *Les règles de la méthode sociologique*, Paris: Presses Universitaires de France (English version, *The Rules of Sociological Method*, New York, Free Press, 1982).

———, 1960 (1912), *Les formes élémentaires de la vie religieuse*, Paris: Presses Universitaires de France (English version, *The Elementary Forms of Religious Life*, Glencoe Ill: Free Press, 1947).

——— and M. Mauss, 1901–2, 'De quelques formes primitives de classification', *L'Année sociologique* (English version, University of Chicago Press, 1963).

Eagleton, T., 1991, *Ideology: an introduction*, London: Verso.

Easton, D., 1957, 'An Approach to the Analysis of Politics Systems', *World Politics*, 9.

Eatwell, R. (ed.), 1997, *European Political Cultures: conflict or convergence?*, London: Routledge.

Eboussi Boulaga, F., 1977, *La crise du Muntu. Authenticité africaine et philosophie*, Paris: Présence Africaine.

Eckstein, H., 1982, 'A Culturalist Theory of Political Change', *American Political Science Review*, 82.

Edelman, M., 1964, *The Symbolic Uses of Politics*, Urbana, IL: University of Illinois Press.

———, 1971, *Politics as Symbolic Action*, Chicago, IL: Markham.

———, 1988, *Constructing the Political Spectacle*, University of Chicago Press.

Edgerton, R., 1978, *Rules, Exceptions and Social Order*, Berkeley: University of California Press.

———, 1992, *Sick Societies: challenging the myth of primitive harmony*, New York: Free Press.

Eisenstadt, S. and R. Lemarchand (eds), 1981, *Political Clientelism, Patronage and Development*, London: Sage.

Elcock, H., 1976, *Political Behaviour*, London: Methuen.

Elias, N., 1968 (1939), *The Civilizing Process*, vol. I: *The History of Manners*; vol. II: *State formation and Civilization*, Oxford: Blackwell.

———, 1974, *La société de cour*, Paris: Calmann-Lévy (English version, *The Court Society*, Oxford: Blackwell, 1969 (1936)).

———, 1991 (1987), *La société des individus*, Paris: Fayard.

Eliasoph, N., 2000, *Avoiding Politics*, Cambridge University Press.

Ellen, R., 1982, *Environment, Subsistence and System: the ecology of small-scale social formations*, Cambridge University Press.

Elliott, A. (ed.), 1999, *Contemporary Social Theory*, Oxford: Blackwell.

Ellis, S., 1999, *The Mask of Anarchy: the destruction of Liberia and the religious dimension of an African civil war*, London: Hurst.

——— and G. Ter Haar, 2004, *Worlds of Power: religious thought and political practice in Africa*, London: Hurst.

Elster, J. (ed.), 1986, *Rational Choice*, Oxford: Blackwell.

———, 1989, *Nuts and Bolts for the Social Sciences*, Cambridge University Press.

———, 1989, *Solomonic Judgements: studies in the limits of rationality*, Cambridge University Press.

Enayet, H., 1982, *Modern Islamic Political Thought*, London: Macmillan.

Englebert, P., 2000, *State Legitimacy and Development in Africa*, Boulder, CO: Lynne Rienner.

Eribon, D., *Michel Foucault*, Paris: Flammarion (2nd edn), 1991, *Michel Foucault*, Cambridge, MA: Harvard University Press.

Eriksen, H. T., 2001, *Small Places, Large Issues: an introduction to social and cultural anthropology*, London: Pluto Press (2nd edn).

Erikson, E., 1958, *Young Man's Luther*, New York: Norton.

———, 1969, *Gandhi's Truth*, New York: Norton.

Esaiasson, P. and S. Holmberg, 1996, *Representation from Above: members of parliament and representative democracy in Sweden*, Dartmouth: Aldershot.

Esaiasson, P. and K. Heidar (eds), 2000, *Beyond Westminster and Congress: the Nordic experience*, Colombus, OH: Ohio University Press.

Escobar, A., 1995, *Encountering Development: the making and unmaking of the Third World*, Princeton University Press.

Esping-Andersen, G., 1990, *The Three Worlds of Welfare Capitalism*, Cambridge: Polity Press.

Esposito, J., 1992, *The Islamic Threat: myth or reality?*, Oxford University Press.

——— and F. Burgat, 2003, *Modernizing Islam: religion in the public sphere in Europe and the Middle East*, London: Hurst.

Etzioni-Halevy, E., 1993, *The Élite Connection: problems and potential of Western Democracy*, Cambridge: Polity Press.

Evans-Pritchard, E., 1937, *Witchcraft, Oracles and Magic among the Azande*, Oxford University Press.

———, 1940, *The Nuer*, Oxford University Press.

Fabian, J., 1983, *Time and the Other: how anthropology makes its object*, New York: Columbia University Press.

———, 1998, *Moments of Freedom: anthropology and popular culture*, Charlottesville, VA: University of Virginia Press.

Fabre, P., 1996, *L'Europe entre cultures et nations*, Paris: MSH.

Fardon, R. (ed.), 1990, *Localizing Strategies: the regionalization of ethnographic accounts*, Washington, DC: Smithsonian Institution Press.

Farouk-Sluglett, M. and P. Sluglett, 1990, *Iraq Since 1958: from revolution to dictatorship*, London: I. B. Tauris.

Farr, J., J. Dryzek and S. Leonard (eds), 1995, *Political Science in History: research programs and political traditions*, Cambridge University Press.

Fauchois, Y., 1997, 'L'absolutisme: un colosse aux pieds d'argile' in *L'histoire grande ouverte: hommages à Emmanuel Le Roy-Ladurie*, Paris: Fayard.

Fawaz, L. T., C. A. Bayly and R. Ilbert (eds), 2001, *Modernity and Culture from the Mediterranean to the Indian Ocean, 1890–1920*, New York: Columbia University Press.

Featherstone, M. (ed.), 1990, *Global Culture: nationalism, globalization and modernity*, London: Sage.

———, 1991, *Consumer Culture and Post Modernism*, London: Sage.

Febvre, L., 1930, 'Civilisation' in *Civilisation: le mot et l'idée*, presented by Lucien Febvre, Emile Tonnelat, Marcel Mauss, Alfredo Niceforo and Louis Weber, Paris: La Renaissance du livre.

Feierband, I. *et al.*, 1972, *Anger, Violence and Politics*, Englewoods Cliffs, NJ: Prentice-Hall.

Feierman, S., 1990, *Peasant Intellectuals: anthropology and history in Tanzania*, Madison: University of Wisconsin Press.

Ferguson, J., 1990, *The Anti-Politics Machine: 'development', depoliticization and bureaucratic power in Lesotho*, Cambridge University Press.

———, 1999, *Expectations of Modernity: myths and meanings of urban life on the Zambian Copperbelt*, Berkeley: University of California Press.

Ferguson, M. and P. Golding (eds), 1997, *Culture Studies in Question*, Thousand Oaks, CA: Sage.

Fernandes, J., 1982, *Bwiti: an ethnography of the religious imagination in Africa*, Princeton University Press.

Feyerabend, P., 1975, *Against Method*, London: Verso.

Figes, O., 2002, *Natasha's Dance: a cultural history of Russia*, London: Allen Lane.

Finkelkrault, A., 1987, *La défaite de la pensée*, Paris: Gallimard.

Firth, R., 1973, *Symbols: public and private*, London: George Allen and Unwin.

Fiske, D. and R. Shweder, 1986, *Metatheory in Social Science*, University of Chicago Press.

Flora, P. and J. Heidenheimer, 1981, *The Development of Welfare States in Europe and America*, New Brunswick, NJ: Transaction.

Fodor, J., 1979, *The Language of Thought*, Cambridge, MA: Harvard University Press.

——, 1981, *Representations*, Cambridge, MA: MIT Press, 1981.

Fogelkou, A., 1987, 'Law as an Ornament of Power' in Arvidsson, C. and L. Blomquist (eds), *The Esthetics of Political Legitimation in the Soviet Union and Eastern Europe*, Stockholm: Almqvist and Wiskell.

Forgacs, D. and R. Lumley (eds), 1996, *Italian Cultural Studies*, Oxford University Press.

Forsythe, D., 2000, *Human Rights in International Relations*, Cambridge University Press.

Fortes, M., 1949, *The Web of Kinship among the Tallensi*, Oxford University Press.

——, 1987, *Religion, Morality and the Person: essays on Tallensi Religion*, Cambridge University Press.

—— and E. Evans-Pritchard (eds), 1940, *African Political Systems*, Oxford University Press.

Foster, R., 1995, *Social Reproduction and History in Melanesia: mortuary ritual, gift exchange and custom in the Tanga Islands*, Cambridge University Press.

Foucault, M., 1966, *Les mots et les choses*, Paris: Gallimard (English version: *The Order of Things: an archeology of the human sciences*, London: Tavistock, 1970).

——, 1969, *L'archéologie du savoir*, Paris: Gallimard (English version, *The Archeology of Knowledge*, London: Tavistock, 1972).

——, 1980, *Power/Knowledge: selected interviews and other writings, 1972–77*, New York: Pantheon.

Fraser, N., 1989, *Unruly Practices: power, discourse and gender in contemporary social theory*, Cambridge: Polity Press.

Frazer, E. (ed.), 1993, *The Politics of Community: a feminist critique*, New York: Harvester Wheatsheaf.

Freilich, M. *et al.* (eds), 1989, *The Relevance of Culture*, New York: Bergen and Garvey.

Friedman, J., 1994, *Cultural Identity and Global Process*, London: Sage.

Friedmann, Y., 1989, *Prophecy Continuous: aspects of Ahmadi religious thought and its medieval background*, Berkeley, CA: University of California Press.

Freidman, J. (ed.), 1996, *The Rational Choice Controversy: economic models of politics reconsidered*, New Haven, CT: Yale University Press.

Friedrich, C. with M. Horwitz, 1968, 'The Relation of Political Theory to Anthropology', *American Political Science Review,* 52.

Freund, B., 1984, *The Making of Contemporary Africa,* Bloomington: Indiana University Press.

Freyre, G. 1938. *Casa-grande e senzala. Formação da família brasileira sob o regimen de economia patriarchal* Rio de Janeiro: Schmidt.

Frost, M., 1986, *Towards a Normative Theory of International Relations,* Cambridge University Press.

Fukuyama, F., 1992, *The End of History and the Last Man,* New York: Free Press.

———, 1995, *Trust: the social virtues and the creation of prosperity,* New York: Free Press.

Gamble, A., D. Marsh and T. Tant (eds), 1999, *Marxism and Social Science,* Basingstoke: Macmillan.

Gamson, W., 1992, *Talking Politics,* Cambridge University Press.

Gamst, F. and E. Norbeck (eds), 1976, *Ideas of Culture: sources and uses,* New York: Holt, Rinehart and Winston.

Gardner, K and D. Lewis, 1996, *Anthropology, Development and the Post-Modern Challenge,* London: Pluto Press.

Gellner, E., 1974, *Legitimation of Belief,* Cambridge University Press.

———, 1981, *Muslim Society,* Cambridge University Press.

———, 1982, 'Relativism and Universals' in M. Hollis and S. Lukes (eds), *Rationality and Relativism,* Oxford: Blackwell.

———, 1983, *Nations and Nationalism,* Oxford: Blackwell.

———, 1984, *Rationality and the Social Sciences,* Cambridge University Press.

———, 1985, *Relativisim in the Social Sciences,* Cambridge University Press.

———, 1988, *Plough, Sword and Book: the structure of human history,* London: Collins Harvill.

———, 1992, *Postmodernism, Reason and Religion,* London: Routledge.

———, 1992, *Reason and Culture: the historic role of rationality and rationalism,* Oxford: Blackwell.

———, 1994, *Conditions of Liberty: civil society and its rivals,* London: Hamish Hamilton.

———, 1995, *Anthropology and Politics: revolutions in the sacred grove,* Oxford: Blackwell.

———, 1997, *Nationalism,* London: Weidenfeld and Nicolson.

Geschiere, P., 1997, *The Modernity of Witchcraft: politics and the occult in postcolonial Africa,* Charlottesville, VA: University of Virginia Press.

———, 2003, 'On Witch Doctors and Spin Doctors; the role of 'experts' in African and American politics' in P. Pels and Meyer, B., *Magic and Modernity,* Stanford University Press.

Geuss, R., 1981, *The Idea of Critical Theory*, Cambridge University Press.

Gibbons, M., 1987, *Interpreting Politics*, Oxford: Blackwell.

Giddens, A., 1979, *Central Problems in Social Theory*, Basingstoke: Macmillan.

———, 1984, *The Constitution of Society*, Cambridge: Polity Press.

———, 1985, *The Nation State and Violence*, Cambridge University Press.

———, 1990, *The Consequences of Modernity*, Cambridge: Polity Press.

———, 1991, *Modernity and Self-Identity: self and society in the late modern age*, Stanford University Press.

Giere, R., 1979, *Understanding Scientific Reasoning*, New York: Holt, Rinehart and Winston.

Gilbert, N., 1993, *Researching Social Life*, London: Sage.

Gilovitch, T., 1991, *How We Know What Isn't So: the fallibility of human reason in everyday life*, New York: Free Press.

Gilroy, P., 1993, *The Black Atlantic: modernity and double consciousness*, London: Verso.

Gintis, H., 2000, *Game Theory Evolving*, Princeton University Press.

Gledhill, J., 2000, *Power and its Disguises: anthropological perspectives on politics*, London: Pluto Press.

Godechot, J., 1968, *Les institutions de la France sous la Révolution et l'Empire*, Paris: Presses Universitaires de France.

Godelier, M., 1973, *Horizons, trajets marxistes en anthropologie*, vol. II, Paris: Maspéro (English version, *Perspectives in Marxist Anthropology*, Cambridge University Press, 1977).

———, 1996, *L'énigme du don*, Paris: Flammarion (English version, *Enigma of the gift*, Cambridge: Polity Press, 1999).

Goffmann, E., 1959, *The Presentation of Self in Everyday Life*, Garden City, NJ: Anchor Books.

Goldstein, J. and R. Keohane (eds), 1993, *Ideas and Foreign Policy: beliefs, institutions and political change*, Ithaca, NY: Cornell University Press.

Goldstone, J., 1991, *Revolution and Rebellion in the Early Modern World*, Berkeley, CA: University of California Press.

Gomard, K. and A. Krogstad (eds), 2001, *Instead of the Ideal Debate: doing politics and doing gender in Nordic political campaign discourse*, Aarhus University Press.

Goode, W., 1978, *The Celebration of Heroes: prestige as a social control system* Berkeley: University of California Press.

Goodin, R. (ed.), 1996, *The Theory of Institutional Design*, Cambridge University Press.

——— and H. Klingemann (eds), 1996, *A New Handbook of Political Science*, Oxford University Press.

Goody, J., 1956, *The Social Organisation of the Lo Wiili*, Oxford University Press.

————, 1971, *Technology, Tradition and the State in Africa*, Oxford University Press.

————, 1992, 'Local Knowledge and Knowledge of Locality: the desirability frames', *Yale Journal of Criticism*, 5 (2).

Gottlieb, A., 1992, *Under the Kapok Tree: identity and difference in Beng thought*, Bloomington: Indiana University Press.

Grafstein, R., 1999, *Choice-Free Rationality: a positive theory of political behaviour*, Ann Arbor: University of Michigan Press.

Gramsci, A., 1971, *Selections from Prison Notebooks*, London: Lawrence and Wishart.

Graubard, S. (ed.), 1986, *Norden: the passion for equality*, Oslo: Norwegian University Press.

Gray, C., 1997, *Postmodern war: the new politics of conflict*, New York: Guildford Press.

Gregory, C., 1982, *Gifts and Commodities*, New York: Academic Press.

————, 1997, *Savage Money*, Amsterdam: Harwood Academic Press.

Green, D. and I. Shapiro, 1994, *Pathologies of Rational Choice Theory: a critique of applications in political science*, New Haven, CT: Yale University Press.

Grillo, P. (ed.). 1981. *Nation and State in Europe: anthropological perspectives.* London: Academic Press.

Grimal, P., 1981 (1960), *La civilisation romaine*, Paris: Flammarion.

Griswold, W., 1994, *Culture and Societies in a Changing World*, Thousand Oaks, CA: Pine Forge Press.

Grunebaum, G. E. von, 1962, *Modern Islam: the search for cultural identity*, New York: Vintage Books.

Gupta, A. and J. Ferguson (eds), 1997, *Culture, Power and Place: explorations in critical anthropology*, Durham, NC: Duke University Press.

Gurr, T., 1970, *Why Men Rebel*, Princeton University Press.

Gurvitch, G., 1966, *Les cadres sociaux de la connaissance*, Paris: Presses Universitaires de France (English version, *The Social Frameworks of Knowledge*, Oxford, Blackwell, 1971).

Gustafsson, H., 1994, *Political Interaction in the Old Regime: central power and local society in the eighteenth-century Nordic States*, Lund: Studentlitteratur.

Gutmann, A. (ed.), 1994, *Multiculturalism*, Princeton University Press.

Gutting G. (ed.), 1980, *Paradigms and Revolutions*, South Bend, IN: University of Notre Dame Press.

Guyer, J., 1995, 'Wealth in People as Wealth in Knowledge: accumulation and composition in Equatorial Africa', *Journal of African History*, 36.

———— (ed.), 1995, *Money Matters: instability, values and social payments in the modern history of West African communities*, Porstmouth, NH: Heinemann.

Habermas, J., 1971, *Knowledge and Human Interests*, Boston, MA: Beacon Press.

————, 1987, *The Philosophical Discourse of Modernity,* Cambridge: Polity Press.

————, 1989, *Jürgen Habermas on Society and Politics: a reader,* Boston, MA: Beacon Press.

————, 1991, *The Theory of Communicative Action,* Cambridge: Polity Press.

Hague, R. *et al.,* 1998, *Comparative Government and Politics,* Basingstoke: Macmillan.

Hahm, P. C., 1987, *The Korean Tradition and Law,* Seoul: The Royal Asiatic Society, Korean Branch.

Haj, S., 1997, *The Making of Iraq, 1900–1963: capital, power and ideology,* New York: State University of New York Press.

Halfpenny, P. and P. McMylor (eds), 1994, *Positivist Sociology and its Critics,* London: Unwin Hyman.

Hall, J. (ed.), 1996, *Civil Society: history, theory, comparison,* Cambridge: Polity Press.

————, 1998, *The State of the Nation: Ernest Gellner and the theory of nationalism,* Cambridge University Press.

———— and I. Jarvie (eds), 1992, *Transition to Modernity: essays on power, wealth and belief,* Cambridge University Press.

Hall, S., 1996, 'Cultural Studies: two paradigms' in J. Storey (ed.), *What is Cultural Studies? A Reader,* London: Edward Arnold.

————, D. Morley and K.-H. Chen (eds), 1996, *Critical Dialogues in Cultural Studies,* London: Routledge.

———— and P. du Gay (eds), 1996, *Questions of Cultural Identity,* London: Sage.

Halliday, F., 1994, *Rethinking International Relations,* Basingstoke: Macmillan.

Hammersley, M., 1991, *Reading Ethnographic Research: a critical guide,* London: Longman.

————, 1992, *Social Research: philosophy and practice,* London: Sage.

Hannerz, U., 1992, *Cultural Complexity: studies in the social organization of meaning,* New York: Columbia University Press.

————, 1996, *Transnational Connections: culture, people, places,* New York: Routledge.

Harbeson, J. W. and D. Rothchild and N. Chazan (eds), 1994, *Civil Society and the State in Africa,* Boulder, CO: Lynne Rienner.

Harris, M., 1968, *The Rise of Anthropological Theory: a history of theories of culture,* New York: Thomas Cromwell.

————, 1989, *Our Kind: who we are, where we came from, and where we are going,* New York: Harper and Row.

Harrison, L. E., 1992, *Who Prospers? How cultural values shape economic and political success,* New York: Basic Books.

———, 1985, *Underdevelopment is a State of Mind: the Latin American case*, Lanham, MD: University Press of America.

——— and S. Huntington (eds), 2000, *Culture Matters: how values shape human progress*, New York: Basic Books.

Hartstock, N., 1998, *The Feminist Standpoint Revisited and Other Essays*, Boulder, CO: Westview.

Harvey, D., 1989, *The Condition of Postmodernity: an enquiry into the origins of cultural change*, Oxford: Blackwell.

Harvey, L., 1990, *Critical Social Research*, London: Unwin Hyman.

Hausman, D., 1991, *The Separate and Inexact Science of Economics*, Cambridge University Press.

Hawthorn, G., 1976, *Enlightenment and Despair: a history of sociology*, Cambridge University Press.

Hay, C., 2002, *Political Analysis*, Basingstoke: Palgrave.

Heath, A. (ed.), 1991, *Understanding Political Change*, Oxford: Pergamon Press.

Hecht, D. and A. M. Simone, 1994, *Invisible Governance: the art of African micro-politics*, New York: Autonomedia.

Heidenheimer, A., 1978, *Political Corruption: readings in comparative analysis*, New Brunswick, NJ: Transaction.

Held, D., 1982, *An Introduction to Critical Theory*, London: Hutchinson.

———, 1991, *Political Theory Today*, Cambridge: Polity Press.

——— et al. (eds), 1999, *Global Transformations: politics, economics and culture*, Cambridge: Polity Press.

Hellevik, G., 1984, *Introduction to Causal Analysis*, London: George Allen and Unwin.

Hempel, C., 1965, *Aspects of Scientific Explanation and Other Essay in the Philosophy of Science*, New York: Free Press.

———, 1966, *Philosophy of Natural Science*, Englewoods Cliffs, NJ: Prentice-Hall.

Henderson, D., 1993, *Interpretation and Explanation in the Human Sciences*, Albany, NY: SUNY Press.

Hendrickson, H. (ed.), 1996, *Clothing and Difference: embodied identities in colonial and post-colonial Africa*, Durham, NC: Duke University Press.

Henriques, J. et al. (eds), 1998, *Changing the Subject: psychology, social regulation and subjectivity*, London: Routledge.

Hermet. G., 1996, *Histoire des nations et du nationalisme en Europe*, Paris: Seuil.

Herskovits, M., 1938, *Acculturation: the study of culture contact*, New York: Augustin.

Heesterman, J., 1985, *The Inner Conflict of Traditions*, University of Chicago Press.

Heusch, L. de, 1982, *The Drunken King or the Origins of the State*, Blooming-ton: Indiana University Press.

———, 1985, *Sacrifice in Africa*, Bloomington: Indiana University Press.

Hill. P., 1982, *Dry Grain Farming Families: Hausaland (Nigeria) and Karnataka (India) compared*, Cambridge University Press.

Hindess, B., 1988, *Choice, Rationality and Social Theory*, London: Unwin Hyman.

Hinich, M. and M. Munger, 1997, *Analytical Politics*, Cambridge University Press.

Hirschman, Ch., 1987, 'The Meaning and Measurement of Ethnicity in Malaysia: an analysis of census classification', *Journal of Asian Studies*, 46 (3).

Hobbs, D. and T. May (eds), 1993, *Interpreting the Field: accounts of ethnography*, Oxford: Clarendon Press.

Hobsbawm, E., 1991, *Nations and Nationalism since 1780*, Cambridge University Press.

——— and T. Ranger (eds), 1983, *The Invention of Tradition*, Cambridge University Press.

Hofstede, G., 1997, *Cultures and Organizations: software of the mind*, New York: McGraw-Hill (2nd edn).

Hoggart, R., 1957, *The Uses of Literacy*, London: Chatto and Windus.

Höjer, M. and C. Åse, 1999, *The Paradoxes of Politics: an introduction to feminist political theory*, Lund: Academia Adacta.

Hollinger, D., 1995, *Postethnic America: beyond multiculturalism*, New York: Basic Books.

Hollis, M., 1994, *The Philosophy of Social Science*, Cambridge University Press.

———, 1977, *Models of Man: philosophical thoughts on social action*, Cambridge University Press.

——— and S. Lukes (eds), 1982, *Rationality and Relativism*, Oxford: Blackwell.

Holt, R. and J. Turner (eds), 1970, *The Methodology of Comparative Research*, New York: Free Press.

Honig, B., 1993, *Political Theory and the Displacement of Politics*, Ithaca, NY: Cornell University Press.

Hoogvelt, A., 1997, *Globalisation and the Postcolonial World: the new political economy of development*, Basingstoke: Macmillan.

Hountondji, P., 1976, *Sur la 'philosophie africaine'. Critique de l'ethnophiloso-phie*, Paris: Maspéro.

Huff, D., 1991, *How to Lie with Statistics*, Harmondsworth: Penguin.

Hufton, O., 2000 (2nd edn), *Europe: privilege and protest 1730–1789*, Oxford: Blackwell.

Huizinga, J., 1970, *Homo Ludens: a study of the play element in culture*, London: Temple Smith.

Hull, D., 1988, *Science as a Process: an evolutionary account of the social and conceptual development of science*, University of Chicago Press.

Hume, D., 1976, *A Treatise of Human Nature*, Oxford University Press.

———, 1999 (1748). *An Enquiry concerning Human Understanding*, ed. T. Beauchamp, Oxford University Press.

Humphrey, C. and S. Hugh-Jones (eds), 1992, *Barter, Exchange and Value: an anthropological approach*, Cambridge University Press.

Hunter, F., 1953, *Community Power Structure*, Chapel Hill, NC: University of North Carolina Press.

Hunter, J., 1991, *Culture Wars: the struggle to define America*, New York: Basic Books.

Huntford, R., 1971, *The New Totalitarians*, London: Allan Lane.

Huntington, S., 1968, *Political Order in Changing Societies*, New Haven, CT: Yale University Press.

———, 1992, 'The Clash of Civilizations', *Foreign Affairs*, summer.

———, 1996, *The Clash of Civilizations and the Remaking of World Order*, New York: Simon and Schuster.

———, 1996, 'The West Unique, not Universal', *Foreign Affairs*, 75.

———, 2004, *Who are We? The challenges to America's national identity*, New York: Simon and Schuster.

Hutchinson, S., 1996, *Nuer Dilemmas: coping with money, war and the state*, Berkeley: University of California Press.

Hyden, G., 1980, *Beyond Ujamaa in Tanzania*, London: Heinemann.

———, 1997, 'Civil Society, Social Capital and Development: dissection of a complex discourse', *Studies in Comparative International Development*, 32 (1).

Ikels, C., 1996, *The Return of the God of Wealth: the transition to a market economy in urban China*, Stanford University Press.

Iliffe, John, 1995, *Africans: the history of a continent*, Cambridge University Press.

Inglehart, R., 1977, *The Silent Revolution: changing values and political styles among Western publics*, Princeton University Press.

———, 1990, *Culture Shift in Advanced Industrial Society*, Princeton University Press.

———, 1997, *Modernization and Postmodernization*, Princeton University Press.

Inglis, F., 1993, *Cultural Studies*, Oxford: Blackwell.

———, 2000, *Clifford Geertz: culture, custom and ethics*, Cambridge: Polity Press.

Iniesta, F., 1995, *L'univers africain. Approche historique des cultures noires*, Paris: L'Harmattan.

Inkeles, A. and D. Smith, 1974, *Becoming Modern: individual change in six developing countries*, London: Heinemann.

Isichei, E., 1983, *A History of Nigeria*, Harlow: Longman.

Izard, M., 1985, *Gens du pouvoir, gens de la terre: les institutions politiques de l'ancien royaume du Yatenga*, Cambridge University Press.

Jackson, M. and I. Karp (eds), 1990, *Personhood and Agency: the experience of self and other in African cultures*, Washington, DC: Smithsonian Institution Press.

Jackson, R., 1990, *Quasi-states: sovereignty, international relations and the Third World*, Cambridge University Press.

Jaffrelot, C., 1993, *Les nationalistes hindous*, Paris: Presses de la FNSP (English version, *The Hindu Nationalist Movement in India*, London: Hurst, 1996).

———, 1996, 'Le multiculturalisme indien à l'épreuve. Le cas des débats constitutionnels', *L'Année Sociologique*, 46 (1).

——— (ed.), 2000, *Démocratie d'ailleurs*, Paris: Karthala.

———, 2003, *India's Silent Revolution: the rise of the lower castes in north India*, London: Hurst.

Jameson, F., 1991, *Postmodernism or the Cultural Logic of Late Capitalism*, Durham, NC: Duke University Press.

Jahneman, D., P. Slivic and A. Tversky, 1982, *Judgement under Uncertainty: heuristics and biases*, Cambridge University Press.

Jeambrun, P., 1991, *Jules Grévy ou la République debout*, Paris: Tallendier.

Jespersen, L., 2000, 'The Constitutional and Administrative Situation,' in Jespersen, L. (ed.), *A Revolution from Above? The Power State of 16th and 17th Century Scandinavia*, Odense University Press.

Jones, G. and P. Krautz (eds), 1981, *The Transition to Statehood in the New World*, Cambridge University Press.

Jones, K. and A. Jonasdottir (eds), 1988, *The Political Interests of Gender*, London: Sage.

Kahn, J., 1995, *Culture, Multiculture, Postculture*, London: Sage.

Kaldor, M., 1999, *New and Old Wars: organised violence in a global era*, Cambridge: Polity Press.

Kamenka, E., 1992, *Nationalism: the nature and evolution of an idea*, London: Edward Arnold.

Kane, O. and J.-L. Triaud (eds), 1998, *Islam et islamismes au sud du Sahara*, Paris: Karthala.

Kardiner, A., 1939, *The Individual and his Society: the psycho-dynamics of primitive social organization*, New York: Columbia University Press.

Kaplan, R., 2001, *The Coming Anarchy: shattering the dreams of the post cold war*, New York: Vintage Books.

Katzenstein, P., 1991, *Cultural Norms and National Security: police and military in postwar Japan*, Ithaca, NY: Cornell University Press.

Kaviraj, S. and S. Khilnani (eds), 2001, *Civil Society: history and possibilities*, Cambridge University Press.

Kedourie, E., 1960, *Nationalism*, London: Praeger.

———— (ed.), 1993, *Nationalism in Asia and Africa* (4th expanded edn), Oxford: Blackwell.

Keesing, R., 1974, 'Theories of Culture', *Annual Review of Anthropology*, 3.

Keen, D., 1998, *The Economic Functions of Violence in Civil Wars*, Oxford University Press.

Kegley, C. (ed.), 1995, *Controversies in International Relations Theory: realism and the neoliberal challenge*, New York: St Martin's Press.

Keohane, R., 1989, *International Institutions and State Power*, Boulder, CO: Westview.

Kepel, G. 2004. *The War for Muslim Minds: Islam and the West*. Cambridge MA: Harvard University Press.

Kertzer, D., 1988, *Ritual, Politics and Power*, New Haven, CT: Yale University Press.

Kettunen, P., 1999, 'A Return to the Figure of the Free Nordic Peasant', *Acta Sociologica*, 42.

Khilnani, S., 1999, *The Idea of India*, New Delhi: Penguin.

Kiel, L. D. and E. Elliott (eds), 1996, *Chaos Theory in the Social Sciences: foundations and applications*, Ann Arbor: University of Michigan Press.

King, G., 1989, *Unifying Political Methodology*, Cambridge University Press.

————, R. Keohane and S. Verba, 1994, *Designing Social Enquiry: scientific enquiry in qualitative research*, Princeton University Press.

Kirk-Greene, A., 1965, 'Bureaucratic Cadres in a Traditional Milieu' in Coleman, J. (ed.), *Education and Political Development*, Princeton University Press.

Klingemann, H. and Goodin, R. (eds), 1996, *A New Handbook for Political Science*. Oxford University Press.

Kluckhohn, C., 1951, 'Values and Value-orientation on the Theory of Action' in Parsons, T. and E. Shills (eds), *Toward a General Theory of Action*, Cambridge, MA: Harvard University Press.

————, 1955, 'Ethical Relativity: *sic et non*', *Journal of Philosophy*, 52.

Knight, J. and I. Sened (eds), 1995, *Explaining Social Institutions*, Ann Arbor: University of Michigan Press.

Knorr-Certina, K., 1981, *The Manufacture of Knowledge: an essay on the constructivist and contextual nature of science*, Oxford: Pergamon Press.

Knudsen, T., 1991, 'State Building in Scandinavia: Denmark in a Nordic context' in T. Knudsen (ed.), *Welfare Administration in Denmark*, Copenhagen: Ministry of Finance.

Kohli, A. *et al.*, 1995, 'The Role of Theory in Comparative Politics', *World Politics*, 48.

Kohn, H., 1960, *Nationalism: its meaning and history*, Princeton University Press.

———, 1962, *The Age of Nationalism*, New York: Harper and Brothers.

Kontopolous, K., 1993, *The Logics of Social Structure*, Cambridge University Press.

Kopytoff, I. (ed.), 1987, *The African Frontier: the reproduction of traditional African societies*, Bloomington: Indiana University Press.

Kornberg, A. and H. Clarke, 1992, *Citizens and Community: political support in representative democracy*, Cambridge University Press.

Kourouma, A., 1998, *En attendant le vote des bêtes sauvages*, Paris: Seuil.

Kramer, M., 1993, 'Islam v. Democracy', *Commentary*, January.

Kristeva, J., *Pouvoirs de l'horreur: essai sur l'abjection*, Paris: Seuil, 1980 (English version, *Power of Horror: an essay on abjection*, New York: Columbia University Press, 1982).

Kroeber, A., 1952, *The Nature of Culture*, University of Chicago Press.

——— and C. Kluckhohn, 1952, *Culture: a critical review of concept and definitions*, Cambridge, MA: Harvard University Press.

Kuhn, T., 1962, *Structure of Scientific Revolution*, University of Chicago Press.

Kuper, A., 1983, *Anthropology and Anthropologists: the modern British School*, London: Routledge.

———, 1988, *The Invention of Primitive Society: transformations of an illusion*, London: Routledge.

———, 1999, *Culture: the anthropologists' account*, Cambridge, MA: Harvard University Press.

———, 1999, *Among the Anthropologists: history and context in anthropology*, London: Athlone Press.

Lacorne, D., 1997, *Crise de l'identité américaine: du melting-pot au multiculturalisme*, Paris: Fayard.

Lagroye, J., 1991, *Sociologie politique*, Paris: Presses de la FNSP and Dalloz.

Laitin, D., 1986, *Hegemony and Culture: politics and religious change among the Yoruba*, University of Chicago Press.

———, 1995, 'The Civic Culture at 30', *American Political Science Review*, 89.

———, 1995, 'Disciplining Political Science', *American Political Science Review*, 89.

Lakatos, I. and A. Musgrave (eds), 1970, *Criticism and the Growth of Knowledge*, Cambridge University Press.

Lamont, M. and M. Fournier (eds), 1992, *Cultivating Differencies: symbolic boundaries and the making of inequality*, University of Chicago Press.

Lamont, M. and L. Thévenot (eds), 2000, *Rethinking Comparative Cultural Sociology*, Cambridge University Press.

Lan, D., 1985, *Guns and Rain: guerrillas and spirit mediums in the Zimbabwe war of independence*, Berkeley: University of California Press.

Landes, D., 1983, *Revolution in Time: clocks and the making of the modern world*, Cambridge, MA: Harvard University Press.

———, 1998, *The Wealth and Poverty of Nations: why some are so rich and some are so poor*, New York: W. W. Norton.

La Palombara, J. and M. Wiener (eds), 1966, *Political Parties and Political Development*, Princeton University Press.

Lascoumes, P., 1990, 'Normes juridiques et mise en œuvre des politiques publiques', *L'Année Sociologique*, vol. 40.

———, 1997, *Élite irrégulières: essai sur la délinquance d'affaires*, Paris: Gallimard.

Lash, S. and J. Friedman (eds), 1992, *Modernity and Identity*, Oxford: Blackwell.

Lassiter, J., 2001, 'African Culture and Personality: bad social science, effective social activism or a call to reinvent ethnology?', *African Studies Quarterly*, 3.

Lasswell, H., 1948, *Power and Personality*, New York: W. W. Norton.

Layton, R., 1997, *An Introduction to Theory in Anthropology*, Cambridge University Press.

Leach, E., 1961, *Rethinking Anthropology*, London: Athlone Press.

———, 1970, *Political Systems of Highland Burma: a study of Kachin social structure*, London: Athlone Press.

———, 1970, *Claude Lévi-Strauss*, New York: Viking.

Lee, K. B., 1984, *A New History of Korea*, Cambridge, MA: Harvard University Press.

Legendre, P., 1976, *Jouir du pouvoir*, Paris: Minuit.

Le Goff, J. (ed.), 2000 (1989), *Histoire de la France: la longue durée de l'Etat*, Paris: Seuil.

Lehmann, H. and G. Roth (eds), 1993, *Weber's Protestant Ethhic: origins, evidence, contexts*, Cambridge University Press.

Lemarchand, R., 1994, *Ethnocide as Discourse and Practice*, Cambridge University Press.

Leonardo, M. di, 1998, *Exotics at Home: anthropologies, others, American modernity*, University of Chicago Press.

Lerner, D., 1964, *The Passing of Traditional Society*, New York: Free Press.

Le Vine, R., 1973, *Culture, Behavior and Personality*, Chicago, IL: Aldine.

Lévi-Strauss, C., 1949, *Les structures élémentaires de la parenté*, Paris: Plon (English version, *The Elementary Structures of Kinship*, Boston: Beacon Press, 1969).

———, 1955, *Tristes Tropiques*, Paris: Plon (English version, *Tristes Tropiques*, New York: Antheneum, 1974).

———, 1958, *Anthropologie structurale*, Paris: Plon (English version, *Structural Anthropology*, New York: Basic Books, 1963).

————, 1962, *La pensée sauvage*, Paris: Plon (English version, *The Savage Mind*, University of Chicago Press, 1966).

————, 1950, '*Introduction à l'œuvre de M. Mauss*' in Mauss, M., *Sociologie et anthropologie*, Paris: Presses Universitaires de France (English version, *Sociology and Psychology*, London: Routledge, 1987).

Lewin, L., 1988, *Ideology and Strategy: a century of Swedish politics*, Cambridge University Press.

Levinsion, R. and M. Malone, 1981, *Towards Explaining Human Culture: a critical review of the findings of Worldwide cross-cultural research*, New Haven, CT: HRAF Press.

Lewis, B., 1993, 'Islam and Liberal Democracy', *Atlantic Monthly*, February.

Le Wita, B., 1988, *Ni vue ni connue: approche ethnographique de la culture bourgeoise*, Paris: Maison des Sciences de l'Homme.

Lichbach, M. and A. Zuckerman (eds), 1997, *Comparative Politics: rationality, culture and structure*, Cambridge University Press.

Lieberson, S., 1985, *Making it Count: the improvement of social research and theory*, Berkeley: University of California Press.

Lijphart, A., 1971, 'Comparative Politics and Comparative Method', *American Political Science Review*, 65.

————, 1977, *Democracy in Plural Societies*, New Haven, CT: Yale University Press.

Linde, C., 1993, *Life Stories: the creation of coherence*, Oxford University Press.

Linton, R., 1936, *The Study of Man: an introduction*, New York: Appleton Century.

Lipset, S. M. and S. Rokkan (eds), 1967, *Party Systems and Voter Alignment: cross-national perspectives*, New York: Free Press.

Little, D., 1991, *Varieties of Social Explanation: an introduction to the philosophy of science*, Boulder, CO: Westview.

Lloyd, C., 1986, *Explanation in Social History*, Oxford: Blackwell.

Lloyd, P. C., 1954, 'The Traditional Political Systems of the Yoruba', *South-Western Journal of Anthropology*, IV (10).

Lofland, J. and L. Lofland, 1985, *Analysing Social Settings: a guide to qualitative observation and analysis*, Belmont, CA: Wadsworth.

Lowie, R. H., 1942, *Social Organisation*, London: Routledge and Kegan Paul.

Luckham, R. and G. White, 1996, *Democratisation in the South: the jagged wave*, Manchester University Press.

Lukes, S., 1974, *Power: a radical view*, London: Macmillan.

Lupia, A. and M. McCubbins, 1998, *The Democratic Dilemma: can citizens learn what they need to know?*, Cambridge University Press.

Lumsden, C. and O. Wilson, 1981, *Genes, Mind and Culture*, Cambridge, MA: Harvard University Press.

Lyotard, J-F., 1984, *The Postmodern Condition: a report on knowledge*, Minneapolis: University of Minnesota Press.

Maalouf, A., 1998, *Les Identités meurtrières*, Paris: Grasset.

Maffesoli, M., 1988, *Le temps des tribus: le déclin de l'individu dans les sociétés de masse*, Paris: Klinsieck.

Malinowski, B., 1945, *The Dynamics of Culture Change*, New Haven, CT: Yale University Press.

———, 1944, *A Scientific Theory of Culture and Other Essays*, Durham, NC: University of North Carolina Press.

———, 1960, *Sex and Repression in Savage Society*, London: Routledge and Kegan Paul.

Malkki, L., 1995, *Purity and Exile: violence, memory and national cosmology among Hutu refugees in Tanzania*, University of Chicago Press.

Mamdani, M., 1996, *Citizen and Subject: contemporary Africa and the legacy of late colonialism*, Princeton University Press.

Mandelbaum, M., 1987, *Purpose and Necessity in Social Theory*, Baltimore, MD: Johns Hopkins University Press.

Mandrou, R., 1987 (4th edn), *La France aux XVIIe et XVIIIe siècles*, Paris: Presses Universitaires de France.

Manin, B., 1996 (2nd edn), *Principes du gouvernement représentatif*, Paris: Flammarion (English version, *Principles of Representative Government*, Cambridge University Press, 1997).

———, A. Przeworski and S. Stokes, 1999, 'Elections and Representation' in A. Przeworski, S. Stokes and B. Manin (eds), *Democracy, Accountability and Representation*, Cambridge University Press.

Mannheim, K., 1936, *Ideology and Utopia: an introduction to the sociology of knowledge*, New York: Harvest Books.

———, 1952, *Essays on the Sociology of Knowledge*, London: Routledge and Kegan Paul.

Manning, P., 1990, *Slavery and African life: occidental, oriental and African slave trades*, Cambridge University Press.

Mansbridge, J. (ed.), 1990, *Beyond Self-Interest*, University of Chicago Press.

Mansel, Ph., 1987, *The Eagle in Splendour: Napoleon I and his Court*, London: George Philip.

March, J. and J. Olsen, 1989, *Rediscovering Institutions*, New York: Free Press.

Marie, A. (ed.), 1997, *L'Afrique des individus*, Paris: Karthala.

Marsh, C., 1988, *Exploring Data*, Cambridge: Polity Press.

Marsh, D. and G. Stoker (eds), 2002, *Theory and Methods in Political Science*, 2nd edn, Basingstoke: Palgrave.

Martin, D.-C., 1988, *Tanzanie: l'invention d'une culture politique*, Paris: Karthala/Presses de la FNSP.

————, 1989, 'A la recherche des cultures politiques: de certaines tendances récentes de la politologie française', *Cahiers Internationaux de Sociologie*, 87.

————, 1992, 'La découverte des cultures politiques: esquisse d'une approche comparatiste à partir des expériences africaines', Paris: *Les Cahiers du CERI*, 2.

Martin, M. and L. McIntyre (eds), 1994, *Readings in the Philosophy of Social Science*, Cambridge, MA: Bradford Books.

Martin, P., 1995, *Leisure and Society in Colonial Brazzaville*, Cambridge University Press.

Martinez, L., 2000, *The Algerian Civil War, 1990–1998*, London: Hurst.

Martin-Fugier, A., 1990, *La vie élégante ou la formation du Tout-Paris*, Paris: Fayard.

Mason, J., 1996, *Qualitative Researching*, London: Sage.

Mauss, M., 1950 (1924), 'Essai sur le don' in *Sociologie et Anthropologie*, Paris: Presses Universitaires de France.

Mayall, J., 1990, *Nationalism and International Society*, Cambridge University Press.

————, 2000, *World Politics: progress and its limits*, Cambridge: Polity Press.

Mayer, A., 1991, *Islam and Human Rights: tradition and politics*, London: Pinter.

Mayer, L., 1989, *Comparative Political Enquiry: promise versus performance*, Beverly Hills, CA: Sage.

Mazlish, B., 1976, *The Revolutionary Ascetic*, New York: Basic Books.

Mbembe, A., 2000, *De la postcolonie: essai sur l'imagination politique dans l'Afrique contemporaine*, Paris: Karthala.

McBride, I., 1997, *The Siege of Derry in Ulster Protestant Mythology*, Dublin: Four Courts Press.

McCulloch, J., 1995, *Colonial Psychiatry and the 'African Mind'*, Cambridge University Press.

Mead, M., 2001 (1935), *Sex and Temperament in Three Primitive Societies*, New York: Perennial.

Médard, J.-F. (ed.), 1991, *Etats d'Afrique noire: formations, mécanismes, crises*, Paris: Karthala.

————, 1992, 'Le "Big Man" en Afrique: esquisse d'analyse du politicien entrepreneur', *L'Année sociologique*, vol. 42.

Meek, C. K., 1971 (1925), *The Northern Tribes of Nigeria* (2 vols), London: Frank Cass.

Meillassoux, C., 1981, *Maidens, Meal and Money: capitalism and the domestic community*, Cambridge University Press.

———— and C. Messiant (eds), 1991, *Génie social et manipulations culturelles en Afrique du Sud*, Paris: Arcantère.

Melucci, A., 1996, *The Playing Self: person and meaning in the planetary society*, Cambridge University Press.

Mennell, S., 1989, *Norbert Elias: civilisation and the human self-image*, Oxford: Blackwell.

Mény, Y. (ed.), 1993, *Les politiques du mimétisme institutionnel. La greffe et le rejet*, Paris: L'Harmattan.

Merelman, R., 1991, *Partial Visions: culture and politics in Britain, Canada and the United States*, Madison: University of Wisconsin Press.

Merkl, P., 1970, *Modern Comparative Politics*, New York: Holt, Rinehart and Winston.

Merritt, R., 1971, *Systematic Approaches to Comparative Politics*, Chicago, IL: Rand McNally.

Merton, R., 1968 (1949), *Social Theory and Social Structure*, New York: Free Press, 3rd edn.

Meyer, B. and P. Geschiere (eds), 1999, *Globalization and Identity: dialectics of flow and closure*, Oxford: Blackwell.

Michaels, W., 1995, *Our America: nativism, modernism and pluralism*, Durham, NC: Duke University Press.

Micheletti, M., 1995, *Civil Society and State Relations in Sweden*, Aldershot: Avebury.

Michels, R., 1971 (1915), *Les partis politiques: essai sur les tendances oligarchiques des démocraties*, Paris: Flammarion (English version, *Political Parties: a sociological study of the oligarchical tendencies of modern democracy*, London: Jarrold).

Miller, D. (ed.), 1995, *Worlds Apart: modernity through the prism of the local*, London: Routledge.

———, 1997, *Capitalism: and ethnographic approach*, Oxford: Berg.

———, *Material Cultures: why some things matter*, University of Chicago Press.

Mills, Wright C., 1959, *The Sociological Imagination*, London: Oxford University Press.

Miquel, P., 2001, *Les rois de l'Elysée*, Paris: Fayard.

Mishler, W. and D. Pollack, 2003, 'On Culture, Thick and Thin: toward a neo cultural synthesis' in Pollack, D. *et al.* (eds), *Political Culture in Post Communist Europe*, Aldershot: Ashgate.

Mitchell, C., 1987, *Cities, Society and Social Perception: a central African perspective*, Oxford: Clarendon Press.

Mohr, L., 1996, *The Causes of Human Behavior: implications for theory and method in the social sciences*, Ann Arbor: University of Michigan Press.

Monroe, K. (ed.), 1991, *The Economic Approach to Politics: a critical reassessment of the theory of rational action*, New York: Harper Collins.

Moore, B., 1966, *Social Origins of Dictatorship and Democracy: lord and peasant in the making of the modern world*, Boston, MA: Beacon Press.

Moore, H. and T. Sanders (eds), 2001, *Magical Interpretations, Material Realities: modernity, witchcraft and the occult in postcolonial Africa*, London: Routledge.

Moore, S. F., 1994, *Anthropology and Africa: changing perspectives on a changing scene*, Charlottesville: University of Virginia Press.

Morabito, M., 1996, *Le Chef de l'Etat en France*, Paris: Montchrestien.

Morrow, J., 1994, *Game Theory for Political Scientists*, Princeton University Press.

Morton, R., 1999, *Methods and Models*, Cambridge University Press.

Mount, F., 1972, *The Theatre of Politics*, London: Weidenfield and Nicolson.

Mouffe, C., 1993, *The Return of the Political*, London: Verso.

Muchembled, R., 1978, *Culture populaire et culture des élites dans la France moderne (XVᵉ–XVIIIᵉ siècle)*, Paris: Flammarion (English version, *Popular Culture and Elite Culture in France, 1400. 1750*, State University of New York Press, 1985).

Mudimbe, V. Y., 1988, *The Invention of Africa: gnosis, philosophy and the order of knowledge*, Bloomington: Indiana University Press.

——, 1997, *Tales of Faith: religion as political performance in Central Africa*, London: Athlone Press.

Munch, R. and J. Smelser (eds), 1992, *Theory of Culture*, Berkeley: University of California Press.

Murdoch, G., 1965, *Culture and Society*, Pittsburgh, PA: University of Pittsburgh Press.

Myers, F. (ed.), 2001, *The Empire of Things: regimes of value and material culture*, Oxford: James Currey.

Mylroie, L., 2000, *Study of Revenge: Saddam Hussein's unfinished war against America*, Washington, DC: AEI Press.

Myrdal, G., 1970, *Objectivity in Social Science*, London: Duckworth.

Nadel, S. F., 1942, *A Black Byzantium*, London: Oxford University Press.

Nagel, E., 1979, *The Structure of Science*, Indianapolis, IN: Hackett.

Nandy, A., 2002, *Time Warps: silent evasive pasts in Indian politics and religion*, London: Hurst.

Needler, M., 1991, *The Concepts of Comparative Politics*, New York: Praeger.

Nicholson, M., 1989, *Formal Theories in International Relations*, Cambridge University Press.

Nicolson, I., 1969, *The Administration of Nigeria 1900–1960: men, methods and myths*, Oxford: Clarendon Press.

Nisbet, R., 1966, *The Sociological Tradition*, New York: Basic Books.

North, D., 1990, *Institutions, Institutional Change and Economic Performance*, Cambridge University Press.

Nozick, R., 1974, *Anarchy, State and Utopia*, Oxford: Blackwell.

Nwankwo, N., 1975, *My Mercedes is Bigger than Yours*, London: André Deutsch.

Obeyesekere, G., 1992, *European Mythmaking in the Pacific*, Princeton University Press.

O'Donnell, G. *et al.* (eds), 1986, *Transitions from Authoritarian Rule: prospects for democracy*, Baltimore, MD: Johns Hopkins University Press.

Olson, M., 1965, *The Logic of Collective Action: public goods and the theory of groups*, Cambridge, MA: Harvard University Press.

Olukoshi, A. (ed.), 1998, *The Politics of Opposition in Contemporary Africa*, Uppsala: Nordisk Afrikainstitutet.

Olunsaya, G., 1975, *The Evolution of the Nigerian Civil Service 1861–1960: the problem of Nigerianization*, University of Lagos.

Ordeshook, P., 1986, *Game Theory and Political Theory*, Cambridge University Press.

Orstrom, E., 1982, *Strategies of Political Enquiry*, London: Sage.

———, 1990, *Governing the Commons: the evolution of institutions for collective action*, Cambridge University Press.

Ortner, S. (ed.), 1997, *The Fate of Culture: Geertz and beyond*, Berkeley: University of California Press.

Østerud, Ø., 1977, 'Configurations of Scandinavian Absolutism' in P. Torsvik, *Mobilization, Center-Periphery Structures and Nation Building*, Bergen: Universitetsforlaget.

Otayek, R., 2000, *Identité et démocratie dans un monde global*, Paris: Presses de Sciences Po.

Ozouf-Marignier, M.-V., 1989, *La formation des départements: la représentation du territoire français à la fin du 18ème siècle*, Paris: Editions de l'Ecole des Hautes Etudes en Sciences Sociales.

Paige, G. (ed.), 1972, *Political Leadership: readings for an emerging field*, New York: Free Press.

———, 1977, *The Scientific Study of Political Leadership*, New York: Free Press.

Pape, R., 2003, 'The Strategic Logic of Suicide Terrorism', *American Political Science Review*, 97, 2.

Papineau, D., 1978, *For Science in the Social Science*, London: Macmillan.

Parekh, B., 2000, *Cultural Diversity and Political Theory*, Basingstoke: Palgrave.

Parry, J. and M. Bloch, 1989, *Money and the Morality of Exchange*, Cambridge University Press.

Parsons, T., 1937, *The Structure of Social Action*, Glencoe, IL: Free Press.

———, 1951, *The Social System*, Glencoe, IL: Free Press.

——— and E. Shils (eds), 1951, *Towards a General Theory of Action*, Cambridge, MA: Harvard University Press.

Pateman, C., 1989, *The Disorder of Women: democracy, feminism and political theory*, Cambridge: Polity Press.

Patterson, O., 1977, *Ethnic Chauvinism: the reactionary impulse*, Briarcliff Manor, NY: Stein and Day.

Paulme, D. (ed.), 1971, *Classes et associations d'âge en Afrique de l'Ouest*, Paris: Plon.

Pecora, V., 1989, 'The Limits of Local Knowledge' in H. Veeser (ed.), *The New Historicism*, London: Routledge.

Pennings, P., H. Keman and J. Kleinnijenuis, 1999, *Doing Research in Political Science*, London: Sage.

Perkins, D., 2000, 'Law, Family Ties and the East Asian Way of Business' in Harrisson, L. and S. Huntington (eds), *Culture Matters: how values shape human progress*, New York: Basic Books.

Peters, G., 1998, *Comparative Politics: theory and methods*, Basingstoke: Macmillan.

——, 1999, *Institutional Theory in Political Science: the 'new institutionalism'*, London: Pinter.

Phillips, A. (ed), 1998, *Feminism and Politics*, Oxford University Press.

Phillips, R. and C. Steiner (eds), 1999, *Unpacking Culture: art and commodity in colonial and postcolonial worlds*, Berkeley: University of California Press.

Pierson, C., 1986, *Marxist Theory and Democratic Politics*, Cambridge: Polity Press.

Pinches, M. (ed.), 1999, *Culture and Privilege in Capitalist Asia*, London: Routledge.

Piot, C., 1999, *Remotely Global: village modernity in West Africa*, University of Chicago Press.

Pitkin, H., 1967, *The Concept of Representation*, Los Angeles: University of California Press.

Polanyi, K., 1944, *The Great Transformation: the political and economic origins of our time*, Boston, MA: Beacon Press.

——, 1968, *Primitive, Archaic and Modern Economies*, Boston, MA: Beacon Press.

Pontusson, J., 1988, *Swedish Social Democracy and British Labour: essays on the nature and condition of social democratic hegemony*, Ithaca, NY: Center for International Studies, Cornell University.

Popkin, S., 1979, *The Rational Peasant: the political economy of rural society in Vietnam*, Berkeley: University of California Press.

Popper, K., 1959, *The Logic of Scientific Discovery*, London: Hutchinson.

——, 1965, *Conjectures and Refutations: the growth of scientific knowledge*, New York: Harper Torchbooks.

——, 1972, *The Poverty of Historicism*, London: Routledge and Kegan Paul.

Postel-Vinay, K., 1994, *La révolution silencieuse du Japon*, Paris: Calmann-Lévy.

Poulantzas, N., 1973, *Pouvoir politique et classes sociales*, Paris: Naspéro (English version, *Political Power and Social Class*, London: New Left Books, 1970).

Poutignac, P. and J. Streiff-Fenard (eds), 1995, *Théories de l'ethnicité*, Paris: Presses Universitaires de France.

Powell, R., 1999, *In the Shadow of Power: states and strategies in international relations*, Princeton University Press.

Powermaker, H., 1966, *Stranger and Friend: the way of an anthropologist*, New York: W. W. Norton.

Prakash, G., 1990, 'Writing Post-Orientalist Histories of the Third World: perspectives from Indian historiography', *Comparative Studies in Society and History*, 32 (2).

Pratt, M., 1992, *Imperial Eyes: travel writing and transculturation*, London: Routledge.

Presthus, R., 1964, *Men at the Top*, New York: Oxford University Press.

Pridham, G. and P. Lewis (eds), 1996, *Stabilising Fragile Democracies: comparing new party systems in Southern and Eastern Europe*, London: Routledge.

Prunier, G., 1995, *The Rwanda Crisis, 1959–1994: History of a genocide*, London: Hurst.

Przeworski, A., 1991, *Democracy and the Market: political and economic reforms in Eastern Europe and Latin America*, Cambridge University Press.

———— and H. Teune, 1970, *The Logic of Comparative Social Enquiry*, New York: Wiley.

————, S. Stokes and B. Manin (eds), 1999, *Democracy, Accountability and Representation*, Cambridge University Press.

Putnam, H., 1978, *Meaning and the Moral Sciences*, London: Methuen.

————, 1981, *Reason, Truth and History*, Cambridge University Press.

Putnam, R., 1993, *Making Democracy Work: civic traditions in modern Italy*, Princeton University Press.

Pye, L., 1962, *Politics, Personality and Nation Building: Burma's search for identity*, New Haven, CT: Yale University Press.

————, 1985, *Asian Power and Politics: the cultural dimensions of authority*, Cambridge, MA: Harvard University Press.

———— and S. Verba, 1965, *Political Culture and Political Development*, Princeton University Press.

Ragin, C., 1987, *The Comparative Method: moving beyond qualitative and quantitative strategies*, Berkeley: University of California Press.

————, 2000, *Fuzzy-Set Social Science*, University of Chicago Press.

Rahman, F., 1979, *Islam*, University of Chicago Press.

Ramadan, T., 1999, *To Be a European Muslim*, Markfield: Islamic Foundation.

————, 2001, *Islam, the West and the Challenge of Modernity*, Markfield: Islamic Foundation.

Randall, V., 1987, *Women and Politics*, Basingstoke: Macmillan.

———— and G. Waylen (eds), 1998, *Gender, Politics and the State*, London: Routledge.

Ranger, T. and R. Werbner (eds), 1996, *Postcolonial Identities in Africa*, London: Zed Press.

Rasmusen, E., 1989, *Games and Information: an introduction to game theory*, Oxford: Blackwell.

Rawls, J., 1972, *A Theory of Justice*, Oxford University Press.

————, 1996, *Political Liberalism*, New York: Columbia University Press.

Raynaud, P., 1987, *Max Weber et le dilemme de la raison moderne*, Paris: Presses Universitaires de France.

Reddy, W., 1987, *Money and Liberty in Modern Europe: a critique of historical understanding*, Cambridge University Press.

Redfield, R., 1953, *The Primitive World and Its Transformation*, Ithaca, NY: Cornell University Press.

Reed-Danahay, D., 1996, *Education and Identity in Rural France*, Cambridge University Press.

Reno, W., 2000, *Warlord Politics and African States*, Boulder, CO: Lynne Rienner.

Ribeiro, A., 2002, *Dress in Eighteenth-Century Europe, 1715–1789*, New Haven, CT: Yale University Press.

Rice, K., 1980, *Geertz and Culture*, Ann Arbor: University of Michican Press.

Richard, P., 1996, *Fighting for the Rain Forest: war, youth and resources in Sierra Leone*, Oxford: James Currey.

Richards, A., 1982, *Chisungu: a girl's initiation ceremony among the Bemba of Zambia*, London: Tavistock.

Richter, M., 1995, *The History of Political and Social Concepts: a critical introduction*, Oxford University Press.

Riesman, P., 1986, 'The Person and the Life Cycle in African Social Life and Thought', *African Studies Review.*

Riggs, F., 1998, 'The Modernity of Ethnic Identity and Conflict', *International Political Science Review,* 19 (3).

Riker, W., and O. Ordeshook, 1973, *Introduction to Positive Political Theory*, Englewoods Cliffs, NJ: Prentice-Hall.

Ringmar, E., 1996, *Identity Interest and Action*, Cambridge University Press.

Risse-Kappen, T., 1994, *Bringing Transnational Relations back in*, Cambridge University Press.

Ritaine, E., 2001, 'Cherche capital social, désespérément', *Critique internationale,* 12 (July).

Rittberger, V., 1993, *Regime Theory and International Relations*, Oxford University Press.

Rivière, C., 1988, *Les liturgies politiques*, Paris: Presses Universitaires de France.

Robertson, R., 1992, *Globalization: social theory and global culture*, London: Sage.

Roels, J., 1969. *Le concept de représentation politique au dix-huitième siècle français*, Louvain: Nauwelaerts.

Roff, W., 1967, *The Origins of Malay Nationalism*, New Haven, CT: Yale University Press.

Rokkan, S., 1970, *Citizens, Elections, Parties: approaches to the comparative study of the process of development*, New York: David McKay Co.

Rorty, R., 1980, *Philosophy and the Mirror of Nature*, Oxford: Blackwell.

———, 1991, *Objectivity, Relativism and Truth*, Cambridge University Press.

———, 1998, *Truth and Progress*, Cambridge University Press.

Rosaldo, R., 1989, *Culture and Truth: the remaking of social analysis*, Boston, MA: Beacon Press.

Rosanvallon, P., 1990, *L'Etat en France de 1789 à nos jours*, Paris: Seuil.

———, 1998, *Le peuple introuvable. Histoire de la représentation démocratique en France*, Paris: Gallimard.

Rose, M., 1986, *The Relief of Poverty, 1834–1914*, Basingstoke: Macmillan.

Rosenau, J., 1990, *Turbulence in World Politics: a theory of change and continuity*, Princeton University Press.

———, 1992, *Post-Modernism and the Social Sciences: insights, inroads and intrusions*, Princeton University Press.

Rosenberg, A., 1995, *Philosophy of Social Science*, Boulder, CO: Westview.

Rosenthal, E., 1958, *Political Thought in Medieval Islam*, Cambridge University Press.

Rosny, E. de, 1981, *Les yeux de ma chèvre*, Paris: Plon.

Rostow, W., 1958, *The Stages of Economic Growth*, Cambridge University Press.

Roth, P. and T. Ryckman, 1995, 'Chaos, Clio, and Scientistic Illusions of Understanding', *History and Theory*, 34.

Rouland, N., 1995, *L'Etat français et le pluralisme: histoire politique des institutions publiques de 476 à 1792*, Paris: Odile Jacob.

Roy, O., 1994, *Échec de l'Islam Politique*, Paris: Seuil (English version, *The Failure of Political Islam*, London: I. B. Tauris, 1992).

———, 2004, *Globalised Islam: the search for a new 'ummah'*, London: Hurst.

Ruane, J. and J. Todd, 1996, *The Dynamics of Conflict in Northern Ireland: power, conflict and emancipation*, Cambridge University Press.

Rudolph, L. and S. Rudolph, 1967, *The Modernity of Tradition*, University of Chicago Press.

Ruelle, D., 1991, *Chance and Chaos*, Princeton University Press.

Rustow, D. and K. Erickson (eds), 1991, *Comparative Political Dynamics: research perspective*, New York: HarperCollins.

Ruthven, M., 2004, *Fundamentalism: the search for meaning*, Oxford University Press.

Ryan, A., 1970, *The Philosophy of Social Science*, London: Macmillan.

Said, E., 1978, *Orientalism*, New York: Pantheon.

————, 1993, *Culture and Imperialism*, London: Chatto and Windus, New York: Vintage Books.

Salamé, G. (ed.), 1994, *Démocraties sans démocrates. Politiques d'ouverture dans le monde arabe et islamique*, Paris: Fayard.

Salmon, W., 1984, *Scientific Explanation and the Causal Structure of the World*, Princeton University Press.

Sandbrook, R., 2000, *Closing the Circle: democratisation and development in Africa*, London: Zed Press.

Sandel, M., 1982, *Liberalism and the Limits of Justice*, Cambridge University Press.

Sandler, T., 1997, *Global Challenges: an approach to environmental, political and economic problems*, Cambridge University Press.

Sardan, O. de, 1992, 'Occultism and the Ethnographic "I": the exoticizing of magic from Durkheim to "Postmodern" anthropology', *Critique of Anthropology*, 12 (1).

————, 1999, 'A Moral Economy of Corruption', *Journal of Modern African Studies*, 37 (1).

Saro-Wiwa, K., 1991, *Similia: essays on anomic Nigeria*, London: Saros International.

Sawyer, B. and P. Sawyer, 1993, *Medieval Scandinavia: from conversion to reformation, circa 800–1500*, Minneapolis: University of Minnesota Press.

Sayer, A., 1992, *Method in Social Science: a realist approach*, London: Routledge.

Scarbrough. E. and E. Tannenbaum (eds), 1998, *Research Strategies in the Social Sciences*, Oxford University Press.

Schacht, J., 1966, *An Introduction to Islamic Law*, Oxford: Clarendon Press.

Scharpf, W., 1997, *Games Real Actors Play: actor-centred institutionalism in policy research*, Boulder, CO: Westview.

Schatzberg, M., 2001, *Political Legitimacy in Middle Africa: father, family, food*, Indianapolis: Indiana University Press.

Schellin, T., 1978, *Micromotives and Macrobehaviour*, New York: W. W. Norton.

Schemeil, Y., 1985, 'Les cultures politiques' in M. Grawitz and J. Leca (eds), *Traité de science politique*, vol. III, Paris: Presses Universitaires de France.

Schmid, M., 1992, 'The Concept of Culture and its Place within a Theory of Social Action: a critique of Talcott Parsons' theory of culture' in

Munch, R. and N. Smelser (eds), *Theory of Culture*, Berkeley: University of California Press.

Schnapper, D., 1994, *La communauté des citoyens: sur l'idée moderne de nation*, Paris: Gallimard.

Schneider, L. and C. Bonjean (eds), 1973, *The Idea of Culture in the Social Sciences*, Cambridge University Press.

Schrift, A., 1997, *The Logic of the Gift*, London: Routledge.

Schroeder, R., 1992, *Max Weber and the Sociology of Culture*, London: Sage.

Scott, A. (ed.), 1997, *The Limits of Globalization: cases and arguments*, London: Routledge.

Scott, James, 1976, *The Moral Economy of the Peasant: rebellion and subsistence in Southeast Asia*, New Haven, CT: Yale University Press.

———, 1985, *Weapons of the Weak: everyday forms of peasant resistance*, New Haven, CT: Yale University Press.

Scott, John, 1996, *Stratification and Power: structures of class, status and command*, Cambridge: Polity Press.

Seddon, D. (ed.), 1978, *Relations of Production: Marxist approaches to anthropology*, London: Frank Cass.

Seiler, D.-L., 1985, *Comportement politique comparé*, Paris: Economica.

———, 2002, 'L'usage politique de la vie privée des hommes publics en démocratie' in Baudry, P., C. Sorbets and A. Vitalis (eds), *La vie privée à l'heure des medias*, Presses Universitaires de Bordeaux.

Seligman, A., 1992, *The Idea of a Civil Society*, New York: Free Press.

Selznick, P., 1992, *The Moral Commonwealth: social theory and the promise of community*, Berkeley, CA: University of California Press.

Sen, A., 1970, 'Rational Fools', *Philosophy and Public Affairs*, 6.

———, 1983, *Poverty and Famines*, Oxford University Press.

———, 1999, *Development as Freedom*, New York: Knopf.

Seton-Watson, H., 1977, *Nations and States: an enquiry into the origins of nations and the politics of nationalism*, Boulder, CO: Westview.

Sewell, W., 1997, 'Geertz, Cultural Systems and History: from synchrony to transformation', *Representations*, 59 (summer).

Shaikh, F., 1989, *Community and Consensus in Islam: Muslim representation in colonial India, 1860–1947*, Cambridge University Press.

Shankman, P., 1984, 'The Thick and the Thin: on the interpretive theoretical program of Clifford Geertz', *Current Anthropology*, 25 (3).

Shapiro, I. and R. Hardin (eds), 1995, *Political Order*, New York University Press.

Shaw, R., 1997, 'The Production of Witchcraft/Witchcraft as Production: memory, modernity, and the slave trade in Sierra Leone', *American Ethnologist*, 24 (4).

Shepsle, K. and M. Bonchek, 1997, *Analyzing Politics: rationality, behavior and institutions*, New York: W. W. Norton.

Shils, E., 1969, 'Reflections on Deference' in Rogow, A. (ed.), *Politics, Personality and Social Science in the Twentieth-Century: essays in honour of Harold D. Lasswell*, University of Chicago Press.

———, 1992, 'The Virtue of Civil Society', *Government and Opposition*, 26 (1).

Shipton, P., 1989, *Bitter Money: cultural economy and some African meanings of forbidden commodities*, Washington, DC: American Anthropological Association.

Shore, B., 1996, *Culture in Mind: cognition, culture and the problem of meaning*, New York: Oxford University Press.

Shumaker, L., 2001, *Africanizing Anthropology: fieldwork, networks, and the making of cultural knowledge in Central Africa*, Durham, NC: Duke University Press.

Shweder, R. A., 1991, *Thinking Through Cultures: expeditions in cultural psychology*, Cambridge, MA: Harvard University Press.

———, 2000, 'Moral Maps, "First World" Conceits and the New Evangelists' in Harrisson, L. and S. Huntington (eds), *Culture Matters: how values shape human progress*, New York: Basic Books.

——— and R. LeVine (eds), 1984, *Culture Theory: essays on mind, self and emotion*, Cambridge University Press.

Silverman, D., 1993, *Interpreting Qualitative Data: methods for analysing talk, text and interaction*, London: Sage.

———, 1997, *Qualitative Research: theory, method and practice*, London: Sage.

Skinner, Q., 1981, 'The World as a Stage', *New York Review of Books*, 16 April 1981.

——— (ed.), 1985, *The Return of Grand Theory*, Cambridge University Press.

———, 1997, *Liberty before Liberalism*, Cambridge University Press.

Skocpol, T., 1979, *States and Social Revolutions: a comparative analysis of France, Russia and China*, Cambridge University Press.

Smelser, N., 1976, *Comparative Method in the Social Sciences*, Englewood Cliffs, NJ: Prentice-Hall.

———, 2003, 'On Comparative Analysis: interdisciplinarity and internationalisation in sociology', *International Sociology*, 18, 4 (December).

Smith, A., 1971, *Theories of Nationalism*, London: Duckworth.

Smith, A., 1976, *Nationalist Movements*. London: Macmillan, 1976.

———, 1981, *The Ethnic Revival*, Cambridge University Press.

———, 1992, *The Ethnic Origins of Nations*, Oxford: Blackwell.

Smith, K. and M. Light (eds), 2001, *Ethics and Foreign Policy*, Cambridge University Press.

Solomon, R., 1971, *Mao's Revolution and Chinese Political Culture*, Berkeley, CA: University of California Press.

Sørensen, Ø. and B. Stråth (eds), 1997, *The Cultural Construction of Norden*, Oslo: Scandinavian University Press.

Sosa, E. and M. Tooley, 1993, *Causation*, Oxford University Press.

Sperber, D., 1985, *On Anthropological Knowledge*, Cambridge University Press.

Sprenkel, O. Van der, 1958, *The Chinese Civil Service*, Canberra: Australian National University.

Sprenkel, S. Van der, 1977, *Legal Institution in Manchu China*, Oxford: Berg.

Squires, J., 1999, *Gender in Political Theory*, Cambridge: Polity Press.

Stedman Jones, G., 1983, *Languages of Class: studies in English working class history 1832–1982*, Cambridge University Press.

Steinmo, S., K. Thelen and F. Longstreth (eds), 1992, *Structuring Politics: historical institutionalism in comparative analysis*, Cambridge University Press.

Stepan, A., 2001, *Arguing Comparative Politics*, Oxford University Press.

Stigler, J., R. Shweder and G. Herdt, 1990, *Cultural Psychology: essays on comparative human development*, Cambridge University Press.

Stocking, G. (ed.), 1991, *Colonial Situations: essays on the contextualization of ethnographic knowledge*, Madison: University of Wisconsin Press.

Stoller, P., 1995, *Embodying Colonial Memories: spirit possession, power and the Hauka in West Africa*, London: Routledge.

Stove, D. 1973. *Probability and Hume's Inductive Scepticism*. Oxford: Clarendon Press.

Strathern, M., 1988, *The Gender of the Gift: problems with women and problems with society in Melanesia*, Berkeley: University of California Press.

———, 1992, *Reproducing the Future: anthropology, kinship, and the new reproductive technologies*, London: Routledge.

Stocking, G., 1968, *Race, Culture and Evolution: essays in the history of anthropology*, New York: Free Press.

Sugar, P., 1999, *East European Nationalism, Politics and Religion*, Aldershot: Ashgate.

Suleiman, E., 1976, *Les hauts fonctionnaires et la République*, Paris: Seuil.

Svensson, L., 1987, *Higher Education and the State in Swedish History*, Stockholm: Almqvist and Wiskell.

Swanson, R., 1985, *Gourmantché Ethnoanthropology: a theory of human being*, New York: University Press of America.

Swidler, A., 1973, 'The Concept of Rationality in the Work of Max Weber', *Sociological Enquiry*, 43 (1).

Tambiah, S., 1985, *Culture, Thought and Social Action: an anthropological perspective*, Cambridge, MA: Harvard University Press.

Tarrow, S., 1995, 'Bridging the Qualitative-Quantitative Divide in Political Science', *American Political Science Review,* 89.

———, 1989, *Democracy and Disorder: protest and politics in Italy, 1965–75,* Oxford: Clarendon Press.

———, 1998, *Power in Movement: social movements and contentious politics,* 2nd edn, Cambridge University Press.

Taussig, M., 1980, *The Devil and Commodity Fetishism in South America,* Chapel Hill, NC: University of North Carolina Press.

———, 1993, *Mimesis and Alterity: a particular history of the senses,* London: Routledge.

Taylor, C., 1971, 'Interpretation and the Sciences of Man', *Review of Metaphysics,* 25, 1.

———, 1989, *Sources of the Self: the making of modern identity,* Cambridge University Press.

———, 1994, *Multiculturalism: examining the politics of recognition,* Princeton University Press.

Ter Haar, G., 1996, *L'Afrique et le monde des esprits: le ministère de guérison de Mgr Milingo, archevêque de Zambie,* Paris: Karthala. (English version, *Spirit of Africa: the Healing Ministry of Archbishop Milingo of Zambia,* London: Hurst, 1992)

Terray, E., 1972, *Marxism and Primitive Societies,* New York: Monthly Review Press.

Thiesse, A. M., 1999, *La création des identités nationales,* Paris: Seuil.

Thiriot, C., Marty, M. and Nadal, E. (eds), 2004, *Penser la politique comparée. Un état des savoirs théoriques et méthodologiques,* Paris: Karthala.

Thomas, N., 1994, *Colonialism's Culture: anthropology, travel and government,* Princeton University Press.

Thompson, J. and D. Held (eds), 1982, *Habermas: critical debates,* Basingstoke: Macmillan.

Thompson, M., R. Ellis and A. Wildavski, 1990, *Cultural Theory,* Boulder, CO: Westview.

Thompson, M., G. Grenstad and P. Selle (eds), 1999, *Cultural Theory as Political Science,* London: Routledge.

Tilly, C. (ed.), 1975, *The Formation of National States in Western Europe,* Princeton University Press.

Tipps, D. C., 1973, 'Modernisation Theory and the Comparative Study of Societies', *Comparative Studies in Society and History,* 15.

Tocqueville, A. de, 1968 (1835–40), *De la démocratie en Amérique,* Paris: Gallimard (English version, *Democracy in America,* New York: Harper and Row, 1967).

Toennies, F., 1955, *Community and Association,* London (Original: 1887, *Gemeinschaft und Gesellschaft,* Leipzig).

Tonkin, E., 1995, *Narrating our Pasts: the social construction of oral history,* Cambridge University Press.

Todorov, T., 1989, *Nous et les autres. La réflexion française sur la diversité humaine,* Paris: Seuil.

Torga, M., 1986, *L'universel, c'est le local moins les murs,* Bordeaux: William Blake.

Tripp, C., 2000, *A History of Iraq,* Cambridge University Press.

Tsebelis, G., 1990, *Nested Games: rational choice in comparative politics,* Berkeley: University of California Press.

Tucker, R. C., 1973 'Culture, Political Culture and Communist Society', *Political Science Quarterly,* 88.

Tu Wei-ming (ed.), 1996, *Confucian Traditions in East Asian Modernity: moral education and economic culture in Japan and the four mini-dragons,* Cambridge, MA: Harvard University Press.

Turner, B., 1974, *Weber and Islam: a critical Study,* London: Routledge and Kegan Paul.

Turner, E., 1992, *Experiencing Rituals: a new interpretation of African healing,* Philadelphia, PA: University of Pennsylvania Press.

Turner, V., 1967, *Schism and Continuity in an African Society,* Manchester University Press.

———, 1967, *The Forest of Symbols,* Ithaca, NY: Cornell University Press.

———, 1986, *The Anthropology of Performance,* New York: PAJ Publications.

Unger, D., 1998, *Building Social Capital in Thailand,* Cambridge University Press.

Van Parijs, P., 1981, *Evolutionary Explanation in the Social Sciences: an emerging paradigm,* London: Tavistock.

Vanderlinden, J., 1996, *Anthropologie politique,* Paris: Dalloz.

Vanhanen, T., 1997, *Prospects of Democracy: a study of 172 countries,* London: Routledge.

Vansina, J., 1990, *Paths in the Rainforest: toward a history of political tradition in Equatorial Africa,* Madison, WI: University of Wisconsin Press.

Verba, S., N. Nie and J. Kim, 1978, *Participation and Political Equality: a seven-nation comparison,* Cambridge University Press.

Vincent, J., 1990, *Anthropology and Politics: visions, traditions and trends,* Tucson, AZ: University of Arizona Press.

Volkan, V., 1988, *The Need to Have Enemies and Allies: from clinical practice to international relationships,* New York: Jason Aronson.

Voslensky, M., 1980, *La Nomenklatura: les privilégiés en URSS,* Paris: Belfond (English version, Voslenskii, M., *Nomenklatura: the Soviet ruling class,* Garden City, New York: Doubelday, 1984).

Vovelle, M., 1982, *Idéologies et mentalités,* Paris: Maspéro.

Wagner, R., 1981, *The Invention of Culture,* University of Chicago Press.

————, 1986, *Symbols that Stand for Themselves*, University of Chicago Press.

Waldrop, M., 1992, *Complexity: the emerging science at the edge of order and chaos*, New York: Viking.

Walker, R., 1993, *Inside/Outside: international relations and political theory*, Cambridge University Press.

Waltz, K., 1979, *Theory of International Politics*, Reading, MA: Addison-Wesley.

Ward, H., 1996, 'The Fetishisation of Falsification: the debate on rational choice', *New Political Economy*, 1, 283–96.

Warnier, J.-P., 1999, *La mondialisation de la culture*, Paris: La Découverte.

Waterman, C., 1990, *Juju: a social history and ethnography of an African popular music*, University of Chicago Press.

Wearne, B., 1989, *The Theory and Scholarship of Talcott Parsons to 1951*, Cambridge University Press.

Weber, E., 1976, *Peasants into Frenchmen: the modernization of rural France, 1870–1914*, Stanford University Press.

Weber, M., 1946 (more recent edn 1991) *From Max Weber: essays in sociology*, translated and edited by H. Gerth and C. Wright Mills, New York: Oxford University Press.

————, 1949, *The Methodology of the Social Sciences*, translated and edited by E. Shils and H. Finch, New York: Free Press.

————, 1951, *The Religion of China: Confucianism and Taoism*, translated by H. Gerth, New York: Free Press.

————, 1961 (1923), *General Economic Theory*, translated by F. Knight, New York: Collier Books.

————, 1978 (1968), *Economy and Society: an outline of interpretive sociology*, 2 vols, edited by G. Roth and C. Wittich, translated by E. Fischoff *et al.*, Berkeley and Los Angeles, CA: University of California Press.

————, 1985 (1904–5), *The Protestant Ethic and the Spirit of Capitalism*, translated by T. Parsons, London: George Allen and Unwin.

————, 1919 (1959), *Le savant et le politique*, Paris: Plon.

Weigert, S., 1996, *Traditional Religion and Guerrilla Warfare in Modern Africa*, Basingstoke: Macmillan.

Weiner, A., 1992, *Inalienable Possessions: the paradox of keeping-while-giving*, Berkeley: University of California Press.

Weiner, A., 1994, 'Cultural Differences and the Density of Objects', *American Ethnologist*, 21 (2).

Weiner, M. and S. Huntington (eds), 1987, *Understanding Political Development*. Boston, MA: Little, Brown.

Weisberg, H. (ed.), 1986, *Political Science: the science of politics*, New York: Agathon Press.

Welsh, S., 1993, *The Concept of Political Culture*, New York: St Martin's Press.

Werbner, P., 2002, *Imagined Diasporas Among Manchester Muslims*, Oxford: James Currey.

Werbner, R., 1989, *Ritual Passage Sacred Journeys: the process and organization of religious movement*, Manchester University Press.

―――― (ed.), 2002, *Postcolonial Subjectivities in Africa*, London: Zed Press.

―――― and T. Ranger (eds), 1998, *Memory and the Postcolony: African anthropology and the critique of power*, London: Zed Press.

Westwood, R. and A. Chan, 1992, 'Headship and Leadership' in Westwood, R. (ed.), *Organizational Behaviour: Southeast Asian perspectives*, Hong Kong: Longman.

Whitaker, C., 1970, *The Politics of Tradition: continuity and change in modern Nigeria*, Princeton University Press.

White, H., 1973, *Metahistory: the historical imagination in nineteenth-century Europe*, Baltimore, MD: Johns Hopkins University Press.

―――― , 1987, *The Content of the Form: narrative discourse and historical representation*, Baltimore, MD: Johns Hopkins University Press.

White, L., 2001, *Speaking with Vampires: rumor and history in East and Central Africa*, Berkeley: University of California Press.

White, S., 1979, *Political Culture and Soviet Politics*, London: Macmillan.

Wiarda, H. (ed), 1990, *New Directions in Comparative Politics*, Boulder, CO: Westview.

Wickham, A. and S. Coignard, 1986 (2nd edn), *La Nomenklatura française. Pouvoirs et privilèges des élites*, Paris: Belfond.

Wight, M., 1991, *International Theory: the three traditions*, Leicester University Press for the RIIA.

Wilks, I., 1975, *Asante in the Nineteenth Century: the structure and evolution of a political order*, Cambridge University Press.

Williams, M. and T. May, 1996, *Introduction to the Philosophy of the Social Science*, London: UCL Press.

Williams, R., 1958, *Culture and Society*, London: Chatto and Windus.

―――― , 1981, *Culture*, Harmondsworth: Penguin.

Wills, G., 1990, *Under God: religion and American politics*, New York: Simon and Schuster.

Wilshire, R., 1982, *Role Playing and Identity: the limits of theatre as methaphor*, Bloomington: Indiana University Press.

Wimmer, A., 2002, *Nationalist Exclusion and Ethnic Conflict: shadows of modernity*, Cambridge University Press.

Winch, P., 1958, *The Idea of a Social Science*, London: Routledge and Kegan Paul.

Wolf, E., 1982, *Europe and the People without History*, Berkeley: University of California Press.

Wolfenstein, V., 1967, *The Revolutionary Personality: Lenin, Trotsky, Gandhi*, Princeton University Press.

Wolferen, K. van, 1990 *The Enigma of Japanese Power: people and politics in a stateless nation*, New York: Vintage Books.

Wright, L., 1976, *Teleological Explanations*, Berkeley: University of California Press.

Wrigley, R., 2002, *The Politics of Appearances: representation of dress in revolutionary France*, Oxford: Berg.

Young, C., 1994, *The African Colonial State in Comparative Perspective*, New Haven, CT: Yale University Press.

Young, I., 1990, *Justice and the Politics of Difference*, Princeton University Press.

Young, R., 1990, *Colonial Desire: hybridity in theory, culture and race*, London: Routledge.

Zahab, M. and O. Roy, 2004, *Islamist Networks: the Afghan-Pakistan Connection*, London: Hurst.

Zaller, J., 1992, *The Nature and Origins of Mass Opinion*, Cambridge University Press.

Zahan, D., 1979, *The Religion, Spirituality and Thought of Traditional Africa*, University of Chicago Press.

Zartman, I., 2000, *Traditional Cures for Modern Conflicts: African Conflict 'Medicine'*, Boulder, CO: Lynne Rienner.

Zelizer, V., 1994, *The Social Meaning of Money*, New York: Basic Books.

Zeiltin, I. M., 1990, *Ideology and the Development of Social Theory* (4th edn), Englewood Cliffs, NJ: Prentice Hall.

Ziff, B. and P. Rao, 1997, *Borrowed Power: essays on cultural appropriation*, New Brunswick, NJ: Rutgers University Press.

Zuckerman, A., 1991, *Doing Political Science: an introduction to political analysis*, Boulder, CO: Westview.

——, 1997, 'Reformulating Explanatory Standards and Advancing Theory in Comparative Politics' in Lichbach, M. and A. Zuckerman (eds), *Comparative Politics: rationality, culture and structure*, Cambridge University Press.

INDEX